A World in Flames

A World in Flames

*A Concise History of
World War II*

*With new Preface, Introduction, Appendix I,
and Bibliography*

Martha Byrd

SMITHMARK

PUBLISHED BY ARRANGEMENT WITH MARTHA BYRD, P.O. BOX 1659, DAVIDSON, NORTH
CAROLINA 28036.

MAPS BY JOAN EMERSON
DESIGNED BY KATHLEEN CAREY

THIS EDITION PUBLISHED IN 1992 BY SMITHMARK PUBLISHERS, INC., 112 MADISON
AVENUE, NEW YORK, NEW YORK 10016

SMITHMARK BOOKS ARE AVAILABLE FOR BULK PURCHASE FOR SALES PROMOTIONS AND
PREMIUM USE. FOR DETAILS WRITE OR TELEPHONE THE MANAGER OF SPECIAL SALES,
SMITHMARK PUBLISHERS, INC., 112 MADISON AVENUE, NEW YORK, NEW YORK 10016.
(212) 532-6600

0-8317-9604-9

PRINTED IN THE UNITED STATES OF AMERICA

For Skip

WE SHALL NOT CAPITULATE—NO, NEVER.
WE MAY BE DESTROYED, BUT IF WE ARE,
WE SHALL DRAG A WORLD WITH US—
A WORLD IN FLAMES.

Adolf Hitler, 1932

Preface

This book was written to answer a basic question about World War II: *who did what, and where and when did it take place?*

The reader who approaches the war as history faces a sobering challenge. The volume of literature is immense, for not only did a great deal happen between 1939 and 1945, but many of the events were significant in terms of their continuing effects on the post-war world. I sensed the need for a book that would merge separate events into a whole and provide a foundation for broader reading.

The first edition of *A World in Flames* was published in 1970. Since then additional records have been opened; hundreds of new books have been published. For the most part, however, the newly available material sheds light on *why* events unfolded as they did. It fleshes out the skeleton without altering the structure.

This book—the skeleton, if you will—now offers a new generation of readers a place to begin. The Introduction, rewritten for this edition, alerts the reader to new information and suggests a way to view the war in pieces so that the whole is easier to grasp. The Bibliography, updated and arranged by theater to facilitate use, includes a number of new works plus those originally cited in the text.

Every writer is indebted to hundreds of others—scholars, publishers, archivists, librarians, friends, and family. I take this opportunity to express special gratitude to the staff of the Davidson College E. H. Little Library for their unfailing courtesy, help, and friendship.

February 1990, Davidson, North Carolina
Martha Byrd

Introduction

From the perspective of half a century, World War II falls into place as the last of those great national struggles that began with the American and French revolutions. For a century and a half these national wars escalated in size and scope until World War II achieved totality. The shock value of totality, culminating in the realization of atomic power, enforced retrenchment. Since 1945 the trend has been to reduce the scale of conflict—to limit war—while holding atomic power as a threat. Perhaps the most compelling reason to study World War II is to grasp what might take place should we fight a total war with atomic weapons.

Without doubt world War II had the scale of the grand finale: some fifty million dead, with vast areas of the globe reduced to an economic wasteland. The totality of the destruction went far beyond humans and physical objects. Political, economic, and social institutions, having failed to prevent disaster, came under serious question. The war cleared the stage, figuratively and often literally, for new approaches.

When we look at World War II as a finale, we see the post-war years as a search for new structures, an experiment with different patterns for the ordering of human affairs. From human rights to economic opportunity, from life styles to political systems, this experimentation proceeds at a near-frantic pace. It thus seems appropriate to note Hitler's observation that gives this book its title. He spoke the words in 1932 to express his determination. We might apply them today as a warning against the blind pursuit of a course that has failed of its objective: *We shall not capitulate—no, never. We may be destroyed, but if we are, we shall drag a world with us—a world in flames.* (Quoted in H. Rauschning, *The Voice of Destruction*, 1940, 5.)

Hitler did, indeed, drag down with him a world in flames. The complete story continues to develop. The most dramatic information released since this book was written concerns Ultra, the intelligence the British obtained by successfully cracking and reading German codes and ciphers. The comparable American Magic (reading the Japanese codes) was revealed early because it formed a vital part of the national inquiry into the U.S. defeat at Pearl Harbor. The Ultra secret, however, was successfully kept all during the war and for thirty years thereafter. Starting with F.W. Winterbotham's *The Ultra Secret* in 1974, the story has gradually unfolded. (See the bibliography, under intelligence.) Fascinating to read, the Ultra accounts raise some intriguing questions. No code or cipher, it seems, can be completely secure against a determined, intelligent enemy. Both Axis and Allies, however, believed their own codes to be secure, even when they were successfully reading those of their enemy. What does war do to our thought processes?

Ronald Lewin's *Ultra Goes to War* provides the best concise summary of how Ultra was used by the Allies in waging the war. In a few critical instances—most notably the Battle of Britain—information obtained through Ultra bestowed a vital advantage. Other campaigns were largely unaffected. Even though the code-breaking achievement was significant, at no time were the Allies privy to *all* information about their enemy, while the interpretation of the intelligence they did have was subject to human failing. The Battle of the Bulge in December 1944, for instance, achieved complete surprise because the Germans had imposed strict radio

raised a red flag. Analyzing the effects of Ultra on Allied decision-making in Western Europe, Ralph Bennett (*Ultra in the West*) concludes that it brought manifest advantages through the battles of the Falaise Gap in August 1944. After Falaise, Ultra seems to have been almost ignored, perhaps the victim of over-confidence or war-weariness. The losses at Arnhem in September 1944 might have been averted had Ultra information been heeded.

If the leading Allied generals left any written analyses of how they applied Ultra, those accounts remain closed. Yet as Winterbotham put it (*The Ultra Secret*, p. 188), "This new dimension of war needed a new dimension of thinking on the part of our commanders, and the different ways in which they either used or misused these opportunities was a measure of the men themselves." Perhaps the most important long-term effect of Ultra on the historiography of the war will be seen in biography.

Although it was one single, global conflict, World War II can be viewed as a number of smaller wars, each distinct even though vitally connected to all the others. The war between Germany and Western Europe in the spring of 1940 is memorable for the near-flawless military performance of the German war machine, contrasted to the psychological, political, and military reasons for the West's rapid defeat.

Starting in the summer of 1940, the Battle of Britain witnessed the first full-scale test of strategic air power in a conflict of high drama, personal heroism, and national sacrifice. When Britain refused defeat, Hitler turned on the Soviet Union in the summer of 1941. The ensuing war on the Eastern Front was the largest in terms of forces committed and lives lost. Most of Germany's mass extermination and slave labor efforts centered on this front, where the war was brutal, oppressive, and disregarded all accepted codes of military conduct.

Mussolini's Italy carried the war into North Africa, where armored battles in the desert offered a conventional competition, a battle of wits and tactical skill in which one's enemy could be—and was—respected. General Erwin Rommel assumed near heroic proportions; he would have given his British opponents an even closer contest had Ultra not enabled the British to play hob with his supply convoys.

he would have given his British opponents an even closer contest had Ultra not enabled the British to play hob with his supply convoys.

Lasting from the first day of war until the last, the Battle of the Atlantic formed a critical background. Although victory in the Atlantic alone could not win the war for the Allies, defeat there could lose it for them: they could not afford to launch a major campaign in Europe until they controlled the Atlantic sea lanes for the transport of men and supplies. During much of 1942 and early 1943, the Germans were reading Allied convoy codes and came close to victory. The advantage returned to the Allies in mid-1943 when Ultra cracked a key German cipher and the British simultaneously changed their own codes.

The war became global in December 1941 when Japan, involved since 1937 in a campaign of conquest in China and the Far East, precipitated war with the United States. Germany, aligned with Japan through the Tripartite Pact, declared war on the United States but made little effort thereafter to coordinate action with Japan. The wars in Europe and the Pacific remained separate and distinct.

The far-flung theaters of war converged as the Allies returned to the continent of Europe. Starting with an invasion of North Africa in late 1942, one prong moved across the Mediterranean, into Sicily, and up the peninsula of Italy. A second and larger prong invaded Normandy in June 1944 and advanced steadily toward Germany from the west. Soviet forces, which held the initiative after Stalingrad in late 1942, simultaneously advanced against Germany from the east. The final European campaigns saw the commitment of enormous quantities of war material and thousands of men. With the course of these campaigns shaped by political as well as military decisions, they provide an absorbing study of a massive endeavor and the complexities of coalition warfare.

Geography dictated an entirely different nature for the Pacific war, which saw naval engagements and amphibious landings pushing a bomber line ever closer to the Japanese home islands. Strategic air warfare, which began to reach significant proportions in Europe in 1943, provided the culminating campaign against Japan in 1945. In its political aspects, the Pacific (including the China-Burma-India theater) offers a powerful example of peoples in rebellion against power structures that no longer suited existing circumstances. The fighting and the treatment of prisoners were often characterized by startling cruelty.

The war took place on different levels as well as in different theaters. Pursue the theme of national politics, international diplomacy, grand strategy, military operations, personal experience, or technological competition. By providing a summary, *A World in Flames* serves as an introduction to one of the most complex and fascinating dramas of human history.

Contents

xvii

Maps

PART I

The Axis Advance

Preface to War

ON SEPTEMBER 1, 1939, the most devastating war of recorded history broke over the central European plains. Three years later the swastika of Nazi Germany flew over a prostrate Europe, while in Asia the Rising Sun of Japan waved from the mainland across the vast expanses of the Pacific to New Guinea and the Solomon Islands. The Second World War lasted for six years and engulfed every major world power and most lesser ones. At its end more than forty million people lay dead [1] and the living knew the world could never be the same again.

As late as September 1938, only a year before the war commenced, some dared to hope that the problems of an ailing world could be solved without a major war. The World War of 1914–18 had left Europe exhausted and vulnerable. In Russia, the Czars had given way before a revolution that had changed not only Russia but all of

---

[1] See Appendix I, p. 323.

Europe as well, since Communism implied a threat to all established institutions. In Italy, the King and Parliament had retained their titles but had yielded their power to a militant young fascist named Benito Mussolini. In Germany, the ill-starred Weimar Republic had fallen before the oratory of an intense, fiery-eyed Austrian, Adolf Hitler, who became Chancellor, then Fuehrer, of the German Reich. In Japan, a growing group of militarists loudly advocated their country's right to a place in the sun. The whole world was suffering from the Great Depression, and a struggling League of Nations fought with meager resources to keep the peace so dearly bought and so precariously held.

Japan Chooses Force

The first serious portent that the peace would not last had come from China in 1931.[2] There the Japanese Army created an incident and within six months had seized control of Manchuria. It was renamed Manchukuo, and Japan controlled its puppet government. The Manchurian affair was the beginning of a steady expansion of Japanese control on the Chinese mainland. Japan, beset by economic and social problems, had turned to a policy of foreign expansion to seek their solution. A united "Asia for the Asians," with China, Manchukuo, and Japan cooperating under Japanese leadership, was the goal.

The Chinese had no intentions of bowing to Japanese leadership, but China was weakened by civil war and was unable to rally effective force to stop the Japanese. The League of Nations condemned Japan for the Manchurian affair, but it took no further action, and Japan left the League and continued to extend her control in China. Winston Churchill wrote that China was being eaten "like an artichoke, leaf by leaf,"[3] but no one was willing to take military action to bring the meal to an end.

In 1937 the Japanese began full-scale warfare against China. Al-

[2] For background on Japan and the war see Borton, *Japan;* Beasley, *The Modern History of Japan; The China Handbook*, published by the Chinese Ministry of information; Butow, *Tojo and the Coming of the War.*
[3] Churchill, *Step by Step*, p. 137.

though persisting in calling the conflict the "China Incident," the Japanese soon found it was more than an incidental task to conquer China. The Chinese retreated to the interior of their vast homeland and by the end of 1938 a dismal stalemate had been reached. Japan's aggressive action antagonized the rest of the world, and the Japanese Army acquired a reputation for barbarism and irresponsibility. Tension with other countries rose. The army was accused of mistreating foreign nationals in China, indiscriminately bombing civilians, and senselessly destroying business and educational property. The United States, Britain, France, and Russia began giving China active aid and support. Japan and Russia clashed over the Manchukuo border, and in 1936 Japan further alienated Russia by joining Germany in an Anti-Comintern Pact. By the late thirties Japan considered herself friendless in a hostile world. The outbreak of war in Europe in 1939 cast a new light on Japan's ambitions for economic hegemony in the Far East.

The Birth of Fascism

In Europe during the 1930's the fascist governments of Italy and Germany led their people on a course of rearmament and military aggression that challenged the rest of Europe to fight or to be overcome. Italy's goal was a new Roman Empire that would bring back the days of Italy's power and glory, while Germany sought an expanded German Reich that would not only incorporate all German-speaking peoples, but also acquire space for them at the expense of the non-Germans of central Europe.

The rebirth of the Roman Empire was less the dream of the Italian people than of their dictator, Benito Mussolini,[4] a strange combination of demagogue and poseur, who combined skill and strength with weakness and unscrupulousness. While a young man he affiliated with the Socialists and made a name for himself as a speaker and journalist. By 1919 he had founded his own political movement, which became the Fascist Party. At that time Italy was plagued by economic

[4] For bibliographical data see Kirkpatrick, *Mussolini, A Study in Power;* Finer, *Mussolini's Italy.*

instability and social unrest. Strikes, violence, demonstrations, and Communist threats of revolution began to reach grave proportions. Capitalizing on the public's fears and the government's inability to maintain order, Mussolini organized armed squads and began making open war on the Communists and Socialists. The Fascist movement grew. Not hesitating to use violence, Mussolini's squads became famous for the black shirts they wore and the doses of castor oil they administered to their victims. Gradually, through force and elections, the Fascists took control of Italy's larger cities. Fascist demands for political power increased, though they had few specific measures to propose. In October 1922, when Mussolini and the Black Shirts organized the March on Rome to demand political power, King Victor Emmanuel, reluctant to risk civil war and endanger the throne, extended to Mussolini an invitation to form a new government.

What could Italy expect from its new government? The only consistent themes of Fascism had been nationalism and intense patriotism. Mussolini later claimed that Fascism was born of the need for action and was more practical than theoretical. In 1922 the Fascists attempted to solve Italy's practical problems by restoring order (by force when necessary), ending strikes, and establishing firm financial measures to bring about a resumption of foreign trade and credit. The government began extensive public works measures, built roads and public buildings, and drained swamplands. Mussolini modernized railroads, and tourists claimed that he had "made the trains run on time." By 1929, when he settled a long-standing dispute between Italy and the Pope by negotiating the Lateran Agreements, Mussolini had reached a peak of popularity with the Italian people and had acquired a measure of worldwide respect.

But behind Fascism's concrete achievements, and hidden by a propaganda program of public spectacles and celebrations, speeches and slogans, Italy was changing. By steady and often ruthless measures the Fascists disposed of all political opposition. Mussolini, as Il Duce (leader) of the Fascist Party as well as of the State, became "Italy." The Party, itself highly centralized, became closely woven into the organs of state so that government, from Rome to the smallest province, became a vast bureaucracy of government from above, not below. The growing and inefficient bureaucracy offered unique opportunities for corruption. As the Italian people gradually lost their civil and personal liberties, they also lost any semblance of efficient government, sound economic growth, or realistic military development. At its core Italy was rotting, but this did not become apparent until she began to play a militant role in world affairs.

In 1933 the climate of Europe was altered by the establishment of a fascist dictatorship in Germany under Adolf Hitler.[5] Before long, it became obvious that Nazi Germany was outdoing Fascist Italy not only in the degree of government and party control, in the use of brutality and violence, in the fanaticism of its cause, but in aggressive foreign policy as well. Mussolini reacted with admiration and fear.

Hitler was born in Austria in 1889. He had little taste for formal schooling and spent his formative years living a hand-to-mouth existence in Vienna. Politics intrigued him, and he became a passionate German nationalist and a violent anti-Semite. He joined the German Army in World War I, and although he did not advance beyond the rank of corporal, he won the Iron Cross for bravery. His political career began in Munich in 1919, when he joined an obscure political group later known as the National Socialist German Workers' Party (Nazis). Hitler's work and talent changed the party from a small group of malcontents to a vast organization that ruled a nation. The German leader believed that a successful political movement was based on a strong mass movement, effective use of propaganda, and free employment of spiritual and physical terror. The Nazi Party acquired its own newspaper and its own army—brown-shirted ruffians known as the SA, who adopted the stiff-armed Roman salute of Italy's Black Shirts as well as their free use of force and intimidation. Most dramatic was Hitler's tireless and impressive oratory. He could grip an audience with nearly hypnotic emotional intensity. The Nazi movement grew, and with uncanny persuasion Hitler advocated the union of all Germans, a strong central government, anti-Communism and anti-Semitism, and, above all, abrogation of the Treaty of Versailles.

The Treaty of Versailles, drafted by the Paris Peace Conference at the end of World War I, redrew the map of Europe, established a League of Nations to provide collective security against aggression, and imposed severe reparations and military restrictions on the Ger-

[5] For biographical data and early history of Nazism see Heiden, *Der Fuehrer;* Bullock, *Hitler: A Study in Tyranny;* Shirer, *The Rise and Fall of the Third Reich.*

man state. From the first it was extremely unpopular with the German people. Also unpopular was Germany's post-war government, the Weimar Republic. It was the first democratic government in German history, and from its inception in 1918 the political parties supporting it had trouble maintaining a workable majority in the Reichstag. The early twenties witnessed widespread civil unrest, and in November 1923 Hitler made an unsuccessful attempt to overthrow the government. As a result of his Beer Hall Putsch he was sentenced to five years' imprisonment. However, he served less than nine months, and spent much of his time writing *Mein Kampf* (*My Struggle*)—a turgid volume that accurately forecast much of the horror of the Nazi regime.

The failure of the Beer Hall Putsch convinced Hitler that a revolution must be well organized in advance, must be achieved through strictly legal channels, and must have the support of the army. Therefore he campaigned to establish the Nazi Party, and by September 1930 it was the second party in the Reichstag. During the next three years election followed election as the government of President Hindenburg sought to find a coalition that would give the Reichstag a working majority. Finally, threatened by continued stalemate and the possibility of Communist exploitation of the government, Hindenburg offered Hitler the chancellorship of Germany. The new leader was sworn in on January 30, 1933.

The Nazi Reich

Hitler wasted no time in establishing the Nazi dictatorship. Intimidated by the SA, the Reichstag passed the Enabling Act that granted the cabinet exclusive power for controlling legislation, the budget, foreign treaties, and constitutional amendments. Under the legal cloak of this act, Hitler proceeded to consolidate his power and destroy all opposition to Nazi control of social, cultural, educational, and governmental life. In 1934, when President Hindenburg died, Hitler combined the offices of Chancellor and President and declared himself Fuehrer. To cement his authority, he exacted from the armed

8

forces an oath of loyalty, which was sworn not to their country but to their Fuehrer:

> I swear by God this sacred oath, that I will render unconditional obedience to Adolf Hitler, the Fuehrer of the German Reich and people, Supreme Commander of the Armed Forces, and will be ready as a brave soldier to risk my life at any time for this oath.[6]

Hitler's control over the Third Reich was complete. He vowed that what he was building would last a thousand years.

Germany rearmed. Under World War I fighter pilot Hermann Goering, the Luftwaffe (Air Force) began to develop. The army's General Staff, pleased to be released from the shackles of the Versailles Treaty, studied the military lessons of the past war and began training men and building an armored force. The rest of Europe, hoping for peace, urged treaties and agreements, to which Hitler was receptive. He talked of peace but prepared for war, and with a political cunning that approached genius, divided or soothed his opposition and re-established Germany's power. In March 1935 Hitler announced that Germany was beginning universal military service and would build a standing army of roughly half a million men—larger than that of France. Mussolini, encouraged by Hitler's show of strength, began his pursuit of empire by invading Ethiopia. Britain and France, hoping to keep Italy's friendship to help them restrain Germany, did not take drastic action against Italy. The United States, fearing involvement in another "foreign war," passed a Neutrality Law that set the pattern for U.S. foreign policy for the remainder of the decade.

In March 1936 Hitler sent German troops back into the Rhineland, which had been demilitarized by the Versailles Treaty. No troops marched to stop them, and the Germans began building the West Wall (Siegfried Line) behind the Franco-German frontier. In May Italy brought the Ethiopian affair to a successful conclusion, and in October Italy and Germany signed a secret protocol that Mussolini christened an "axis" around which the other European states could revolve. Few realized how much the Axis alliance jeopardized the peace of Europe.

[6] Shirer, *The Rise and Fall of the Third Reich*, p. 227.

9

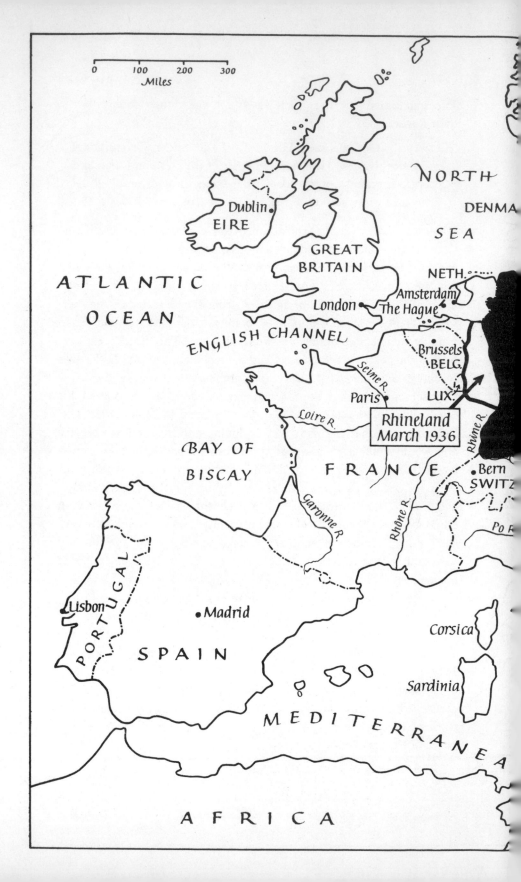

Memel
March 1939

Sudetenland
Sept. 1938

March 1939

March 1938

EUROPE, 1939

By November 1937 Hitler had decided to go to war. In a lengthy conference with his military commanders he outlined his intentions. Germany's aim was to "preserve the racial community." Her future was "wholly conditional upon the solving of the need for space." Germany "had the right to a greater living space than other peoples." [7] Between February 12 and March 11, 1938, Hitler incorporated Austria into the Reich.[8] Although the armed forces were mobilized, no blood was shed. The Anschluss (Union) was a political victory, won by a combination of Nazi infiltration, threats of force, and appeals to the emotional issue of greater German nationalism. A "free and secret" plebiscite, influenced by Nazi storm troopers and propaganda, made the Austro-German union legal and surrounded Czechoslovakia on three sides by the Third Reich. She would be next to be incorporated into the German state.

The Sudetenland, the western province of Czechoslovakia, contained a large German-speaking minority, and their alleged mistreatment by the Czech government was the issue on which Hitler based his demands for this area.[9] Throughout the summer of 1938 the air was heavy with accusations, counteraccusations, threats, and the fear of war. Neither Britain nor France was militarily prepared for another conflict, and by September, as the crisis approached its climax, the "solution" to give Hitler the Sudetenland was gaining support. To see if such an arrangement would avert war, Prime Minister Neville Chamberlain, supported by French Premier Edouard Daladier, flew to Germany to confer with Hitler. After the first conference, held at Hitler's retreat high in the Bavarian Alps at Berchtesgaden, the British and French governments agreed that Czechoslovakia must give up the disputed area, but at a second conference a week later Hitler increased his demands. These the British cabinet could not accept, nor could it urge the Czechs to do so. Hitler called up his troops. France was bound to Czechoslovakia by a mutual defense treaty. Britain assured France that if she found herself at war because of it, Britain would support her. An emissary was sent to Berlin to make sure Hitler understood that Britain would stand beside France

[7] *Ibid.*, pp. 303–8.
[8] Brook-Shepherd, *The Anschluss.*
[9] Wheeler-Bennett, *Munich, Prologue to Tragedy;* Churchill, *The Gathering Storm;* Feiling, *The Life of Neville Chamberlain.*

if there was war. Hitler insisted, "It is a matter of complete indifference to me . . . by next Monday we shall all be at war." [10]

Although military preparations proceeded, the doors were still open for negotiation. Chamberlain urged a conference which convened at Munich, September 29, 1938. There Hitler declared he would occupy the Sudetenland on October 1. Anxious to absolve this action from the character of violence, the Nazi leader assured the world that this would be his last territorial demand in Europe. Was Czechoslovakia too high a price for peace? The agreement was signed in the early morning hours of September 30, and Czechoslovakia as a nation was ruined. She lost extensive lands and economic resources. The Czech Minister to Britain, Jan Masaryk, spoke with dignity and feeling when he told the British, "If you have sacrificed my nation to preserve the peace of the world, I will be the first to applaud you. But if not, gentlemen, God help your souls!" [11]

The Steps to War

The policy of appeasement that culminated in Munich did not preserve the peace. Hitler did not hesitate to order his armed forces to be prepared for the liquidation of the remainder of Czechoslovakia. Throughout the winter Nazi-inspired agitation kept the Czech state in turmoil. When political crisis came to a head in March 1939, Hitler summoned President Hacha of Czechoslovakia to Berlin. The Czech leader was told that German troops would invade Czechoslovakia the following morning, March 15. If the Czechs fought, they would be overwhelmed; if they accepted peacefully, they would have a "generous way of life." [12] Hacha advised his government to surrender. A document which had been prepared previously was presented and signed. When German troops began pouring across the border into Czechoslovakia two hours later, they met no resistance.

Hitler's occupation of Czechoslovakia was a turning point in prewar diplomacy. In Britain appeasement gave way to determination; in

[10] Henderson, *Failure of a Mission,* pp. 164–65.
[11] Wheeler-Bennett, *Munich, Prologue to Tragedy,* p. 171. Masaryk was present in the House of Commons on August 5, 1942, when the British Foreign Secretary, Anthony Eden, made the formal statement renouncing the Munich agreement.
[12] Shirer, *The Rise and Fall of the Third Reich,* p. 446.

the United States President Franklin Roosevelt and his Secretary of State, Cordell Hull, urged amendment of the U.S. neutrality laws so that U.S. force could be applied against Axis aggression. The Neutrality Law of 1935 called for an embargo of arms and munitions from the United States to any belligerent. As one European crisis led to another and Japan threatened the peace in the Far East, the neutrality legislation had been amended several times, always with the aim of insuring that the U.S. would not get involved in any conflict. Isolationist sentiment was strong, but as crisis deepened, anti-Fascist sentiment grew. Hemisphere defense became an issue, and in December 1938 Secretary Hull attended an inter-American conference at Lima, Peru, to lay the groundwork for inter-American cooperation to meet a foreign threat. The Declaration of Lima reaffirmed the principle of continental solidarity and recognized that a threat to any of the American republics was a threat to all. The Lima Conference was followed by talks in Panama City the next September. There, means were studied for strengthening the hemisphere's economy and defenses, and ways were sought to prevent the New World from becoming involved in the conflicts of the Old. The Declaration of Panama designated a 300-mile zone off American coasts as a neutral area which the American republics would patrol. Belligerents were warned to refrain from hostilities within this area.[13] United States relations with Canada also were strengthened, and during the crisis in Czechoslovakia in 1938, President Roosevelt and Prime Minister Mackenzie King exchanged policy commitments. Roosevelt assured the Canadians that the U.S. would not stand idly by if Canadian soil was threatened, and King reciprocated by declaring that Canada accepted the duty of defending herself against invasion so that enemy forces should not be able to pursue their way across Canadian territory to the U.S. The Americas were aligning themselves against Axis aggression. Meanwhile in Europe Hitler pursued a course that could lead only to conflict.

Everyone could see that Poland was now at the top of Hitler's list. One of the most unpopular provisions of the Treaty of Versailles was the incorporation of a strip of German territory, the Corridor, into

---

[13] For the United States during the pre-war period see Langer and Gleason, *The Challenge to Isolation 1937–1940* and *The Undeclared War 1940–1941*.

Poland to give Poland an access to the sea at Danzig. Although such an outlet was considered essential to Poland's economic survival, the boundary arrangement was awkward in the extreme. East Prussia was separated from the remainder of Germany by the Corridor, and in this strip there were German-speaking people under foreign rule. Less than a month after the conference in Munich, Poland was alerted that Germany wanted Danzig as well as extraterritorial rights to build a superhighway and rail line across the Corridor to East Prussia. The Polish government replied that any attempt to incorporate Danzig into the Reich would lead to conflict.

Poland's defiance did not deter Hitler. Before turning on Poland, however, he decided to clear up the situation involving a small strip of territory on the north edge of East Prussia—Memel, which had been given up by Germany in 1919 and later had become part of Lithuania. When Hitler demanded that she return it, Lithuania followed the now familiar course and signed the German government's ultimatum on March 23, 1939. Hitler had made his last bloodless conquest. On March 31, Chamberlain told the House of Commons:

> In the event of an action which clearly threatened Polish independence . . . His Majesty's Government would feel themselves bound at once to lend the Polish Government all support in their power.[11]

Hitler was furious. He ordered his armed forces to be ready by September 1, 1939, for the military destruction of Poland.

For Britain, France, and Poland, the remaining five months of peace brought a stiffened resolve to resist Axis aggression, coupled with diplomatic activity aimed at avoiding war if possible but securing allies if not. On April 6 Britain and Poland signed a temporary mutual assistance pact, and a week later—after Mussolini had conquered Albania in a rapid campaign—France and Britain gave guarantees to Greece and Rumania. By the middle of April the British began talks with the Russians. Britain, France, and Poland were aware that if war broke out they would need Russia's assistance if aid was to reach Poland or if a strong eastern front against Germany was to be maintained. But Germany, to deal effectively with Poland and the

---

[14] Churchill, *The Gathering Storm*, pp. 345–46.

Western powers, also needed Russia's passive acquiescence if not her active support. Otherwise Germany would be faced with a war on two fronts, and this had caused her defeat before. Germany and Britain both sought an understanding with the Soviets.

Negotiations proceeded with difficulty for both sides. The Soviet regime's revolutionary threats and oppressive domestic policies made Russia feared by all, but Hitler was willing to bow to Russian terms. On August 23 Germany and Russia signed a non-aggression pact. The price Hitler paid for Russia's non-interference with his war was half of Poland, the province of Bessarabia (which had been part of Rumania since 1920), and the Baltic states. Fascism and Communism, mortal enemies, had signed a truce. Few doubted that it meant war.

Mussolini wavered. In May, in a burst of martial enthusiasm, he had committed Italy to the Pact of Steel, a military alliance that bound Italy to march at Germany's side. Now he realized that Hitler was drawing him into a war for which Italy was by no means prepared, and he tried to wiggle free of his alliance. He wrote Hitler warning him that Italy could not take the initiative in a war with Britain and France. Hitler was shaken. He wrote Mussolini an understanding letter promising German aid in building up Italy's war machine. Then the German leader made one last attempt to persuade Britain not to interfere with his designs on Poland.

On August 25 Hitler proposed that Britain accept his solution for Poland in return for his guarantee to defend the British Empire. Germany wanted a British-German alliance, the return of Germany's African and Asian colonies (lost in World War I), a guarantee for the German minority in Poland, and Britain's help in securing for Germany Danzig and the Corridor. In return Germany would pledge to defend the British Empire and guarantee the new Polish frontiers. The British had never felt the need of German help in defending their empire, and the other points seemed reminiscent of those preceding the sacrifice of Czechoslovakia. Nevertheless a flurry of round-the-clock diplomatic activity began.

On August 28 the British told the Germans that a settlement of Polish-German differences must be made before anything else could be considered. On August 29 Hitler agreed to German-Polish negotiations, but insisted that a Polish emissary must be in Berlin the next

16

day. It was a trap. If the Polish emissary did arrive (most unlikely on such short notice) and refused to capitulate, or even if he did not come, Poland could be blamed for sabotaging a peaceful settlement.

During the last day of peace, August 31, the Polish Ambassador in Berlin, Josef Lipski, requested an interview with the German Foreign Minister, Joachim von Ribbentrop. He was put off for five hours. When he was received he told von Ribbentrop his government was considering the suggestion for negotiations and the official reply, probably a favorable one, would arrive within a few hours. Lipski returned to his embassy to find the telephone lines with Warsaw severed. Hours before, shortly after noon, Hitler had signed his first war directive. He had decided on a "solution by force" because "all the political possibilities of disposing by peaceful means of a situation on the Eastern Frontier which is intolerable for Germany are exhausted." [15]

At daybreak, September 1, 1939, German armies began pouring across the Polish frontiers from north, south, and west. World War II had begun.

[15] Shirer, *The Rise and Fall of the Third Reich*, p. 589.

Poland, the Atlantic, Scandinavia

WORLD WAR II began with the blitzkrieg. Although it was not solely a German idea, the Germans perfected the technique and gave it a name, which translates literally as "lightning war." The blitzkrieg moved with speed and ruthlessness, leaving death and destruction in its wake and spreading terror ahead.

The Blitzkrieg Destroys Poland

The concept of the blitzkrieg is based on a highly mobile, armored striking force centered around tanks, self-propelled guns, and trucks to transport the infantry. The mechanized columns penetrate rapidly into enemy territory, breaking front lines, wrecking command areas, and cutting off rear supply routes. Disorganized and without means of direction or resupply, the enemy is unable to offer a coordinated defense against the slower, non-motorized infantry that follow to "mop up." Coordination is provided by radio, telephone, telegraph, and the airplane—the second arm of the blitzkrieg. Bombers range far behind enemy lines, destroying bridges, railroads, communication centers, and industrial plants. The blitzkrieg deals the enemy a triple blow: his ability to mobilize, direct, and supply his forces is impaired; the industrial base for his long-range supply is crippled; the terror and destruction raining from the skies undermine civilian morale.

The blitzkrieg broke over Poland at dawn on September 1, 1939. The Germans employed two Army Groups—North, under General Fedor von Bock, and South, under General Gerd von Rundstedt.[1] Their total strength was approximately one and a half million men. In a force of more than fifty divisions, five were panzer [2] and four were motorized infantry. With approximately 1400 offensively armed aircraft at their disposal, the Luftwaffe opened hostilities with concentrated, well-timed attacks on Polish airfields and communication centers. The Stuka dive bomber proved a particularly efficient weapon. Most of the Polish planes were destroyed in the opening hours of the war; by September 3 the Polish Air Force was eliminated as a fighting unit. The Luftwaffe, now in command of the skies, turned to direct support of the ground forces by bombing and strafing Polish troops. By that time Army Group North had cut the Polish Corridor by simultaneous thrusts from East Prussia and Pomerania and had turned south toward Warsaw; Army Group South had crossed the Polish frontiers on a broad front and were pressing toward Lodz, Warsaw, and Cracow.

The Poles had expected war but were tactically surprised. Negotiations for a peaceful settlement were being considered, apparently by both sides, right up to the moment of attack. Not only was Poland's mobilization incomplete, but her task in defense was formidable. Poland is a vast plain providing a path between Germany and Russia. For centuries, since Poland has no natural eastern or western boundaries to protect her territory, this plain has been trampled by armies moving between east and west. In addition, in 1939 Poland was so constituted that to protect her vital industrial and agricultural areas, she must spread her armed forces over a broad perimeter and expose their flanks. Troops in the Corridor could easily be cut off, as the

[1] For the military action in Poland see Kennedy, *The German Campaign in Poland*.
[2] The term "panzer," meaning "armor," is applied to individual German tanks as well as to armored divisions.

19

German thrusts
→ 1st stage ⇢ 2nd stage

BALTIC SEA

LITHUANIA

Pomerania

KÖNIGSBERG

DANZIG

East Prussia

OLD CURZON LINE

Army Group North, Bock

Narew R.

GERMANY

Poznan

Vistula R.

Bug R.

•Kutno

WARSAW

•Brest

U.S.S.R.

POLAND

•Lodz

•Lublin

Silesia

Gleiwitz

Vistula R.

San R.

CRACOW

Lwow•

Moravia

C A R P A T H I A N   M T S.

Army Group South, Rundstedt

SLOVAKIA

AUSTRIA

HUNGARY

RUMANIA

GERMAN CONQUEST OF POLAND, SEPTEMBER 1939

Germans so ably demonstrated, while units in the area around Poznan and Cracow would be vulnerable to encirclement. Yet these areas contained a large part of Poland's agricultural, mineral, and industrial resources. To lose them would make continued defense almost impossible. Rather than concentrate her forces on a narrow front, Poland elected to defend her entire area. If Britain and France could attack in the west before Polish forces had to capitulate, there was a chance of success.

British and French help did not come. The German blitzkrieg moved with startling rapidity, and the war in Poland was over before Poland's allies could come to grips with the military situation confronting them. The Poles fought with valor but with little chance of success. Most of their weapons were of World War I vintage; they had almost no tanks; horse cavalry pitted against panzers resulted in cruel slaughter that scarcely hindered the German advance. By the 6th Cracow had fallen and the Polish armies were either surrounded or in retreat. German mechanized units raced ahead to cut off retreat routes and to prevent the Poles from organizing a coordinated resistance. Roughly one third of the Polish ground forces, surrounded in the Kutno area, made a desperate attempt to break out toward Warsaw. They failed. The survivors surrendered on September 17. The same day Brest, to the east, fell before the armored assault of General Heinz Guderian's Panzer Corps.

On September 17 Russian troops began pouring across Polish frontiers from the east. By the terms of the August 23 Pact, Russia was to receive half of Poland. On September 3 Hitler invited Stalin to occupy his half. Not only did the Fuehrer want to dispose of Poland in a hurry so he would be free to face Britain and France, but if Russia participated in the military destruction of Poland, the stigma of aggression would not be borne by Germany alone.[3] Perhaps because Russia's forces could not be mobilized quickly enough to begin earlier (a small war with Japan was being concluded in the Far East), perhaps because she was willing to let Germany carry the burden of Poland's defeat, Russia refrained from direct action until the 17th.[4] By that time Poland was dying; the Russian armies merely claimed

---

[3] Shirer, *The Rise and Fall of the Third Reich*, pp. 621–22.
[4] Britain did not declare war on Russia for her violation of Poland, since the British-Polish Treaty promised aid in the event of German aggression only.

their half of the corpse. Calling their advance a "liberation march," [5] the Russians explained their action to the world as a move to protect the Slavs in eastern Poland, since the Polish state had disintegrated.

Poland was doomed. Warsaw was under siege and a wider German encirclement was closing its arms around those Polish forces who had sought escape to the east. The Polish government crossed into Rumania—the first step toward exile in London. Lwow held out until the 21st, Warsaw until the 27th. Isolated units did not surrender until the first week in October, but Poland was essentially destroyed in seventeen days.

The morning of September 1, when the blitzkrieg was making its debut on Polish soil, Hitler addressed the Reichstag. The Germans had not responded to the news of war with enthusiasm, and it was now up to Hitler to defend his action. Earlier he had told his generals:

> The victor will not be asked afterward whether he told the truth or not. In starting and waging a war it is not right that matters, but victory.[6]

Hitler lied when he assured the German people that German armed forces had invaded Poland in self-defense. Apparently Polish soldiers had violated the German frontier and fired on German forces, and Polish corpses were left as evidence. After the war it was established that the whole affair was staged by the secret police, the SS. The Polish corpses were not Poles, but German convicts who had been drugged and dressed in Polish uniforms.[7]

Sitzkrieg

During the first day of the war against Poland Hitler anxiously awaited the reaction of Britain and France. That evening they delivered identical messages: unless German forces halted their aggressive action and withdrew from Polish soil, Britain and France would fulfill

[5] Erickson, *The Soviet High Command*, p. 539.
[6] Shirer, *The Rise and Fall of the Third Reich*, p. 593.
[7] *Ibid.*, pp. 518–20, 594–95.

their obligations to Poland. Mussolini continued to press for an international conference, but the British insisted that Germany must evacuate Poland as a prerequisite. Hitler refused. On September 3 Great Britain and France declared war on Germany. They were shortly joined by Australia, New Zealand, the Union of South Africa, and Canada. Hitler had a world war on his hands, and he is reported to have said, "What are we going to do now?" [8]

First, Hitler wanted to finish up in Poland so that troops could be transferred to the west, where the West Wall was manned by only a minimum force. The transfer began as soon as the Polish issue was beyond doubt, but, as it turned out, there was no need for haste. For eight months—until May 1940—the war in the west was a "phony" or "twilight" war, a "sitzkrieg" (sitdown war). The French Army had planned for a defensive war, with the massive fortifications of the Maginot Line as their fort. They were not ready to take the offensive, either in terms of equipment, training, planning, or state of mind. It took time for the British Expeditionary Force (BEF) to arrive on the continent where its effectiveness could be brought to bear. Belgium continued to insist on her strict neutrality, and Hitler took advantage of the absence of military action to initiate another verbal peace campaign. He assured the world that he had no war aims against Britain or France; Germany wanted nothing in the west. Apparently Hitler did not believe he would achieve victory through peaceful persuasion, for on October 10, without waiting for replies to his peace feelers, Hitler signed Directive No. 6, outlining the invasion of France through the neutral Low Countries. Two days later Chamberlain replied to the Fuehrer's olive branches by saying that it was no longer possible to rely on the "unsupported word of the present German government." Peace would have to be based on "acts, not words alone." [9]

Hitler was not about to undo what he had done to Poland, and the acts he was contemplating now were not acts of peace, but acts of war. Oddly enough, despite the dramatic military success in Poland, he was meeting opposition from his generals. The Nazi propaganda machine had made the victory in Poland appear much greater than it

---

[8] Wiskemann, *The Rome-Berlin Axis*, p. 175.
[9] Taylor, *The March of Conquest*, p. 39.

actually was. Weaknesses in equipment and procedures had been brought to light, and opinion was divided on the best way to employ the armored divisions. The generals knew that war against Britain and France would be immeasurably more difficult than war against Poland, and they wanted time to prepare tactical plans, to overhaul equipment, to replace losses, and to train more men. Some of the generals were convinced that war with the West was folly, and at least one objected to the invasion of Belgium, a neutral country, on moral grounds.[10] Hitler was impatient to proceed against the West, but perhaps because he sensed he could not act unless his generals were with him, he kept postponing the attack. It was first definitely set for November 12, 1939. Before it was actually launched, the attack was put off no less than fourteen times. The reason usually given was "meterological conditions."

The United States was gravely concerned about the outbreak of war. For months sentiment had been growing that the Allies should be helped, and after Poland fell Congress amended the Neutrality Laws to allow "cash and carry." Belligerents could buy arms and munitions in the U.S., but they must pay cash and transport them in their own ships. While technically giving both sides the right to buy goods, the amendment favored Britain and France because of their greater sea power.[11]

By spring 1940 all aid short of joining the conflict was gradually becoming U.S. policy, but few realized the degree of threat that an Axis victory might impose. Congress appropriated funds for increases in the Navy, Army, and National Guard, as well as expanded plane production, but the increases were modest and little was done to begin mobilizing the nation's economy for war production.

During the Phony War President Roosevelt made several unsuccessful diplomatic efforts to bring an end to hostilities before the devastation became more widespread. He sent a representative to the Vatican to see what could be done through cooperation with the Pope, and in February he dispatched the Undersecretary of State,

[10] General Wilhelm von Leeb, who overcame his scruples and served the German Army, predicted the world would turn against Germany for breaking the neutrality of Belgium twice within 25 years. See Shirer, *The Rise and Fall of the Third Reich*, pp. 646–47; Goerlitz, *The German General Staff*, p. 366.

[11] Langer and Gleason, *The Challenge to Isolation*, pp. 45–51, 78–82, 136–47, 218–35.

Sumner Welles, to visit the European capitals and explore the possibilities of a mediated settlement. Mr. Welles's mission was discouraging. Hitler seemed determined to continue the war, and Mussolini seemed eager to join him. Events soon confirmed this to be the case.

The War at Sea

The war at sea experienced no phony phase. On September 3, just hours after Britain declared war, the British liner *Athenia,* unarmed and unescorted, was torpedoed and sunk with a loss of 112 lives, 28 of them Americans.[12] For several reasons Berlin promptly denied being responsible for *Athenia*'s fate. The London Naval Conference of 1930 had established the principle of submarine warfare that a U-boat must not sink a merchant vessel without first putting passengers and crew in a place of safety, and the Reich had subscribed to that principle in 1936.[13] In addition there was the touchy business of the Americans, and it was no part of Hitler's scheme to draw the United States into the war. Despite Berlin's denials, the British took the sinking of the *Athenia* as evidence that Germany did not intend to abide by her treaty commitments. Merchant vessels, previously unarmed, would be armed in self-defense.

The war at sea was to be a life-and-death struggle waged by Britain to preserve her lifelines—her sea communications with her empire and other nations. Since Britain must import much of her foodstuffs and raw materials, Germany could strangle her by driving her commerce off the seas. The Battle of the Atlantic, the most continuous struggle of the entire war, did not reach its peak until 1942, but it began immediately. During September 1939, 26 British merchant ships were sunk by U-boats, 2 by mines, and 1 by a surface raider.[14]

The British inaugurated defensive measures at once. Not only did the Royal Navy impose a blockade on Germany to halt the flow of Germany's seaborne supplies, but the Royal Navy took steps to protect its own shipping by reviving the convoy system used in the First World War. Merchant ships sailed in disciplined formation,

12 Churchill, *The Gathering Storm,* p. 423.
13 Morison, *The Battle of the Atlantic,* p. 8.
14 Churchill, *The Gathering Storm,* p. 436n.

escorted by warships to afford protection against enemy ships. Although there were too few escort vessels to protect all merchant shipping, scientists had developed a sound-wave device called Asdic (the Americans called it Sonar) that enabled surface ships to locate submerged submarines.

Asdic was one of the first scientific devices utilized in the Second World War—a war in which science and technology played a major role.[15] The battle of wits—called by Churchill the "Wizard War"—was fought in the laboratories as each side raced to develop newer and more effective weapons and devise defensive measures. Shortly after the war commenced the Germans began using a magnetic mine that defied traditional methods of minesweeping. Not until a mine was taken from the ocean intact and its mechanism studied were the British able to find ways to cope with it. Minesweepers thereafter used electric cables, and ships were degaussed, or demagnetized, by winding electric cables around their hulls. Even so, the magnetic mine and its variations continued to be a problem.

During the first four months of the war at sea the British suffered their share of reverses. In September the aircraft carrier *Courageous* was sunk while on escort duty. In October the battleship *Royal Oak,* at anchor in the harbor at Scapa Flow, the Royal Navy's wartime base in the Orkney Islands off the north coast of Scotland, was torpedoed and went down. The battleship was sunk by the cunning of a lone German U-boat, which had slipped past the British defenses and through the dangerous channel, fired her torpedoes, and made her escape.

Germany's pocket battleship, *Admiral Graf Spee,* sank ship after ship, and not until December 12, by which time *Spee* had accounted for nine British ships, was she located off the coast of South America.[16] Three British cruisers engaged *Spee,* and although the cruisers were lighter and their guns were outranged by those of *Spee,* it was three to one. *Spee* sustained damage that drove her to take refuge in Montevideo harbor. According to neutrality laws, she could remain there no longer than 72 hours, and the British waited for her to emerge. *Spee* had the choices of internment, doing battle, or scuttling.

15 See Eggleston, *Scientists at War.*
16 Roskill, *The War at Sea 1939–1945,* Vol. I, pp. 113–21.

She chose the latter. Late in the day, December 17, she blew up in the River Plate. The British began a search for *Spee*'s auxiliary ship, the *Altmark,* which carried the passengers and crew that had been rescued from *Spee*'s victims. Before the *Altmark* adventure was concluded, interest shifted to Russia and the Baltic, where war had broken out between Russia and Finland.

The Winter War

Only weeks after extending her frontier to the old Curzon Line, Russia began strengthening her position in the Baltic. Russia had lost Estonia, Latvia, and Lithuania in 1918 when she concluded the peace of Brest-Litovsk with Germany. After Germany was defeated by the West, the Baltic states were established as independent countries. If Russia ever intended to reclaim them, now was the time. Germany had granted the Baltic area to Russia in the August 23 Pact, and no one else was in a position to interfere. In October 1939 the three states were requested by Russia, who added a certain show of force to hasten their decision, to allow Russian troops to occupy strategic bases on their soil. They complied. It was the first step toward incorporation of the Baltic states into the USSR, which was completed the following summer.

Having greatly improved her strategic position in the west, Russia looked to her northern flank and Leningrad. The city built by Peter the Great was not only Russia's major seaport but also her second largest city and an important industrial center. The Finnish frontier came to within fifteen miles of the city on the north. To increase Leningrad's defensive potential, Russia requested that Finland grant some territorial concessions: the Karelian Isthmus up to Viipuri, four small islands in the Gulf of Finland, and the use of Hangö as a Russian naval and air base. Finland, like the other Baltic states, had been a part of Russia before 1919, though in the semi-independent capacity of a grand duchy. Although Finland could appreciate Russia's position and was willing to make certain concessions toward Leningrad's defense, she was not willing to grant all that Russia asked. When requests and negotiations failed, Russia invaded Finland on November 30, 1939, and the Winter War began.[17]

The Russian forces outnumbered the Finns three to one and they expected to cross the Karelian Isthmus to Viipuri and Helsinki without delay. But they reckoned without the Finns. The Russians were stopped at the Mannerheim Line, a fortified zone across the Isthmus some twenty to forty miles from the frontier. While one Russian Army battered itself against reinforced concrete fortifications, the Finns applied themselves to the north, where the Russians had made initial gains in Finnish territory. The Finns knew how to use the ruggedness of the terrain, and they were ably led by Field Marshal Mannerheim. In the engagements around Suomussalmi during December and the first week of January, the Finns suffered only minimum casualties while annihilating one Russian Army and part of another. The Russians, having been dealt a humiliating defeat, were forced to pause. They had been defeated by small, mobile units, often operating on skis, who made maximum use of rugged terrain and bitter weather. The Finns moved easily through the forests and across the frozen lakes, but the Russians were tied to the roads by their heavy equipment and cumbersome supply lines. When the Russians renewed their assault in February 1940, it was soon apparent that they had profited from their mistakes. The Mannerheim Line was broken by the middle of February and on March 12 the Finns capitulated, granting all the Russian demands.

The Winter War had interesting diplomatic undercurrents. The Finns had ties with Germany as well as with the Western Allies, and for a time it looked as though both might intervene on her behalf. Germany was forced to stay out because of the Nazi-Soviet Pact. Under its terms she was receiving foodstuffs and raw materials from Russia—more important than ever now that the Baltic ports were under blockade—and until the war in the west was won, Germany could ill afford to endanger her truce in the east. The Allies also were in a dilemma. The League of Nations, in a last desperate attempt to halt the onrush of tragedy, expelled Russia for her aggression and urged its members to aid Finland. But assistance could reach Finland only through Sweden and Norway, and these countries took a position of strict neutrality. Although sympathetic to Finland's cause,

[17] See Tanner, *The Winter War*.

28

SCANDINAVIA

Sweden and Norway could not grant right of transit for military forces or supplies without exposing themselves to war with Russia and turning all of Scandinavia into a major battlefield. Although France and Britain sent weapons, and a volunteer Expeditionary Force reached Finland (but never got into action), the Allies did not enter the Winter War. Had they done so, conceivably the whole nature of the Second World War would have been different, with Russia and Germany allied against Scandinavia and the West.

The *Altmark* Affair; Invasion of Denmark and Norway

Between September 1939 and April 1940 Scandinavia was the object of close scrutiny by Germany and the Allies. For Germany there were two considerations. Much of Germany's iron came from northern Sweden, and when the Swedish port of Lulea was icebound, the ore had to travel by rail to the Norwegian port of Narvik and thence by ship to Germany. Consequently Norway's neutrality or friendship was essential if the iron was to be obtained. The German Navy also wanted control of the Norwegian coast because its harbors and fiords offered access to the open sea. If the Germans controlled the long Norwegian coastline, the British blockade would be less easily enforced, and the German Navy could play a more vigorous role in the war.

The Allies were primarily concerned with the iron ore traffic. Since most of its journey could be made within Norwegian territorial waters, the First Lord of the Admiralty, Winston Churchill, urged that the Allies mine the Norwegian Leads, the inland waterway between the mainland and the offshore islands, and force the ore traffic onto the open seas, where the Royal Navy could reach the German boats. The British government hesitated. Pursuing a policy that Churchill called "honourable correctitude," [18] they were loath to violate Norwegian neutrality by mining her neutral waters. Not until early April 1940 was the Admiralty told to proceed, and by then it was too late. Meanwhile the German Navy was appealing to Hitler to take the Norwegian ports. Admiral Raeder presented his plan in September

[18] Churchill, *The Gathering Storm*, p. 573.

30

1939, but it was not until the first of the year that Hitler ordered OKW, the Armed Forces High Command, to work out the plans for an operation in Norway. They were shortly to be speeded up, for in February came the sequel to the sinking of the *Graf Spee*—not in the South Atlantic, but off the Norwegian coast.

On February 14 the Royal Navy located the *Altmark* in Norwegian territorial waters.[19] A flotilla of British destroyers, commanded by Captain Philip Vian, intercepted the *Altmark,* which took refuge in a narrow inlet. When the destroyers pursued they were met by two Norwegian gunboats who told them the *Altmark* had been inspected, was unarmed, contained no prisoners, and had been given permission to use Norwegian waters. The British withdrew, but Churchill, feeling quite certain that *Altmark* was loaded with *Spee*'s victims and was violating Norwegian neutrality by using her waters to convey prisoners of war, ordered Captain Vian to board the *Altmark.* Vian did so the night of February 16, and released 299 British prisoners who had been stuffed into storerooms and empty oil tanks to escape Norwegian detection. Germany decided that if the Royal Navy was going to act so aggressively in Norwegian waters, then those waters must be more important to Germany's cause than had been realized. On February 19 Hitler ordered OKW to complete the plans for seizing Norway. On the 21st he named General Nikolaus Falkenhorst to command; on the 29th he decided to occupy Denmark as well.

Denmark posed few problems for the Wehrmacht, the German armed forces. At 4:00 a.m., the morning of April 9, the German Minister in Copenhagen told the Danish Foreign Minister that German troops were moving into Denmark to prevent an attack by the British. These troops came as friends, but if Denmark resisted, she would be crushed. While the Danish government pondered their predicament, German troops crossed the Schleswig border, and German ships moved into Denmark's ports. The large airfield at Aalborg—the Germans' major objective—was taken by paratroopers and airborne infantry. When German bombers appeared over Copenhagen about 7:00 a.m., King Christian X capitulated. The Germans quickly assumed complete control of the country, and the Luftwaffe moved into Aalborg to support the operations in Norway, where King Christian's

[19] See Frischauer and Jackson, *The Altmark Affair.*

brother, King Haakon VII, had been given the same alternative—capitulate or be crushed.

The campaign in Norway was the only German operation of the war in which the Navy played a leading role. Admiral Raeder had warned that success would depend on "boldness, tenacity, and skill," [20] and the Wehrmacht lived up to his exhortation. General Falkenhorst decided to seize simultaneously the major cities and ports —Oslo, Christiansand, Bergen, Trondheim, and Narvik. (See map, page 29.) The detailed planning was difficult, for the ports were widely scattered. Success would depend on surprise and coordination, and opposition from the Royal Navy could be expected. Despite the difficulties, German forces appeared off shore at all five ports shortly before 5:00 a.m. on April 9. Narvik, Trondheim, Bergen, and Christiansand fell by noon, and the Sola airfield, between Christiansand and Stavanger, was captured by paratroopers. At Oslo the Wehrmacht met a temporary reversal. While still some fifteen miles from Oslo, the task force came under heavy and accurate fire from Norwegian forts and was forced to retreat. Alerted by the gunfire in the Oslofiord, the cabinet went into midnight session and were still convened when the German Minister arrived, shortly before 5:00 a.m., with the Fuehrer's ultimatum. The Norwegians vowed they would not submit without a fight, but failed to take vigorous steps to counter the German threat. Nevertheless they managed to foil the German plans, for the King and government fled to the mountains and escaped capture. Norway would require more than a day of the Wehrmacht's time.

Oslo was occupied by noon April 9 by airborne troops that landed at a nearby airfield and marched into the city. The government had departed, and Vidkun Quisling, a man who played a small but despicable role in the capture of Norway and whose name became synonymous with traitor, assumed control of the government. The leader of an insignificant fringe of Norwegian Nazis, for months Quisling had been in contact with Hitler and the German Foreign Office. The latter planned to use him to help take Norway from within, the way Austria had been captured. When the Germans demanded that King Haakon accept Quisling as the head of the

[20] Taylor, *The March of Conquest*, p. 102.

government, the Norwegians were outraged and they set about the task of resisting the Germans as long as possible. General Otto Ruge, Commander-in-Chief of Norway's meager forces, barricaded the road north of Oslo and prepared to contest the German advance. He received indirect assistance from the Royal Navy.

Although caught off balance by the German action, and hampered in reconnaissance by bad weather, the British dealt the German Navy some severe blows. At Narvik they disposed of the German task force, and the occupying Germans fled into the hills behind Narvik. The British began preparations to occupy Narvik and to keep the northern portion of Norway out of German control. British action was also planned to help liberate Trondheim, but the extremity of the northern weather and the undisputed German air control defeated it, and the Trondheim force was evacuated at the end of April.

On May 10 the blitzkrieg exploded against Holland and Belgium, dwarfing the significance of the fight for Norway. Nevertheless, British efforts to take Narvik and hold northern Norway, still valuable to Germany as an access to the Swedish ore fields, continued. On May 14 General Claude Auchinleck, who a year later would oppose the Germans in the African desert, was put in command in northern Norway. At first it seemed that Auchinleck and his force of 25,000 British, French, Poles, and Norwegians [21] might succeed. The Germans were cut off from naval reinforcement, but although the Allies captured Narvik on May 28, they had already decided that it must be evacuated, for every man was needed to plug the gap in the defense of France and Britain. The King and his government were transported to London, and Norway began the long night of Nazi occupation.

The Norwegian campaign was a tremendous boost to German confidence and a severe blow to Allied morale. Were the Germans invincible? Many began to think so, especially when the Norwegian triumphs were followed by those in the Low Countries and in France. Germany continued to receive the much needed iron ore; the British blockade of Germany was weakened; Luftwaffe bases in Norway were a serious threat to the British-Russian convoys that began operating early in 1941. There was, however, another side to the German victory. Although ground and air casualties were relatively

[21] *Ibid.,* p. 142.

low on both sides, German naval losses were extremely high in proportion to her total naval strength. She lost 10 out of 20 destroyers and 3 out of 8 cruisers. In addition, the cruisers *Scharnhorst* and *Gneisenau* and the pocket battleship *Luetzow* sustained damage that put them out of action for many months.[22] Germany's losses in Norway were greater than she could afford, since when France fell in June and only Britain remained to be defeated, Germany did not have the naval strength to cross the English Channel. But before coming to grips with the problem of invading Britain, Hitler had a further taste of victory. On May 10, with fighting still going on in northern Norway, the Wehrmacht began the long-expected and often postponed assault on the West.

[22] *Ibid.*, p. 153. See also Roskill, *The War at Sea,* Vol. I, Chapter 10.

Germany Subdues Holland, Belgium, and France

THE GERMAN VICTORY over the Low Countries and France in the spring of 1940 is one of the most dramatic military campaigns on record. The West was overwhelmed by the blitzkrieg: the German forces overran Holland in five days, subdued Belgium in eighteen days, conquered France in six weeks, and took over tiny Luxembourg, with only a token army, in a matter of hours.

Allied Preparations

During the Phony War and the not-so-phony Norwegian campaign, neutral Holland and Belgium followed events with concerned interest. As time went by they became doubtful as to whether their neutrality would be respected and braced themselves for self-defense. The Netherlands shared a 200-mile frontier with Germany and had only slender military forces with which to defend it. Her plans were to flood the eastern lowlands to delay the German advance, and to concentrate her strength along the Grebbe-Peel Line, where natural defenses were reinforced with fortifications. In the western area that

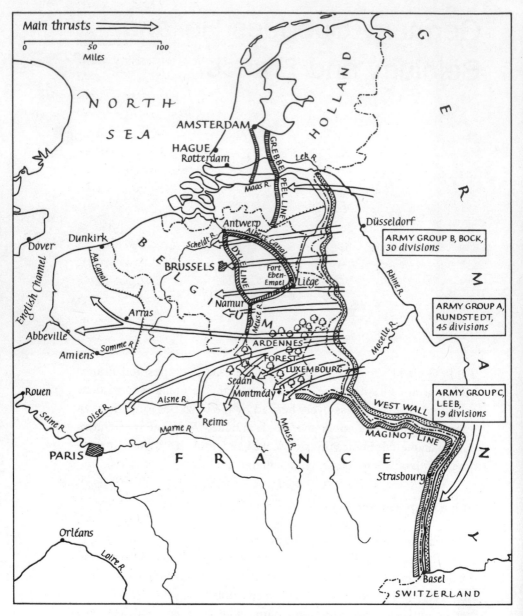

Main thrusts

0   50   100
      Miles

NORTH
SEA

HOLLAND

GERMANY

AMSTERDAM
HAGUE
Rotterdam

GREBBE PEEL LINE

Lek R.

Maas R.

Düsseldorf

ARMY GROUP B, BOCK,
30 divisions

Antwerp
Albert Canal
Scheldt R.
DYLE LINE
Fort
Eben-
Emael
Liége

BELGIUM
BRUSSELS

Namur
Meuse R.

Rhine R.

ARMY GROUP A,
RUNDSTEDT,
45 divisions

Dover
Dunkirk

English Channel

Aa Canal

Arras
Abbeville
Somme R.
Amiens

ARDENNES
FOREST
Sedan
Montmédy

LUXEMBOURG

Moselle R.

Rouen
Seine R.
Oise R.
Aisne R.
Reims
Marne R.
Meuse R.

WEST WALL

ARMY GROUP C,
LEEB,
19 divisions

MAGINOT LINE

PARIS

FRANCE

Strasbourg

Orléans
Loire R.

Basel
SWITZERLAND

GERMAN CAMPAIGN, MAY 10–JUNE 5, 1940

included Amsterdam, Rotterdam, and the Hague, the Dutch reserves were held in readiness. There, to protect "Fortress Holland," the Dutch planned to make their most determined resistance. Although alerted to the possibilities of airborne attack, when the assault came on May 10 countermeasures were incomplete and ineffective.

Belgium had proclaimed her independent neutrality shortly after Germany reoccupied the Rhineland in 1936, but she had also made clear her intention to defend herself if necessary. Although King Leopold III refused to jeopardize his country's neutrality by close staff planning with the British and French, both Allies and Axis accepted that Britain and France would march to Belgium's assistance if Germany invaded. Until then, Belgium planned to hold the invaders behind prepared defenses on her eastern frontier. A fortified line had been constructed from Antwerp to Namur (the Dyle Line), and the waterway defense lines of the Meuse River and the Albert Canal were reinforced by modern forts near Liège, the most likely avenue for a German assault. The newest and strongest fort, Eben Emael, was considered a masterpiece of fortification, rivaling anything in either the West Wall or the Maginot Line. The Belgians, who so often had seen blood spilled on their soil, awaited developments with a healthy determination.

In Britain the respite provided by the Phony War was used to build up British armed strength. Industry was mobilized for wartime production, the British Expeditionary Force (BEF) was sent to France, and action in Norway was contemplated. Failure of British Operations in Norway precipitated a government crisis early in May. Neville Chamberlain stepped down and was replaced by Winston Churchill, who became Prime Minister on May 10, the day Germany invaded the West. Churchill was almost 66 years old. A distinguished career of public service lay behind him, but ahead were five years of grave challenge. As the German armies swarmed across Holland and Belgium, he told the House of Commons that the policy of the new government would be to "wage war, by sea, land, and air, with all our might and with all the strength that God can give us." The aim was victory, but until it was attained, he had nothing to offer but "blood, toil, tears and sweat." [1]

[1] Churchill, *Their Finest Hour*, p. 25.

When France declared war in September 1939, she mobilized her available strength and waited for the Germans to strike. After World War I France had suffered economic, governmental, and social crisis. Anxious to avoid another war, her military leaders had put their resources into a massive fortified line along the Franco-German frontier. The forts and guns of the Maginot Line were formidable and modern; behind them the French believed they could wage a defensive war. But the Maginot Line proper extended only along the Franco-German border to the vicinity of Montmédy. What of the Franco-Belgian border? It was protected only by scattered field fortifications, yet the area between Brussels and Paris—the "pit of the French stomach"—had been the critical battlefield of previous French wars. There, surely, lay the danger. But to fortify the Franco-Belgian border would be pointless unless the French planned to fight behind the fortifications, and to do so would mean abandoning Belgium to fight alone in the event of German aggression. Also the northeastern area of France was her most valuable industrial area; to protect it France would have to fight in front of it—in Belgium. Accordingly the French High Command planned to meet a German threat to the north by advancing into Belgium while the Maginot Line protected the southern flank. Such a plan would suggest that the armies in northern France would be equipped and trained as a mobile striking force, but that was not the case.

During the 1930's a tall and outspoken French officer named Charles de Gaulle urged the formation of an army of maneuver—an army of tanks, motorized transport, and planes. Only with such a mobile force could the armies of the north hope to challenge successfully Germany's mobile, armored war machine. The French High Command did not agree. Although the French Army had good tanks, most of them were divided among the infantry for supporting tactics rather than grouped into armored divisions. The few armored divisions the French possessed were scattered along the front, not grouped into a powerful armored army. The French Air Force was obsolescent and small. The Navy, modern and well trained, was to have little chance to fight.

In May 1940 the Maginot Line was fully manned. Two armies, poorly equipped and with a minimum of training, faced the Ardennes

Forest region of southern Belgium. It was the most weakly held sector of the front, for the Ardennes Forest was considered impenetrable and the sector not dangerous. To the north, facing the expected avenue of assault through Belgium, were two of the best French Armies plus the British Expeditionary Force. The BEF, nine divisions strong, was commanded by Lord Gort. French Generalissimo Maurice Gamelin commanded the Allied force. When the Germans struck, that force would march into Belgium, but for the Allies the German plans held a bitter surprise.

The German Plan

During the fall of 1939 many of Germany's military leaders had been in a state of doubt and disenchantment over Hitler and his designs against the West, but as the winter passed, so did the disagreement. By March the tactical plans were ready, and it was a matter of waiting for suitable weather and the conclusion of the Norwegian campaign. The German plan incorporated innovations in the use of armor and air power as well as a shrewd analysis of how the enemy would react. General Erich von Manstein, a capable staff officer under von Rundstedt, figured prominently in the development of the war plan. Von Manstein and Guderian, the tank expert, both believed that armor could move efficiently through the so-called impenetrable Ardennes Forest of southern Belgium and based the German plan on this theory. Along the Franco-German border, where the French Army waited behind the bristling Maginot Line, Army Group C, under General Wilhelm von Leeb, would conduct limited operations to hold the French troops on that front. At the opposite end of the long front, Army Group B, under von Bock, would seize Holland and simultaneously launch an attack through Belgium north of Liège, aiming toward Brussels. It was anticipated—accurately—that the violation of Belgium would draw the British and French armies forward from northern France into Belgium. The *coup de grâce* would then be administered by Army Group A under von Rundstedt, which would strike with the heaviest force [2] through the Ardennes

---

[2] Von Rundstedt had 45 divisions as compared to 19 for von Leeb and 30 for von Bock. The Germans held 42 divisions in reserve, and another 20 in Norway, Den-

39

Forest south of Liège. It was anticipated—again accurately—that this portion of the front would be weakly held. The Germans would break through the Allied defenses quickly and drive straight for the Channel coast north of the Somme River. The Belgians, the BEF, and the best French armies would be cut off from the body of France and destroyed. The remaining French forces would then be easy prey for the Wehrmacht. The German plan, unfolding almost exactly as intended, has been judged "one of the most shrewdly and skillfully contrived plans in the annals of modern warfare." [3]

Five Days for Holland

On May 10, 1940, Holland was subjected to the first large-scale airborne invasion in military history. The Dutch were informed at dawn that they were being invaded to forestall an Anglo-French invasion. Although they refused to accept this, they could do little. Luftwaffe bombers struck barracks, hangars, and defenses at Holland's western airfields and the Dutch Air Force was neutralized at once. Transport planes disgorged paratroopers, who held the airfields and seized nearby bridges. Within hours the Hague was invested, the Dutch reserves were tied down, and, most important for the Axis, General Kurt Student's paratroopers secured two large bridges over the Maas that gave access to Fortress Holland from the south.

Flooding the eastern lowlands did not delay the German ground forces as much as had been hoped, for the Germans seized some bridges intact and built temporary bridges over other water barriers. As the Dutch forces fell back, a French Army under General Henri Giraud moved toward Holland's assistance from the south, but it was as vulnerable as the Dutch to the combination of panzer and Stuka. On May 12 the advancing German armies made contact with Student's paratroopers at the Maas bridges south of Rotterdam; on May 13 the main body of Dutch forces was withdrawn from the Grebbe-

---

mark, East Prussia, and Poland. French, British, Belgian, and Dutch divisions totaled 135, but their action was not closely coordinated. See Taylor, *The March of Conquest*, p. 181 and Appendix C.

[3] Taylor, *The March of Conquest*, p. 179. See Manstein, *Lost Victories*, Chapter 5, for von Manstein's role.

Peel Line into Fortress Holland. Queen Wilhelmina and the government left the Hague to join a growing colony of exiled rulers in London.

On May 14 the Dutch began negotiations for surrender. After conferring with the German commanders, the Dutch officer in charge was returning to Rotterdam with the surrender terms when Luftwaffe bombers appeared overhead and proceeded to drop their deadly loads on the city. More than eight hundred persons were killed, thousands made homeless, and the heart of the city was completely destroyed.[4] Rotterdam had no anti-aircraft defenses, and controversy over its bombing still goes on. The issue involved is what constitutes a military target in a total war in which the civilian resistance and industrial potential are of as much importance as the military establishment to the prosecution of the war. The Luftwaffe bombed Rotterdam because the German High Command wanted to finish with Holland quickly and get on into Belgium, where the bulk of the Allied opposition was expected. Since the surrender was already in progress, the raid added to a growing contempt and hatred for Nazi Germany. The Dutch surrender was completed late on May 14, and the German occupation that began at once was one of the most brutal and notorious in all of Hitler's New Order.

The Battle for Belgium, May 10–15

By the time Holland fell, the Allied positon in Belgium was in doubt. There also the war had begun at dawn on May 10, with gliders rather than paratroopers announcing the invasion. Three groups of gliders landed on the west bank of the Albert Canal, and within minutes key bridges giving access to southern and western Belgium were in German hands. Paratroopers followed to reinforce the glider units and hold the bridges until the advancing ground forces reached them in the afternoon. Fort Eben Emael, on which such high hopes had rested, was also assaulted at dawn by gliders. Specially prepared explosives were dropped down the gun turrets, and flames and gas spread rapidly within the fort. In less than an hour the fortress was

---

[4] Taylor, *The March of Conquest*, p. 200.

rendered totally ineffective, and its capture cost the Wehrmacht only 6 dead and 19 wounded.[5]

By the time Eben Emael fell, General Reichenau's Sixth Army was pushing rapidly into northern Belgium. Tanks poured across the bridges of the Meuse River and the Albert Canal, and on the evening of May 11 the Belgian Army began a gradual withdrawal to the Dyle Line. By May 14 they were joined by the British and French forces, who, according to German expectation, moved forward into Belgium. With 36 Allied divisions now concentrated in northern Belgium,[6] it was time for von Rundstedt's Army Group A, already through the Ardennes Forest, to deliver the decisive blow.

Army Group A had been only slightly hampered by the light resistance and narrow roads encountered in the Ardennes Forest. On the right of its front, General von Kluge's Fourth Army reached the Meuse by the afternoon of May 12. An enterprising general, Erwin Rommel, led his 7th Panzer Division across the river in rubber boats on May 13—the first crossing.[7] Two days later Rommel's force was assembled on the west bank of the Meuse and ready for a major thrust.

Meanwhile, on Rommel's left, General List's Twelfth Army had surged across Luxembourg and southeast Belgium. By the evening of May 12 General Guderian's XIX Panzer Corps had taken Sedan. The Germans began to pour over the river barriers. The Luftwaffe, especially the dreaded Stuka dive bomber, kept the French forces from moving to meet the German threat by attacking the French columns on the roads as well as bombing railroads and communication lines in the French rear. The French Air Force and the RAF struggled to counter the Luftwaffe, and at the same time to knock out the bridges over the Meuse that the Germans were using to such good advantage. They had little success and lost heavily.

Army Group A was opposed by only two French Armies, the Second and the Ninth. These two armies were outnumbered, lacked proper equipment, were poorly trained, and were so completely bewildered by the nature of the task they confronted they literally

[5] Taylor, *The March of Conquest*, p. 214; Shirer, *The Rise and Fall of the Third Reich*, p. 725.

[6] Taylor, *The March of Conquest*, p. 216. For Battle of France see Draper, *The Six Weeks' War*.

[7] Liddell-Hart, *The Rommel Papers*, pp. 6–13.

collapsed. By May 14 Army Group A had opened a 50-mile gap in the line and faced no opposition. The Battle for Belgium became the Battle for France. It began the morning of May 15, as the Stuka and panzer spearhead set out for the Channel coast. Reynaud, the French Premier, called Churchill and said, "We have been defeated. We are beaten; we have lost the battle." [8]

The Battle for France, May 15–June 4

Between May 15 and May 20 the armored corps of Generals Guderian, Hoth, and Reinhardt cut a swath across northeastern France from the Belgian border to Abbeville on the coast. French attacks, directed by de Gaulle, were made against the German's south flank on May 17 and 19, but they scarcely hindered the German advance. When the Ardennes sector collapsed, General Giraud was sent to reorganize and reassemble the troops and plug the gap, but his efforts were unavailing and he himself was taken prisoner on May 18. The German surge westward continued, and Guderian reached the coast on May 20. Hitler began plans for the peace treaty.

Although their situation was desperate, the Allies were not quite ready to sign a peace treaty. The northern armies were under heavy pressure from Army Group B on the east and north. Army Group A had cut these armies off from the remainder of the Allied forces south of the Somme River, and behind them lay the English Channel. Their alternatives, if they were to avoid destruction, were to strike south, break the German corridor, and reunite with the rest of the French forces, or evacuate the continent. The strike south, if conducted at once and in cooperation with an attack on the German corridor by forces south of the Somme, might succeed. General Gamelin issued orders for the operation on May 19, but on that day he was relieved of command and General Maxim Weygand became Generalissimo. Weygand canceled the orders pending a conference with the field commanders. Delay ensued. Confusion, misunderstanding, and a lack of urgency plagued the Allied High Command. The northern armies were fighting without clear and decisive direction, and they were

---

[8] Churchill, *Their Finest Hour*, p. 42.

nearly out of touch with the forces to the south. Lord Gort directed part of the BEF to secure Arras, an important road junction, on May 21, but by then no one could expect more than a local success. The British held Arras until May 23, when Lord Gort judged further attacks to the south to be unfeasible. The forces not actively engaging the enemy began to withdraw toward Dunkirk.

Meanwhile the Germans had been pouring every unit that could be spared into their salient across the Somme valley. By May 24 Army Group A had been strengthened to more than seventy divisions.[9] Most of its armored or motorized units were concentrated on the far left, close to the English Channel, where Guderian had already begun to advance northward along the coast toward Dunkirk and Calais. By May 24 the German panzers were poised along the Aa Canal, pointed north, nearer Dunkirk than the Allied forces, and ready to cut the Allied armies off from the coast. It looked as though the northern armies were doomed, but on the same day the German panzers were halted by order of the German High Command.

Because the two-day delay that ensued before the panzers were again ordered to advance enabled the Allied armies to reach the coast and seal off a defensive perimeter around Dunkirk, the origin and reasons for the order have been debated. Both Hitler and von Rundstedt appear to have been responsible, and there were several reasons.[10] (1) The area between the Aa Canal and the coast was marshy and unsuitable for tanks. Since many tanks had already been lost in the Battle for France, the desire to husband the remaining tank forces for the conclusion of operations was a factor. (2) Although the German panzer advance had completely disrupted the Allied forces, it had cut only a very narrow corridor through France, and the German infantry divisions often faced heavy fighting to secure the areas the tanks had already passed through. The infantry needed time to consolidate the gains. (3) The German leaders sensed no need for haste, since the northern armies were considered beaten and Goering was confident the Luftwaffe could finish their annihilation. (4) Evacuation from the insignificant harbor at Dunkirk seemed improbable. But

[9] Taylor, *The March of Conquest*, p. 240.

[10] Taylor, *The March of Conquest*, pp. 255–61; Shirer, *The Rise and Fall of the Third Reich*, pp. 731–35; Churchill, *Their Finest Hour*, pp. 76–78; Liddell-Hart, *The German Generals Talk*, pp. 132–36.

while the German armor was halted and the Allied armies fought their way to the coast, the Royal Navy gathered its forces for an evacuation—Operation DYNAMO.

The Miracle of Dunkirk

Evacuations are usually acknowledgments of serious military defeats, and Dunkirk was no exception. Nevertheless, what happened there has been called a miracle. As early as May 19 Admiral Bertram Ramsay and the Royal Navy had begun preparations for possible evacuation of the BEF from France.[11] Thousands of non-combatants had already been carried to England before full evacuation was ordered on May 26. Although the German armor renewed its advance, the Allies were in position to hold a perimeter around Dunkirk. The fighting was severe, and on May 28 King Leopold surrendered the Belgian forces which held the northeastern end of the ever-shrinking pocket. He received harsh criticism for his action, but Lord Gort closed the gap left by the departing Belgians and the evacuation went on.

The heaviest burden and most spectacular success of Operation DYNAMO fell to the destroyers. Destroyers are fast and maneuverable, but not designed to carry large numbers of men. Nevertheless, in steady succession they pulled alongside Dunkirk's narrow mole, or breakwater, and took aboard as many men as could be crammed below and lined up on their decks. Clumsy and slowed by their unwieldy load, they steamed to Dover, constantly manning their guns to protect themselves and unarmed craft from the Luftwaffe. The destroyers could not carry out the evacuation alone, and all manner of available craft were pressed into service. Dunkirk's harbor was too small for all the craft to load at the mole, and many of the larger ships had to lie offshore while the men were ferried from the open beaches in smaller boats. The process was slow, but when they realized that small craft could play a vital role in the proceedings, the seafaring

[11] For Dunkirk see Divine, *Dunkirk;* Roskill, *The War at Sea,* Vol. I; Ellis, *The War in France and Flanders.*

British manned their pleasure yachts or fishing boats and headed for Dunkirk. The armada of little boats began to operate on May 29; hundreds were involved.

As the days went by, the German pressure on the Dunkirk perimeter intensified. The area was marshy and flooded, and the German armor soon had to withdraw in favor of the infantry and Luftwaffe. The Luftwaffe struck so severely at the town and harbor of Dunkirk that on May 27 the Allies were forced to carry out the loading from the open beaches. Bad weather gave the Allies a reprieve on the 28th, but by May 29 the Luftwaffe realized what the British were accomplishing and turned their full force against the evacuation fleet. They met severe opposition from the RAF. The aerial battlefield was by now as close to English as to German bases, and the RAF could operate on almost even terms. The Spitfire, Britain's newest fighter, appeared in combat for the first time and proved a worthy match for the German Messerschmitt. Even so, the RAF could not provide constant air cover, and on the 29th five ships were sunk in the harbor. The following day bad weather again favored the British, and General Franz Halder, Chief of Staff of the German Army, wrote with some bitterness that "The bad weather has grounded the Luftwaffe and we must now stand by and watch countless thousands of the enemy get away to England right under our noses." [12] Even though the skies cleared the next day, the RAF was able to disrupt the Luftwaffe attacks and more than 60,000 men were evacuated on that day alone. One of them was Lord Gort, who was ordered to turn over his command to a junior officer.

June 1 was the crucial day in the air battle over Dunkirk. Not only the harbor and the ships, but the men assembled on the beaches were targets for the German fliers. Three more destroyers and numerous small craft were sunk; each air force lost about thirty planes. Daytime evacuation proceedings were abandoned, but by night the rescue mission went on. The relentless advance of the German infantry with its heavy artillery made the beachhead untenable and necessitated ending the evacuation after the night of June 3. More than 338,000 men had been saved; one third of them were French. The French High Command did not order evacuation proceedings as early as did

[12] Shirer, *The Rise and Fall of the Third Reich*, p. 736.

the British, for they hoped to hold the Germans long enough to organize a defense. It proved a futile hope. The Germans quickly overwhelmed the remaining resistance in the northern pocket, and by June 5 were ready to move south. The final phase of the Battle of France began.

The Battle for France, June 5–25

When the German offensive began on May 10, German and Allied forces numbered roughly the same. Less than a month later the Dutch, Belgian, British, and elite of the French armies were gone, and Allied strength was almost cut in half. Sixty-five Allied divisions remained to face the Wehrmacht with its 120 divisions.[13] With amazing speed and efficiency, the Wehrmacht turned around, regrouped, reorganized, and attacked again. Three major blows fell in quick succession. The first was struck by Army Group B on the west, the second by Army Group A in the center, the third by Army Group C on the east against the Maginot Line.

Army Group B reopened the battle on June 5 and reached the Seine River, the waterway defense line before Paris, on June 8, after what Rommel called "glorious days in pursuit."[14] While part of the Army Group fanned out toward the coast and pressed an Allied force into a pocket at Saint Valéry,[15] the remainder concentrated on the Seine for a thrust toward the capital. On June 9 von Rundstedt's Army Group A crossed the Aisne River to deliver the second blow. Within three days Guderian's armor was through the French defenses near Chalon and racing south. At this point Italy entered the war.

The preceding nine months had been a time of chafing frustration for Mussolini. Unready to engage in a European war, he had been forced to declare Italy a "non-belligerent" when Germany invaded Poland. The Italian people rejoiced at his proclamation and he was irritated. Inactive while Hitler basked in the glory of dramatic conquest, he vacillated between hoping for an early peace and fearing the

---

[13] Taylor, *The March of Conquest*, pp. 282–84.
[14] Liddell-Hart, *The Rommel Papers*, p. 57.
[15] After Dunkirk the Royal Navy evacuated some 200,000 more British and Allied troops. Roskill, *The War at Sea*, Vol. I, p. 230.

war would be over before Italy could enter. France, Britain, and the United States did what they could to persuade Italy to stay neutral, but their appeals received cold replies. When the German armies lunged through France, Mussolini could stand it no longer. On May 30 he wrote Hitler that he had decided to enter the war, and on the evening of June 10 he spoke from the balcony of the Palazzo Venezia to inform his people. The Fascist Grand Council was not convened; the King did nothing. The Italian people seemed depressed and stunned.

The Italian forces made little contribution to the Axis effort, but their help was scarcely needed. By June 12 the French efforts to hold the Germans had collapsed, and the advancing German armies were spreading over France. On June 10 the French government fled Paris for Tours and later Bordeaux; on June 12 Paris was declared an open city; on June 14 the Germans flew the swastika from the Eiffel Tower. The same day Army Group C assaulted the Maginot Line. The French were defeated. On June 17 they requested an armistice, and on June 25 the battle came to an end.

U.S. Neutrality Weakens

On June 4, as the Dunkirk evacuation ended, Winston Churchill delivered one of his most masterful wartime speeches. Expressing British determination to continue the war, he promised that Britons would never surrender, but "we shall defend our island, whatever the cost may be, we shall fight on the beaches, we shall fight on the landing-grounds, we shall fight in the fields and in the streets, we shall fight in the hills." [16] He closed with a moving appeal to the New World to come to the assistance of the Old.

The United States, still unready to take up arms against the Axis, was moved by the plight of Europe and gradually committed itself to undisguised economic warfare. As Denmark, the Low Countries, and France fell before German might, Roosevelt, by executive order, froze the funds of these countries in the U.S. so that Germany could not seize them. After Denmark fell, Greenland asked for American

[16] Churchill, *Their Finest Hour*, p. 118.

protection and it was gradually extended. When the British saved their army at Dunkirk at the expense of losing its arms and equipment, the U.S. dug into its arsenals and sent emergency weapons to Britain. And on June 10, the day Italy entered the war, Roosevelt made a speech that left no doubt about America's intention to throw her economic weight behind the Allies. In strong language he expressed contempt for Italy's action by saying "the hand that held the dagger has struck it into the back of its neighbor." The United States would now follow two courses:

> We will extend to the opponents of force the material resources of this nation; and, at the same time, we will harness and speed up the use of those resources in order that we ourselves in the Americas may have equipment and training equal to the task of any emergency and every defense.[17]

Roosevelt had sound backing for his policy of strengthening U.S. defenses while aiding Britain, but there were legal difficulties involved in extending the nation's material resources. While seeking a solution to them, Roosevelt took several steps to strengthen the nation internally. In June he appointed an eminent group of civilians to a National Defense Research Committee, and in mid-summer he strengthened his cabinet by the addition of two widely respected Republicans. Frank Knox became Secretary of the Navy and Henry L. Stimson Secretary of War. Stimson's first move was to urge upon Congress the adoption of a Selective Training and Service Act. It became law on September 16, 1940. Never before had the United States resorted to compulsory military training in time of peace.

[17] Rosenman, *The Public Papers and Addresses of Franklin D. Roosevelt*, Vol. IX, pp. 263–64.

The Battle of Britain

AN INTERLUDE followed the Battle of France. The Fuehrer, triumphant, visited fallen Paris; the soldiers of the Reich rested and digested their victories. Marshal Pétain, who had replaced Reynaud as Premier of France, established the government of Unoccupied France at Vichy; Charles de Gaulle formed the Free French in London. The Germans waited for the British to sue for peace; the RAF girded itself for the storm to come. During this interlude the Wehrmacht recognized, for the first time, that it must come to grips with Britain.

Vichy and Free France

After the armistice at the end of June, Marshal Pétain moved the French government to Vichy. Under the leadership of Pierre Laval, the Vichy government adopted a new constitution and began to move toward the fascist pattern. Vichy supporters ranged in sympathy from those who thought the Nazis would prevail in Europe and therefore the best course would be to collaborate with them, to those who felt they must accept the consequences of defeat and live with the changed situation as best they could until the balance of European power shifted again. The most Vichy could accomplish for the time being was to make Germany abide by the terms of the armistice, which left the Vichy government a reasonable degree of freedom, and in this course Vichy received the support of the United States, which recognized the Vichy regime as the lawful government of France. Most of France also recognized Vichy as the legal government, but a few rebellious Frenchmen gave their allegiance to de Gaulle, who refused to acknowledge that France had surrendered. De Gaulle had been brought into the French government during the Battle for France in June, and he had urged that France continue to resist, if necessary, from her empire. When Pétain became Premier and requested an armistice on June 17, de Gaulle fled to London.[1] He had few assets and fewer supporters, but his desire to save the honor of France was intense. On June 28 the British recognized de Gaulle as the leader of all the Free French who might rally behind the Allied cause. Churchill and de Gaulle, so much alike in some respects, so different in others, so strong, and so intensely wrought up in the welfare of their respective nations, were bound to clash. Each admired the other, but the degree to which each would go to protect the vital interests of his own country was cogently demonstrated on July 3, when the British attacked the French Fleet.

The French Fleet had been a problem for Britain from the beginning of France's collapse. Since June Churchill had urged that the Fleet not be allowed to fall into German hands, and Admiral Jean Darlan had assured him it would not. But the Fleet did not sail from French ports, as Churchill had urged, and although Germany promised not to use the Fleet for her war effort, Germany's promises no longer carried much weight. On July 3 the British moved to seize, destroy, or disable all the accessible French Fleet. Churchill called the decision the "most unnatural and painful in which I have ever been

---

[1] For bibliographical data on de Gaulle and the Free French movement, see de Gaulle, *The Call to Honour;* Churchill, *Their Finest Hour;* Spears, *Assignment to Catastrophe;* Werth, *De Gaulle.*

51

concerned." [2] French vessels in British harbors were seized; many volunteered to sail with the Royal Navy. In the eastern Mediterranean, at Alexandria, the French ships were demilitarized under British direction. In the western Mediterranean ports of Oran and Mers El Kebir, a powerful French force, including two modern battle cruisers and two battleships, was asked to decide whether it would (1) join the British, (2) sail under British supervision to ports where it could be interned out of Germany's reach, or (3) scuttle.[3] When the French admiral in command refused all of these choices, the British attacked. Britain disabled enough of the French Fleet so that she felt she could face her forthcoming ordeal with Germany assured that the Fleet could not be employed to shift the maritime balance of power against her.

To many Frenchmen, this action of the British seemed unnecessarily harsh. The Vichy government promptly broke off formal relations with Britain, but de Gaulle, to whom the events brought "pain and anger," accepted it: "I considered that the saving of France ranked above everything, even above the fate of her ships, and that our duty was still to go on with the fight." [4]

Operation SEA LION

With the fall of France, the British braced themselves to defy Germany without assistance. Hitler hoped the stubborn islanders would sue for peace. He maintained that since all he wanted from the British Empire was its acceptance of his control of the continent, there was no reason for the war to continue. As the days passed and Britain remained silent, the German High Command began discussing possibilities for concluding the war. Admiral Erich Raeder thought an invasion should be attempted only as a last resort, and War Directive Number 16 ordered planning for a landing operation in England only "if necessary." [5] The English Channel makes, as the French leaders

[2] Churchill, *Their Finest Hour*, p. 232.
[3] *Ibid.*, p. 235; Cunningham, *A Sailor's Odyssey*, Chapter 21.
[4] De Gaulle, *The Call to Honour*, p. 92.
[5] Trevor-Roper, *Blitzkrieg to Defeat*, p. 34. For SEA LION, see Fleming, *Operation Sea Lion*; Shirer, *The Rise and Fall of the Third Reich*; Taylor, *The Breaking Wave*.

told Churchill, a fine anti-tank ditch, and to cross it and land on a hostile shore was a problem that bedeviled German as well as British and American planners. In July 1940 the Wehrmacht, undefeated in a series of campaigns that made it master of the continent from northern Norway to the Pyrenees, lacked the means to invade Britain. It lacked the landing craft and supporting fleet, and its air force was not designed for long-range strategic missions. The Third Reich had reached its first big military crisis—a crisis that came about because it had not counted on a war that would take it off the continent of Europe.

Planning for the invasion of Britain—Operation SEA LION—brought frustration and friction into the German High Command. At the end of July Hitler called his military chiefs into conference and made a crucial decision. Since air supremacy over the Channel was essential to SEA LION's success, the Luftwaffe would begin concentrated attacks against southern England. If the British Air Force was severely weakened, SEA LION would begin in mid-September; if not, it would wait until spring. On August 1, Hitler signed the directives that launched the Battle of Britain. "The German Air Force is to overpower the English Air Force with all the forces at its command, in the shortest possible time. . . . The intensification of the air war may begin on or after 5th August." [6]

The Battle of Britain

The Battle of Britain was already under way when Hitler signed the directives on August 1. For weeks the Luftwaffe had been striking at British shipping and the Channel ports, since Goering hoped to loosen the blockade and also to lure the British fighters into battle. But when the aerial war began in earnest in mid-August, the Luftwaffe had accomplished little, because the Air Chief Marshal, Sir Hugh Dowding, refused to risk his Fighter Command in unfavorable conditions. Goering approached the coming trial of strength with self-confidence that marred his strategic thinking. He believed that four days would suffice to eliminate the RAF fighters and two weeks

[6] Trevor-Roper, *Blitzkrieg to Defeat*, pp. 37–38.

would conclude the campaign to achieve German air superiority. He called his operation EAGLE.

Goering had three air fleets, together comprising more than a thousand bombers and more than a thousand fighters.[7] The bulk of this airborne armada was concentrated in Field Marshal Albert Kesselring's Second Fleet, stationed in the Low Countries, and Field Marshal Hugo Sperrle's Third Fleet, in northern France. A much smaller Fifth Fleet, under General Hans Stumpff, was in Norway. On August 13 the Luftwaffe flew more than a thousand sorties over southeastern England. On August 15 came the first full-strength attack, utilizing all three fleets. Confident that Dowding would have concentrated all his fighter defenses in southern England to protect London, General Stumpff's Fifth Fleet attacked without fighter protection, expecting no opposition. But Dowding had rotated his squadrons, sending some to rest in the quieter northern sector before they returned to the more active southern area. Stumpff's Fleet was met by British fighters that shot down 16 bombers and 7 fighters with no loss to their own force.[8] EAGLE was not going to be a four-day pushover; Stumpff's Fleet was withdrawn from daylight action in the Battle of Britain.

RAF Fighter Command had fewer planes than did the Germans, but the Hurricane and Spitfire were good fighters and the aircraft plants were turning them out at a satisfactory rate. Fighter Command held another advantage: since the war would be fought over Britain, pilots who bailed out would be saved to fly again. More important, the British had given much thought to the subject of aerial defense. During the 1930's a Scottish scientist, Robert Watson-Watt, developed a means of using radio waves to give a "picture" of distant objects. Those responsible for Britain's aerial defense were quick to see the possibilities this provided for an early warning system against enemy aircraft. In 1936, when Hitler was remilitarizing the Rhineland and building an air force, a chain of radar towers began to appear on the cliffs and bluffs of southern England. By 1940 the long-range "eyes" of the radar towers had been improved so that they could

[7] For an analysis of the comparative strengths of the Luftwaffe and RAF, see Collier, *The Defense of the United Kingdom*, pp. 161–62; Taylor, *The Breaking Wave*, pp. 96–99.

[8] Collier, *The Defense of the United Kingdom*, pp. 192–95.

detect aircraft, indicate their direction, and distinguish between friend and foe. Ground control rooms and sector stations could plot the entire air battle on large boards and could direct the British fighters to the areas most threatened, for the fighter planes themselves were equipped with very high-frequency radio-telephones that gave them direct contact with their ground control stations. The Luftwaffe was aware of radar but had not thoroughly developed it. Nor did they appreciate its value. During the early days of the battle the Germans bombed the English radar stations, but they concluded the attacks were worthless and abandoned them. The radar towers stood, and through the ensuing months served Fighter Command well.

After abandoning the strikes on the radar towers, Goering directed the Luftwaffe to concentrate on harbors, port facilities, and airfields. Southern England was subjected to heavy attacks, but the RAF fighters inflicted heavy losses on the Luftwaffe. On August 19 Goering shifted the target to Fighter Command itself—the airfields and bases in southeastern England. Fighter battles would be the object of the daylight raids, and the Luftwaffe would use only enough bombers to lure Fighter Command into battle. The weight of the Luftwaffe now fell on Air Vice Marshal K. R. Park's Number 11 Group, and Park instructed his fighters to concentrate on the enemy bombers and avoid their fighters. His decision ultimately forced Goering to divert more and more fighters to close escort duty. Unsuited to the task, the escorting fighters could not challenge Fighter Command as easily.

The most critical two weeks of the battle opened with a massive raid on August 24. The Luftwaffe flew more than a thousand sorties. One airfield was knocked out of action. Two others sustained serious damage. Fighter Command lost 22 planes to the Luftwaffe's 38.[9] The intense battle continued, and Fighter Command's efficiency diminished. During this critical fortnight it lost nearly 300 planes. Though the Luftwaffe's total losses were higher, their fighter losses were lower than the RAF's.[10] Attrition in men was severe. Between August 24 and September 6, Fighter Command lost 103 pilots and another 128 were wounded. Newly trained replacements were not sufficiently battle-tried to hold their own in the aerial dog fights, and the experienced

[9] *Ibid.*, p. 208.
[10] Taylor, *The Breaking Wave*, p. 150.

pilots were wearing down from the constant strain.[11] The airfields and control centers were operating on a reduced scale, and the entire defense system was on the verge of collapse. Then, on September 7, the Luftwaffe switched its attention from the airfields to the city of London.

Why the change? On August 24 some German planes strayed from course and dropped their bombs on the center of London. Homes were destroyed and civilians killed. The RAF retaliated and bombed Berlin, and although the damage done was slight, Berliners were killed in their own capital, and Goering had promised that this would never happen. Hitler was furious and vowed that British cities would be razed. The Luftwaffe command felt that the battles of the past two weeks had brought Fighter Command near to collapse, but they thought the RAF was holding a reserve which the attacks on London would bring out. The Luftwaffe effort was switched from Fighter Command to London. It was the most important decision of the battle.

On the afternoon of September 7 the blitz on London began with the largest bombing raid ever made on a city. Day after day the bombing went on, but as far as the outcome of the air war was concerned, the damage done to London was minute, since the airfields and sector stations could be repaired while the bombing of London continued. Fighter Command gradually regained its strength, and on September 15, when Goering planned to polish the British off with a massive daylight raid, Fighter Command was again ready for the contest. This was a decisive battle in the war, and Churchill himself was at the headquarters of Park's Number 11 Group, fifty feet underground at Uxbridge.[12] There the group commanders watched the plotting board track the progress of the German bombers, heavily escorted and enroute to London. Directed by their ground control, the RAF fighters scrambled to intercept. All reserves were committed. The citizens of London, knowing that their government expected invasion, watched the battle taking place four miles above them with grave concern. That day the Luftwaffe lost 60 planes to Fighter Command's 26.[13] Goering could not continue to take such losses, and

[11] Collier, *The Defense of the United Kingdom*, p. 205.
[12] Churchill, *Their Finest Hour*, pp. 332–37.
[13] Collier, *The Defense of the United Kingdom*, pp. 244–45.

large-scale daylight missions were abandoned. The blitz would go on by night in an effort to break the British morale and induce surrender, but Operation SEA LION was indefinitely postponed. It was obvious that the Germans had not secured the necessary air control over England.

September 15 was the turning point in the air war over Britain, but it was not the end. London was bombed for 57 consecutive nights. The massive nighttime raids were supplemented by smaller daylight sorties, so sirens wailed and bombs exploded nearly continuously. Londoners did not break under the blitz. Parliament continued to sit in defiance of the enemy who sought to destroy the free government it represented. Citizens carried out their daily lives, seeking protection in shelters and the subway tubes during attacks and emerging afterward to resume their work. At the beginning of the blitz, the Luftwaffe dropped high-explosive bombs, occasionally supplemented by delayed-action bombs and land mines. In mid-October the Luftwaffe began to drop incendiary bombs as well, and many Londoners had to stay above the ground during the raids as roof-watchers and fire-fighters.

Early in November the blitz on London lessened and the Luftwaffe began a blitz on other cities. Designed to bring Britain to her knees by destroying her industrial potential, the new blitz lasted well into the spring. Coventry was bombed on November 14. The heart of the city, including the magnificent cathedral, was destroyed; 554 people died; [14] but within a week the city, including the aero-engine and machine-tool factories, was functioning again. On November 15 the Luftwaffe struck London; on November 19–22, Birmingham. Then the ports and the munitions centers—Bristol, Southhampton, Liverpool, Plymouth, Sheffield, Manchester, Leeds, Glasgow—were bombed. Dispersal of vital industries to smaller, scattered locations was begun and carried out as rapidly as possible. Production, while hampered, was not halted.

On December 29 the Luftwaffe returned to London. This climactic raid, the last of 1940, seemed to express the fury the Nazis felt toward the British, who would not give in. Thousands of incendiary bombs were dropped; 1500 fires were started. Railways and docks were

[14] *Ibid.,* p. 263.

severely damaged. Yet even though the Luftwaffe could inflict such punishment on the British cities, Britain had won the aerial battle. Churchill paid his well-known tribute to Fighter Command: "Never in the field of human conflict was so much owed by so many to so few." [15] Less eloquent than Churchill, Hitler spoke to his troops on New Year's Eve:

> It is the will of the democratic war inciters and their Jewish-capitalistic wire-pullers that the war must be continued . . . We are ready! . . . The year 1941 will bring completion of the greatest victory in our history.[16]

Few knew what Hitler meant by "the greatest victory in our history," but the shrewd could guess. By the end of 1940 Hitler had decided to turn his back on the British—those "little worms" that he had been so sure would not have the spunk to defy him—and invade Russia. The decision was crucial, and to follow its development it is necessary to go back to the conclusion of the Battle of France.

Germany and the East

When Hitler turned the Wehrmacht westward in the spring of 1940, he retained only a nominal military force in eastern Germany. The August 23 Pact with Russia gave him security on his eastern frontier, and also provided the Reich with appreciable amounts of raw materials. But Germany was not alone in profiting from the non-aggression treaty; Russia also saw benefits to be derived and did not hestitate to seize them. While the Germans were occupied in the west, Russia had completed incorporating Latvia, Lithuania, and Estonia into the Soviet Union. The Rumanian provinces of Bessarabia and Bucovinia were next on Stalin's list, and on June 23, the day after the French armistice was signed, Russian Foreign Minister Molotov told the Germans that Russia intended to take these provinces and was prepared to use force against Rumania if necessary. The Russian ultimatum was delivered to the Rumanians June 26. The Germans

---

[15] Churchill, *Their Finest Hour*, p. 340.
[16] Millis, *This Is Pearl*, p. 9.

advised them to accept it.

The Nazi-Soviet agreement had placed Bessarabia—but not Buco-vina—within the Russian sphere, and Russia's greed for Rumania distressed Berlin. Germany was dependent on oil from Rumania, especially since the British blockade had cut her off from other sources, and Germany also got a good deal of grain from Rumania. What if the Russians occupied the whole country? They did not, but Russia's attitude had been drawn in bold relief and Hitler felt he should turn his attention to the east. His intention to destroy the Russians was not new—it was plainly stated in *Mein Kampf*—but many times Hitler had insisted he would not involve Germany in a war on two fronts, and he would turn east only when he was free in the west. Yet now, at the end of July 1940, Hitler set the date for the invasion of Russia for spring 1941.[17] Britain was far from defeated. In fact, the Luftwaffe's big battle had hardly begun, and plans for SEA LION were still uncertain. Several reasons seem to have affected Hitler's decision to turn east at this time. The Wehrmacht felt confident of its strength and believed Russia could be defeated quickly. Russia's expansion was causing friction. The invasion of Russia might even help to solve the problem of Britain, who might come to terms and release the German forces for a "holy war" against Communism. If not, conquering Russia might still be the best way to defeat Britain, for with Russia destroyed and the entire continent aligned against her, Britain would be forced to capitulate. Five weeks seemed sufficient time to allow for the Wehrmacht to conquer Russia, and in that time the United States could not intervene. By late August German troops were massing in Poland.

While the Battle of Britain proceeded, Hitler had already turned toward the east. In August a troublesome situation arose when Hungary and Bulgaria demanded part of Rumania and the source of oil was again threatened. This time Hitler acted more vigorously. After forcing Rumania to grant the demands, Hitler occupied the rest of the country (upon the invitation of the pro-Nazi General Ion Antonescu) to "protect" Rumania from further territorial loss. Germany now felt secure about the precious oil, and Rumanian bases would be useful for the forthcoming war with Russia.

[17] Shirer, *The Rise and Fall of the Third Reich*, pp. 796–800.

How to keep Russia from suspecting German intentions was a problem, for troops must be massed in position and preparations on such a grand scale were hard to hide. Diplomatic relations between the two countries were already under a strain, and they scarcely improved when Germany signed the Tripartite Pact with Italy and Japan on September 27. Its main purpose was to scare the United States into staying neutral by threatening her with a war on two fronts if she intervened. To keep from frightening Russia, a specific clause exempted her from the terms of the pact, which stated in part:

> Article I: Japan recognizes and respects the leadership of Germany and Italy in the establishment of a new order in Europe.
>
> Article II: Germany and Italy recognize and respect the leadership of Japan in the establishment of a new order in Greater East Asia.
>
> Article III: Japan, Germany and Italy agree to cooperate in their efforts on the aforesaid lines. They further undertake to assist one another with all political, economic and military means when one of the three Contracting Parties is attacked by a power at present not involved in the European War or in the Sino-Japanese Conflict. . . .
>
> Article V: Japan, Germany and Italy affirm that the aforesaid terms do not in any way affect the political status which exists at present as between each of the three Contracting Parties and Soviet Russia.[18]

Russia, sandwiched between Germany and Japan, was not completely reassured by the exemptive clause, and Molotov was invited to come to Berlin for conferences to ease matters.[19] He did so on November 12, and Hitler and von Ribbentrop held out the possibility of drawing Russia into the Pact as one of the great powers. Her "new order" and sphere of interest could be developed toward the Indian Ocean.

The Russian reaction was cool. Russia wanted access to the sea through the Balkans, not the Indian Ocean, and in the Balkans the

[18] As given in Feis, *The Road to Pearl Harbor,* pp. 119–20.
[19] Shirer, *The Rise and Fall of the Third Reich,* pp. 800–10.

Axis seemed determined to have its own way. Two weeks later Molotov informed the Germans of the conditions under which Russia would consent to join a four-power pact. Russia wanted Finland; she wanted a treaty with Bulgaria and protection of her Balkan interests; she wanted the Persian Gulf area. The price was too high for Hitler. Any doubts about invading Russia were swept aside. On December 18, 1940, Hitler signed War Directive Number 21 for Operation BARBAROSSA. It read, in part:

> The German Armed Forces must be prepared, even before the conclusion of the war against England, to crush Soviet Russia in a rapid campaign. . . . Preparations . . . will be concluded by 15th May 1941. . . . The bulk of the Russian Army stationed in Western Russia will be destroyed by daring operations led by deeply penetrating armoured spearheads. Russian forces still capable of giving battle will be prevented from withdrawing into the depths of Russia. The enemy will then be energetically pursued. . . . The final objective of the operation is to erect a barrier against Asiatic Russia on the general line Volga-Archangel.[20]

[20] Trevor-Roper, *Blitzkrieg to Defeat*, pp. 49–50.

War Approaches the United States

During 1940 and 1941, the United States was pulled toward involvement in the war by a dual threat. (1) German U-boats were threatening to drive the Royal Navy off the seas and seize control of the Atlantic for Germany. (2) Japan was moving toward open aggression in the Far East that challenged U.S. rights and responsibilities in the Pacific.

Battle in the Atlantic, 1940–1941

Before June 1940 German U-boats had not been able to inflict critical loss on British merchant shipping, but the fall of France was a tremendous boost to the German Navy. Not only did the British lose the support of the French Fleet, which had borne the primary responsibility of policing the Mediterranean, but Germany now controlled the coast of Europe from northern Norway to southern France. Blockade, as a weapon against Germany, was weakened, and the

German Navy immensely improved its offensive position by operating from the French ports in the Atlantic, thus shortening the distance to their refueling and supply bases.

Admiral Karl Doenitz, in charge of Germany's submarine warfare, lost no time in taking advantage of his improved situation. He set up his own headquarters at Brest, and St. Nazaire became the chief operating and repair base for his U-boats. At first the U-boats operated individually and with appreciable success. The German U-boat aces called the period between July and October the "happy time." [1] Seeking to increase their kills, Doenitz planned a tactic called the Wolf-Pack, and by October, when he had enough submarines to employ it, the Wolf-Packs went into operation. The U-boats were sent out in a fan-shaped pattern. When one located a convoy, it radioed the location to home base and other U-boats were directed to the scene. By day, submerged and at maximum distance to escape detection, they shadowed the convoys. At night they surfaced, closed distance, and fired their torpedoes. The U-boats could shadow a convoy for days. The system was efficient and deadly. Although the Battle of the Atlantic was not officially proclaimed until March 1941, for Britain its most critical period was the twelve months between July 1940 and July 1941.[2]

The British changed escort techniques and convoy routes, but their losses continued to climb. Shipping was diverted from the southern approaches to the northern ports, but then port congestion became a problem. The weekly tonnage of imports remained too low for security. Churchill admitted that the U-boat peril frightened him.[3]

Action against the U-boats was essential. The RAF Coastal Command was instructed to concentrate all suitable resources in the area of the coastal waters, and their efforts were rewarding, but when German losses in the coastal areas rose, Doenitz began employing the U-boats further out to sea. The answer seemed to be increased convoy protection, improved radar and direction-finding wireless sets, and, of course, more ships. But ships take time to build. The Royal Navy had suffered grievous losses at Norway and Dunkirk, especially in destroyers, and so long as the threat of German invasion remained,

---

[1] Roskill, *The War at Sea,* Vol. I, p. 348.
[2] Churchill, *Their Finest Hour,* p. 599.
[3] *Ibid.,* p. 598.

much of the fleet had to be employed in defensive positions on the east coast of Britain rather than sent out to sea. Britain decided to call on the United States, and on May 15, 1940, Churchill wrote to Roosevelt on the subject of American aid. It was the first of an important series of personal messages, about 1750 in all, exchanged between the two men.[4] Churchill requested the loan of fifty old American destroyers to supplement the Royal Navy's convoy escorts. In September the arrangements were completed and fifty U.S. destroyers became available to the Royal Navy. In return Britain leased to the U.S. certain areas in the western Atlantic to be used as naval, military, or air bases.[5]

During the last months of 1940 and early 1941 the Atlantic struggle intensified. German U-boats were increasing in number and effectiveness. Magnetic mines took a heavy toll of shipping; Germany's long-range aircraft caused heavy losses at sea. Measures taken to protect shipping caused delays that slowed down the volume of imports, so that in January 1941 the total volume of British imports was less than half that of a year ago.[6] Between the end of October 1940 and the beginning of April 1941, the *Scheer* sank 16 ships and successfully evaded the Royal Navy to make her way back to Germany. The *Hipper* berthed at Brest and made forays into the Atlantic to wreak havoc along the sea lanes. *Scharnhorst* and *Gneisenau,* damaged at Norway but since repaired, cruised the North Atlantic, where in a two-month period they sank or captured a total of 22 ships.[7]

In January 1941 Hitler warned the British that in the spring he would launch a U-boat war that would bring about Britain's annihilation. By March the U-boat damage had become so severe that Churchill formally proclaimed the attacks the "Battle of the Atlantic" so that intensified efforts of the government and the armed forces could be focused on Britain's lifelines. In April British naval losses were so high that publication of them was suspended. But in May, when the Luftwaffe was withdrawn from the war at sea to prepare for

---

[4] *Ibid.,* p. 23.

[5] The base sites were in Newfoundland, Bermuda, the Bahamas, Jamaica, Antigua, St. Lucia, Trinidad, and British Guiana. Churchill, *Their Finest Hour,* pp. 398–416; Langer and Gleason, *Challenge to Isolation,* pp. 742–76.

[6] Churchill, *The Grand Alliance,* p. 114.

[7] Roskill, *The War at Sea,* Vol. I, Chapter 18 and Appendix M, pp. 604–5.

the invasion of Russia, some relief came to the Atlantic. But relief for the convoys was short-lived, since as soon as the Royal Navy began to send goods to Russia, these convoys also were hounded.

The war at sea was difficult and drawn out, but in May the Royal Navy sank the *Bismarck* in one of the longest and most dramatic naval engagements in history.[8] The *Bismarck* was a major threat to British shipping, and Allied morale received a welcome boost when she was eliminated. The new German battleship *Bismarck* was the biggest ship afloat, mounting 8 fifteen-inch guns plus 81 smaller ones. She displaced 42,800 tons, yet could steam at 31 knots. Despite the Admiralty's close watch, she eluded the British blockade and escaped from the Baltic Sea. On May 23 she was spotted in the Denmark Strait, and at dawn the next day H.M.S. *Hood* and H.M.S. *Prince of Wales* intercepted her and opened fire. Seventeen minutes later *Hood* was in a watery grave, the victim of a direct hit and explosion, and *Prince of Wales* was so badly damaged she was forced to withdraw. Nineteen warships began to converge on *Bismarck's* course, but in the early morning of May 25 she escaped her shadowers and was not relocated until late in the day. She was heading for St. Nazaire, and it was imperative that the Royal Navy bring her to battle before she reached safety. On May 26 the aircraft from carrier *Ark Royal* so badly damaged *Bismarck's* rudder by torpedo attacks that she became completely unmaneuverable. The British closed in on their prey at dawn, May 27. *Norfolk, Rodney, King George V,* and *Dorsetshire* led the fire. Unable to maneuver, *Bismarck* nevertheless fought back with intense and accurate fire, but the weight of the attack against her began to tell. One by one her guns were knocked out. After an hour and twenty minutes of pounding, *Bismarck* was silent and to all practical purposes defeated, but her flag still flew and she showed no signs of sinking. The British ships, fuel running low, were anxious to sink their foe and go home. *Dorsetshire* moved in close to *Bismarck's* starboard side and fired two torpedoes point blank. One exploded right under the bridge. *Dorsetshire* steered around to port and fired another. With her flag still flying, the *Bismarck* turned bottom up and disappeared.

Throughout the summer the battle of the lifelines remained con-

---

[8] See Grenfell, *The Bismarck Episode.*

stant and unrelenting. Although British losses dropped in mid-summer, Germany's U-boat production was on the increase, and the security of the sea lanes was far from assured. On the other hand, the British and Canadian Navies were strengthening their escort potential, and the United States was steadily moving toward outright assistance in the Atlantic struggle.

The United States Begins De Facto War

The Battle of the Atlantic was almost as important to the United States as it was to Britain. For years U.S. foreign policy had been based on a friendly power maintaining control of the Atlantic while the bulk of the U.S. Fleet was concentrated in the Pacific. After the fall of France, the Chief of Naval Operations, Admiral Harold Stark, requested money to start a massive expansion of the Navy, and Congress appropriated it without hesitation. Shipbuilding takes time, and until the U.S. had a navy ready to fight on two oceans at once, it was imperative that Britain not be defeated.

In November 1940 Roosevelt was elected to an unprecedented third term. For some time he and his advisers had been grappling with the problem of how to aid Britain. Her dollar resources were rapidly decreasing and she could not indefinitely continue the "cash and carry" arrangement. In December Roosevelt introduced the concept of Lend-Lease. As he put it, if a neighbor's house was on fire and one had a hose, he loaned it to the neighbor to help put out the fire. Afterward he would expect to get it back. Instead of the "silly, foolish, old dollar sign," there was a "gentleman's obligation to repay in kind." [9] Next Roosevelt established the Office of Production Management (OPM), representing both labor and management, and endowed with authority to organize and administer defense production. On December 29, the same night that London endured the mammoth fire raid that climaxed the 1940 blitz, Roosevelt went on the radio for his customary "fireside chat." In his strong, resonant voice he spoke about the problems of national security. He warned

[9] Rosenman, *The Public Papers and Addresses of Franklin D. Roosevelt*, Vol. IX, pp. 607–8.

that it was foolish to believe that an Axis victory would not bring a "new and terrible era" to the Western Hemisphere. "There is far less chance of the United States getting into the war, if we do all we can now to support the nations defending themselves against attack by the Axis. . . . We must admit that there is risk in any course we may take. . . . The people of Europe who are defending themselves do not ask us to do their fighting. They ask us for the implements of war. . . . We must be the great arsenal of democracy. For us this is an emergency as serious as war itself." [10]

The response to the President's speech was enthusiastic, and on March 11, 1941, the Lend-Lease bill was signed. The President was authorized, "when he deems it in the interest of national defense," to have manufactured and to "sell, transfer title to, exchange, lease, lend, or otherwise dispose of," "any defense article" for "the government of any country whose defense the President deems vital to the defense of the United States." [11] Congress would appropriate the funds, and conditions for return or payment were to be up to the discretion of the President. The American people were committed. They would not let Britain go under.

Lend-Lease was of no value if the goods were sunk by U-boats before they reached Britain, and all too often this was the case. The security of the Atlantic sea lanes became increasingly important to U.S. security, and although the Lend-Lease bill did not authorize the U.S. Navy to convoy goods, or authorize any U.S. vessel to enter the combat area, these activities were the logical next step in the "short of war" policy. The U.S. Navy began to marshal its forces for more active convoy protection.

Between January and March 1941 U.S. and British service staffs held conferences in Washington to make sure that if the United States were drawn into the war, she would be ready to coordinate her action with that of her ally.[12] From the Washington conferences emerged the basic strategic concept that formed the core of future coalition warfare. Should the United States enter the war, she would join

[10] *Ibid.*, pp. 633–44 for complete speech.
[11] Commager, *Documents of American History*, Vol. II, pp. 449–50; Langer and Gleason, *The Undeclared War*, Chapters 8 and 9.
[12] Langer and Gleason, *The Undeclared War*, pp. 285–89; Greenfield, *Command Decisions*, Chapter 1.

Britain in concerted action against Hitler while maintaining a strategic defensive position against Japan. By concentrating on Germany first, both countries could use their forces in conjunction, whereas if the United States turned her main effort toward Japan, Britain could be of little assistance so long as Hitler remained undefeated.

Shortly after the staff talks were concluded, the United States clarified its relation to Greenland. The U.S. assumed an official protectorate of the island, and became responsible for her supply and defense until Denmark was free. Greenland, the Azores, the Gulf of St. Lawrence, the Bahamas, the Caribbean, and the Gulf of Mexico were proclaimed part of the Western Hemisphere for which the United States assumed the responsibility for defense. Belligerent vessels were warned to stay away. Admiral Ernest J. King, Commander-in-Chief of the Atlantic Fleet, organized patrols and task forces to insure that they did so.[13]

In May a neutral passenger ship, the *Zam Zam,* was sunk by a German raider in the South Atlantic. Shortly afterward the *Robin Moor,* an American freighter enroute to South Africa with a general cargo, was sunk by a submarine. A week later the British sank the *Bismarck,* but her brief career and near escape dramatized the German threat. Patrols were enlarged and extended, but much Lend-Lease material continued to end up on the bottom of the Atlantic.

In July the United States began building escort vessels for the British under the Lend-Lease program. This building program was gradually enlarged to include landing craft—to the mutual benefit of both navies later on. Also in July the United States Marines occupied Iceland, relieving the British garrison for duty elsewhere. A task force was organized to escort convoys of U.S. and Icelandic ships, "including ships of any nationality which may join," between the U.S. and Iceland. While theoretically escorting her own ships in her own hemisphere waters, the "hitch-hiking" clause enabled the U.S. Navy to assume full convoy-escort duties west of Iceland.[14]

As the U.S. Navy assumed its enlarged duties, it faced a dilemma. What should U.S. ships do if they met a German war vessel? Fire? Wait to be fired upon? The U.S. was not at war, but protecting the

[13] Morison, *The Battle of the Atlantic,* p. 61.
[14] *Ibid.,* pp. 74–79.

merchant ships implied destroying any hostile forces. The difficulties were illustrated by an incident involving the U.S. destroyer *Greer*. Early in September, while proceeding toward Iceland, *Greer* was warned by a British plane that a German submarine lay across her path ten miles ahead. *Greer* made sound contact and followed the sub for three hours, but when the plane asked if *Greer* were going to attack, she replied, "No." The British plane dropped its depth charges and withdrew. Shortly, the submarine fired a torpedo at *Greer,* which dodged it but replied by dropping depth charges. The submarine fired a second torpedo, which *Greer* also dodged. *Greer* then lost sound contact on the submarine and proceeded to her destination. That an American naval vessel had been fired on brought matters to a head. On September 11 Roosevelt warned that henceforth "if German or Italian vessels of war enter the waters the protection of which is necessary for American defense, they do so at their own risk." [15] The Navy was authorized to shoot. It was soon operating under wartime conditions, ready for combat.

The Japanese Threat

For the United States, the Atlantic peril had constantly to be viewed in relation to mounting dangers in the Pacific. Since 1937, when Japan's war against China assumed major proportions, Japanese-American relations had grown steadily more strained. American sympathies were overwhelmingly in support of China, and although the U.S. was not eager to go to war in her support, loans were granted to China to bolster her economy and enable her to buy munitions. Meanwhile the U.S. government tried to persuade Japan to abandon her aggressive course. Although there were moderate elements within the Japanese government who felt Japan's wisest course was to retain friendly relations with other countries, the Army and Navy, centers of a militaristic element favoring expansion by force, in large measure controlled the Japanese government.

In 1937 Japan set about securing a position on the Asian mainland and extending her influence toward the South Seas. She justified her

[15] *Ibid.,* p. 80.

action by affirming that the entire region was "geographically, histori-
cally, racially and economically very closely related."[16] Although
Japan emphasized that the aims of unification would be attained
peacefully, the establishment of the Southeast Asia Co-Prosperity
Sphere became the *casus belli* for the greatest war in Japanese
history. In July 1940 Prince Fumimaro Konoye became Prime Minister for the second time. During his first term, from 1937 to 1939, the
war in China had erupted. His reassumption of office contributed to a
growing apprehension in the West that Japan's creeping aggression
was gaining momentum.

The pace of Konoye's new administration was set by his Foreign
Minister, Yosuke Matsuoka. He urged that the government move to
hasten the end of the China Incident by any means, take stronger
measures in dealing with French Indo-China and the Indies, and
make a political arrangement with Germany.[17] Japan officially joined
the Axis by signing the Tripartite Pact on September 27, 1940. All
three countries were thus united in a military alliance against any
power that might enter the war against any one of them. The United
States, though still neutral, was a source of worry, and it was hoped
that the threat of the pact, confronting the U.S. with a war on two
oceans if she intervened, might keep her out.

Keeping the U.S. neutral was Japan's biggest problem, for so long
as the European war continued, only the U.S. would have the available naval strength to challenge Japan's moves in the Pacific. Committed to expansion, but also committed to seeking to avoid war with
other powers, the Japanese government faced the difficult task of
trying to steal the cheese without springing the trap. The fourteen
months between signing the Tripartite Pact and the Japanese attack
on Pearl Harbor were months of delicate negotiations and careful
actions, but grim determination on both sides. Japan wanted economic and political hegemony over an area which both the U.S. and
Japan had pledged to uphold as politically and economically independent. Until Japan crossed the Great Wall of China, the U.S. had
not interfered, although it had disapproved. But Japan's continued
aggression was a threat not only to U.S. economic interests in Asia,

[16] Feis, *The Road to Pearl Harbor*, p. 64.
[17] *Ibid.*, pp. 84–85, 112.

70

but to the Philippines as well, whose defense was a U.S. responsibility. At this point Roosevelt and the State Department took a firm stand against further Japanese aggression by force.

Aside from moral suasion and appeals to treaty commitments, the main weapon by which the United States could seek to influence Japan's actions (short of war) was applying economic embargo. The U.S. showed she was willing to use that weapon in the summer of 1939, when she did not renew her commercial treaty with Japan. Japan did not alter her aggressive course. When the Netherlands fell, Japan began pressuring the Netherlands East Indies to give her economic and political privileges, especially the right to buy a large proportion of her oil production. When France fell, Japan demanded that French Indo-China close the routes by which outside aid could reach China and grant Japan air bases and the right of troop passage through Indo-China. As soon as Britain became helpless, Japan demanded that the Burma Road be closed. China had built the road to connect Kunming with Lashio, Burma. It provided a supply route to the west after Japan closed the Chinese ports. Japan, striving to cut off China's sources of supply, hoped that the huge country might be weakened to the point of collapse. Practically defenseless, the Indies began a delaying series of negotiations, making minor concessions and playing for time. Vichy France also yielded to Japan's demands, and in August the Japanese occupied northern Indo-China and began using the airfields of Tonkin province. The United States responded with economic pressure, stopping the export to Japan of certain implements of war and raw materials. The embargo was steadily expanded to include all iron and steel scrap (important in the Japanese economy), but not all fuel oils.

By using economic pincers the U.S. hoped to convince Japan that she was determined to resist the Japanese policy of expansion by force, as well as determined to weaken Japan's war-making ability. Yet how far could the U.S. go without driving the Japanese to seek to gain by force those raw materials the U.S. was refusing to sell? The Indies were virtually defenseless, and if the U.S. denied Japan the right to buy fuel oils, would not Japan move at once into the Indies, where she could obtain them? No force in the Pacific was capable of halting Japan should she choose to press south at once, and if Britain fell, as seemed likely until late in 1940, the United States would need its entire naval resources in the Atlantic. Economic pressure was tempered by the necessity not to drive Japan into the very war the U.S. was seeking to avert, for if war had to come, the U.S. needed more time to prepare for it. This carefully paced game of negotiations, appeals, and economic pressures continued through the first eleven months of 1941.

The ARGENTIA Conference and the Atlantic Charter

On Saturday, August 9, 1941, Churchill and Roosevelt met at Placentia Bay, Newfoundland, for the first of nine meetings they would hold before Roosevelt's death in April 1945. Although this first conference (code-named ARGENTIA) came before the United States formally stood by Britain's side, it laid the foundation on which all succeeding conferences were to be based. At its conclusion Roosevelt and Churchill issued what amounted to their war aims in the Atlantic Charter, but perhaps more important, they established a warm and deep personal understanding and assumed leadership of the principles of cooperation and coalition warfare.

There was much for Churchill and Roosevelt to discuss. The Lend-Lease bill of March had made American policy clear—she would support Britain. Lend-Lease, joint staff talks, the exchange of scientific information, the pool of military intelligence, increasing cooperation between military and civilian specialists, the repair of British warships in American shipyards—all these were in progress, plus the aid the U.S. was supplying in the Atlantic. Russia had been invaded in June (see page 85) and in this vast country also the Wehrmacht had made dramatic gains. How long could Russia resist? If she could hold, Britain and America would do well to help her, but if she were on the verge of collapse they could ill afford to deplete their own stocks of war materials. Harry Hopkins, Roosevelt's friend and adviser, just back from Moscow, was convinced Russia would fight, and hard. Arrangements for Lend-Lease to Russia were begun. Could Japan be dissuaded from her militant course? Churchill urged making a strong warning to Japan that further aggression would mean war. Roosevelt was not free to make such a threat, since under the U.S. Constitution only Congress can make such a decision. Nor was Roosevelt free to give Churchill a definite answer as to whether the U.S. would fight for the Pacific, or at what point in Japan's expansion would the U.S. draw the line. Appreciating his position, Churchill left Japanese diplomacy in Roosevelt's hands.

As the conference closed, Churchill and Roosevelt issued the Atlantic Charter:

Joint Declaration by the President and the Prime Minister
August 12, 1941

The President of the United States of America and the Prime Minister, Mr. Churchill, representing His Majesty's Government in the United Kingdom, being met together, deem it right to make known certain common principles in the national policies of their respective countries on which they base their hopes for a better future for the world.

First, their countries seek no aggrandisement, territorial or other.

Second, they desire to see no territorial changes that do not accord with the freely expressed wishes of the peoples concerned.

Third, they respect the right of all peoples to choose the form of government under which they will live; and they wish to see sovereign rights and self-government restored to those who have been forcibly deprived of them.

Fourth, they will endeavour, with due respect for their existing obligations, to further the enjoyment by all States, great or small, victor or vanquished, of access, on equal terms, to the trade and to the raw materials of the world which are needed for their economic prosperity.

Fifth, they desire to bring about the fullest collaboration between all nations in the economic field, with the object of securing for all improved labour standards, economic advancement, and social security.

Sixth, after the final destruction of the Nazi tyranny they hope to see established a peace which will afford to all nations the means of dwelling in safety within their own boundaries, and which will afford assurance that all the men in all the lands may live out their lives in freedom from fear and want.

Seventh, such a peace should enable all men to traverse the high seas and oceans without hindrance.

Eighth, they believe that all the nations of the world, for realistic as well as spiritual reasons, must come to the abandonment of the use of force. Since no future peace can be maintained if land, sea, or air armaments continue to be employed by nations which threaten, or may threaten, aggression outside of their frontiers, they believe, pending the establishment of a wider and permanent system of general security, that the disarmament of such nations is essential. They will likewise aid and encourage all other practicable measures which will lighten for peace-loving peoples the crushing burden of armaments.[18]

If Churchill and Roosevelt hoped to dissuade Germany from her U-boat warfare by warning her that they were united morally if not militarily, they failed. In October U-boats attacked a slow convoy four hundred miles south of Iceland. Three ships were sunk and five U.S. destroyers rushed to the convoy's defense. Despite the increased protection the U-boats attacked again. Seven more vessels were sunk and the U.S.S. *Kearney* was torpedoed. She reached Iceland, but some of her men had been killed. Two weeks later the U.S.S. *Reuben James,* the first U.S. Navy casualty in the undeclared war, was sunk about six hundred miles west of Ireland.[19] Congress amended the Neutrality Laws to permit merchant vessels to be armed and to enter war zones. How long would Hitler put up with America's flagrant violation of neutrality?

[18] Churchill, *The Grand Alliance,* pp. 443–44.
[19] Morison, *The Battle of the Atlantic,* p. 94.

War Comes to the Mediterranean

LATE IN 1940 a new theater of war erupted when Italy opened hostilities in the Balkans and North Africa. Although the war in the Mediterranean was begun on a small scale, it gradually expanded into a major conflict.

Italy Attacks Greece and Egypt

Mussolini, annoyed that he had not been consulted when Hitler partitioned Rumania in August 1940, began casting about for an easy victory that would enhance his prestige and raise his bargaining power with Hitler. He decided to take Greece, a poor country with a small army and navy. In addition to offering the victory he needed, it would afford bases that would weaken Great Britain's position in the Mediterranean. He ordered his generals to be ready by October.

In North Africa, also, Mussolini saw opportunities to expand his New Roman Empire. Italy had taken the provinces of Tripolitania

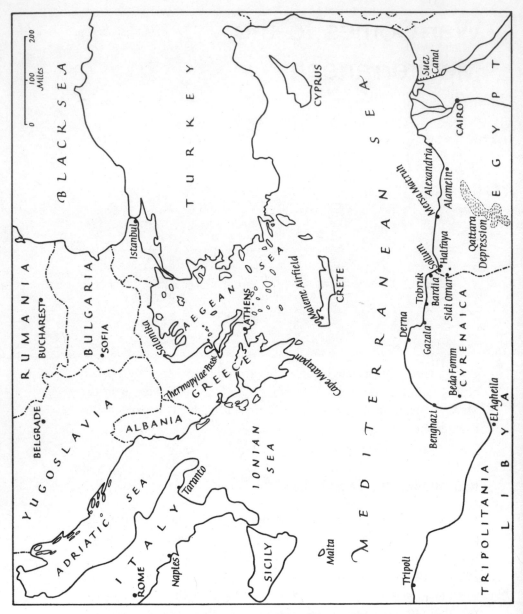

EASTERN MEDITERRANEAN AREA

76

and Cyrenaica from Turkey in 1912. During the succeeding years she had suppressed native resistance, and in 1939 the two provinces were incorporated into the kingdom of Italy as Libya. There, Mussolini had been building up his military strength for some time. Planning to attack Egypt and the Suez Canal, he had built a road along the coast to the Egyptian frontier and stockpiled supplies along the way at Benghazi, Derna, Tobruk, Bardia, and Sollum. By September his armies were ready to move, but Italian preparations had not eluded the British. As early as 1936, after Italy had annexed Ethiopia, Great Britain and Egypt concluded a treaty which gave Britain the right to base troops in Egypt for the protection of the Suez Canal. In 1939 Lieutenant General Sir Archibald Wavell went to Cairo to head the Middle East Command. Although he had few men, Wavell made his plans with confidence. Lieutenant General Sir Richard O'Connor was given two divisions with which to defend northwest Egypt, and when the Italians began their advance he was ready. With O'Connor harassing them, the Italians advanced cautiously to Sidi Barrani, just over the Egyptian frontier, where they halted to bring up more supplies. Through October and November the two armies contemplated each other in the desert heat, while across the Mediterranean the Italians began their assault on Greece.

The Greeks were no more surprised by the Italian attack than the British had been. Ever since Mussolini had annexed Albania in 1939, the Greeks had been preparing for defense; and when the Greek government refused to yield to Mussolini's ultimatum of October 28, 1940, the Italo-Greek war began.[1] Its progress surprised everyone except perhaps the Greeks, who fought with a morale that transcended poor equipment and supplies, bitter weather and deprivation. The Italians expected to reach Salonika in two weeks and Athens in four. Instead, by mid-November the Greeks had not only stopped the Italian advance, but they had begun to drive the invaders back. Before a stalemate was reached at the end of the year, the Greeks had pushed Mussolini's armies some thirty miles back into Albania. There, both Italians and Greeks spent a miserable winter, suffering from extreme cold, exposure, inadequate supplies, and hunger.

[1] Kirkpatrick, *Mussolini: A Study in Power,* Chapter 17; Shirer, *The Rise and Fall of the Third Reich,* pp. 815–17.

In December General O'Connor's forces in Egypt took action. Moving by night and hiding in the desert by day, the British moved around the Italian positions and attacked them from the rear. Surprised, the Italians floundered. By December 10 Sidi Barrani was in British hands and thousands of Italians had surrendered: "five acres of officers and two hundred acres of other ranks." [2] Capitalizing on his enemy's disorder, O'Connor pressed on. Bardia fell to the British on January 4, 1941, and the victors moved toward Tobruk, a small town built around a harbor and encompassed by a ring of Italian earthworks and fortifications. It fell to O'Connor's force on January 21 and he immediately turned toward Benghazi, a larger port on the western side of the Cyrenaican Bulge. (See map, page 76.) On the bulge between Gazala and Benghazi the Western Desert gives way to a region of olive groves, small villages, hills and valleys, and fresh water. Mussolini's road followed the coast between the towns, and along it moved the remnants of the retreating Italian Army. Directing the 6th Australian Division to pursue them, O'Connor sent the 7th Armored Division across the uncharted desert at Mechili to intercept the Italians south of Benghazi. The 7th Armored reached the coast ahead of the retreating Italians, and on February 5 the opposing forces met at Beda Fomm, where the British annihilated the Italian Tenth Army.

The British were jubilant, and O'Connor wanted to continue his advance to Tunisia, drive the Italians out of Africa, and secure the southern shores of the Mediterranean. But, instead, O'Connor was forced to deplete his troops and put them on the defensive, because the British planners felt it was necessary to send military aid to Greece.

Germany Subdues Yugoslavia and Greece

Hitler was furious when he heard of Mussolini's unilateral action in Greece. Not only did Italy's aggressive attack provide the RAF with an excuse to move onto Greek airfields, putting the British within range of the vital Rumanian oil fields, but Hitler wanted the Balkan

[2] Churchill, *Their Finest Hour*, p. 611.

area secured before he began his assault on Russia. He decided to send German forces to Greece to insure an Axis victory. Meanwhile, he sought to bring the other Balkan states into the Axis alliance. Rumania and Hungary formally joined the Axis in November 1940, and in March 1941 Bulgaria and Yugoslavia signed the Tripartite Pact. On March 26 the Yugoslav government was overthrown and an anti-Nazi government assumed power. Such disrespect triggered the Fuehrer's unstable temper, and in a rage he ordered Yugoslavia crushed in a merciless campaign called Operation PUNISHMENT. It was planned to coincide with the attack on Greece. BARBAROSSA, the cherished assault on Russia, would have to wait until the Balkan affair was concluded.[3]

German intentions against Greece were divined by both Greeks and British, and for the latter they posed a problem. Britain had signed an agreement with Greece in 1939 promising help in the event of attack. When the Italo-Greek war began in October, Greece requested aid. Since few ground forces could be spared, the Royal Navy took up the challenge. Admiral Sir Andrew Cunningham's Mediterranean Fleet, stationed at Alexandria, conducted a torpedo bomber raid on the Italian Fleet at its main base at Taranto on November 11. More than 20 aircraft, flying from the carrier *Illustrious*, surprised and sank at their moorings 3 Italian battleships Only 2 British aircraft were lost. Combined with a successful attack on an Italian convoy the next day, the Taranto raid vigorously reasserted British maritime power in the Mediterranean.[4]

With a German invasion in the offing, Greece needed more help than the Royal Navy could provide. The British were facing a numerically superior Italian force in Egypt, the RAF was engaged in the Battle of Britain, and the material losses of Dunkirk had not yet been made good, but nevertheless the British sent what support they could muster to the Greeks. Unfortunately it was insufficient, and when the German assault began, the outcome was not long in doubt.

Operation PUNISHMENT began on April 6. Belgrade, which possessed no anti-aircraft defenses, was bombed for three days and

---

[3] Shirer, *The Rise and Fall of the Third Reich*, pp. 822–26.
[4] Roskill, *The War at Sea*, Vol. I, pp. 296–301; Cunningham, *A Sailor's Odyssey*, pp. 273, 283–87. The Taranto raid attained significance when the Japanese attacked Pearl Harbor using similar tactics.

nights. The city was destroyed, more than 17,000 persons were killed, and Yugoslavia's defense was crippled since the High Command's communications with the army were annihilated.[5] The Yugoslav Army, hampered by internal strife between Serbs and Croats, was easy prey for the efficient Germans and was essentially defeated in the first few days of the campaign. On the 17th Yugoslavia surrendered, but many of the soldiers slipped away into the rugged mountains to begin a guerrilla war that brought Hitler many headaches.

The German campaign in Greece progressed almost as rapidly as the one in Yugoslavia. Although the Greeks fought with bravery, resourcefulness, and determination, these qualities did not compensate for German superiority on land and in the air. The German advance was swift and sure. By the 17th, when Yugoslavia surrendered, the British and Greek forces were retreating to the Thermopylae Pass. The Greek Army in Albania was cut off by a German column that captured Jannina April 23, and on April 24 the Greeks signed an armistice. Admiral Cunningham's Mediterranean Fleet, having given the Italian Navy another major trouncing at Cape Matapan on March 28, now moved in to evacuate the British forces from Greece.[6] The British had sent some 68,000 men to Greece and now they had to be lifted from a shore where harbors were inadequate or unusable and where the military situation was virtually out of British control. The Germans controlled the skies, necessitating that evacuation ships move into Greek waters only at night. Despite the difficulties, 80 percent of the forces sent to Greece were successfully lifted between April 24 and April 29. Naval losses, however, were high.

It was apparent that the Germans intended to move on to seize Crete. Although Crete's strategic position for control of the eastern Mediterranean had been appreciated earlier, little had been done to supply or fortify it adequately. Evacuees from Greece reinforced the Crete garrison in late April, and General Bernard C. Freyberg,

---

[5] Shirer, *The Rise and Fall of the Third Reich*, p. 826.
[6] See Heckstall-Smith, *Greek Tragedy;* Roskill, *The War at Sea,* Vol. I; Cunningham, *A Sailor's Odyssey.* For the British campaign in Greece see Buckley, *Greece and Crete;* Playfair, *The Mediterranean and the Middle East,* Vol. I; Churchill, *Their Finest Hour.*

commander of the New Zealand Division, was put in charge. He had only two dozen tanks, almost no transport, no air support, and tenuous communications. He positioned his troops to guard Crete's three airfields.[7]

The German assault, an unprecedented attempt to capture an island with air power, began on May 20 with an intense bombing followed by a massive parachute drop. There was confusion and slaughter as many of the parachutists dropped within the British lines and were dead before they could remove their harnesses. Many others, landing in gliders, were cut down before they could unload. Anxious to help, the Cretans fell upon the invaders with axes, spades, or ancient flintlock rifles. Germany's Seventh Parachute Division was decimated. General Student, in command of the operation, gambled its success by concentrating his forces and committing his entire reserve to capture the Maleme airfield. Although losses were heavy, the Germans secured the field and began to pour in reinforcements and heavy equipment. A British counterattack to regain the field failed, and in the days that followed Freyberg's men suffered mounting losses for no gain. On May 27 Admiral Cunningham began another bitter evacuation. More than 16,000 [8] of the Crete garrison were evacuated to Egypt, but operations in Greece and Crete had cost the British dear. Cunningham's fleet was almost destroyed, and while the British had been occupied in Greece and Crete, the war in Libya, nearly won in February, had come under Axis control.

The War in the Western Desert

In February 1941 General Erwin Rommel and the advance elements of two German divisions arrived in Libya. The African campaign began to acquire a new intensity and a new urgency. Every military campaign derives part of its character from the terrain over which it is fought, for the terrain determines what weapons and tactics will be applicable. The Western Desert of Egypt and Libya, the battlefield for the North African war of 1940–42, is a vast and

[7] Clark, *The Fall of Crete;* Buckley, *Greece and Crete.*
[8] Cunningham, *A Sailor's Odyssey,* p. 389. Roskill, *The War at Sea,* Vol. I, p. 446, credits the Royal Navy with evacuating 18,600.

empty place, bereft of vegetation and life except for patches of camel scrub, a few desert rats and foxes, and a myriad of flies, scorpions, and fleas. The heat is oppressive; the glare of the sun on the sand is blinding; the dust is a torment; the absence of water is a threat. The scanty population lives along the coast, separated from the desert by an escarpment which rises two hundred feet above the coastal plain and runs southeast into the desert east of the Egyptian frontier. The few places where vehicles could mount the escarpment became strategic passes. Otherwise military objectives were limited to the small ports Tobruk and Benghazi, the settlements where wells had been bored to provide a water supply, and some scattered airfields in Cyrenaica which were within operating distance of the Mediterranean supply routes. The possession of territory meant little, for in the desert victory is measured in terms of the destruction of the enemy force.

The desert terrain afforded to ground commanders the opportunity for the free, fluid maneuvers usually associated with war at sea. Vehicles moved freely, unhampered by rivers, forests, towns, or swamps, and not restricted to roads. Such a battlefield is a tank commander's dream, and the desert war became a war of rapid movement of armor against armor, free movement rather than prolonged stalemate, and attrition of equipment rather than of men. A soldier without his tank or gun was no longer a threat to the enemy, so the destruction of equipment took precedence over the destruction of men. Both sides tended to treat prisoners with consideration.

The desert features that provided freedom for the conduct of war also created a major problem. The armies were dependent on their supply bases for every item. Gasoline, food and water, ammunition, equipment, and all other necessities had to come from bases in the rear. These bases had to be stocked from Italy on the one hand and Britain on the other. The British were backed up by Alexandria, the Axis by Tripoli. The two ports in between, Tobruk and Benghazi, were subject to enemy air attack and not dependable. As an army advanced, it found itself becoming weaker as the distance from its source of supply increased. As an army retreated and fell back on its supply port, its position was strengthened. It was as though each side was tied to its base by a huge rubber band which could be stretched just so far before snapping.

The early successes of the British forces against the numerically superior Italians had annoyed Hitler. He decided to send German troops to Africa to bolster the Italians, but he hoped to accomplish nothing more than saving the Italians from disgrace. Some of his advisers tried to persuade him that Africa could be a crucial theater. A victory here could sever Britain's lifelines to the Pacific and to her oil supplies in the Middle East. Hitler was unimpressed. Germany's African war began on a small scale—two divisions and their equipment.[9] The Fuehrer himself was not seeking a major strategic goal, but the general whom he chose to wage his African war was acutely aware of the possibilities before him. Erwin Rommel arrived in Africa in February 1941. Earlier in the war he had established the tenor of his command, one marked by offensive, mobile, and flexible action. A brilliant tactician, he quickly changed the course of the desert war.

On March 31 Rommel's forces began a series of exploratory attacks against the British lines, which were thinly held. Not only had General Wavell sent troops to Greece, but between January and May 1941 Wavell's command conducted a campaign in East Africa that reclaimed British Somaliland (captured by the Italians in 1940) and restored Ethiopia to its people. In May and June British troops went to Iraq and Syria to eliminate pro-Axis forces, and in August a similar operation was conducted in Iran (Persia). When Rommel began his attack, the British position was held by only two weak divisions. Wavell authorized a fighting retreat, but Rommel was a master at perceiving and exploiting his enemy's vulnerability. Realizing that Wavell's opposition was disintegrating, Rommel pursued, capitalizing on every weakness he found and making free use of bluff and ruse. Wherever the British fell back, Rommel's forces were right on their heels. In the confusion of retreat, General O'Connor was taken prisoner, and from then until late 1942 the British suffered from inadequate leadership in the field.

Rommel destroyed the British armored resistance in a series of

---

[9] The 15th and 21st Panzer Divisions, which became the "Afrika Korps." For the desert war see Liddell-Hart, *The Rommel Papers;* Playfair, *The Mediterranean and the Middle East.* For bibliographical data on Rommel see Young, *The Desert Fox.*

skirmishes, and then, employing O'Connor's ruse of the previous winter, he cut across the desert through Mechili. Rommel's advance threatened to capture the 9th Australian Division, in retreat along the coast road, just as the Italians had been trapped at Beda Fomm. A stand had to be made. General Wavell, supported by Churchill and the other Mediterranean commanders, Admiral Cunningham and Air Chief Marshal Longmore, decided the stand must be made at Tobruk. Its defenses were in disrepair and Rommel's men were only seventy miles away, but stores and ammunition were on hand, and Admiral Cunningham felt the Royal Navy could keep the garrison supplied.

The 9th Australian Division got inside the Tobruk defenses just a week after they had begun their demoralizing retreat across Cyrenaica. Morale was low, but General Morshead, their commander, told them with confidence that they would hold Tobruk. The "Diggers," who more than twenty years before had established a reputation as magnificent soldiers, once again began to "dig in." The siege of Tobruk, which began the first week in April, was to last until December. As the summer wore on, the Australians strengthened the Tobruk defenses, and although bitter fighting raged around the perimeter, Rommel was able to accomplish nothing more than a few bulges in the outer lines.[10] The Desert Fox had met his first challenge, for, as Wavell had anticipated, Rommel could not afford to advance into Egypt as long as the garrison at Tobruk was in a position to strike at his rear. In April Rommel halted his first desert drive in the Bardia-Sollum area. British attacks failed to dislodge him or to re-establish land communications with Tobruk. Until November the desert war quieted into a temporary stalemate, but elsewhere the summer months brought the Nazis stunning victories.

[10] Heckstall-Smith, *Tobruk, The Story of a Siege.*

Blitzkrieg to Moscow

ON JUNE 22, 1941, Hitler's Wehrmacht invaded Russia. The German leader had predicted that "When BARBAROSSA commences, the world will hold its breath and make no comment." [1] He was right. The largest land battle in the history of warfare began with startling German success.

Operation BARBAROSSA

For sixteen months after the blitzkrieg had struck Poland, the Germans enjoyed almost unqualified military victory. Except for the Battle of Britain, in which the armies had played no part, not one major catastrophe had halted the development of the most efficient military goliath the world had yet seen. At 7:00 a.m. on June 22, as 2700 tanks and 6000 guns advanced on Russia, the German radio broadcast a message from Hitler: "I have decided again today to

[1] Shirer, *The Rise and Fall of the Third Reich*, p. 822.

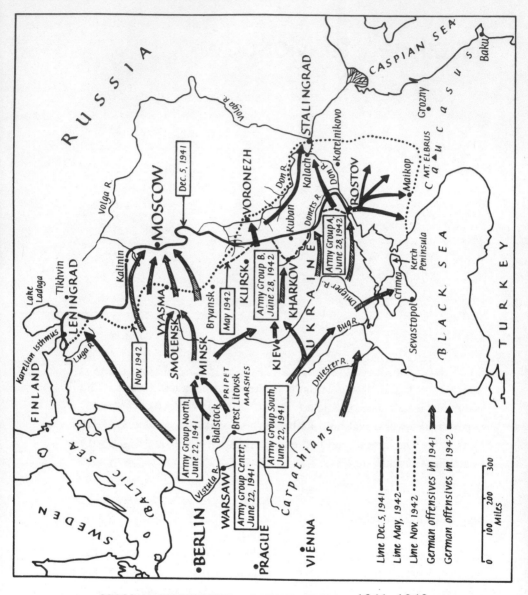

GERMAN OFFENSIVES AGAINST RUSSIA, 1941–1942

place the fate and future of the Reich and our people in the hands of our soldiers." [2] Despite the evidence that such an assault was imminent, the Germans achieved tactical surprise. Russian frontier troops were caught off guard. Messages flew to headquarters: "We are being fired on; what shall we do?" [3] The answer came: "Resist." Although eventually the Germans would have to fight with all the resources at their command, Russia's initial, uncoordinated resistance counted for little. She sustained heavy casualties in men and tanks; in the first forty-eight hours she lost more than two thousand aircraft.[4] Spearheaded by four armored groups, the Germans advanced as much as fifty miles in the first day. Within three weeks they were some five hundred miles inside Russia. On the far left of the front, von Leeb's Army Group North penetrated Leningrad province in eighteen days. Von Bock's Army Group Center carried out a vast pincers movement around Bialystok and Minsk and on July 10 announced victory and capture of nearly 300,000 prisoners.[5] Between July 16 and August 7 Army Group Center conducted another pincers operation around Smolensk and claimed 100,000 prisoners. Moscow was only two hundred miles away. On the far right, von Rundstedt's Army Group South advanced steadily toward Kiev, capital of the Ukraine. Hitler's prediction of victory before winter seemed to be coming true.

After the Smolensk battle, the generals, led by von Brauchitsch, Halder, and von Bock, wanted to push an attack directly on Moscow. Hitler overruled them. The prime objectives at this point, he insisted, were the Crimea and Caucasus in the south and Leningrad in the north. To the south he saw the chance of another huge encirclement of Russian forces around Kiev. He directed Army Group Center to go on the defensive and divert its armored strength due south to form one arm of a Kiev pincer. The Kiev encirclement was the largest yet achieved. The Russian forces were trapped and surrounded by the combined strength of von Rundstedt's Army Group South and Guderian's armored group. By late September the Germans again claimed a staggering victory—600,000 Russian prisoners in the one opera-

---

[2] Clark, *Barbarossa*, p. 44.
[3] Freidin and Richardson, *The Fatal Decisions*, p. 56.
[4] Clark, *Barbarossa*, p. 50.
[5] Figures vary on the number of prisoners taken in the encirclement battles. Information from the files of the German High Command set the total Russian prisoners taken in 1941 at 3,335,000. See Werth, *Russia at War*, p. 708.

tion.[6] On October 3 Hitler broadcast "without any reservation" that Russia had been "struck down and will never rise again." [7]

Meanwhile Army Group North pressed closer and closer to Leningrad. In mid-July it crossed the Luga River and faced the Russian's last prepared defenses short of the city. Under relentless German pressure these defenses steadily crumbled, and by the end of August Leningrad seemed on the verge of falling into Hitler's grasp. The Germans had severed all land routes leading into the city from the west and south. When German forces were only seven miles from Leningrad, General Georgi Zhukov, Chief on Staff, was dispatched from Moscow to the Leningrad front. Under his direction the opposition tightened and the German advance was stopped.

Hitler had counted on Finnish help in securing Leningrad, for he had expected Finland to welcome the opportunity to strike back at Russia after being defeated in the Winter War. Russia, doubting Finnish neutrality, attacked Finland when BARBAROSSA began. The Finns declared war, but, insisting theirs was a "separate" struggle, refused to cooperate with the Germans. The Finns advanced to the narrowest part of the Karelian Isthmus, just over their old boundary line, and were content to go no further. The result, much to Hitler's chagrin, was that Leningrad was never completely surrounded. A gap remained between the German and Finnish troops at Lake Ladoga, and through it the Russians were able to squeeze enough supplies into the city to ward off its capitulation.

The siege of Leningrad began when, in September, Hitler ordered part of Army Group North to move south to support a drive on Moscow. The remaining forces were to isolate and blockade the city. Hitler intended to starve its population to death. Shortages of food were accompanied by shortages of fuel for cooking or heating. Those who escaped death from starvation and exposure faced death from the intensive artillery barrage and aerial bombardment that lasted for much of the 900-day siege. Late in the year, when the German offensive on the center front threatened Moscow, the Russians used Leningrad to draw off German strength. The forces defending Leningrad expended their energy in continuous attacks designed to keep

[6] Guderian, *Panzer Leader*, p. 225, gives the figure 665,000.
[7] Shirer, *The Rise and Fall of the Third Reich*, p. 854.

88

the Germans from sending more divisions south. Even though depleted and exhausted, the Russians were able to hold when the Germans attempted to take Tikhvin and close the supply route across Lake Ladoga—Leningrad's only lifeline. The end of 1941 did not see the end of Leningrad, as Hitler had hoped, but rather witnessed the astounding ability of a people to endure.

While Army Group North brought Leningrad under seige, von Rundstedt was directing Army Group South toward distant objectives. Hitler wanted him to clear the Black Sea coast as far as the Don River and Rostov, take the Crimea, push on past the Don to secure the Maikop oilfields in the Caucasus, and seize Voronezh on the Don and Stalingrad on the Volga. Von Rundstedt was one of Hitler's most capable generals, but he could not work miracles. Winter was threatening when the ambitious offensive began, and he was hampered from the first by the diversion of forces needed for the attack on Moscow. The left flank of von Rundstedt's force was halted far short of Voronezh; beyond Kursk it was blocked by Russian forces which Hitler insisted did not exist. On the extreme south of the front, von Manstein's tanks took the Crimea, except for Sevastopol and the Kerch peninsula, but the operation drained strength from General von Kleist's main drive to Rostov and the oilfields. The German forces became dangerously overextended; bad weather closed in, and supplies, especially oil, ran short. Late in the year the Russians brought up fresh divisions and the opposition stiffened daily. Rostov, a vital railway junction called the "gateway to the Caucasus," was finally taken in November, but Russian forces threatened to recapture it. In late November von Rundstedt requested permission to withdraw and consolidate on the Mius River, just west of Rostov. Hitler refused. Von Rundstedt retorted it was nonsense to try to hold Rostov and resigned his command. The withdrawal to the Mius was later approved and the line held throughout the winter.

The Battle of Moscow

BARBAROSSA was fourteen weeks old when Hitler announced that Russia would never rise again, and on that day Army Group Center lunged forward to begin the Battle of Moscow. This battle was executed in four phases. The first began with the opening of BARBA-ROSSA itself and lasted through the envelopment at Smolensk. At that time—July—Army Group Center halted and sent part of its force south to Kiev. The Kiev operation caused delay on the central front, and after it was over, valuable time was lost in indecision. In September the weather turned wet, forecasting an early fall. Hitler finally decided that Army Group Center, reinforced with units from both von Leeb's and von Rundstedt's groups, would drive on Moscow. After a necessary lapse of time to recondition the equipment and rest the men, this second phase of the battle began on October 3. A renewed German assault, the Autumn Offensive, began on November 16 and marked the third phase, which lasted until the first week in December. The fourth phase was an unexpected and successful Russian counterattack, which stopped the German advance just short of the city.

The second phase of the Moscow offensive seemed at first to justify the German decision to force a decisive battle for the capital. Following the pattern that had been successful at Minsk, Smolensk, and Kiev, the armored groups of Generals Hoth, Hoepner, and Guderian forged ahead and turned in to draw a noose around the Russian armies near Vyasma and Briansk. After three weeks of bitter fighting the Germans claimed the capture of 650,000 prisoners.[8] Russia seemed doomed. Hitler repeatedly said so, and his claims were believed not only in Germany but in Britain and in the United States. Hopes that Germany had sealed her fate by risking a war on two fronts faltered. Russia's enormous losses in men, planes, tanks, and guns exceeded many estimates of her total armed strength. But on the Eastern Front a subtle change was taking place in the complexion of the battle.

BARBAROSSA caught the Russian people off balance. Dazed and overwhelmed by the suddenness and fury of the invasion, they looked for leadership. It was ten days before Stalin addressed them, but when he did he supplied the essential orientation. The German-Russian war would be a war for the defense of Mother Russia. He challenged the people to:

[8] *Ibid.*, p. 859.

Abandon all complacency . . . the issue is one of life or death of the Soviet state . . . whether . . . peoples of the Soviet Union shall remain free or fall into slavery.

He made an appeal for partisan warfare, which, coupled with Germany's war of terror, was to turn the Russian war into a deadly, oppressive carnage:

Peoples of the Soviet Union must rise against the enemy and defend their rights and their land . . . all citizens must defend every inch of Soviet soil. . . . In occupied regions conditions must be made unbearable for the enemy and all his accomplices. They must be hounded and annihilated at every step, and all their measures frustrated.

Stalin also called for the "scorched earth" policy, used by Sherman when he marched through Georgia and by Kutuzov when he fought Napoleon in 1812:

In case of forced retreat of Red Army Units, all rolling stock must be evacuated, the enemy must not be left a single engine . . . not a single pound of grain or gallon of fuel.

Stalin characterized the enemy as "cruel and implacable." "This war with Fascist Germany," he said, "cannot be considered an ordinary war." [9]

Hitler had already decreed that this would be no "ordinary" war. Since it was a struggle of ideologies and racial differences, it would have to be conducted with "unprecedented, unmerciful and unrelenting harshness." [10] Political Commissars [11] were not to be taken prisoner, but shot. Traditional military court-martial was suspended; justice rested with individual officers; prosecution was not required for German soldiers who abused the civilian population. Alfred Rosenberg, self-styled philosopher of the Nazi Regime, was named

---

[9] Quotations from Stalin's July 3, 1941 speech, as given in *The Voice of Fighting Russia*.

[10] Shirer, *The Rise and Fall of the Third Reich*, p. 830.

[11] Political Commissars were Party "Watchdogs"—loyal Communists stationed at the elbow of army officers to countersign their orders and insure that they acted in the best interests of the regime. Nikita S. Khrushchev was a Commissar on the southern front.

Minister of the Eastern Territories; his plans included using the Russian resources to feed the German people while the Russians starved. Heinrich Himmler, head of the German Secret Police, the SS, was charged with "special tasks" designed to eliminate the Russian people. Shortly after the invasion commenced, the oppressive German policies began to make themselves felt. As civilian supplies and foodstuffs were confiscated, the people experienced severe deprivation. Large numbers of hostages were shot in retaliation for minor incidents of resistance; slave labor was recruited and shipped back to Germany like cattle. The SS seemed bent on the wholesale slaughter of the Slavic people. Under this unrelenting Nazi persecution, the Russian people, if they had ever entertained any doubts about the relative merits of their government, were driven to its fanatical defense as the lesser of two evils.

The Russians gradually found their "battle legs." Partisan units began to form in the rear areas to fight the Germans from behind, and in the front lines the Russian armies ceased to flounder and began to conduct a skillful and stubborn defense. On October 8 General Zhukov took command of the Russian forces defending Moscow. Russia's situation was critical. Her losses had been severe, and even though the Russians concentrated 40 percent of their troops on the Western Front, the Germans continued to advance.[12] By October 16 the Russian capital was in a state of panic and the government (though not Stalin himself) began to evacuate to Kuibyshev. But though the Germans advanced, victory remained elusive.

German morale deteriorated in the face of the fanatical resistance. The Russian T-34 tank, better than any previous Russian model and impervious to the German infantrymen's anti-tank guns, appeared. A new Russian mortar, the Katyusha, made itself felt, and as the Germans neared Moscow the Red Air Force, little in evidence since the mass destruction of the first days of the war, began to dominate the skies. German air power suffered from lack of suitable airfields and from lengthy supply lines. The autumn rains started shortly after the second phase of the battle began, and German armor and motorized transport found itself immobilized by mud. Troops were ex-

[12] Erickson, *The Soviet High Command*, pp. 618–25.

hausted by the continuous fighting, and Hitler's glorious offensive slowed to a demoralized crawl.

In November the German High Command held a conference to decide what to do. Moscow seemed within their grasp; but were the tired and weakened troops able to take it? Should they stop now and build defensive positions to hold for the winter? Already snow had begun. Hitler urged "one final heave." Even though on the day it began the temperature dipped well below the freezing point, the drive was named the Autumn Offensive.

The plan for the Autumn Offensive, which was plagued by snows and below-freezing temperatures, called for the reinforced Fourth Army, under von Kluge, to make a frontal assault toward Moscow while the armored groups of Hoth and Hoepner encircled the capital from the west and north and Guderian's armor swung up to meet them from the south. The Germans lunged forward and gained ground. By November 28 Hoth reached the Moscow-Volga Canal, less than twenty miles from the Kremlin. Zhukov, realizing that he could not continue to take losses on the scale of the previous months, husbanded the remaining Russian soldiers with care. Reserves, rushed to Moscow from the Far East, were held back until their strength was sufficient to have a positive effect on the battle. Civilian armies were sent into the lines to hold the Germans short of the city until a counterattack could be launched. With little training or equipment, these *Opolcheniye,* or "home guard" battalions, died by the thousands.[13] But Moscow held. During the first few days of December the German generals realized that their armies simply could not go on. Then, on December 6, Zhukov opened a major offensive against the German armies.

Zhukov's offensive, which coincided with Japan's air attack against the U.S. at Pearl Harbor, began with a break through the German lines near Kalinin. Other breaks followed, and gradually the offensive settled down to a steady hammering at weak spots in the lines, forcing the Germans to withdraw all along the front. Although Russian strength was not sufficient to eliminate the German threat or surround and destroy the German armies (as happened at Stalingrad the

---

[13] Kerr, *The Russian Army,* p. 42. Opinion differs on how much civilian units were employed. See Clark, *Barbarossa,* pp. 117n, 180n.

following winter), the immediate danger to Moscow was removed. The Russians continued to batter the Germans until spring 1942, when the rain and mud called a dreary halt to all operations.

When the Russians first broke through the German lines, Chief of Staff Halder urged a general withdrawal. Hitler refused. Blaming defeat on his generals, he began a drastic shake-up in personnel. Von Bock, ill and disheartened, was replaced by von Kluge. Guderian and Hoepner were dismissed for falling back without authority. Field Marshal von Brauchitsch asked to be relieved as Commander-in-Chief of the Army, and Hitler assumed the position himself, telling Halder that "This little matter of operational command is something anyone can do." [14] Hitler ordered his troops to fall back on their supply dumps, which were turned into fortified positions called "Hedgehogs." There the armies found a certain amount of shelter, and when necessary, supplies were airlifted in by the Luftwaffe. Winter clothing, much of it donated by civilians, was rushed to them. Hitler had neither planned nor prepared for a winter campaign, and the Germans spent their first winter on the Eastern Front in misery. But no disorderly retreat took place, such as had spelled the doom of Napoleon's Grand Army, and in the summer of 1942 the powerful German Army struck once more deep into Russia.

Why did BARBAROSSA fail? The German Army had scored one dramatic victory after another. The encirclement battles, each the size of a minor theater of war, were skillfully executed. The Kiev battle area was almost as extensive as the Western Front in France the year before.[15] The Germans had brought Leningrad under seige and captured most of the Crimea. Although military defeats of such magnitude would have toppled a lesser foe, there is no evidence that Russia considered surrender. During the first weeks of the war she began uprooting her vital industries in European Russia and transporting them beyond the Ural Mountains, well out of reach of the Luftwaffe. In every area the government tightened its grip. The manufacture of consumer goods was stopped; food was severely rationed; all transport and material was confiscated for the army. An American war correspondent in Russia wrote, "I doubt whether any army in the world

[14] Shirer, *The Rise and Fall of the Third Reich,* p. 866.
[15] Fuller, *The Second World War,* p. 125.

has ever received such total support from its civilian population as the Red Army received in the first two years of the German invasion." [16] If civilians were required to die—as they were at Leningrad and Moscow—they did so. The patriotic love of Mother Russia, largely ignored since 1918, was revived, and the Russians, primarily a peasant people with close ties to the soil, defended their homeland with stoicism and intensity. The German soldier began to fear his Russian counterpart. When wounded the Russian soldier did not cry out; when faced with death he did not flinch. Infantry marched against armor, and the number of Russian forces seemed unending.

Russia's hard climate and great size were in her favor.[17] The severe winter decreased the efficiency of German vehicles, and the shortage of hard-surfaced roads hampered German mobility. As the Germans advanced into Russia they had to spread out like a fan to north and south. Divisions were spread thin; supply lines grew longer; partisan activities disrupted rear areas. Weaknesses in the German command contributed to BARBAROSSA's failure. Conflict between Hitler and his generals and lack of agreement among the generals themselves cost time and efficiency. Hitler had set his sights on three divergent goals—Leningrad, Moscow, and the Caucasus. In 1941 he had attained none of the three; next year he would concentrate on the Caucasus.

[16] Kerr, *The Russian Army*, p. 172.
[17] For Russia as a military obstacle see Jackson, *Seven Roads to Moscow*.

Japan Enters the War

DURING 1941 the Japanese waged battles of policy and negotiation. Within the Japanese government the struggle between militarists and moderates continued, its progress closely connected to a diplomatic battle that sought to persuade the United States to accept Japan's demands for expansion in Asia.

Japan Decides for War

Neither Japan nor the United States wanted to fight the other, but Japan wanted a free hand in Asia and the U.S. objected. If war was to be avoided, one or the other must change its stand. In February Admiral Kichisaburo Nomura went to Washington as the new Japanese Ambassador. He was charged with securing an understanding with the United States. In March he and the U.S. Secretary of State, Cordell Hull, began an exhausting series of talks—about fifty sessions in all—which went on until the morning of December 7, 1941.[1] Their aim was to try to settle Japanese-American differences by peaceful means. The United States insisted that Japan subscribe to four minimum points: (1) territorial integrity and national sovereignty; (2) non-interference in internal affairs of other countries; (3) commercial equality (the Open Door); (4) no alteration of the status quo by force. Japan wanted the United States to stop helping China; to lift the embargoes; and to allow Japan to establish a commanding position in the Pacific. Despite the apparent futility of their task, both Hull and Nomura applied themselves with diligence and sincerity. Nomura worked under the handicap of not always knowing the policy of his government, or, many times, of disagreeing with it. More than once he asked to be relieved.

Meanwhile in Tokyo the ardent militarists and the cautious moderates continued their tug-of-war. The two groups were forced to a showdown in April, when Nomura cabled his government the basic proposals the United States put forward for peace negotiations. The moderates, led by Konoye and wishing to avoid war with Britain and the United States, were of sufficient strength to insure that efforts toward a peaceful settlement would continue. The militarists, led by Matsuoka and backed up by a Neutrality Treaty with Russia (concluded in April and making it possible for Japan to face south with a secure rear), were strong enough to make sure that nothing was done to compromise Japan's membership in the Tripartite Pact. U.S. cryptographers had deciphered Japan's main diplomatic code, providing a "magic" window through which the U.S. followed the inner struggle of the Japanese government. Disunity within the Japanese government encouraged the United States to keep the talks open. Necessity dictated a policy of extending all possible aid to Britain, seeking to restrain Japan by embargo, attempting to settle the Far East problems by negotiation, and, if that should fail, using the time gained to prepare for war.[2]

On July 2 the Japanese government made a policy decision. She would not attack Russia for some time; efforts would be intensified to end the China war; advances would be made into the Southern

---

[1] See Feis, *The Road to Pearl Harbor,* primary source for this section.
[2] See Langer and Gleason, *The Undeclared War.*

Resources Region, especially French Indo-China; and preparations for war with England and America would be made "in case the diplomatic negotiations break down." The policy stated that:

> The Imperial Government is determined to follow a policy which will result in the establishment of the Greater East Asia Co-Prosperity Sphere and world peace, no matter what international developments take place.[3]

At the end of July, Japanese troops moved into the previously unoccupied parts of Indo-China. The United States responded by freezing Japanese assets in the United States. Similar action was taken by Britain. The Japanese government was shaken. Prime Minister Konoye forced Matsuoka to resign, but the composition of the new cabinet was still half militarist. Through Magic, the U.S. learned that the Tripartite Pact would continue to be the keystone of Japanese policy. In Washington, the talks between Nomura and Hull came to a temporary halt. In August, after the ARGENTIA conference, Roosevelt warned Japan that the United States would be compelled to "take steps" if she did not cease her policy of military domination.[4] The door to negotiation was left open, and once more Hull and Nomura began to meet for talks.

By fall Japan had to make a decision. U.S. embargoes had hampered her economy. She was virtually cut off from oil imports, and her oil reserves were sufficient only for a war lasting twelve to eighteen months. The militarists urged beginning war at once. The General Staff warned that, because of weather and the state of reserves, December was the latest month that war could begin, and a decision must be made by October to give time for troops and ships to be moved into position. The Washington talks deadlocked, and on October 16 Konoye resigned. He was succeeded by a former War Minister, Hideki Tojo, a militarist, an authoritarian, and a fervent patriot.[5]

When Tojo became Premier, Emperor Hirohito instructed him to examine the current situation and propose the best solution. The government must be in agreement. The Army and Navy, which had

---

[3] Feis, *The Road to Pearl Harbor*, p. 215.
[4] *Ibid.*, pp. 255–57.
[5] See Butow, *Tojo and the Coming of the War.*

different views on the possible war, must agree and cooperate.[6] Tojo's cabinet considered three possibilities: (1) No war; this would mean giving up much of what Japan had fought for since 1931. (2) Immediate war. (3) Renewed efforts at a negotiated agreement, with the condition that if this last effort failed, war would be declared. The cabinet chose the third. A final set of revised conditions for a settlement was sent to Nomura, and a special envoy, Saburo Kurusu, hurried to Washington to assist the Japanese Ambassador in persuading the United States to accept them. If the conditions were rejected, it would mean war. The deadline for reply was November 25 (later it was extended to November 29).

Japan's "Last Proposals" offered little that had not been talked about before. She would withdraw from Indo-China when peace was made with China, and she would promise to advance no further into Southeast Asia. In return Japan asked the U.S. to restore commercial relations, supply her with oil, help her get what she wanted from the Indies, and let her have a free hand in China.[7] The United States could not accept Japan's terms, even though Magic intercepts left no doubt that there would be war if the proposals were refused.[8] On November 26 Hull told the Japanese ambassadors that the U.S. could not accept Japan's terms. The U.S. reasserted that the Japanese must withdraw from both China and Indo China, recognize Chiang Kai shek's regime as the lawful government of China, and sign a non-aggression pact regarding further expansion into Asia. The Japanese government rejected Hull's reply as a humiliating ultimatum and began to draft a response. On November 26 a Japanese task force began to move from the Kurile Islands toward Pearl Harbor.

The American government braced itself for war. Messages were drafted and sent to Generals MacArthur in the Philippines, Short in Hawaii, and Andrews in Panama. They were told that the Japanese negotiations "appear to be terminated," that "Japanese future action unpredictable but hostile action possible at any moment." They were directed to take such measures "as you deem necessary" for defense. The message from Admiral Stark, Chief of Naval Operations, to

[6] *Ibid.*, p. 301; Feis, *The Road to Pearl Harbor*, p. 286.
[7] Feis, *The Road to Pearl Harbor*, pp. 291–97.
[8] Hull gives his reasons for refusing the proposals in *Memoirs*, Vol. II, p. 1070.

Admiral Hart in the Philippines and Admiral Kimmel in Hawaii began: "This dispatch is to be considered a war warning." [9]

In Japan the last peacetime Imperial Conference convened on December 1. The war plans were reviewed and accepted. War would commence December 8, Tokyo time. A final message to the United States, declaring that the talks were at an end, would be delivered to Hull at 1:00 p.m. December 7, Washington time, some twenty minutes before Japanese planes would appear over Pearl Harbor.

On December 6 Washington received information that two large Japanese fleets, transports and warships, were moving around the southern point of Indo-China, headed west into the Gulf of Siam. An attack on Malaya seemed imminent. Roosevelt appealed directly to Emperor Hirohito to halt the impending conflict. The message was delayed and did not reach the Japanese Emperor until 3:00 a.m., Monday, December 8, Tokyo time. By then, Japanese planes were already in the air, streaking toward Oahu.[10] During the night of December 6, Washington time, Magic began to intercept the Japanese formal reply to Hull's answer of November 26. On reading the first portion, Roosevelt declared, "This means war." [11] By Sunday morning, December 7, Roosevelt had the complete Japanese message. It formally ended the already defunct negotiations and put the blame for their failure on the United States. The message was not a declaration of war, and the American government could do nothing but wait to see what Japan's moves might be. A further Magic intercept alerted the White House that Nomura would deliver the message at 1:00 p.m. The hour might or might not have significance. No further warnings were issued to military commanders except through General George C. Marshall's office. Because of radio static these went through Western Union rather than direct communication. The warning reached Pearl Harbor after the raid was over.

At 2:00 p.m. Nomura and Kurusu arrived at Secretary Hull's office. They were late, for their lengthy message, eleven typewritten pages, had taken time to decipher and type. They did not know that it had already been decoded and read by the Americans, or that Hull had just received a phone call from the President saying that Hawaii

[9] Morison, *The Rising Sun in the Pacific*, p. 77. See also Millis, *This Is Pearl!*
[10] Grew, *Ten Years in Japan*, pp. 486–89.
[11] Sherwood, *Roosevelt and Hopkins*, p. 426.

was reporting "Air raid on Pearl Harbor. This is no drill." Hull received the spokesmen coldly. He read their message to make sure it was the same as the intercepted one. When the envoys left, Japan and the United States were at war.

Japanese War Plans

During 1941, as the relations between Japan and the United States became more strained, Japanese leaders had worked on plans for war should it become necessary. The plans ultimately implemented were for a limited war.[12] In its opening phases Japan would take her prime objectives: Malaya and the East Indies, the heart of a rich area called the Southern Resources Region. As quickly as possible she would move on to the Philippines, the Celebes, and New Guinea to protect her eastern flank. To guard her conquests and obtain room to maneuver she would establish an outpost line some distance away. Similar in purpose to the entrenched zone of land warfare, the outer line would run from the Kurile Islands to the north of Japan across the Pacific through Wake Island, the Marshall, Gilbert, and Ellice Islands, westward through the Solomons and New Guinea, and around the Indies to Burma. Once the outer defensive perimeter was taken and fortified, Japan could incorporate the captured areas, exploit their resources, and wage a war of exhaustion on the Allied powers. If the defensive perimeter could be held until Britain and the United States decided it would cost too much to destroy it, Japan could negotiate peace, bargaining to keep the Southern Resources Region and her Chinese gains in return for giving up the outpost line and ending the war.

Chances for success were reasonable. The Japanese military machine was ready; the soldiers had been well trained in the China war. The tactics and weapons necessary for the type of combat expected had been tested. Japan held air and naval superiority over her opponents in the Pacific, and the European war would prevent the Western powers from amassing too much strength in the Pacific before Japan had seized her outpost line. Once it was occupied and fortified, this line would be a strong and defensible position.

[12] United States Strategic Bombing Survey, *The Campaigns of the Pacific War*, Chapter 1.

PACIFIC BATTLE AREA

The biggest obstacle to the success of Japan's short-range plans was the United States Pacific Fleet. Since April 1940 it had been stationed at Pearl Harbor on Oahu, Hawaii, for the Americans hoped it would serve as a deterrent to Japanese aggression. Admiral Isoroku Yamamoto, Commander-in-Chief of the Combined Fleet, began work on a plan for destroying it by a surprise raid as the opening move of the Japanese offensive. Yamamoto had been quick to appreciate the role of air-sea warfare and the possibilities of carrier-based planes. To avoid U.S. detection, a route far to the north of the usual shipping lanes was mapped out, despite the hazards of refueling in bad weather and rough seas. The Japanese consul in Hawaii kept the Japanese Navy posted on details of the U.S. Fleet's movements and the exact layout and berthing plan of the harbor. A torpedo was perfected that would be effective in the shallow waters of Pearl Harbor. By September the plan was fairly complete and crews began specialized training.

The Pearl Harbor attack outraged the American public, but it was only a hit-and-run raid, a very small part of Japan's opening offensive. Her plans called for attacks on Malaya, Hong Kong, Thailand, Guam, Wake, and the Philippines on the opening day of the war. Malaya and the Philippines were to be occupied within fifty days; the entire southern area was to be secured in ninety days. It was a daring and complicated plan that called for close attention to detail and hairbreadth coordination of all military forces. It was executed with remarkable smoothness and precision. By March 1942, when the Indies surrendered, the first phase of Japan's war plan was essentially complete.

Pearl Harbor Attack; the U.S. Enters the War

At 6:00 a.m., December 7, the first planes of the Japanese Pearl Harbor Striking Force took off from their carrier decks and set course south for Pearl Harbor, 275 miles away. A total of 363 planes, organized into two waves, took part.[13] At 6:45 a.m., while the unsuspected Japanese planes streaked toward Pearl, the first shots of the U.S.-Japanese war were fired by the U.S. destroyer *Ward*. While on patrol off Oahu, the *Ward* spotted a small submarine where it

[13] See Morison, *The Rising Sun in the Pacific.*

knew no friendly submarine would be. *Ward* fired, destroyed the submarine, and radioed its report to base. But false alarms had been frequent at Pearl, and *Ward*'s message did not serve to put the Fleet or the base on full alert.

A few minutes after 7:00 a.m. two U.S. privates, stationed for training at the Army's radar station on the northern tip of Oahu, sighted blips on their screen larger than any they had seen before. The inexperienced soldiers at first suspected the set was broken, but on checking, they realized it was a huge flight of planes, 137 miles to the north, approaching rapidly. They phoned their news to the Information Center at Fort Shafter, the "mind" that would make use of the information the radar "eyes" provided. A lone lieutenant on duty considered the information was "nothing to worry about." The large flight was doubtless Navy planes, or perhaps an expected flight of B-17's from the West Coast. The two privates continued to watch the incoming flight "for fun" until 7:39, when it disappeared from their screen behind the neighboring hills.

Just before 8:00 a.m. the first Japaneses planes reached Pearl Harbor. Below them lay a perfect target—almost a hundred ships riding quietly at anchor in the early morning sunlight. For a few moments after the attack began, the dazed Americans could not grasp what was happening. Doubt was short-lived, and short-lived also was the fighting strength of both Army and Navy at Oahu. The primary target for the Japanese striking force was the seven battleships moored in a tidy row along the southeastern shore of Ford Island, in the middle of the harbor. Within half an hour after the first torpedo struck, *Arizona* had blown up; *Oklahoma* had capsized; *West Virginia* was sunk; *California* was sinking; and *Tennessee, Nevada,* and *Maryland* were damaged. *Pennsylvania,* in dry dock, received lesser damage later in the attack.[14] While torpedo bombers struck the battleships, dive bombers swept over the airfields, where the planes were lined up wing tip to wing tip so as to be more easily guarded against sabotage. Few were able to take to the air to meet the enemy.

Americans at Pearl Harbor responded to the shock that their country was at war with incredulity followed by anger. The defense

---

[14] All but two battleships were later salvaged, repaired, and returned to service. *Arizona* was a total loss; *Oklahoma* was raised but sold for scrap. *Maryland* was first to rejoin the Fleet, in February 1942.

was spirited, but surprise had given the Japanese the vital margin they needed for success. By ten o'clock, when the raid was over and the last Japanese planes were winging their way, unpursued and unmolested, back to their waiting carriers, Japan had successfully accomplished the first step in her war plans—to eliminate the ability of the U.S. Pacific Fleet to interfere when she began to secure her goals in Asia. The raid cost Japan only 29 planes, 5 midget submarines, possibly 1 large submarine, and approximately 100 lives.[15]

On the morning of December 8, President Roosevelt asked Congress to declare that since December 7, a "date which will go down in infamy," a state of war had existed between the United States and Japan.[16] Americans put aside their isolationist hopes and peacetime complacency and plunged into the prosecution of the war with a national will more fervent and united than at any time in the nation's history. At the same time a cry was raised over why the Army and Navy had been caught napping at Pearl Harbor. Investigations began at once, culminating in a Joint Congressional Investigation after the war. Thirty-nine volumes of testimony were produced, but even with so much information it is no simple matter to understand why events unfolded as they did at Pearl Harbor.[17] The simplest, and perhaps best, explanation is that the United States was not prepared for war, and especially not prepared for an air raid on Pearl Harbor.

Pearl Harbor was a humiliating defeat for the Americans, but it turned out to be a strategical error on the part of the Japanese. One reason Japan achieved such complete surprise was that the Americans did not think Japan would commit national suicide by provoking war with the United States. Japan's best course toward achieving her aims in the Pacific was to avoid any direct attack on the United States that would crystallize public opinion and commit the U.S. to fight for the Far East. All through 1941 Roosevelt and his advisers had pondered what they should do if Japan attacked Thailand, Malaya, or the Indies, and did not directly assault American territory. Would Congress declare war? Would the American people support it? Washington assumed that Tokyo appreciated America's political dilemma and

[15] USSBS, *The Campaigns of the Pacific War*, pp. 18–19.

[16] Rosenman, *The Public Papers and Addresses of Franklin Roosevelt*, Vol. X, pp. 514–15.

[17] For an account and an analysis of the results see Wohlstetter, *Pearl Harbor, Warning and Decision* and Morison, *The Rising Sun in the Pacific*.

would capitalize on it. Even an attack on the Philippines might not have roused the Americans to fight, but the assault on Pearl Harbor struck too close to their honor and pride to be ignored. Japan's chances for a negotiated peace sank with the *Arizona* and *Oklahoma;* Japan began the war in the one way which would insure her defeat.

Samuel Eliot Morison called the Pearl Harbor raid a "strategic imbecility," directed on the wrong targets and politically disastrous.[18] But even though it was a long-term mistake, Pearl Harbor was a short-term stunning success. American casualties were high. The Navy lost about three times as many men in that one brief action as it had lost in the Spanish American War and World War I combined. Total dead or missing numbered 2280; more than 1000 more were wounded.[19] Two battleships, 2 destroyers, and a target ship were total losses; the other 6 battleships were temporarily disabled; 3 cruisers and a destroyer were seriously damaged. Oahu's air strength was almost wiped out. And Pearl Harbor was just the beginning. The main Japanese assault fell in the Far East.

On December 22 Roosevelt and Churchill opened a three-week conference in Washington. This, their first wartime meeting, was code-named ARCADIA and produced three decisions of lasting importance. First, the strategy of "Germany first" was reaffirmed. Second, the Combined Chiefs of Staff (CCS) was established. General George C. Marshall, Chief of Staff of the U.S. Army, insisted that only the complete fusion of the General Staffs of the two countries would suffice to insure that the coalition worked with maximum efficiency. The Combined Chiefs made their headquarters in Washington, and the British Chiefs of Staff were represented on the CCS by colleagues in constant communication with London. All military decisions for the rest of the war came through the Combined Chiefs, who worked in close cooperation with Roosevelt, Churchill, and their advisers. The third achievement of the ARCADIA talks was the Declaration of the United Nations. Twenty-six nations subscribed to the principles of the Atlantic Charter, pledged themselves to employ their full resources toward victory, and promised not to make a separate peace.

[18] Morison, *The Rising Sun in the Pacific*, p. 132.
[19] Morton, *The Fall of the Philippines*, p. 79.

Japanese Advance
in the Pacific

JAPAN'S version of the blitzkrieg enjoyed an initial success fully as dramatic as Germany's early conquests. Characterized by the daring use of air power and amphibious assault, within six months it swept over Hong Kong, Malaya and Singapore, Burma, the Netherlands East Indies, Guam, Wake, the Gilbert Islands, and the Philippines, as well as crippling the U.S. Pacific Fleet at Pearl Harbor. During these battles the British and Americans sustained the bitterest defeats in their history.

Midway, Guam, and Wake Island

Moving west across the Pacific from Hawaii, the United States held three steppingstones to the Philippines—Midway, Wake, and Guam.[1] (See map, page 102.) All three of these islands received blows on December 8 (across the international date line, Sunday, December 7,

[1] Heinl, *The Defense of Wake;* Morison, *The Rising Sun in the Pacific,* Chapter 7.

was Monday, December 8). Midway, closest to the United States, was shelled by warships, but only minor damage was done. Guam, the only U.S. foothold in the Japanese-held Marianas, received more vigorous attention. Air raids on the 8th and 9th were followed by landings early on the 10th. No realistic effort was made to hold Guam, for its forces were too meager, its facilities too inadequate, and its communications too undependable. Guam could do little more than wait for the Japanese to seize her.

Wake Island was another matter, and here the Japanese met a spirited defense. Although air attacks on the 8th destroyed much of the island's air strength, a Japanese landing, attempted on December 10, was beaten back. While their would-be invaders made an ignominious departure, the jubilant Marine battalion prepared to hold Wake until reinforcements could reach them. With good spirits and much improvisation they countered almost daily air attacks until December 23, when the Japanese returned with a stronger invading force, which succeeded where the first had failed. Realizing that relief would not reach him, the island commander surrendered to avoid unjustified casualties.

Hong Kong, Malaya, and Singapore

British positions in the Far East also came under immediate Japanese assault. Knowing that the crown colony of Hong Kong could not be held against a major assault, the British planned that its small garrison deny the Japanese the use of the harbor for as long as possible. In a valiant struggle that began on December 8, the Hong Kong defenders held the Japanese at bay until Christmas Day.

Although Hong Kong was regarded as an untenable outpost, the Malay peninsula, with the island of Singapore guarding its tip, was another matter.[2] Singapore measures approximately 28 miles east-west by 14 miles north-south. It is separated from the mainland by the Strait of Johore, less than a mile wide. Its location is strategic. Not only does it lie between the rich areas of the Indies and Malaya,

[2] Kirby, *The Loss of Singapore;* Churchill, *The Hinge of Fate*, Book I, Chapters 3 and 6.

but any country controlling Singapore controls the main sea route from Europe to Asia through the Malacca Strait and the South China Sea. The British possessed a naval base on the north shore of the island which offered excellent anchorage, docks, and equipment. Its defenses were considered impregnable, yet this stronghold fell in a little over two months.

The Japanese assault on Malaya began December 8 with air attacks on Singapore and airfields in Malaya. Landings followed immediately at Singora and Patani in southern Thailand, and at Kota Bharu in northern Malaya. The Japanese forces, under Lieutenant General Tomoyuki Yamashita, consisted of four army divisions supported by the Japanese Second Fleet and the Third Air Army. Yamashita, who had studied German tactics at first hand during the 1940 campaigns, was throughly competent and professional. His army was well trained and well equipped, knew the terrain, and had adopted tactics designed to turn all factors to their advantage.

More than half of the Malayan peninsula is dense jungle, which the British had assumed would render Singapore almost unapproachable

MALAYA

from the landward side. The Japanese turned the jungle to their advantage, and their rapid sweep from the Thai border to Singapore was a sobering demonstration of their mastery of jungle warfare. Bicycles were used for rapid movement on narrow jungle trails; equipment was light and mobile and easily handled; the troops were clad for the tropical heat and lived off the land. They carried only water and a ball of rice, and they showed the same facility for taking care of themselves that marked the Russian soldiers. The Japanese took full advantage of the concealment of the jungle vegetation to infiltrate British positions, and they utilized all varieties of small native craft to navigate the rivers and streams and to make coastal landings behind the British lines. The entire campaign was characterized by the action of small, highly mobile units, using infiltration as their basic approach.

Under Lieutenant General A. E. Percival, the British forces defending Malaya were on the defensive from the first moments of attack. Unable to counter the rapid Japanese advance and infiltration, they were forced into a costly and despairing retreat southward. Morale, which was low, plummeted when Japanese planes sank the British battleship *Prince of Wales* and the battle cruiser *Repulse* on December 10.[3] These two ships had arrived at Singapore only days before, and when war broke out, Admiral Sir Tom Phillips immediately sortied with his ships to attack the Japanese assault forces. He knew he was running a grave risk, since Japanese attacks on the Malayan airfields had eliminated land-based air support for his fleet. Yet the desperate nature of the British position made it unbearable for the naval forces to do nothing, and Admiral Phillips steamed north, searching for the Japanese forces. Japanese planes attacked the ships about 11:00 a.m. on December 10. An hour and a half later *Repulse* rolled over and sank; 45 minutes after that, *Prince of Wales* was gone. The planes that sank them were the first to sink a free-moving battleship by air power alone.

Through December and January of 1942 the forces on the mainland fought a costly and demoralizing delaying battle and fell back steadily before the Japanese advance. The time they bought was used

---

[3] Brown, *Suez to Singapore*, pp. 293–336. See also Roskill, *The War at Sea*, Vol. I, Chapter 26.

to pour reinforcements into Singapore. In January General Wavell assumed command of a newly established American-British-Dutch-Australian unified command (ABDA). He reported to Churchill that Singapore had no defenses against an assault from land across the Strait of Johore, and it was obvious that the Japanese would attack across the Strait. Churchill was dumbfounded. That Singapore might not have landward defenses had no more entered his mind than that a battleship might be "launched without a bottom." [4] Militarily Singapore was doomed to fall, but to abandon the native population and scuttle responsibility without a stubborn defense would do irreparable harm to the honor of British commitments and to relations between East and West. General Percival was admonished to exert every effort to defend Singapore and, if necessary, to fight to the last man.

The last week in January the British forces withdrew onto Singapore and blew up the causeway. The Japanese immediately positioned their artillery on Johore and began a close-range bombardment. On February 8, when the invasion came, it was met by only one inexperienced division that could not hold. Communications had been practically destroyed by the bombardment. British movements to meet the invasion were slow, poorly coordinated, and hesitant. By the 13th General Percival felt that the time was rapidly approaching when further resistance would serve no useful purpose. The British were being forced into a shrinking area around Singapore City. Exhausted, discouraged, disorganized, and running out of supplies, they could do no more. Percival was given permission to surrender, and he did so the evening of February 15. The Malayan campaign had lasted 69 days; it had cost the British more than 138,000 casualties, 130,000 of them taken as prisoners of war.[5]

The Netherlands East Indies and Burma

The Netherlands East Indies, a string of islands stretching south and east from the Malay peninsula toward Australia, were Japan's prime objective and the next to fall. The Japanese began the Indies

[4] Churchill, *The Hinge of Fate*, p. 49.
[5] Kirby, *The Loss of Singapore*, p. 473.

111

assault in December. It was a step-by-step, nibbling campaign that resulted in complete victory by March 9, 1942. Two powerful attack groups, the Eastern under Vice Admiral Takahashi and the Western under Vice Admiral Ozawa, "slithered into the Netherlands East Indies like the arms of two giant octopi." [6] Here, as in Malaya, Japanese tactics were ideally suited to the area and its existing defense. The islands were many and scattered; Allied defense forces were few and scattered. The Japanese destroyed them by attacking one objective at a time with overwhelming power. First, land-based planes were used to wipe out Allied air power at a given location. Then ground troops landed and wiped out existing ground defenses. Air power moved in and the process began again. At the end of February General Wavell felt nothing further could be done. He left the Indies, and the short-lived ABDA Command was dissolved. Now it was up to the Dutch, and their only hope lay in their naval forces.

Rear Admiral Karel Doorman was in charge. He had at his disposal the U.S. heavy cruiser *Houston,* the H.M.S. *Exeter* (also a heavy cruiser), three light cruisers (one Australian and two Dutch), and ten destroyers (four American, three British, three Dutch). They had never worked together, possessed no common set of signals or tactics, and had difficulty communicating because of the need for translation. When Doorman received word of a Japanese convoy approaching Java, he signaled "Follow me," and the force was off. Doorman hoped to get around the fighting ships that protected the convoy and to raise havoc among the vulnerable transports in the rear. He was unable to do so. The Japanese warships sank five of the Allied ships, including Doorman's flagship, with which he went down. The Japanese force proceeded intact to Java. The Dutch capitulated March 9. Rich in resources, especially oil and rubber, the Indies would make Japan self-sufficient. These islands would also provide a strong frontier for her new empire, since control of the Indies meant control of the vital straits giving access from the Indian Ocean to the South China Sea.

Six weeks after the Indies capitulated, Burma fell. There, too, Japanese tactics were right for terrain and defense.[7] While the defend-

[6] Morison, *The Two Ocean War,* p. 88.
[7] See Owen, *The Campaign in Burma;* Slim, *Defeat into Victory.*

ing forces (mostly Burmese, poorly trained and equipped) were held by frontal assault, flanking columns moved through the jungle to establish road blocks and cut them off from the rear. The Japanese moved steadily toward Rangoon, Burma's only port of entry, which had to be held if Burma was to be saved. General Sir Harold Alexander, whose imperturbability at Dunkirk had helped turn disaster into a moral victory, was sent to Burma, but he could do nothing. Rangoon was evacuated on March 7, and the British began a hopeless withdrawal up the river valley toward Mandalay.

China had a stake in the Burmese campaign, since her only link to the outside world was by the Burma Road from Kunming to Lashio. Chiang Kai-shek sent three Chinese armies, under the command of his American Chief of Staff, Major General Joseph Stilwell, to help hold Burma, but even so Lashio fell on April 29 and Mandalay on April 30. Retreat became a rout, and the defending forces escaped as best they could, through uncharted jungle and roadless mountains, to India or China. After a grueling march to Homalin, Stilwell summed it up: "We got a hell of a beating." [8]

Luzon, Bataan, and Corregidor

Across the South China Sea, the Filipinos and Americans were suffering a defeat as bitter as that of the British and Dutch. The 7100 islands that comprise the Philippines were included in Japan's plans for conquest not for their riches, but because of their geographic position. Five thousand miles from Honolulu but only 1800 miles from Tokyo, the Philippines represented an advance base from which the United States could conduct operations against the Japanese mainland while mounting naval attacks on the Japanese flank. Recognizing that in a U.S.-Japanese war the Philippines would be involved, Manuel Quezon, the first President of the Commonwealth,[9] was anxious to develop a Philippine defense force. In 1937 he had asked Major General Douglas MacArthur, who had already retired from the

[8] Stilwell, *The Stilwell Papers*, p. 106. See also Romanus and Sunderland, *Stilwell's Mission to China*.

[9] Under the terms of the Tydings-McDuffie Act, the Philippines were to receive independence in 1946, after 10 years as a Commonwealth. See Morton, *The Fall of the Philippines*, Chapter 1.

U.S. Army after a noteworthy career, to come to the Philippines as military adviser.

MacArthur, who had often served in the Philippines and knew and loved the islands, hoped to establish a citizen-conscript army, welded together by a small corps of professionals, that would make the Filipinos so able to defend themselves that no enemy would dare molest them. Economy largely dictated what could be done, and when war came in 1941 the Filipinos were far short of their goal. In July 1941 MacArthur was recalled to active duty, and the Philippine Army was incorporated into the U.S. service. MacArthur, though 61, had lost none of his self-confidence, optimism, or willingness to voice his opinions. He insisted that with proper equipment and troops the Philippines could be defended, and his optimism, supplemented by the Air Force's enthusiasm over the potential of the new B-17 heavy bomber, led the War Department to begin a last-minute effort to supply the Philippines with all manner of military necessities. But the Japanese onslaught fell before preparations were complete.

The Japanese intended to seize the Philippines in a quick campaign carried out by Lieutenant General Masaharu Homma's Fourteenth Army. While Army and Navy planes destroyed the Philippine air strength, small landings would be made at five different points to seize airfields for future operations. The main landings would come two weeks later at Lingayen Gulf and Lamon Bay, and Homma intended to defeat the Philippine forces in battle around Manila, in the central plains of Luzon.

The early stages of the Japanese campaign went off as planned. The morning of December 8 was heavily overcast on Formosa, and only a small Japanese striking force was able to take off at dawn. It attacked targets in central Luzon, and it served to alert the B-17's at Clark Field north of Manila, which were sent aloft to escape being caught on the ground. By 11:30 a.m. the B-17's were back on the field, refueling and taking on bombs for a proposed offensive mission against Formosa. They were still on the airstrip when the main Japanese strike hit Clark Field shortly after noon. As at Pearl Harbor, the defense could do little to hamper the attack. When it was over, hangars, barracks, and warehouses were a burning ruin, and the strength of the air force was reduced by half. Of 35 B-17's, only 17 remained. Eighty-one other aircraft were destroyed and many were severely damaged.[10]

Between December 8 and 22, the Japanese virtually eliminated Philippine air and naval strength and conducted five small landings. The landings received little opposition, for MacArthur, anticipating Homma's strategy, held the bulk of his forces intact in central Luzon. Nevertheless, as General Wainwright caustically observed, "the rat was in the house, and it was no comfort." [11] Major General Jonathan M. Wainwright, commanding the North Luzon Force, met the major Japanese assault at Lingayen Gulf on December 22. From the beaches the Japanese moved quickly inland, leaving the consolidation of their beachheads to follow-up troops. Some of the poorly trained Filipino units broke and fled in disorder before the Japanese advance, unable to execute the sophisticated maneuvers necessary to halt the rapid penetration. By afternoon the Japanese had sizable forces ashore and were pressing rapidly south toward Manila. Two days

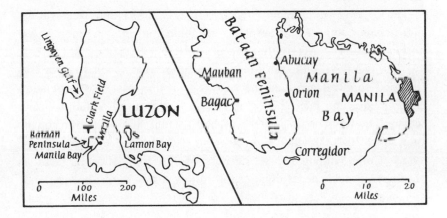

---

[10] Morton, *The Fall of the Philippines*, p. 88. See also Craven and Cate, *The Army Air Forces in World War II*, Vol. I, Chapter 6.
[11] Wainwright, *General Wainwright's Story*, p. 27.

later a smaller force came ashore at Lamon Bay and began a pincer movement from the southeast. Brigadier General George M. Parker, commanding the South Luzon Force, did his best to hold them, but both Wainwright and Parker were hard pressed. MacArthur ordered all forces to withdraw into the Bataan peninsula to establish a defensive line.

The following two weeks were marked by bitter fighting and heavy loss, but the withdrawal was successfully accomplished. MacArthur moved his headquarters from Manila to Corregidor, a fort in the harbor, and declared Manila an open city. His action did not spare Manila the force of Japanese bombs, but after occupying Manila, General Homma faced a problem. So long as MacArthur's forces held Bataan and Corregidor, the Japanese could not use Manila Bay, and Homma could not claim victory. The Americans and Filipinos must be driven out of Bataan. MacArthur held the advantage of a naturally strong defensive position but had very few stockpiled supplies. The Japanese had the islands blockaded by air and sea, and if they could maintain the blockade, the garrison was doomed.

The defense of Bataan lasted for three months and was waged more against hunger and despair than against a fanatical enemy. As early as January 5 MacArthur's forces were put on half rations, 2000 calories per day. Although drastic measures were taken to increase the food supply (including the slaughter of the local work animals, the carabao, and later the cavalry horses), the food situation grew worse. The number to be fed was high, about 80,000 fighting men plus some 26,000 civilian refugees who had crowded into the peninsula.[12] Compounding the seriousness of the food shortage was a shortage of medicine, clothing, shoes, mosquito netting, shelters, and sun helmets. Disease was inevitable. The two hospitals on Bataan could not handle the large numbers of battle casualties plus the disease-stricken men. Beri-beri, dysentery, dengue, hookworm, and malaria struck down more than did the Japanese guns.

Both sides began the siege of Bataan with more determination than optimism. Homma had few men (some of his force had been taken away for the assault against the Indies) and they, too, were plagued by shortages. On January 9 the Japanese struck against the

[12] Morton, *The Fall of the Philippines*, p. 254.

far right of the Abucay Line. Behind their defense line, which stretched across the peninsula from Abucay through Mt. Natib to Mauban, the defenders were organized into the I Corps under General Wainwright and the II Corps under General Parker. Parker and II Corps met the Japanese assault with a ferocious response. Two days later the Japanese began a heavy infantry attack with a banzai charge. Wave after wave of screaming Japanese threw themselves on the barbed-wire entanglements, forming with their tortured bodies a human stile for their comrades to climb over. The attack was contained only after Parker sent up part of his reserve, and the following morning there were more than two hundred Japanese dead on the battlefield.[13]

Stalled on the far right, the Japanese struck in the Mt. Natib sector, and by the 16th they were breaking through the defense line. Wainwright's I Corps also came under serious attack, and on January 22 MacArthur ordered a general withdrawal to the prepared rear defenses, the Orion-Bagac Line. The front would be shorter—only 13 miles—but there was a grim finality about taking up the rear battle position. Further retreat was impossible, and MacArthur wrote General Marshall, "I intend to fight it out to complete destruction." [14]

On January 22 the Japanese, employing the tactics that worked so well in Malaya, made the first of several amphibious landings in the rear of the defense line. They were met by an "ill-assorted band" of sailors without ships, airmen without planes, Philippine constabulary (police), a few U.S. Marines, and some Philippine Army units. The makeshift defense was able to contain the Japanese on the craggy coastal points until reinforcements moved up to assist them. Advancing units of Japanese penetrated the Orion-Bagac Line, only to be cut off into isolated pockets of resistance. In the fighting, both at the front and in the rear, the Japanese displayed the fanatical fight to the last man that characterized much of the Pacific war. The Japanese soldiers, trained to consider that dying for the Emperor was an honor and that surrender was a disgrace, fought until whole units were totally annihilated.

By mid-February General Homma realized he could not break the

13 *Ibid.*, p. 270.
14 *Ibid.*, p. 295.

Orion-Bagac Line without reinforcements. He withdrew his men into defensible positions to await help, and not until the end of March was there another major military clash on Bataan. During the six-week calm the Filipinos and Americans strengthened their positions and trained for the coming battle. No relief could be expected. Malaya and Singapore had already fallen; the Indies were almost gone; the first week in March the Japanese landed in New Guinea. The Philippines were on their own and isolated in a Japanese sea. President Quezon, tortured by the plight of his country, proposed that the Philippines be granted immediate independence and that both Americans and Japanese evacuate the islands and make them neutral. Roosevelt rejected his plan. The United States would not quit the Philippines "until the forces which are now marshaling outside the Philippine Islands return to the Philippines and drive the last remnant of the invaders from your soil." [15]

In February the British and Americans divided the strategic responsibility of the Pacific between them, the British taking India and Burma, the Americans Australia, the Indies, and the Philippines.[16] It was up to the Americans to halt the Japanese. The prime essential was to preserve the air-sea communication links between Australia and the United States, for Australia must be saved from Japanese assault to serve as a base for future operations. The Americans needed a supreme commander for their new Southwest Pacific theater, and MacArthur, because of his knowledge and experience in the area, his military ability, and his almost revered position with the Philippine people, was the logical choice. At the end of February Roosevelt ordered MacArthur to Australia to take over the new command.

MacArthur was reluctant to leave, but the night of March 12 he and his family and part of his staff departed Corregidor by PT boat for Mindanao. From there, they were taken to Australia by B-17. On his arrival, when asked by the press for a statement, MacArthur assured the Filipinos that he had left in order to organize a force for their redemption: "I came through and I shall return." Surveying the forces beginning to assemble in Australia, MacArthur realized it

---

[15] *Ibid.*, p. 355.
[16] Morton, *Strategy and Command: The First Two Years,* Chapter 11; Matloff and Snell, *Strategic Planning for Coalition Warfare 1941–1942,* Chapter 7.

would be some time before he could return. Every effort was made to send food and supplies to the beleaguered Philippines, but the results were negligible and the ordeal of Bataan went on.

General Wainwright, in command of all forces in the Philippines after MacArthur's departure, moved into headquarters on Corregidor and named Major General Edward P. King, Jr., commander of the Bataan forces. Their duty was to put up a determined fight with what they had, and hope their sacrifice would buy time for the Allied forces to organize for the defense of Australia.

During March General Homma received reinforcements and renewed his assault on Bataan. Under intense air and artillery bombardment the weakened condition of the defenders became more apparent daily. By March the men were receiving only 1000 calories per day. Disease reached alarming proportions, with as many as 1000 malaria cases reporting to the hospital every day.[17] Of those at the front, at least 75 percent were ill. Nerve fatigue mounted with decreased physical resistance. The men expressed their bitterness in the doggerel:

> We're the battling bastards of Bataan;
> No mama, no papa, no Uncle Sam;
> No aunts, no uncles, no cousins, no nieces;
> No pills, no planes, no artillery pieces.
> . . . And nobody gives a damn.[18]

The Japanese opened a devastating artillery bombardment early on the morning of Good Friday, April 3. It marked the beginning of the now inevitable disaster. For three days the Japanese advanced, each penetration preceded by an intensive bombardment. The defenders were too ill and too weak to resist. By the 8th General King felt his men could no longer even slow down the Japanese advance. Only one issue of half rations remained. Assuming complete responsibility for his decision, King sent a flag of truce to the Japanese. He urged that his sick and starving men be given decent treatment; he received the disdainful reply: "The Imperial Japanese Army are not barbarians." [19] Yet in the days that followed, the survivors of Bataan

---

[17] Morton, *The Fall of the Philippines*, p. 378.
[18] *Ibid.*, p. 367.
[19] Falk, *The Bataan Death March*, p. 27.

fell victim to one of the most tragic and irresponsible episodes of the entire war. The Battling Bastards, assembled at the tip of the Bataan peninsula, were marched to prison at Camp O'Donnell, some 65 miles to the north. To a healthy soldier the march would have been an ordeal. What made it a tragedy was the sick, starved, and weakened condition of the men and the lack of discipline in the Japanese Army that permitted rampant mistreatment and murder. Although individual officers and men treated their charges with decency, all too many did not. Prisoners were denied food and water even when it was available. On one occasion between 350 and 400 men were tied together with telephone wire and butchered. It is impossible to say how many perished on the Bataan Death March. General King estimated that 25,500 men of his original command did not reach Camp O'Donnell. Many of them were killed in the final offensive; some escaped to Corregidor; some escaped into the hills and disappeared among the civilian population. But thousands died on the road to Camp O'Donnell, and 22,000 more died at the Camp during the first two months of captivity.[20] General Homma paid little attention to the fate of his prisoners. Once the forces on Bataan surrendered, he immediately focused his mind and his artillery on Corregidor.

Corregidor was the largest of four fortified islands in the mouth of Manila Bay. Shaped like a tadpole, it lay only two miles from the southern tip of Bataan. For months it had been bombed and shelled, and everything possible had been moved underground. A large tunnel under Malinta Hill, on the tail of the tadpole, became Corregidor's nerve center. Constructed with many lateral tunnels and a lighting and ventilation system, Malinta Tunnel housed a hospital, an Army headquarters, supplies, and living quarters. Accommodations were crowded, crude, and uncomfortable, but they afforded protection. Nothing could counter the effects of the close-range bombardment on above-ground installations, however, and as April wore on into May the devastated island found its position growing daily more helpless.

The invasion came on May 5. By then the beach defenses were demolished, the huge guns silenced, and communications destroyed. As the Japanese advanced relentlessly toward Malinta Tunnel, where 1000 hospital cases lay helpless, Wainwright came to grips with the

[20] *Ibid.,* p. 137.

inevitable. Late on the morning of May 6 he surrendered the island. Wainwright hoped to surrender only Corregidor, but Homma took advantage of the garrison's helplessness to force the General to surrender all the remaining forces in the Philippines. The Japanese had exerted little effort against the southern islands until the end of March, but since that time they had landed forces on Panay, Cebu, and Mindanao. The defending garrisons had planned and prepared for guerrilla war, and surrender to the Japanese had little appeal. Many managed a timely disappearance into the hills, and not until June 9 were the Japanese satisfied that the southern forces had surrendered. Wainwright was then informed that he was now officially a prisoner of war. It was a status he would hold for three years, three months, and eighteen days, during which time he would play 8632 games of solitaire, take much abuse, and think that Corregidor's half rations had been a feast.[21]

The Doolittle Raid

On April 18, 1942, shortly after the surrender of Bataan and while General Homma's artillery was pounding Corregidor, U.S. Army planes bombed Tokyo.[22] The mission was executed by 16 B-25 bombers that took off from the deck of the carrier *Hornet*.

The planning and execution of this daring mission was entrusted to Lieutenant Colonel James H. Doolittle, an outstanding airman whose quiet competence did much to insure its success. Doolittle, his volunteer crews, and the specially modified planes were escorted into Japanese waters by the task force of Vice Admiral William F. Halsey. Halsey could not risk his carriers in an action with the Japanese, but he must get Doolittle's planes close enough to Japan so that they would have a reasonable chance of flying on to safety in China. When the task force was spotted by Japanese vessels early on April 18, Halsey decided that Doolittle's planes must be launched. The task force was more than six hundred miles from Japan.

None of the pilots had launched a B-25 from a carrier deck before,

---

[21] Wainwright, *General Wainwright's Story*, p. 262.
[22] See Glines, *Doolittle's Tokyo Raiders;* Morison, *The Rising Sun in the Pacific*, pp. 389–98.

and tension was high as Doolittle, in the lead plane, took off into a gale wind. He had no trouble, and the remaining planes left the carrier without mishap. While the task force "got the hell out" of enemy waters, the B-25's winged their way toward Tokyo. They reached their target about noon, dropped their bombs on a startled nation, and headed for the China coast.

The damage done by the Tokyo Raid was not great, but as an Allied morale booster it was an unqualified success, and the Japanese reaction was grim. Thereafter they diverted more strength to home defense, and since it was not known where the planes had come from (Roosevelt hinted they had taken off from "Shangri-la"), the raid influenced the Japanese to extend the defensive perimeter beyond original plans. The Tokyo Raid was the first of a succession of set-backs that caused doubt to penetrate centuries of propaganda which had assured the Japanese they were divinely protected and secure from foreign invasion.

PART II
The Axis Contained

The United States Halts Japan

WHILE THE Malayan, Burmese, Indies, and Philippine campaigns were underway, Japan also occupied the outer defensive perimeter she thought necessary to maintain if she were to protect her conquests. The Gilbert Islands were occupied in December 1941. Kawieng in New Ireland and Rabaul in New Britain were taken in January 1942. (See map, page 203.) At Rabaul the Japanese began to develop a major naval and air base to support their southern operations. From Rabaul they leapfrogged to Gasmata in New Britain (February 1942) and to Lae and Salamaua in Northeastern New Guinea (March). To the southeast they swept along the chain of the Solomon Islands to Buka and Bougainville.

Early in 1942 Japan decided to extend her defensive perimeter by making three further advances to the south and east. The first step would be to secure air mastery of the Coral Sea by occupying Tulagi in the Solomons and Port Moresby on the southern coast of New Guinea. Next she planned to occupy Midway and the western Aleutians, a move calculated to lure the U.S. Pacific Fleet into battle so that the Japanese could destroy it. The third step would be to take New Caledonia, Fiji, and Samoa, thus isolating Australia from the United States. The first step led to the Battle of the Coral Sea. The second led to the Battle of Midway. Both times the Japanese met defeat; the third step was never taken.

The Battles of the Coral Sea and Midway

The Battle of the Coral Sea, fought between May 3 and May 8, was the first naval battle in history in which the two opposing forces did not sight or fire their guns on each other. Carrier planes were the offensive weapons.[1] Vice Admiral Inouye's forces began moving south early in May. One group swung left to take Tulagi, one swung right to take Moresby, while Vice Admiral Takagi's Carrier Striking Force, centered around the carriers *Shokaku* and *Zuikaku,* advanced into the Coral Sea to prevent any U.S. opposition. The U.S. forces, centered around the carriers *Lexington* and *Yorktown,* searched for the Japanese, and on May 7 planes located and sank the Japanese light carrier *Shoho. Shoho's* loss so discouraged Inouye that he ordered the Port Moresby invasion force to turn back. On May 8 the planes from both the U.S. and Japanese carriers met in a lively contest. After the fray both sides claimed victory. The Japanese had inflicted higher loss than they had sustained, for *Yorktown* was damaged and the *Lexington* had to be scuttled. On the other hand, the Americans had thwarted the Moresby invasion, and had inflicted so much damage and plane loss on the Japanese carriers that they were unable to participate in the Battle of Midway, which was a more important battle, a month later.

Luckily Admiral Chester W. Nimitz, who had replaced Admiral Kimmel as Commander of the Pacific Fleet, knew through decrypted messages from Tokyo of the Japanese plans for Midway. Otherwise the Americans might have lost the balance of their Pacific Fleet, for the Japanese force directed on Midway totaled 162 warships and auxiliaries, including 4 large carriers, 3 light carriers, and 9 battle-

[1] Detailed account in Morison, *Coral Sea, Midway and Submarine Actions,* pp. 21–64.

126

ships. Against this armada Nimitz could pit only 76 ships—no battle-ships, and only 3 carriers, *Hornet, Enterprise,* and *Yorktown.*[2] Admiral Yamamoto commanded the Japanese expedition, but Admiral Nagumo, who had commanded the Pearl Harbor raid, was in command of the Japanese carriers.

The Japanese struck at Dutch Harbor in the Aleutians on June 3, but the major U.S. force was not lured north, as was hoped would happen. Attu and Kiska, undefended islands, were occupied June 7, but the major battle occurred farther south. Shortly after dawn on June 4 a U.S. search plane spotted the Japanese carriers 240 miles northeast of Midway. While the three American carriers set an interception course, the unsuspecting Japanese began attacking Midway. Having completed their strike, Nagumo's planes had just landed on their carrier decks when the first American planes appeared overhead. The first three U.S. strikes, by torpedo bombers, scored no hits and their losses were disastrous. Only 6 of the 41 torpedo planes returned to their carriers, but their sacrifice enabled the dive bombers from *Enterprise* and *Yorktown,* swooping down minutes after the torpedo attack, to catch the Japanese defenses off guard and destroy three of Nagumo's carriers. Only *Hiryu* remained, and in a desperate effort to recover the initiative, Nagumo ordered his planes to attack *Yorktown.* *Hiryu*'s planes damaged the U.S. carrier, who was abandoned and later sunk, but not before *Yorktown*'s planes sank *Hiryu.* Admiral Yamamoto assembled his decimated fleet and withdrew. He had lost 4 carriers, 250 planes, and more than 2000 men[3] He had also lost the initiative in the war.

Although the Japanese Command recognized the extent of the Midway defeat, they did not abandon the New Guinea or Solomon Island projects. In July they began an overland assault on Port Moresby, and at Tulagi they established a seaplane base. On Guadalcanal, near Tulagi, the Japanese began to construct an airfield.

Since each Japanese move threatened the vital U.S.-Australian sea-air communication line, the United States felt it must establish bases and begin to wrest control of the Pacific war from the Japanese.

---

[2] *Ibid.,* pp. 87–93. Detailed account pp. 69–159. See also Fuchida, *Midway: The Battle that Doomed Japan.*
[3] Morison, *Coral Sea, Midway and Submarine Actions,* p. 140n.

In December 1941, Admiral Ernest J. King [4] became Commander-in-Chief of the United States Fleet, a position that absorbed the functions of the former Chief of Naval Operations. Early in the war he had envisioned the broad strategy that would defeat Japan. The initial problems were shortages in trained men, ships, planes, and guns. Naval limitations were especially important, since only through her Navy could the U.S. operate in any theater of war. Troops for ground action on any front would have to be transported, reinforced, and supplied by the Navy. The Navy must get supplies to Russia and Britain, fight the U-boats preying on shipping, meet any threat by Axis surface vessels, and protect American shores against foreign invasion. In the Pacific, every step against Japan must involve an amphibious assault, and distances from base to target were great.

In March, when the Americans assumed responsibility for most of the Pacific, they set up several command areas. The Southwest Pacific, under MacArthur, included Australia, New Guinea, most of the Indies, and the Philippines. The remainder of the Pacific was designated the Pacific Ocean Area (POA) and placed under Admiral Nimitz, whose headquarters were at Pearl Harbor. Pacific Ocean Area was in turn divided into South, Central, and North Pacific Areas. (See map, page 102.) Admiral Nimitz retained command of the Central Pacific (including the Hawaiian, Gilbert, Marshall, Caroline, and Mariana Islands), but command of the South Pacific Area was given to Vice Admiral Robert L. Ghormley, whose headquarters were in Auckland, New Zealand. [5] The Southwest and South Pacific Areas, where the Japanese were still advancing, the Americans saw as most immediately crucial, and in the last half of 1942 two offensive actions were initiated to halt the Japanese conquest. One was the Papuan campaign, directed by MacArthur, to secure the Papuan peninsula of New Guinea and free Australia from the threat of invasion. The other was the Guadalcanal campaign, directed by Ghormley, to take Guadalcanal and Tulagi and end the Japanese threat to the U.S.-Australian supply routes. The two operations coincided and were actually two prongs of the same offensive, aimed ultimately at Rabaul.

[4] See King and Whitehill, *Fleet Admiral King, A Naval Record.*
[5] See Morton, *Strategy and Command, The First Two Years,* for the complex command and strategical arrangements for the Pacific.

Guadalcanal

On August 7, 1942, the 1st Marine Division (reinforced), commanded by Major General Alexander A. Vandegrift, landed on Guadalcanal and Tulagi Islands in the U.S. Navy's first amphibious assault since 1898. The operation was hastily planned and executed under far from ideal conditions. Appalling shortages later prompted the unofficial name "Operation Shoestring," but the task force was undetected enroute and the landings on Guadalcanal were unopposed. By the evening of August 8 the Marines had established a beachhead, had overrun the Japanese encampment, and had occupied the airfield. Opposition was negligible, casualties few. Eighteen miles across the sound, on Tulagi and its small adjacent islands, the Japanese put up a vicious defense that was overcome late on August 8. After this initial success a desperate and grueling war of attrition began.

The Guadalcanal landings were covered by the planes from *Wasp, Saratoga,* and *Enterprise,* commanded by Rear Admiral Frank Jack Fletcher. Aerial fighting was vigorous, and in view of

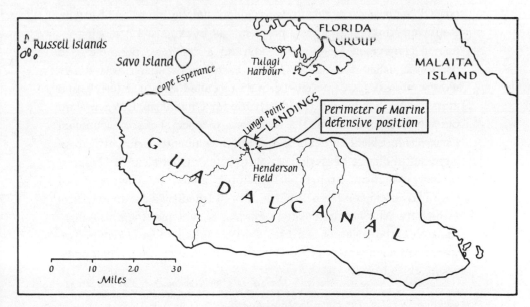

GUADALCANAL

his plane losses, on August 8 Admiral Fletcher decided he could keep the carriers off Guadalcanal no longer. The Admiral withdrew his forces, leaving the men on Guadalcanal without air support. Rear Admiral Richmond Kelly Turner, in charge of the remainder of the amphibious force, put all available warships on patrol to the north and south of Savo Island—a high, round hump that bisects the channel between Guadalcanal and Tulagi. Northwest from Guadalcanal, the Solomon Islands stretch, like a double strand of pearls, across five hundred miles of ocean toward Rabaul. The channel between the two strands, named the Slot, affords a direct route from Rabaul to Guadalcanal. On August 8 Japanese warships steamed down the Slot, arriving off Savo Island after midnight. Tactical surprise and night-fighting skill enabled the Japanese to destroy four heavy cruisers and three other ships before retiring, hardly scratched, back up the Slot. The Battle of Savo Island forced Admiral Turner to withdraw his forces. By nightfall of August 9 the Marines were on their own, exposed to Japanese air and naval attack, and with only thirty days' rations and meager supplies.[6]

First, the Marines had to put the airfield in operating order so they could be covered by air support. Their beachhead was in a sodden coastal plain surrounded by dense jungle fed by almost daily rains. Rank and stinking mud was a problem, but by August 17 the airstrip, named Henderson Field, was ready and a defensive perimeter had been established around it. On the east the perimeter was drawn along a sluggish stream that the Marines called Alligator Creek, and at its mouth they fought their first battle for Guadalcanal. When word of American landings in the Solomons reached Tokyo, Lieutenant General Harukichi Hyakutake and the Seventeenth Army at Rabaul were put in charge of ground action to retake Guadalcanal. Underestimating American strength, a light force landed on August 18 and began advancing on the beachhead. Forewarned by a Japanese patrol (which the Marines annihilated), the Americans met them at Alligator Creek the night of August 21. The Japanese attacked in two waves and each was annihilated in close, intense combat. The oppos-

---

[6] For naval action see Morison, *The Struggle for Guadalcanal.* For the struggle ashore see Miller, *Guadalcanal: The First Offensive;* Zimmerman, *The Guadalcanal Campaign;* Griffith, *The Battle for Guadalcanal.*

ing forces then began to exchange a deadly close-range artillery and mortar barrage, while a battalion of Marines crept through the jungle and launched a surprise attack at the Japanese rear. By early afternoon the remaining Japanese were compressed into a small point between the river and the sea, and when they attempted to break out the Marines held and then counterattacked successfully. The Marines had defeated the Japanese soldier on his own terrain with his own tactics, and the myth of Japanese invincibility was shattered.

The Japanese organized a second force to recapture the island, and it was escorted down the Slot by a major naval force of 64 vessels, including 3 carriers and 3 battleships. The armada was spotted enroute and Ghormley's naval forces met it on August 24 in the Battle of the Eastern Solomons. American planes sank the Japanese carrier *Ryujo,* but *Enterprise* took three bombs and was put temporarily out of action. The transports attempting to land the Japanese invading forces were driven off by the small but spirited air forces now using Henderson Field. After this battle the Japanese aggressive spirit seemed dulled and its Navy became increasingly reluctant to risk a battle by daylight. Reinforcements and supplies for Guadalcanal were sent on fast destroyers that steamed down the Slot by night and left before dawn. Dubbed the Tokyo Express, the destroyers brought 6000 Japanese troops into Guadalcanal between August 29 and September 11,[7] and on September 13 the Marines fought their second battle.

Just south of Henderson Field was a key ridge, where Vandegrift had stationed a battalion of Marines under the command of Colonel Merritt Edson. As expected, the main weight of the Japanese attack was thrown against them, and from the night of September 12 to dawn of September 14 the Marines and Japanese tangled in a fierce, close-range contest for the hill, afterward known as Bloody Ridge. Edson's lines swayed, but did not break. The Japanese were thrown back into the jungle with heavy loss.

So far Guadalcanal had been a sinkhole into which Japanese soldiers, ships, and planes had disappeared without furthering the Japanese cause. They were also fighting a grim struggle for Port Moresby and needed all their resources on Papua. They decided to

---

[7] Miller, *Guadalcanal: The First Offensive,* pp. 112–14.

make a major effort to finish Guadalcanal, and during September and October the Tokyo Express operated steadily, running by night to discharge men and supplies. The Americans were also building up their strength on Guadalcanal, and naval and air clashes were frequent and costly. In mid-September *Wasp* was sunk by a submarine while protecting transports coming into Guadalcanal, and *Saratoga* was put out of commission. Only *Hornet* remained active in the Pacific, and when the next large group of U.S. reinforcements was dispatched to Guadalcanal on October 9, its protection was a cruiser group—no carriers—commanded by Rear Admiral Norman Scott. Scott's force tangled with the Japanese the night of October 11 in the Battle of Cape Esperance, but Scott had trained his men for night fighting and the Japanese took more losses than the Americans.

On October 21 the Japanese land forces opened a major assault on the American beachhead, but their efforts were dispersed and poorly coordinated. After a week of constant struggle, the Japanese effort died away. Their supporting fleet, waiting in the distance, was located and attacked by the Americans on October 26. *Hornet* was sunk but *Shokaku* sustained damages that put her out of action for nine months.

In mid-October Admiral Ghormley was replaced by Vice Admiral William F. Halsey, who brought a spirit of confident aggressiveness to the South Pacific at a critical time. Both Japanese and Americans were suffering heavy losses but a decision seemed no nearer than before. Both sides now intensified their efforts to run in supplies and reinforcements, and the result was a decisive three-day series of air and naval clashes known as the Battle of Guadalcanal. It began in the air, November 12. A formidable array of Japanese fighter-escorted bombers flew down the Slot, but a coastwatcher [8] on Buin spotted them and radioed warning. Almost the entire air group was destroyed, and immediately Rear Admiral Daniel Callaghan, having received warning that a heavily escorted Tokyo Express was enroute, went on patrol with a force of 5 cruisers and 8 destroyers. Nighttime naval battles are confusing, and a wild melee resulted. After half an

---

[8] After the Australians evacuated the southeastern Pacific, individuals remained behind as coastwatchers. Living in extreme hazard, they assisted the Allies by giving advance warning of fleet and air movements.

hour of desperate slugging, the U.S. force was ordered to retire, but only 5 of the original 13 ships were able to do so. Both Admiral Callaghan and Admiral Scott lost their lives. The Japanese lost only 2 destroyers, but a battleship was badly damaged. The next morning planes from Henderson Field, assisted by planes from *Enterprise,* disposed of the damaged Japanese battleship and also located a large Tokyo Express of 11 destroyers escorting 11 troop-laden transports. All the transports were destroyed, and of their 10,000 troops, only 4000, with little of their equipment or supplies, managed to land.[9] On November 14 two U.S. battleships, *Washington* and *South Dakota,* tangled with the Tokyo Express and sent the Japanese battleship *Kirishima* to the bottom. All told, losses during the air and naval battles of November 12–15 were high on both sides, but the U.S. inflicted heavier losses than she sustained and prevented a major reinforcement of the Japanese garrison on Guadalcanal. The U.S. had reached a turning point in the long battle of attrition.

By December the Marines were exhausted and ill. Fighting had been almost constant, disease prevalent, living conditions crude, food and other supplies short. Now it was time for fresh forces to finish up at Guadalcanal. Vandegrift and the 1st Marine Division were evacuated, and Major General Alexander M. Patch moved in with Army and Marine units. General Tojo had by this time realized that the Japanese were fighting a losing battle, and the Tokyo Express began to run in reverse. Some 13,000 [10] Japanese were evacuated before February 9, the day on which General Patch's men cleared Cape Esperance and declared the Battle for Guadalcanal at an end.

The Papuan Campaign

While the struggle for Guadalcanal was going on, American and Australian forces were fighting a nasty campaign on the Papuan

[9] Morison, *The Struggle for Guadalcanal,* pp. 263–85; Miller, *Guadalcanal: The First Offensive,* pp. 185–89.

During the Guadalcanal Campaign General Vandegrift was asked if he could hold Guadalcanal. His reply was, "Hell yes, why not?" Twenty-four years later, on the anniversary of the Guadalcanal landings, the author talked with the General and asked if at any time he had wondered if Guadalcanal could be held. His answer was to remind me of the former question and answer, but when I asked at what time during the campaign he was most concerned, he replied that it was when this large body of troops was enroute. "Fortunately," he said, "they did not land." Printed with permission of General A. A. Vandegrift.

[10] Zimmerman, *The Guadalcanal Campaign,* p. 161.

peninsula of southeastern New Guinea. The Japanese had first moved into New Guinea in March 1942 when they took Lae and Salamaua and began using them as advance bases. Their next goal was Port Moresby, from which Japanese planes could dominate the heavily populated and industrialized Brisbane-Melbourne sector of Australia. Amphibious assault having failed, in July the Japanese landed a force in the Buna-Gona area and began an overland advance on Moresby from the northern side of the peninsula.

Papua's terrain is varied, but all of it is extreme. The Owen Stanley Mountains, among the most rugged in the world, send their saw-toothed peaks towering to a height of 13,000 feet. Their slopes, sometimes almost vertical, are covered by a dense tropical rain forest, fed by a daily soaking that measures as much as ten inches during the rainy season. Only narrow foot trails cross the Owen Stanleys, and the best of these was through Kokoda. On the Moresby side of the peninsula the mountains press their precipitous cliffs and narrow gorges almost to the sea. The Buna side possesses a coastal plain of matted jungle and reeking swamp, alive with malarial mosquitoes, leeches, dreaded tropical fevers, and unknown terrors that made fighting a matter of psychological as well as physical endurance.[11] With amazement and consternation, the Allies watched the Japanese advance over the Kokoda trail until they took Kokoda and its small airstrip on August 12. During the next month Major General Tomi-taro Horii and some 11,000 men continued their difficult advance, fighting tenacious Australian troops as well as the extreme terrain. The Allies had meanwhile thwarted a Japanese attempt to seize their airfield at the tip of the peninsula, at Milne Bay, and the air forces were able to maul Horii's supply lines and force him to halt. In September the Allies began an offensive that gradually pushed the Japanese back on Buna, where the Japanese Command ordered Horii to hold.

By early November the Japanese were compressed into a fairly small perimeter around Buna-Gona, but it took three months of bitter battle to dislodge them. This was the Allies's first experience with the Japanese soldier in a well-fortified defensive position. The Buna defenses utilized bunkers built of coconut logs reinforced with steel

[11] See Milner, *Victory in Papua.*

134

rails. These were covered with more logs reinforced with either sheet iron or 40-gallon steel oil drums full of sand. The bunkers were covered with earth and planted for concealment. Entrances were at the rear and angled for protection from grenades. They were sited so that they not only protected each other by covering fire, but canalized the Allied attack to those areas where defense was the strongest. The 7th Australian Division and the 32nd American Division did not have the proper weapons to reduce the bunkers. Few flamethrowers were available and their design was not yet perfected. Weapons jammed from dampness. The force was dependent for supply on airlifts, native carriers,[12] and small barges or outrigger canoes which could slip along the coast by night. They were short of food, medicine, and even clothes. They were fighting in a swamp, for although the Japanese defenses were mostly on dry land, a morass of streams and swamps surrounded them. More and more men succumbed to malaria and other tropical diseases. Morale was low.

At the end of November General MacArthur, distressed by reports that the Americans were not fighting well, sent Lieutenant General Robert Eichelberger to Buna. Eichelberger and Major General George Vasey, in command of the Australians, made slow but steady progress.[13] By mid-January the Japanese knew they would be exterminated if they remained at Buna. Some Japanese were evacuated, but the remainder fought to the death, and not until January 22, 1943, could the campaign be considered over. Allied losses from disease as well as battle made it one of the costliest operations of the war in terms of the proportion of casualties to the total forces involved.[14] On the other hand, the Allies had gained valuable experience in jungle fighting, in providing air support and supply for ground forces, and in reducing a bunker defense system. Improved tactics and weapons were a result of the campaign. Guadalcanal and Papua halted the Japanese offensive and marked the beginning of an Allied advance that did not end until the war was over, thirty-one months later.

[12] The Papuan natives were primitive Melanesians. They dressed sparsely, lived in thatched huts, had frizzly hair, and many of them served the Allies loyally. They could march further and faster than most soldiers, yet carry a forty-pound pack of supplies. Their gentleness, devotion, and courage as stretcher-bearers earned them the affectionate title, "the Fuzzy-Wuzzy Angels of the Owen Stanley Range."
[13] See Eichelberger, *Our Jungle Road to Tokyo.*
[14] Milner, *Victory in Papua,* pp. 369–72 for casualty analysis.

The Battle for the Atlantic

DURING the early months of 1942, when the Japanese were dealing the Allies bitter defeats in the Pacific, their fortunes in the Atlantic sank to a critical low. In the first six months of the year German U-boats sent more than three million gross tons of Allied merchant shipping to the bottom of the seas.[1] The losses of the United States Merchant Marine alone surpassed their entire losses in World War I. Allied shipyards were unable to match in new production the amount of shipping lost,[2] and German shipyards were building U-boats at a rate almost six times as fast as they were being sunk.[3]

War on the U-Boats

The most critical areas of the Atlantic during the early part of 1942 were the shipping lanes along the United States coast. These

[1] Morison, *The Battle of the Atlantic*, p. 412, Appendix I.
[2] *Ibid.*, pp. 198–200.
[3] *Ibid.*, pp. 410, 415, Appendixes I and II.

lanes run from the Saint Lawrence River, down the coast to New York, Hatteras, and Florida, where they divide, one going into the Gulf of Mexico and the other through the Old Bahama Channel to the Windward Passage. New York, in 1942, was the busiest port in the world, and the Caribbean was rich in ships enroute to or from South America and the Dutch West Indies. The shipping lanes were busy and completely unprotected except for mines in the capes of the Chesapeake and nets and booms in the larger Atlantic harbors. Small craft for anti-submarine warfare had been neglected so that the larger vessels needed for a two-ocean navy could be built. Vessels for convoy escort were scarce. Few merchant ships were armed, and their guns were often inadequate. Americans suffered a shortage of airplanes for coastal patrol, and the U.S. had few pilots trained for flying over water or hitting small, moving targets such as submarines.

It took only six German U-boats (commanded by Admiral Doenitz's top aces) to sink thirteen vessels in the coastal area between New York and Cape Hatteras in the last two weeks of January alone.[4] In February more U-boats joined them and the field broadened to include the Caribbean. In May, when U.S. defense measures began to take effect, the U-boats shifted to the area around the Gulf of Mexico, and Allied losses continued high. By mid-July, when the U.S. Navy scored its eighth kill on a German submarine, more than 360 merchant ships, totaling about 2,250,000 gross tons, had been lost in United States coastal waters.[5] It was vital that the U.S. seize the initiative from the German U-boats.

Anti-submarine warfare was waged in many ways. Convoys were the prime essential. Small craft for escort duty were put on intensive production, and by March a Submarine Chaser Training Center had been set up in Miami. Coastal convoys were expanded until by September the United States had an efficient Interlocking Convoy System that enabled ships to move through the coastal waters under escort and with minimum delays. Losses began to drop, but convoys alone were not enough. Convoys were primarily a defensive measure, since escorts could not leave the convoy to pursue a U-boat. Additional groups of escorts were formed to give chase when a U-boat contact was made.

4 *Ibid.*, p. 131.   5 *Ibid.*, p. 157.

The war against the U-boats was in many respects a scientific war, and playing the most important part in the effectiveness of the anti-submarine craft were three technical devices—sonar, radar, and HF/DF (called huff-duff). Sonar enabled anti-submarine craft to listen for submerged U-boats; radar provided means of locating surfaced U-boats; HF/DF employed high-frequency direction finders to pick up radio transmissions by which operators could locate U-boats by the radio messages they sent. All were effective, but Hitler and Doenitz gave micro-wave radar credit for playing the greatest part in the ultimate defeat of the U-boat.[6]

Aircraft played an important role in the war at sea, not only for reconnaissance but for destroying the submarines. Air cover over the convoys greatly increased their efficiency, and as more bases were built, more planes constructed, and longer-range planes designed, all except the mid-ocean areas could receive land-based air support. Admiral Doenitz began to complain that his field of operation was sorely limited, and in time even the "Black Pit"—the mid-Atlantic—had air cover for its convoys. Small escort carriers gradually took their place among the other anti-submarine craft.

In August 1942 Brazil entered the war and her excellent small navy became available to the Allies. By operating from Brazilian fields, aircraft closed the Atlantic Narrows (between the eastern bulge of South America and the western bulge of Africa) to Axis blockade runners and extended convoy air cover.

Anti-submarine warfare was also waged in the shipyards. Doenitz's strategy was to keep Allied losses well above their construction rate. Until August 1942 Doenitz was ahead in the race, but Allied shipyards were gradually closing the gap, and in August new construction equaled the shipping sunk. In November Doenitz again pulled ahead, but Allied construction jumped forward in December to keep the lead.[7]

This type of warfare involved no single decisive battles, no dramatic turning points. The outcome would be decided by the endurance of the men manning the planes and ships, by the moral stamina of the nations behind them, and by the weapons and vessels those nations could produce. The Battle of the Atlantic did not come to an

[6] *Ibid.*, p. 251.   [7] *Ibid.*, p. 404.

end until the war itself was over.

During the first half of 1942, as anti-submarine measures began to make U.S. coastal waters a less fertile field, the U-boats began once more to concentrate on the Atlantic convoys. By now the United States was moving large numbers of American troops to Britain. Hard as it was to lose a cargo ship full of food, fuel, or munitions, it was worse to lose a ship crammed with men. Fast luxury liners were adopted as troop transports and sent across the Atlantic nearly unescorted. By the end of the year, 194,850 American servicemen had been safely carried across the Atlantic.[8]

Late 1942 and early 1943 was the turning point for the war in the Pacific, Russia, and Africa. In the Atlantic, however, the situation was far from secure, and on its outcome all else depended. British and American European offensives could not be maintained unless the Atlantic lifelines could be depended upon to get the vital supplies across. When Churchill, Roosevelt, and the Combined Chiefs of Staff met at Casablanca for a major strategy conference in January 1943, they agreed that the defeat of the U-boat must have priority. Simultaneously Hitler made Doenitz Commander-in-Chief of the German Navy and ordered top priority in personnel, construction, repair, and support to go to the submarines. The war against the merchant ships was approaching its climax.

By early 1943 Doenitz had about one hundred U-boats operating in the north and central Atlantic. The Wolf-Packs were stationed across every known convoy route. A particularly rough winter and spring worked to Doenitz's advantage. Storm followed storm, and in the heavy seas and gale winds ships had difficulty maintaining convoy position. The vile weather often grounded the convoys' air cover, and losses from marine casualties alone were distressing. February losses showed an alarming increase, running up to 63 ships. Losses during the first ten days of March were 41, during the next ten days, 54. March losses came to more than one-half million tons, but most alarming was that most losses had occurred *in convoy*. Was it possible that the convoy system, upon which the entire Allied strategy was based, was no longer adequate as a defense? Later the Admiralty admitted that during the first twenty days of March, the Germans

[8] Roskill, *The War at Sea*, Vol. II, pp. 211–12.

came as close as they ever did to disrupting communications across the Atlantic.[9] March was the peak of U-boat success. In April and May shipping losses dropped and the number of U-boats sunk rose. Allied anti-submarine measures at last began to swing the pendulum in the Allies' favor.

Increased coverage by long-range aircraft, the use of support groups, and the appearance of escort carriers for the convoys were the most important measures enabling the Allies to gain control over the U-boat. Long-range (Liberators, Flying Fortresses, Catalinas) and very-long-range (modified Liberators and Coronados) aircraft gradually extended air cover over the convoy routes to an extreme radius of nine hundred miles from Newfoundland, five hundred miles from Iceland, and nine hundred miles from the British Isles. The planes prevented many U-boats from ever coming close to a convoy. The Black Pit, the area not under the land-based air umbrella, began in March to receive air cover from the escort carriers. The combination of intensified measures brought success. On May 17, *Aymeric* went down—the last merchant ship sunk in a transatlantic convoy until mid-September.[10] When German submarine losses for May jumped to 41, the U-boats were withdrawn from the North Atlantic to hunt in less heavily defended waters, and Doenitz applied himself to devising new tactics and pushing the development of improved submarines.

By the last half of September Doenitz had a group of 21 U-boats ready for a new convoy strike. Most of them were supplied with full anti-aircraft armament, as well as a new acoustic torpedo and a radar decoy device. They did some damage to two convoys in late September, sinking six merchantmen and three escort vessels,[11] but the heyday of the acoustic torpedo did not last long. The National Defense Research Council had long been at work devising countermeasures, and by the end of September they had developed "Foxer," a noise-making device which was towed behind the ship. It attracted the torpedo and exploded it harmlessly.

Diplomacy also helped defeat the U-boat threat. For some time the British had been urging the Portuguese government to grant Britain

[9] *Ibid.*, pp. 356, 357, 367.   [10] Morison, *The Atlantic Battle Won*, p. 77.
[11] *Ibid.*, p. 146.

the right to base planes in the Azores, Atlantic islands owned by Portugal. Although Portugal was determined to stay neutral in the war, she had a treaty with Britain that dated back to 1373 and had been reinforced in succeeding centuries. The original treaty stated that the two powers would "from this day forward . . . be friends to friends and enemies to enemies." [12] On the basis of this long-standing and unmarred friendship, in October the Portuguese government granted the British the use of bases in the Azores provided the British guarantee the Portuguese protection against German aggression. The RAF lost no time taking advantage of their new base, and it wasn't too long before U.S. planes began flying with them.

The North Russia Convoys

The transatlantic convoys, hazardous at best, were not as hazardous as the North Russia Run, which went from Iceland through the Barents Sea to the north Russian ports of Murmansk, Molotovsk, and Archangel. When BARBAROSSA catapulted Russia into the war against Germany, Britain at once extended the hand of friendship and help. Hitler and Nazism were the enemies, Churchill stated, and anyone who would fight against them would get all the aid Britain could give.[13] Stalin replied that Britain must establish a second front in Europe to draw off some of the German divisions. Such a task was beyond British capabilities in 1941, but Britain, later joined by the U.S., extended help to Russia through Lend-Lease. The agreement was to make war materials available in British or U.S. ports, but in practice much of the material was transported to Russia by British and U.S. forces.

By far the shortest route to Russia was the North Russia Run, but convoying along this route was the most dangerous and unpleasant task to fall on the Allied navies. The crews combatted cold, snow, ice, fog, high seas, and freezing water. The Arctic ice pack narrowed the seas and forced the convoys to pass within range of German aircraft stationed in Norway and Finland. German submarines, painted po-

---

[12] Churchill, *Closing the Ring*, p. 167.
[13] Churchill, *The Grand Alliance*, p. 371.

lar-white to escape detection, were plentiful, and German surface ships lurked in Norwegian waters and threatened to pounce on every convoy. Perpetual daylight made it hard to hide from pursuers. If a ship did reach Murmansk safely it was subject to air attack while it was in the harbor. Despite the hardships and high losses, the North Russia convoys ran until March 1943, when Axis forces were cleared from the Mediterranean, in order to convince Stalin that his allies were doing their best. Lend-Lease was the subject of bitter exchanges between Russia and her allies. The Soviet government did not publicize the Lend-Lease assistance they were receiving. In fact the government made definite accusations of the Allies' bad faith and half-hearted efforts, meanwhile demanding that a Second Front be opened immediately.[14]

The Commandos and Combined Operations

The war of the U-boats against merchant shipping does not tell the complete story of the Battle of the Atlantic. Germany had a respectable surface fleet, and during February 1942 it dealt a startling blow to the Royal Navy. The German battle cruisers *Scharnhorst, Gneisenau,* and *Prinz Eugen* had been blockaded in the French port of Brest for almost a year, but on February 11 the ships evaded the blockade and slipped through the English Channel to reach Norway.

Britain's reply to this humiliating incident was to send two Commando raids to France as a reminder to Hitler that he had not yet defeated his island antagonist. Bruneval, near Le Havre, was the site of a German radar station. British scientists wanted a sample of the German equipment for evaluation, and the Commandos procured it in a daring but successful raid. In March the Commandos blew up the locks at St. Nazaire. This port was the only one on the Atlantic coast that had adequate facilities for repairing the larger ships, and the British reasoned that if no dock facilities existed, the Germans would be less likely to send big ships like the *Tirpitz, Bismarck's* sister

[14] For relations between Russia and the Western Allies see Churchill, *The Grand Alliance, The Hinge of Fate,* and *Closing the Ring;* Feis, *Churchill, Roosevelt, Stalin: The War They Waged and the Peace They Sought.*

ship, into the open seas.

To the staff of Combined Operations Headquarters, these Commando raids were lessons in how to coordinate air, land, and sea forces. Combined Operations Headquarters came into being shortly after the fall of France in 1940. Their purpose was to study the ways and means to strike back at the Germans holding the continent. As part of its organization, it would direct small, specially trained units, the Commandos, in raids against the continent to keep the British on the offensive on a small scale. In October 1941 Lord Louis Mountbatten became its head. In May 1942 nine American officers joined the staff, making it the first inter-allied as well as inter-service staff. Combined Operations dealt with a magnitude of problems. The design and procurement of landing craft, the prerequisite to a continental invasion, was only one part of its achievement. For example, before the Allies could invade the continent, they must be assured of being able to get enough petrol ashore to prevent vehicles from becoming immobilized in the beachheads. PLUTO (Pipe Line Under The Ocean) was the answer, and at its peak PLUTO delivered from England to France one million gallons of oil a day.[15]

In planning the invasion of the continent, the staffs needed to know what kind and how much equipment would be required to breach the Atlantic Wall, and above all how hard it was going to be to take a port. To obtain this information, a raid was planned at Dieppe. Conducted by the 2nd Canadian Division on August 18, 1942, the raid was costly in lives but contributed to the ultimate success of the Normandy invasion launched in 1944. The main question—was it practical to take a port by head-on assault—was answered. The Allies abandoned the idea of capturing a port from the sea, while the Germans assumed they would definitely strike for a port and prepared accordingly. To compensate for not taking a port in the initial assault, Combined Operations began to plan the "mulberry," an artificial port that could be made in England and towed across the Channel.

The Battle of the Atlantic continued until May 1945, but 1942–43 were the years when Germany might have defeated Allied strategy with the U-boat. In March 1943 Germany made her highest bid, but by the end of the year there was no doubt but that the essential troops

[15] Fergusson, *The Watery Maze*, p. 195.

143

and supply convoys could continue to steam fairly safely across the Atlantic. The Battle of the Atlantic, although not over until the end of the war, was under control. The Allied offensives in Europe could proceed, and during 1942–43 they began to reclaim Axis gains on both Eastern and Western Fronts.

German Thrust to the Caucasus

THE LAST MONTHS OF 1942 and the early months of 1943 marked the turning point in the war. In the Atlantic the crisis was reached and passed in March 1943. In the Pacific, the combined effects of Midway, Guadalcanal, and Papua blunted the Japanese thrust. In Africa Rommel was defeated at Alamein, and the Allies invaded Africa in Operation TORCH in November 1942. On the Eastern Front, the crisis came at Stalingrad late in 1942.

Russia Attempts to Seize the Initiative

In December 1941 the German armies had come almost within sight of the Kremlin towers before being thrown back by the Russians. Moscow was saved, but Russian gains during December and January were slight, and at the end of February a temporary lull descended over the battlefield. The Russian High Command, overestimating both their own offensive ability and the German losses of the previous year, planned three offensive operations. In the south, in April, they would try to retake the Crimea and relieve the siege of Sevastopol. In the north, in May, attempts would be made to restore land communications with Leningrad. A third and larger effort would be made in May to recapture Kharkov, thereby disrupting the communications of the German armies in the south and eliminating the German capacity to stage a major offensive in that area. All three efforts failed.

In the Crimea, winter weather did not particularly hamper operations, and there was sporadic activity throughout the winter and early spring. Between December and the end of March the Germans defeated three separate Russian attempts to break into the Crimea, and Russia's larger offensive in April also met disastrous failure. More than 100,000 men were taken prisoner, and the Russians' efforts had accomplished nothing.[1] Von Manstein and the Eleventh Army proceeded to clear the Kerch peninsula and turn their full resources on Sevastopol. Heavy artillery was brought in and the German bombardment began in June. After a month of bitter fighting in severe heat, the Germans broke through the outer ring of defenses, but the more formidable inner defenses seemed too much for their dwindling strength. Von Manstein, perhaps the most capable of the German generals, moved assault forces across the bay on the north of the city and stormed the cliffs. Catching the defenders by surprise, he knocked out one of their most important defense positions, dooming the garrison. It surrendered July 1.

Russia's attempts to relieve the siege of Leningrad were equally disastrous. In January an entire army was captured when it attempted to open the main rail route to Moscow. In May a larger effort to break the siege, led by General Vlasov, met initial success and managed to force a break in the German lines, but had not the strength to sustain it. Vlasov's force was encircled and destroyed, and in Leningrad, where thousands lay dead and dying, the people resigned themselves to continued hardship and suffering. All supplies, for civilians as well as military personnel, had to enter the city by crossing Lake Ladoga. At first they came only in dribbles—not enough to sustain life—but early in 1942 the situation improved.

[1] Clark, *Barbarossa*, p. 199.

After the lake froze, a road was built over the ice, and trucks began rushing food to the starving city. The ice road did not reach peak efficiency until late in February, and by then famine was widespread. During January and February 1942 the death rate reached its peak, at times as high as 3500 to 4000 persons *per day*.[2] Most deaths resulted from starvation, malnutrition, and exposure, but people also died in the almost unceasing artillery barrage the Germans poured on the city.

By March Leningrad began to recover from its first disastrous winter. Adequate supplies began to reach the city, and as many as possible of its citizens were evacuated. Despite continued hardship, few thought of surrender, for not only did the Leningraders doubt that their situation would improve under German occupation, but their pride was stirred by their very endurance. The factories and industries continued to function, even with only 50 percent of the labor force. Although the people criticized the government and the authorities, no riots, demonstrations, or rebellions broke out. By late 1942 the population of Leningrad had been reduced, through death and evacuation, to less than a million.[3] Those remaining were primarily essential personnel for maintaining the city and operating its industries. Knowing that their fate depended on what happened on the more active southern front, Leningraders watched anxiously as Germany drove into Russia's economic heartland.

Russia's third attempt to regain the initiative was commanded by Marshall Timoshenko, who directed two armies and nearly six hundred tanks in an assault on the German lines south of Kharkov on May 12. The armies quickly broke through and began steamrolling west. After a five-day advance Timoshenko's armor was drawn out over seventy miles in a long, vulnerable corridor, and on the 18th the Germans attacked both flanks. By the 23rd the Russians were encircled and the Germans captured 240,000 men and vast amounts of armor.[4] A month later the Germans opened their 1942 campaign.

---

[2] Goure, *The Siege of Leningrad*, p. 217. See also Werth, *Leningrad*.

[3] Goure, *The Siege of Leningrad*, p. 286. Three million persons were originally under siege. Figures vary on the number of deaths, but Soviet Russia acknowledges that 632,000 persons died as a direct result of the blockade. Werth, *Russia at War*, p. 324

[4] Clark, *Barbarossa*, p. 203.

Germany Drives South

Hitler's gamble on a quick war of annihilation against Russia had failed. He decided that Germany's 1942 effort would be in the south. He not only needed the oil of the Caucasus for the German war machine, but if Russia was deprived of her oil, she might be defeated by economic strangulation. She had already lost her greatest agricultural and industrial districts in the 1941 campaigns. Placing the Army Groups facing Leningrad and Moscow on the defensive, Hitler reinforced Army Group South and reorganized it as Army Groups A and B, under List and von Bock. Army Group A, spearheaded by von Kleist's armor, was to strike for the Caucasus, while Army Group B secured and held its left flank from Voronezh on the Don River to Stalingrad on the Volga. (See map, page 86.)

Was the campaign beyond German capabilities? Some of the generals thought so. Germany had lost more than a million men in the Russian campaign of 1941,[5] and though replacements had greatly restored the armies, the Wehrmacht was weaker than when BARBAROSSA commenced, and the war on other fronts had intensified. Although he refused to accept sobering estimates of Russian strength, Hitler called on his satellites for help. Rumanians, Italians, Hungarians—all sent divisions to bolster the Reich on the Eastern Front. Hitler planned to use them to man the long and vulnerable flank from Voronezh to the Volga and beyond.

When Army Group B began its advance from the Kursk area on June 28, they met little opposition. How could they? The Russians, still reeling from their losses in May, could only fall back. The main difference between this advance and the one of the year before was that the Germans no longer took so many prisoners. The Russians seemed to fade over the horizon, drawing the Germans deeper and deeper into the basins of the Don and Donetz Rivers.

On July 5 elements of Army Group B reached Voronezh on the

[5] Figures from Halder's Diaries, quoted in Baldwin, *Battles Lost and Won*, p. 157. Estimates of Russian losses during the 1941 battles vary between 2 and 3 million. *Ibid.*, p. 157.

Don and met their first serious resistance. The Russians had concentrated there a force under General Vatutin to halt the Germans in case they swung north toward Moscow. Von Bock wanted to eliminate Vatutin's force before turning south and sweeping down the corridor between the Don and Donetz. Hitler overruled. Von Bock was dismissed, and Hitler ordered part of his Army Group south to assist von Kleist in forcing the Don at Rostov. Hoth's Fourth Panzer Army assisted von Kleist in taking Rostov, but von Kleist later claimed that the help was not needed and it merely clogged up the roads.[6] With Rostov secured by July 28, Hoth was ordered back to rejoin Army Group B. To the Germans (and others) it appeared that Russia was finished. So far there had not even been a major battle.

Von Kleist's armored spearhead continued to enjoy dramatic success. On August 9 it reached the Maikop oilfields (destroyed by the retreating Russians); on August 22 the Nazi flag was flown from Mt. Elbrus. The Germans pressed on toward the oilfields at Grozny and Baku. By September their momentum was slipping. Hitler dismissed List, and von Kleist was given command of Army Group A. Changing the commanders in no way altered the situation, which was deteriorating because of shortage of supplies—especially oil. All supplies for the German forces in the Caucasus had to come through Rostov, and the rail lines were insufficient to handle the vast amounts needed. By mid-September the German advance had come to a halt, short of its objective, but far enough from its starting point to form a German front, from Kursk into the Caucasus, which was more than 1250 miles in length. Figuring another eight hundred miles for the front from Kursk north to Leningrad, makes the total Russo-German front more than two thousand miles long.[7]

Meanwhile Army Group B, pressing for Stalingrad, had run into trouble. At first Hoth's armor made rapid progress, but after taking Kotelnikovo on August 3, it met a stiffened defense. All units were beginning to experience fuel shortage, and the shifting around of Hoth's Army had spent effort and time—time used by the Russians to move troops to Stalingrad's defense. Behind the Russian front a race of men against time, of hope against despair, was in progress. Not

[6] Liddell-Hart, *The German Generals Talk*, p. 205.
[7] Fuller, *The Second World War*, pp. 529–30.

149

only did the Russians face a tremendous task in moving reserves and organizing forces for the defense of Stalingrad, but morale had plummeted. In August, Churchill had gone to Moscow to tell Stalin that there would be no Second Front in Europe in 1942. The Western Allies had not the strength to mount it. The Russians, meeting the full fury of the Wehrmacht, were bitter. The failure of their spring offensives, followed by the rapid German penetration, had left the Russians demoralized. The main task the Russian generals faced in the fall of 1942 was gathering the masses of tattered, disheartened soldiers and welding them into a fighting force. The defense of Stalingrad testifies the extent of their success.

The Battle of Stalingrad

Stalingrad, a long narrow city of half a million people, stretched for some thirty miles along the west bank of the Volga River. By August 23 General Friedrich Paulus and his Sixth Army had penetrated the outer defenses protecting the city, and were established on the Volga north of Stalingrad on a five-mile front. From there, their artillery could halt the flow of Caucasian oil that traveled up the Volga to central Russia, as well as disrupt Russian supplies being carried into Stalingrad itself. Victory seemed imminent, and on the night of August 23 the Luftwaffe delivered a massive terror raid on the city that killed thousands of civilians and burned nearly every wooden building in Stalingrad. The Russian reply was to exhort the citizens to "barricade every street; transform every district, every block, every house, into an impregnable fortress." [8] In the next two days the Germans were halted in their tracks. Hitler ordered Paulus to capture the city at once; the Russians sent General Zhukov to Stalingrad.

Hitler's offensive was in trouble. Both Army Groups were short of supplies and the German forces were spread dangerously thin. As more and more of the better divisions were withdrawn from other sectors and thrown into the Battle of Stalingrad, the satellite forces moved in to man the flanks. That portion of the vulnerable north (left) flank between Voronezh and Kletskaya was held by the Hun-

[8] Clark, *Barbarossa*, p. 218.

garian Second, the Italian Eighth, and the Rumanian Third Armies
—the weakest of the Axis forces. South of Stalingrad lay another long
and vulnerable flank, to which the Rumanian Fourth Army was
assigned. General Halder, the Chief of the Army's General Staff,
upset by reports of massing Russian strength and by the exposed
positions of the armies, urged withdrawal. For voicing his opinion,
Halder was replaced by General Kurt Zeitzler, who found the atmos-
phere at Supreme Headquarters "not only weird but positively
incredible." [9]

In mid-September the Germans renewed their assault, and the fight
for Stalingrad began in earnest. Although the Luftwaffe had complete
mastery of the air and Paulus had an overwhelming superiority in
men and tanks, the nature of the battle had changed. The Germans
were no longer pushing across the open steppes, but this time were
pushing into the rubble of a city. Here, they found themselves involved in a military situation outside their experience, and they
showed less skill than the Russians when advances came to be
measured in yards rather than miles, and battles resolved into personal combat between individuals. The steady destruction of Stalingrad from artillery and bombs helped the Russian cause, for the
streets became full of debris that slowed the advance of the German
tanks, and ruined buildings afforded excellent cover for snipers and
individual weapons. Of the nature of the battle a German lieutenant
wrote:

> We have fought during fifteen days for a single house, with
> mortars, grenades, machine-guns and bayonets. Already by the
> third day fifty-four German corpses are strewn in the cellars, on
> the landings, and the staircases. The front is a corridor between
> burnt-out rooms; it is the thin ceiling between two floors. Help
> comes from neighboring houses by fire escapes and chimneys.
> There is a ceaseless struggle from noon to night. From storey to
> storey, faces black with sweat, we bombard each other with
> grenades in the middle of explosions, clouds of dust and smoke,
> heaps of mortar, floods of blood, fragments of furniture and
> human beings. Ask any soldier what half an hour of hand-to-

[9] Freidin, *The Fatal Decisions,* p. 135.

hand struggle means in such a fight. And imagine Stalingrad; eighty days and eighty nights of hand-to-hand struggles. The street is no longer measured by metres but by corpses. . . .[10]

By the end of September the Germans had driven a corridor through Stalingrad to the Volga, and General Vasili Chuikov's Sixty-Second Army, defending the city, was cut in two. During October the fighting was especially intense around the factories in the northern part of the city, where more than a fourth of Russia's tractors, tanks, and mechanical vehicles were produced. Many of the factory workers stood by their machines until the last minute, only to pick up a weapon and join the defense when the Germans were at the door. In mid-October Russian casualties reached their peak. The night of October 14 the Volga ferries evacuated 3500 Russian wounded to the east bank of the river.[11]

By November most of the city was in German hands. Chuikov and the Sixty-Second Army controlled the small bridgeheads along the Volga, but their backs were to the river, and the Germans were only some one thousand yards away. Following the same strategy that had worked at Moscow, Zhukov husbanded his reserves, throwing into Stalingrad only enough men to avert complete collapse. Meanwhile, Russian armies were quietly massing in the forests north of the Don River. Generals Golikov, Vatutin, and Rokossovsky commanded three groups of armies (the Russians used the term "Front," whose size was roughly equivalent to a western "Army") along the Don west of Stalingrad; a fourth Front, under Yeremenko, was assembling south of Stalingrad. Silently they waited the winter freeze.

Some German planners had presentiments of disaster, but Hitler refused to stop the Stalingrad assault and withdraw to defensive lines for the winter. Stalingrad had become an obsession, a symbol, a test of wills. Between November 11 and 19 the Germans once more split Chuikov's Army and reduced the bridgehead along the Volga to a scant one hundred yards from the riverbank. The soldiers fought like animals and kept awake on alcohol and benzedrine. On November 19 Zhukov unleashed his reserves. North and

[10] Clark, *Barbarossa*, p. 238.
[11] Chuikov, *The Beginning of the Road*, p. 181.

south of Stalingrad Rokossovsky and Yeremenko struck against the Rumanian armies protecting Sixth Army's vital flanks. Three days later the Russian pincers closed at Kalach and Sixth Army was surrounded in a classic trap.

The Russian pincers were weak, and Sixth Army could probably have broken out of its pocket had it moved at once. Hitler, ordering Paulus to hold Stalingrad and the land along the Volga, allowed no retreat. Goering irresponsibly promised Hitler that the Luftwaffe could keep Sixth Army supplied, but it could not provide Paulus with even his minimum needs. If the Germans were not going to retreat from the Volga, then land communications with Paulus's Army must be restored. Hitler called on the hero of the Crimea, General von Manstein, gave him a newly organized force, Army Group Don, and instructed him to restore the German front at Stalingrad.

Von Manstein was slow to arrive at his new post (partisans were playing havoc with the railroads), and gathering the forces for his new Army Group took even longer. Army Group Don could not begin the major part of its rescue mission until December 12, and by then the full fury of the Russian winter had broken over the steppes, and the Russians had become firmly entrenched around Paulus's Army. Von Manstein did not have the force to dislodge them. The better part of Army Group Don was Sixth Army itself, and von Manstein had no hopes of being able to fight through to Sixth Army if Paulus did not break out to meet him. Paulus was unwilling to break out if it meant disobeying orders from his High Command, and Hitler refused to let Paulus give up an inch of the bridgehead.

Von Manstein's rescue mission failed.[12] It got within 25 to 30 miles of Sixth Army by advancing from the southwest, but it could go no further. Along the vulnerable satellite flank stretching westward along the Don, the Russians were attacking in force. The airlift to Sixth Army had failed, the rescue mission had failed, and the front was disintegrating—but Paulus's orders remained to hold Stalingrad. After the first of the year, it was crucial to Army Group A that he do so, for after much persuasion Hitler authorized a retreat for the forces in the Caucasus. While von Manstein fought desperately to hold open

---

[12] See Manstein, *Lost Victories*.

the Rostov gateway, von Kleist extricated Army Group A from the Caucasus, and in Stalingrad Sixth Army continued to resist.

Within the Stalingrad pocket, life had become a blur of hunger, cold, and misery. Temperatures ranged far below the freezing point. Shelter was almost non-existent, medical facilities scant, and daily rations dropped to two hundred grams of bread per day for each person.[13] Ammunition was almost exhausted. A supply plane landed only occasionally, so the feeble trickle of material it provided made little impression on the quarter of a million men under siege.

Outside the Stalingrad pocket, the Russians massed for the final annihilation. On January 8 Rokossovsky gave Paulus a chance at honorable surrender. To Hitler surrender was out of the question. On January 10 the Russians began a massive bombardment aimed at the destruction of Sixth Army. By January 24 the last airstrips had fallen and the Sixth Army had been cut in two. Again Rokossovsky sent Paulus a request for surrender. Paulus radioed: "Further defense senseless. Collapse inevitable. Army requests immediate permission to surrender in order to save lives of remaining troops." [14] Hitler answered:

> Surrender is forbidden. Sixth Army will hold their positions to the last man and the last round and by their heroic endurance will make an unforgettable contribution toward the establishment of a defensive front and the salvation of the Western world.[15]

The battle was resumed, but Sixth Army was soon incapable of doing more. Late on January 31 Paulus, newly promoted to Field Marshal, quietly surrendered to a squad of Russians who broke into his bunker.[16] In the north of the city a small pocket of Germans held out for two more days. Then the Battle of Stalingrad was over.[17]

---

[13] Goerlitz, *Paulus and Stalingrad*, p. 274.
[14] Schroter, *Stalingrad*, p. 218.
[15] Shirer, *The Rise and Fall of the Third Reich*, p. 930.
[16] Werth, *Russia at War*, pp. 540–41.
[17] German casualties were close to a quarter of a million men. On November 23 Paulus set the strength of Sixth Army at 220,000. Some 42,000 wounded and specialists were evacuated from the pocket. The Russians took 107,000 prisoners; 72,000 Germans died during the battle. See Goerlitz, *Paulus and Stalingrad*, p. 272n.

German Disaster on the Don

By the time Sixth Army surrendered, the entire Eastern Front was in turmoil. Army Group A had gotten out of the Caucasus, although Hitler insisted on holding the Crimea. The Russians, breaking through the Axis lines all along the Don flank, began steamrolling west. Kursk, the starting point of the German offensive, was captured on February 7. Ten days later the Russians reclaimed Kharkov. Again Hitler called on von Manstein, who was given Army Group South (the remnants of Army Group B and Army Group Don) with which to stem the Russian tide. In a brilliantly planned and well-executed campaign, von Manstein rallied his shattered forces and launched an offensive that reclaimed Kharkov in mid-March and established the Germans once more on the Donetz River line. But there his advance petered out in the mud of spring. Although the German Seventeenth Army still held the Crimea, the German lines on the southern end of the long Eastern Front were in essentially the same positions as when they began their ambitious bid for the Caucasus nine months before.

Not only in the south, but all along the vast battle line the Russians prevailed. Army Group Center was forced back behind Vyasma, and in the far north a Russian offensive in January partially restored the rail link between Leningrad and Moscow. Then, toward the end of March, a lull fell over the entire Eastern Front. Both sides had battled to exhaustion and the end of their resources. Not until July 1943 were the armies again on the move, and by that time Germany was in retreat in Africa as well.

The War in North Africa

THE LAST HALF OF 1941 was quiet in the Western Desert of Libya, but in November the lull was broken, and did not fall again until Rommel's Afrika Korps had been defeated and driven out.

Auchinleck and CRUSADER

In July 1941 General Wavell was sent to India, and his place in the Middle East was taken by General (later Field Marshal) Sir Claude Auchinleck. A professional military man of imposing appearance and businesslike manner, Auchinleck faced a challenge of considerable proportions. Although the forces committed were insignificant when compared with the massive deployment on the Russian Front, North Africa was the only theater where British troops were actively engaging the Axis forces. Churchill urged Auchinleck to bring the African campaign to a successful conclusion at once.[1] Auchinleck, convinced

[1] Churchill, *The Grand Alliance*, pp. 396–409, 543.

that Eighth Army (new name for reinforced, reorganized Desert Force, now composed of two corps) needed further training to conduct successfully the mobile, armored warfare that desert fighting required, refused to begin an offensive until his forces were ready. Equipment and supply difficulties had to be overcome, for many of the British tanks were no match for the German panzers in firepower, range, or mechanical dependability. Not only their tanks, but also their anti-tank gun, the deadly, dual-purpose 88mm., gave the Germans an advantage that only improved equipment could counteract.

Rommel also faced supply shortages that made him unable to do more than keep up a steady pressure on the defenses of Tobruk, where the besieged British garrison, supplied by sea, continued to resist. The aims of Auchinleck's first desert offensive were to relieve the siege of Tobruk and to recapture Cyrenaica. The offensive was code-named CRUSADER and got underway on November 17, 1941.

CRUSADER began in confusion and was waged in confusion. It opened with a hugh clash of armor that brought a heavy loss of tanks for both sides, but Eighth Army committed its tanks piecemeal, and the Afrika Korps disposed of them at a favorable ratio. By November 23 Rommel believed the battle had passed its crisis and his fronts would hold. With characteristic bravado he sent his Afrika Korps on a mad dash around and through the British lines toward Egypt. He hoped to create enough confusion and panic to force a withdrawal, but for once the Desert Fox's ruse backfired. General Auchinleck assumed personal command of his forces and forbade any retirement, and since Eighth Army neither retreated nor surrendered, Rommel's armor, after reaching the Egyptian frontier, had to backtrack. By November 27 General Freyberg and the New Zealanders had joined forces with the garrison which was fighting its way out of Tobruk, and by December 7, the day the Russians were beginning to push the Germans back from Moscow and the Japanese were beginning the war in the Far East by attacking Pearl Harbor, Rommel had been pushed back to Gazala. Threatened with envelopment, he withdrew again, and by the end of December he was once more at El Agheila, his starting point of almost a year before.

The Japanese threat in the Pacific made it necessary to send two Australian divisions from Eighth Army home for Australia's defense.

Other Eighth Army forces were also sent to the Far East, and Rommel, always ready to exploit his opponent's weakness, began his usual tactics—probing weak spots in the British lines, concentrating his armor, and wiping out one isolated group after another. Three days of such nibbling and Eighth Army was again in retreat. Like a jack-in-the-box Rommel sprang back to retake half of Cyrenaica— the half including the airfields that were within range of the British base at Malta.

Malta

It is quite possible that Rommel could have won a decisive victory in Egypt had the British not held Malta.[2] Nearly one thousand miles from Gibraltar and more than eight hundred miles from Alexandria, Malta afforded a strategic naval and air base for striking the Axis supply routes across the Mediterranean. Its importance in the crucial battle for supplies was appreciated early in the conflict, and in June 1940 Mussolini began regular bombing attacks. Despite his efforts the British were able to keep the island supplied.

When Rommel found his campaign of January 1942 dragging to a halt for lack of supplies, he flew to Germany to ask Hitler for more men and equipment. Hitler refused. He informed Rommel that he was husbanding every resource for the summer offensive to be directed toward Stalingrad, but to pacify his vigorous general Hitler agreed to "take care" of Malta. More bombers would be sent to Sicily, and after they had neutralized the naval and air bases on Malta, the island would be taken by airborne assault. Rommel returned to Africa encouraged; Malta's ordeal began.

Sicily had half a dozen good airfields, particularly Catania and Palermo. Under the direction of Field Marshal Albert Kesselring, the Luftwaffe took them over and began a concentrated blitz on Malta that left it one of the most-bombed places on earth. The Luftwaffe also preyed heavily on the ocean surrounding the island fortress to

---

[2] Playfair, *The Mediterranean and the Middle East,* Vol. III, Chapter 8; Churchill, *The Hinge of Fate,* Book I, Chapter 17; Liddell-Hart, *The Rommel Papers,* pp. 120, 203, 288.

insure that no convoys of supplies reached its besieged garrison. Displaying stoic stubbornness, the Maltese burrowed into the soft rock of the island and literally lived underground. Supplies diminished. Food, ammunition, planes, and guns were needed if the people were to exist. The war in the Mediterranean grew more critical by the hour.

Malta's prime need was fighter planes with which to meet the Axis attacks. The Spitfires, with their limited range, could not fly to Malta from any Allied-held base, and no British aircraft carriers were available to take them within range. The U.S.S. *Wasp* assumed the mission, and twice, in April and in May, she was able to take planes far enough into the Mediterranean so they could fly on to Malta. What saved Malta, however, was that Hitler cooled to the idea of taking it by airborne assault. Did he remember his losses in the skies over Crete? As the months went by and no German invasion came, Malta eventually recovered her fighting strength. The Axis had made an important mistake.

Rommel's Summer Offensive

During the bombing of Malta Rommel's supplies got through with less loss than at any other time in the war,[3] and by the end of May Rommel was ready to launch a major drive for Cairo. The first obstacle was the British defensive positions around Gazala. In the absence of natural defensive barriers, the British had fortified a number of strong points, or "boxes," scattered in and behind an extensive minefield. Undismayed, Rommel began his summer offensive on May 26 with what had by now become standard procedure in the desert—a holding frontal assault and a wide armored sweep around the exposed south flank. The British mobile units proved unable to halt Rommel's armor, which swept around the southernmost box, Bir Hacheim, and headed for Tobruk. The British armor, reinforced with some of the new American Grant tanks, hastened into battle and inflicted such heavy losses on the Axis that Rommel was forced to break off and withdraw his units into a bridgehead in the

[3] Playfair, *The Mediterranean and the Middle East*, Vol. III, p. 189.

middle of the British minefield. From this "cauldron" he countered the British armored attacks. British armored strength gradually dwindled, and without armored support, Bir Hacheim could not hold. The front began to crumple, and on June 13 the Afrika Korps began a spectacular dash across the desert. Within a week Tobruk, including a large number of prisoners and supplies, was in Rommel's hands. A gratified Fuehrer made his desert general a field marshal, but to Rommel the title was small compensation for his shortages in men and supplies.

Despite his tightening supply situation, Rommel decided to press his advantage on into Egypt. At first the decision seemed the correct one. Sollum, Halfaya, and Sidi Omar fell without a fight, and a delaying battle fought at Mersa Matruh was over quickly. The last two days of June saw the armies racing each other across the desert to Alamein—the British hoping to get there in time to make an effective stand, the Germans and Italians hoping to push them beyond Alamein before they could turn to fight. Much was at stake. Cairo was only 150 miles away.

Alamein

There were two battles at El Alamein. The first, waged in July by a battered and torn Eighth Army, called on every reserve of human fortitude to stop the German advance to the Nile. If Eighth Army had not won the first battle of Alamein, the second, whose victory overshadows the first, could never have been fought.[4]

Why at Alamein? Because at Alamein there could be a "top" and a "bottom" to the battle line. It is only forty miles from the Mediterranean coast to the Qattara Depression, a desert peculiarity believed to have once been an inland sea. The Depression is a mass of salt flats below sea level, separated from the desert by precipitous cliffs and rough terrain. Many areas contain quicksand and few could support vehicles. To go around the Depression would be too wide a movement. At Alamein geography dictated that military forces would

[4] Majdalany, *The Battle of El Alamein;* Liddell-Hart, *The Rommel Papers,* Chapters 13, 14, 15.

meet in a frontal clash. No longer could Rommel swoop around the open southern end to crumple a vulnerable flank.

Rommel attacked the Alamein positions on July 1. His men were tired from the continuous fighting of the last five weeks. Casualties had been heavy and he had not received replacements. Supplies were running short, but the chances for victory seemed so great that Rommel, himself sick and exhausted, urged his men to make one final effort to take Egypt. By the end of only one day's fighting, the Afrika Korps was showing unmistakable signs of exhaustion and shortages. The next day Auchinleck ordered a counterattack that threw the Axis off balance. For two weeks the exhausted forces battled, but the Eighth Army never surrendered the initiative. Gradually the spent Axis forces realized they could do no more. Rommel and the Afrika Korps had seen their last desert victory.

Early in August Churchill and the Chief of the Imperial General Staff, General Alan Brooke, flew to Cairo for a conference. Just as in the summer of 1941, when the theater had suffered a series of reverses, Churchill wanted a change of command. He named General Sir Harold Alexander the new Commander-in-Chief, and General Bernard L. Montgomery the new field commander for Eighth Army. Alexander had handled two disastrous defeats—at Dunkirk and in Burma—with quiet competence and a steady hand. He applied the same calm proficiency in North Africa and, later, in the broader Mediterranean theater. Montgomery was not only capable but colorful, and with his appointment Eighth Army acquired its first field commander since O'Connor who could rival Rommel as a hero. The two were unlike in approach, for Montgomery's battle plans usually called for a steady hammering at enemy resistance with a head-on assault by superior forces. Persistence was one of his outstanding characteristics; the conduct of the set-piece battle was his talent. At Alamein, in the fall of 1942, Eighth Army was in position to fight this type of battle for the first time since the desert war began.

The first clash of the renewed struggle at Alamein came in September. Rommel's supply lines were being strangled, thanks to Malta's recovery and the increasing superiority of the RAF, but his High Command urged him to attack the British positions, and when he was promised adequate fuel for the task, Rommel agreed. Employing the same pattern that had begun the successful action in May, Rommel launched a frontal assault to hold the line, and pushed his armor through the defenses on the southern end. It was not as easy this time, for he could not go below the defenses and had to allow time to break through them. It took longer than expected; they encountered soft sand that slowed up the tanks and caused fuel to disappear at an alarming rate; the RAF pounded them relentlessly. Even so, the German armor advanced, taking a course so obviously dictated by the terrain that both Auchinleck and Montgomery had foreseen it and had planned accordingly. At the foot of the Alam Halfa Ridge, a line of low hills that dominated the area, the Afrika Korps encountered a tight Eighth Army defense—heavy tanks, which had been dug in hull down to fight in fixed positions. Had Rommel possessed freedom of maneuver he might even yet have been able to save his troops from defeat, but the promised fuel had not arrived. The Afrika Korps began to withdraw. An attempt to cut it off from its retreat route failed, but the Eighth Army was in the position of winning a victory simply by not being defeated.

After the battle of Alam Halfa, there was no longer a chance for Rommel's forces to change the course of the African war. Rommel wrote that the battle had reached a point where material resources alone would decide the issue.[5] His health had begun to fail, and at the end of September he went on sick leave to Germany. He was still in the hospital when the second battle of Alamein erupted, and a distraught Fuehrer called him to ask if he felt he could return to Africa. He left at once, but it was too late for good generalship to change the course.

Montgomery and the Eighth Army began the second battle of Alamein on October 23. They had overwhelming superiority in men and equipment,[6] but the Axis defenses were formidable, comprising an elaborate minefield and well-sited anti-tank guns to a depth of five miles. Montgomery planned for the infantry to fight ahead of the tanks and clear two corridors through the minefield for the tanks to follow. After two days of nightmarish effort, the corridors were still

[5] Liddell-Hart, *The Rommel Papers*, p. 280.
[6] Majdalany, *The Battle of El Alamein*, pp. 78–79, 155–56; Barnett, *The Desert Generals*, pp. 256, 258; Liddell-Hart, *The Rommel Papers*, pp. 296, 297, 302.

not open. Montgomery then switched the main effort to the extreme north of the line, where the Australians had made progress in chopping out a salient. The Australians continued to hack their way toward the coast and they reached it October 31. On November 2 the British armor began a decisive push just south of the Australian sector, and by the 4th the Axis defenses had been penetrated. The fight for Alamein lasted two weeks and was a grueling battle for both sides. They were weeks of bloody attrition and of tense expectancy for the British, since the British knew that the Allied invasion of Morocco and Algeria was pending, and the Allies hoped Rommel would be defeated before these battles began. They were weeks of steady persistence by Montgomery, who knew he could win if he persevered despite his losses; they were weeks of heartbreak for Rommel, who knew the forces under his command did not have a chance. On the 2nd he requested permission from Hitler to retreat. On the 3rd he received his answer: ". . . there can be no other thought but to stand fast, yield not a yard of ground and throw every gun and every man into the battle. . . . As to your troops, you can show them no other road than that to victory or death." [7]

Hitler's order demanded the impossible. It was issued for propaganda only, and the next day its restrictions were lifted and the Afrika Korps began the long retreat that was not to end until the Axis were forced out of Africa the following spring. As he retreated by forced steps across the well-worn desert, Rommel faced another foe to his rear, for on November 8 the Americans and British landed on the west coast of Africa in Operation TORCH.

Background for TORCH

TORCH, the Allied invasion of French North Africa, marked the beginning of a series of campaigns that eventually took Allied forces through Sicily and up the Italian boot to Austria. The wisdom of a campaign against what Churchill called the "soft underbelly" of Europe was warmly debated, both before and after the event. [8]

[7] Liddell-Hart, *The Rommel Papers*, p. 321.
[8] Matloff and Snell, *Strategic Planning for Coalition Warfare 1941–1942;* Churchill, *The Hinge of Fate*, Book II, Chapter 2.

The decision to invade North Africa in November 1942 was made in July of that year—just four short months before it took place. During the early months of 1942, Allied strategy was based on three plans that went by the code-names of BOLERO, SLEDGEHAMMER, and ROUNDUP. BOLERO was the build-up of United States strength in the British Isles to form the nucleus of an invasion force for the continent. SLEDGEHAMMER was the name for the landings to be carried out on the northwest coast of France in the fall of 1942. Resources for such an invasion would necessarily be limited, and this operation was considered an emergency measure should a Russian collapse seem imminent and drastic measures be called for. ROUNDUP was the plan, nurtured chiefly by the Americans, to invade the continent from across the English Channel in 1943. It was intended as a major operation, one which would eventually move on into the heart of Germany. Planners agreed that such an operation would eventually be necessary, for a cross-Channel attack afforded advantages that could not be found elsewhere. Not only was it the shortest route from Allied territory to the German homeland, but by using the British Isles as a base on which to accumulate men and supplies, more of both could be transported to the invasion beaches in less time and with less shipping. Air superiority could be built up in the British Isles prior to invasion; British troops could be used with maximum participation; maximum help could be afforded the Russians. However, as the months of 1942 slipped by it became obvious that the Allies did not have the strength to conduct a cross-Channel invasion in the immediate future.

Churchill advocated action in North Africa, which would be possible with existing resources. The American Chiefs of Staff were opposed, for they favored holding their fire until ROUNDUP could be launched. Yet during 1942 Russia's soldiers were dying by the millions as the Germans drove into the Caucasus, and if Russia collapsed before ROUNDUP was launched, a cross-Channel invasion against the full resources of the Wehrmacht would be extremely difficult, if indeed it could be brought off. If a Second Front could not be established where it was most desirable, then it must be established where it was possible. Roosevelt directed his military advisers to reach an agreement with the British on an operation that could be conducted in 1942. North Africa offered positive advantages because the Mediterranean could be opened to Allied shipping, eliminating the time-consuming route around the Cape. Lend-Lease materials could be sent to Russia with less loss through the Persian Gulf. A toe-hold would be acquired from which to squeeze Italy out of the war and coax France back in. The hard-pressed Eighth Army in Libya could be assisted in eliminating the Germans in Africa. Pressure on the Russians would be eased, since Germany would doubtless send both air and ground forces to counter the invasion.

After agreement was reached on TORCH, Marshall named Major General Dwight David Eisenhower Commander-in-Chief. A friendly and forthright mid-westerner who combined a keen professionalism with an easy grin and relaxed manner, Eisenhower applied himself to building an Allied Command and working out detailed plans. D-day was set for November 8. TORCH would be the largest amphibious operation yet undertaken, with landings at Casablanca, Oran, and Algiers. From Algiers a British Army would at once begin a drive toward Tunisia. TORCH was unprecedented both militarily and politically, since the French, whose territory was to be assaulted, were not the enemy.

The TORCH Is Lit

Three separate task forces transported soldiers to North Africa for TORCH. One, the Western, came directly from the United States. It transported some 34,000 American soldiers, mostly young and inexperienced. They were the first American forces to enter combat against Germany, and they made up the largest amphibious assault yet attempted so far from its base of operations.[9] Morale was high. Their commander, Major General George S. Patton, Jr., told the Navy that if they would land him within fifty miles of the right beaches within one week of the right day, he could go ahead and win. In the pre-dawn hours of November 8 Patton's troops began going ashore at three separate points on the Moroccan coast. All three

[9] Morison, *Operations in North African Waters;* Roskill, *The War at Sea,* Vol. II, pp. 312–33.

landings were successful in spite of a disturbing loss of landing craft. As expected, the French Navy offered opposition. Shore-based guns and vessels opened fire, although it came to light later that many of the French did not know the nationality of the invaders they were ordered to repel.

The Center Task Force, which had sailed from England, was largely unopposed in landing. Its main objective was to seize the seaports of Oran, Mers-el-Kebir, and Arzeu, since their possession was vital to control of the Mediterranean, and their harbor facilities were essential for supplying the Allied armies. Once ashore and moving inland, the invaders met heavy opposition that kept up until November 10.

At Algiers, the Eastern Task Force met spotty and half-hearted resistance. Early in the day the French in Algiers received an order to cease fire, and they obeyed it. Americans and British began unloading supplies and preparing for the drive east to Tunisia.

France's touchy political situation caused difficulties. The British recognized de Gaulle but the United States recognized the Vichy government,[10] which of course did not recognize de Gaulle. The Vichy government controlled French North Africa, and prior to TORCH American and British planners sought to find a French leader who would be acceptable to all parties. General Henri Giraud, who had escaped from the German prison where he had been held since his capture in May 1940, agreed to assume leadership of a revitalized France. The day after the TORCH landings Giraud and Eisenhower's Deputy Commander, Major General Mark Wayne Clark, went to Algiers to make the necessary political and military arrangements. The French were unwilling to recognize Giraud's authority, but Admiral of the Fleet Jean Darlan agreed to cooperate with the Allies. He tried to obtain permission from Marshal Pétain to order the French to cease resistance, but Pétain, probably unable to do otherwise because of the threat of German retaliation against France, refused to agree. Nevertheless Darlan issued orders to cease fire and the French obeyed. On the 13th Eisenhower flew to Algiers to conclude the arrangements. The French would assist the Allies and provide all rights and privileges of military operation, and the Allies

[10] Eisenhower, *Crusade in Europe*, pp. 106–110; Langer, *Our Vichy Gamble*.

would not interfere with French control in Africa. Darlan was authorized to take charge of French affairs until the Germans were cleared out of Africa, while General Giraud was put in command of all French military forces in northwest Africa.

Eisenhower's agreement with Darlan caused a furor in the United States and Britain. Why a "deal" with a Vichyite? The French were needed as Allies, not as defeated enemies. Not only would a prolonged battle do permanent damage to future relations with France, but the TORCH forces were not strong enough to defeat the French, institute military occupation of the whole of French North Africa, and move on to Tunisia to meet the main enemy, the Germans. Nevertheless the situation remained controversial, and the episode came to a tragic end on Christmas eve 1942 when Darlan was assassinated by a young French fanatic. General Giraud was named to replace him and work was begun to bring Giraud and de Gaulle together, to move away from the authoritarian Vichy trend, and to end the political strife among Frenchmen.

Drive to Tunis, November 1942–May 1943

Immediately following the TORCH landings, Eisenhower ordered Lieutenant General Kenneth Anderson and the British First Army to begin their push toward Tunisia. A brilliant strategical victory would be won if the Allies could assume control in Tunisia before the Axis could send enough forces there to turn it into a major battlefield. The Allies were sure that the Germans would attempt to occupy and hold Tunisia, for control of its ports was essential for pumping supplies to Rommel's Afrika Korps. Although separated by some 1200 miles, Anderson's First and Montgomery's Eighth Armies were now part of the same campaign—to drive the Axis out of Africa. Anderson's attempt to take Tunisia before the Axis did so was a race against time. He was hampered by shortages in supplies and motor equipment, a poor railroad and highway system, and winter rains that turned roads and airfields into seas of mud.

On November 9 Hitler began pouring into Tunisia the reinforcements he had been unwilling to send Rommel before, and General

167

Dietloff Jürgen von Arnim was sent to take command. The Axis held the advantage of shorter supply lines, which enabled them to reinforce the area more quickly than the Allies. Also, Tunis and Bizerta lay in coastal basins ringed by hills to the west, and since the passes through the mountain ranges determined the route of an army's advance, they could be defended easily.

Undismayed by these odds, General Anderson started the 540-mile push for Tunis on November 11. Bougie, Djidjelli, and Bône were taken, and the Eastern Air Command moved its forward base to the Bône airfield. By November 16 First Army had penetrated Tunisia in two places, and on the 17th the first ground clash, which ended indecisively, took place just east of Tabarka. On November 19 and 20 the forces fought the first of many battles at Medjez el Bab, a road junction of importance, but again neither side had the strength to conduct a decisive action.

Realizing that Anderson did not have the strength to take Tunis alone, Eisenhower began committing units of Americans to the front. On November 25 the Allies began another drive toward Tunis. Despite stiffening opposition and Axis air superiority, Anderson pushed beyond Tebourba before stalling. An Axis counterattack on December 1 could not be contained, and by December 4 the Allies were drawing back. There was a halt while both sides sought to accumulate supplies.

Anderson's First Army made one more effort to reach Tunis, but the attack, which began December 23 and 24, never really got going. The first step was the capture of a strategic ridge called "Longstop Hill." The ill-fated attempt to take it began in pouring rain and was hampered by inadequate supplies, since vehicles floundered in the mud. Faulty intelligence and inexperienced soldiers combined to bring about tragic mistakes. After occupying most of the hill, the Allies were pushed off on December 24. Conferring at forward headquarters, Generals Anderson and Eisenhower decided their drive on Tunis must temporarily halt.

After the battle of Alamein, Montgomery's Eighth Army pursued Rommel across the desert toward the port of Tripoli, which fell to Eighth Army on January 23, 1943. As Rommel retreated closer to von Arnim in Tunisia, the Axis forces became essentially one, caught in a double squeeze.

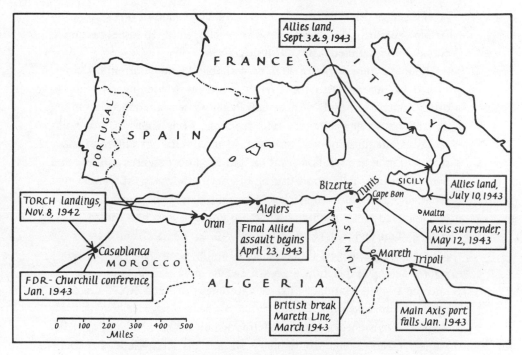

Allies land, Sept. 3 & 9, 1943

FRANCE

ITALY

PORTUGAL

SPAIN

TORCH landings, Nov. 8, 1942

Oran

Algiers

Bizerte
Tunis
Cape Bon

SICILY

Allies land, July 10, 1943

Malta

Final Allied assault begins April 23, 1943

Axis surrender, May 12, 1943

Casablanca
MOROCCO

FDR- Churchill conference, Jan. 1943

ALGERIA

TUNISIA

Mareth
Tripoli

British break Mareth Line, March 1943

Main Axis port falls Jan. 1943

0   100   200   300   400   500
Miles

WESTERN MEDITERRANEAN AREA

During January and February von Arnim and Anderson sparred for positions that would give them a tactical advantage when operations could be resumed on a large scale, and in mid-February Rommel launched a drive against the U.S. II Corps, which held the southern portion of the Allied line. Rommel hoped to drive a wedge through the line to Tebessa. The Afrika Korps poured through Faid Pass and attacked, causing the Americans to retreat toward Kasserine, one of the three major gaps in the mountain range. There, Rommel directed the main weight of his attack on February 19, and the next day his army poured through the narrow defile and thinned out to drive west and north. His overextended forces met a stubborn defense and two days later retreated back through Kasserine Pass, which the Americans reoccupied on February 25.[11] Rommel's bid to disrupt the Allied drive had failed, but the conduct of the battle had emphasized to both sides the necessity for unified command. General

[11] Howe, *Northwest Africa: Seizing the Initiative in the West*, Chapter 23; Blumenson, *Kasserine Pass*.

Alexander, as Eisenhower's Deputy, took command of the 18th Army Group (British, Americans, and French), and Rommel assumed command of a united Army Group Africa.

Rommel, denied permission to pull back and shorten his lines, turned his attention to the Eighth Army at Medenine. Hoping to divide, envelop, and dispose of Montgomery's forces, Rommel opened battle against them on March 6. Four times Rommel attacked. Four times he was repulsed. Montgomery not only had superiority in men and weapons, but he had sited his defenses astutely and had made unusually good use of his anti-tank guns. Medenine was Rommel's last battle in Africa. After his defeat, he turned over his command to von Arnim and left the continent, never to return.

The Tunisian war moved rapidly to a climax. On March 20 Montgomery attacked the Axis at Mareth, where they had built a strong defensive position across a twenty-mile gap between the sea and the rugged Matmata hills. Montgomery ordered XXX Corps to attack at the end near the sea, while General Freyberg led his New Zealand Division around the Matmata hills. When XXX Corps became bogged down, Montgomery shifted his strength to Freyberg, who proceeded to deal the Axis another major defeat. Montgomery pursued relentlessly as the Axis withdrew, and the southern end of the Tunisian rectangle crumpled. Eighth Army occupied Sfax on April 10 and Sousse on April 12, but halted before the formidable Axis defense lines at Enfidaville.

The final push for Tunisia would come from the west. The U.S. II Corps, under Major General Omar N. Bradley, moved across the rear areas to the extreme north of the front in order to participate in the final battle. When the battle began in late April, progress was steady. Tunis and Bizerta fell on May 7, and two days later the Germans in the northern area surrendered. By May 11 Eighth Army controlled the Cape Bon peninsula, the only possible Axis escape route, but no evacuation was attempted. Hitler ordered his forces to fight to the death, but by May 12 more than a quarter of a million had decided on life as a POW rather than death for the Fuehrer.[12] The war in North Africa, begun so confidently by Mussolini in September 1940, ended in Axis disaster.

[12] Eisenhower, *Crusade in Europe*, p. 156.

Conference at Casablanca, January 14–24, 1943

Churchill and Roosevelt decided to meet at Casablanca to formulate plans for 1943.[13] Stalin was urged to join them but declined. Churchill and his military staffs urged that the Allies pursue the Mediterranean campaign by attacking Sicily, Italy, and the "soft underbelly." Although the British thought of an Italian campaign as a "bleeding ulcer" to drain strength away from Hitler's Germany, the Americans tended to regard it as a "vacuum" into which Allied resources would be sucked at the expense of an assault on northern France. Marshall and his colleagues felt that diversionary action that took strength away from the cross-Channel attack was a mistake, but British and American planners were agreed that the cross-Channel attack could not be made in 1943. The Battle of the Atlantic was not yet won, and shipping shortages continued to pose limitations on Allied strategy. The objectives decided upon for the coming year were: (1) maintaining the security of the sea lanes, (2) concluding the Tunisian campaign, (3) assaulting Sicily, (4) supplying aid to Russia, (5) continuing to support BOLERO in preparation for the cross-Channel attack, (6) increasing the strategic bombing of Germany's industries, and (7) maintaining pressure on Japan without draining resources from Europe. The decision to take Sicily was a victory for the British, but the U.S. had the final word about the Pacific. What constituted a "drain" on resources for Europe would be the decision of the U.S. Joint Chiefs of Staff alone.

At the conclusion of the Casablanca Conference, "unconditional surrender" was announced as Allied policy. Roosevelt stated: "Peace can come to the world only by the total elimination of German and Japanese war power. . . . The elimination of German, Japanese, and Italian war power means the unconditional surrender of Germany, Italy, and Japan. . . . It does not mean the destruction of the population of Germany, Italy, or Japan, but it does mean the destruction of the philosophies in those countries which are based on con-

[13] Matloff, *Strategic Planning for Coalition Warfare 1943–1944;* Sherwood, *Roosevelt and Hopkins,* pp. 667–97; Feis, *Churchill, Roosevelt, Stalin,* pp. 105–13; Churchill, *The Hinge of Fate,* pp. 674–95.

quest and the subjugation of other people." [14]

Critics have claimed that the policy of unconditional surrender prolonged the war because it encouraged the Germans and Japanese to resist to the death. Yet Churchill and Roosevelt assured the world that unconditional surrender did not mean unconditional harshness or hardships for the conquered peoples, and the first Axis surrender—that of Italy—was far from "unconditional." In January 1943 there were sound reasons for the policy, since it ended suspicion engendered by the Darlan Affair that the United States would entertain the policy of appeasement. It struck a note of defiance at a time when the war was not yet won, and the road ahead looked arduous. And possibly it would soothe Stalin, who had just received news that there would not be a Second Front in Europe in 1943.

[14] Rosenman, *The Public Papers and Addresses of Franklin Roosevelt,* Vol. for 1943, p. 39; Matloff, *Strategic Planning for Coalition Warfare 1943–1944,* pp. 39–40n.

Sicily and Italy

AFTER the conclusion of the Tunisian campaign, Allied forces in the Mediterranean theater assaulted Sicily and began a limited campaign on the mainland of Italy.

Operation HUSKY

The invasion of Sicily was conducted by Montgomery's Eighth Army and Patton's newly activated Seventh Army. Eisenhower, who had ably handled the task of fusing an Allied Command, was Supreme Commander, North African Theater of Operations. Alexander was his Deputy and in charge of the ground forces, and Admiral Cunningham and Air Chief Marshal Tedder commanded the naval and air forces. The plan, largely Montgomery's,[1] was for Eighth Army to land in the southeast corner of the island, take Syracuse and

[1] Garland and Smyth, *Sicily and the Surrender of Italy*, Chapter 3; Baldwin, *Battles Lost and Won*, Chapter 6.

advance north to Messina. Seventh Army would land in the Gulf of Gela to support Eighth Army's left flank. D-day was set for July 10, 1943, and prior to it the Allied Air Forces vigorously attacked enemy positions in Sicily, Italy, Sardinia, and Greece.[2] To obtain closer bases for fighter aircraft, Pantelleria, a rocky island halfway between Tunisia and Sicily, was occupied on June 11.

Although high winds gravely affected paratroop landings behind both Seventh and Eighth Army fronts, the amphibious landings went well. More than one thousand ships landed eight divisions on a 100-mile front—the largest amphibious assault of the war in terms of assault strength alone.[3] Various new types of landing craft were used with great success. The LST (landing ship, tank) and LCT (landing craft, tank) were designed to land vehicles directly on the beaches. The troop transports carried LCVP's (landing craft, vehicle, personnel) with bow ramps to facilitate unloading, and a few LCI's (landing craft, infantry) and LCM's (landing craft, mechanized) were employed. The DUKW (called "Duck"), a two-and-one-half-ton truck that could be launched from an LST and swim through the surf before rolling along the beaches, proved especially useful.

Allied planners expected opposition to be severe, for two German divisions boosted the Axis forces in Sicily to some 230,000 men.[4] Only at Gela, however, did the assaulting forces meet serious opposition. There, the Hermann Goering Division and two Italian divisions were poised to prevent the Allies from seizing an important airfield six miles inland. Axis attacks on July 10 and 11 were halted, but only after German tanks had come unpleasantly close to the vulnerable beaches. Naval gunfire, directed by fire control parties ashore, played an important part in helping the U.S. 1st Division repel the Axis attack, and thereafter this form of cooperation between Army and Navy played an increasing role in Allied operations.

By the night of July 11 the Allied beachheads were reasonably secure. Airborne reinforcements slated to land behind Seventh Army's front that night were fired on by friendly forces,[5] a tragedy

[2] Craven and Cate, *The Army Air Forces in World War II,* Vol. II. Since Sicily was an obvious target, elaborate measures were taken to deceive the Germans.
[3] Morison, *Sicily—Salerno—Anzio,* pp. 28–29.
[4] Garland and Smyth, *Sicily and the Surrender of Italy,* pp. 80–81.
[5] Casualties for the 504th Combat Team (2000 men) were 81 dead, 132 wounded, 16 missing. Garland and Smyth, *Sicily and the Surrender of Italy,* pp. 175–84.

that marred an otherwise encouraging outlook. The Eighth Army had taken the ancient port city of Syracuse, and on July 12 it secured Augusta as well. With two ports to insure its regular supply, Eighth Army was ready to move toward Messina. To win a decisive victory, the Allies must prevent the Axis from pulling their forces into the Messina point and evacuating them across the narrow Straits to the Italian mainland.

Between Eighth Army and Messina rose the massive bulk of Mt. Etna, a 10,705-foot active volcano that dominates the fertile, heavily cultivated, and densely populated area. To the south of the mountain lay Catania and a fertile plain, through which the Axis commanders drew a defensive line to enable them to fight a delaying battle in the northeastern corner of Sicily. As the Axis forces began to withdraw toward the Mount Etna-Messina area, Eighth Army, driving for Catania, met determined opposition and made slight progress. Directing his two corps into widely separated lines of advance, Montgomery ordered the XIII Corps to press toward Catania on the east while the XXX Corps swung around Mount Etna on the west. The change gave

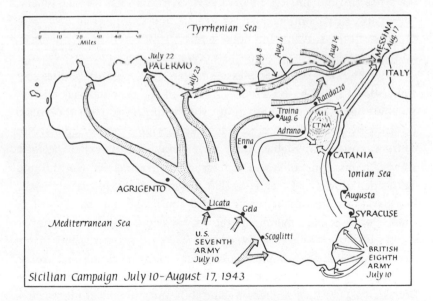

Sicilian Campaign July 10-August 17, 1943

XXX Corps the objectives that Seventh Army was in position to pursue, and the Americans found themselves in the almost passive position of protecting Eighth Army's flank while the latter drove for the prize. General Patton chafed at his supporting role. Hoping for dramatic gain, he sent a reconnaissance in force toward Agrigento and Porto Empedocle the night of July 14. The towns were taken the next day, and with a port to facilitate his army's supply, Patton requested permission to take Palermo. Alexander consented, and the four divisions of Seventh Army swept into western Sicily.

While General Bradley's II Corps (1st and 45th Divisions) struck due north, the 2nd Armored Division began a drive west along the southern coast. Between them the 3rd Division marched from Agrigento to Palermo. By July 22 Palermo was in Seventh Army hands, and the next day II Corps reached the northern coast. Morale soared. The Americans had made their first dramatic and successful offensive; it mattered little that opposition had been light. Next, all eyes turned toward Messina. The Americans were eager to prove their combat worth, and Patton was determined to beat Montgomery to their goal. This healthy but intense rivalry between Patton and Montgomery, forged in Sicily, continued across France and Germany in 1944–45. Opposite in personality and approach, both were talented, eccentric, and nationalistic.

When the final drive for Messina began in August, the Allies met tight opposition. The Axis made full use of the mountainous terrain, narrow roads, and numerous bridges and tunnels to slow the Allied advance by demolitions, minefields, and carefully sited weapons. Not until August 7 did Eighth Army take Catania, and it then began a steady, hammering offensive that gradually forced its way around both sides of Mount Etna. To its left, Seventh Army fought along the coast road and a parallel route to the south. Troina fell August 6, after a week of hard fighting by the 1st Division. Progress was not as rapid as Patton would have liked, and twice, on August 8 and 11, he utilized the Navy to conduct amphibious "end runs" and land troops behind the German lines. They did not decisively affect the German withdrawal, but they impressed Churchill and influenced him in urging a similar outflanking maneuver at Anzio the following January.

As the Axis were steadily compressed into the shrinking Messina

Point, Field Marshal Kesselring and General Hans Hube began directing a skillful evacuation across the Messina Straits. The Straits bristled with defensive guns, and the ferries operating between Sicily and Italy received little harassment from Allied planes or ships. Early in the morning of August 17, the last of the rear guard got safely away. That same morning, just 38 days after the initial landings, advance patrols of Seventh Army entered Messina. Units of the Eighth Army soon followed, but the decisive victory had not been achieved. Although Axis casualties were high, more than 70,000 Italians and 39,000 Germans, with their equipment and vehicles, had already been ferried to the mainland of Italy where the Allies would have to fight them again.[6] Sicily has been called an "Allied physical victory, a German moral victory." [7] The Italian forces did not play a major role in the battle, and the Germans, greatly outnumbered, were able to prolong the contest and inflict substantial casualties. The Allied plan, "sound, cautious, conservative," [8] has been questioned, for it did not use air and naval superiority to maximum advantage. But in one respect Sicily was a clear-cut victory, for it caused the collapse of the Pact of Steel.

Mussolini Falls, Italy Surrenders

As a succession of military fiascos compounded the unrest caused by inflation and corrupt administration, the bonds holding the Fascist regime together began to disintegrate. Responding to public agitation, Mussolini convened the Fascist Grand Council on July 24. It adopted a resolution calling for the King to assume command of the armed forces and restoring King, Parliament, and Council to power. The next day the King asked Mussolini for his resignation and put him in protective custody. Mussolini's New Roman Empire was dead.

Marshal Pietro Badoglio was named Premier of Italy, and although he insisted that his government would continue the war, Hitler discounted his assurance. Plans were drafted for German troops to seize

[6] Garland and Smyth, *Sicily and the Surrender of Italy,* pp. 410, 416n, 417; Morison, *Sicily—Salerno—Anzio,* p. 223.

[7] Baldwin, *Battles Lost and Won,* p. 225.

[8] Garland and Smyth, *Sicily and the Surrender of Italy,* p. 420; evaluation of the campaign, pp. 417–25.

control in Italy the moment they sniffed "surrender," and as a preliminary move German forces, under Rommel's command, began moving into northern Italy. Hoping to forestall an Italian surrender by restoring Mussolini to power, Hitler rescued the Duce and established him as head of a rival Italian government. Although Mussolini held this position until April 28, 1945, when he was shot by partisans, his government was never more than a sham. In the days following his dismissal, it became obvious that Italian Fascism was dead. There was no move to restore the Duce to power or imperil the new regime. The Italians were ready for peace, and the Badoglio government faced the task of getting out of the war. It was obvious the Germans would not allow them a peaceful exeunt. Tension rose. The fighting in Sicily went on, but the Italians began to make secret overtures to the Allies.

The negotiations were complicated.[9] The Italians did not want merely to surrender; they wanted the Allies to save them from the Germans. The Italians were even willing to turn on their old friends and fight beside the Allies, but Churchill and Roosevelt, conferring at the QUADRANT conference (held in Quebec August 14–24), decided that Italy would have to prove her willingness to help the Allies before the status of co-belligerency could be granted. What the Italians did not know was that the Allies were not planning to invade Italy in strength. Although the British favored a major Mediterranean campaign, the Americans insisted on a strong build-up in England preparatory to a cross-Channel invasion in 1944. The Italian campaign was to be conducted with limited means. Partly for that reason it was important to secure the Italian surrender before the Allied invasion.

Fearing that delay in agreeing on detailed terms for the Italian armistice would jeopardize the chances for a speedy Italian surrender before the invasion, Eisenhower urged that he be allowed to conclude a military armistice based on what came to be called the "short terms." Italy bowed to circumstance. On September 3 General Giuseppe Castellano, who had conducted most of the negotiations for the Italians, signed the short-term military armistice which was made

---

[9] See Garland and Smyth, *Sicily and the Surrender of Italy*.

public on September 8, the eve of Allied landings at Salerno.[10] The Badoglio government, however, did not take strong or effective measures to save Italy, while the Germans moved with their customary efficiency. The Germans immediately seized Rome and on September 11 Field Marshal Kesselring declared all Italian territory a theater of war under German control. When the Allies landed in Italy, they were met by determined German resistance.

The Italian Campaign Begins

The immediate goals of the Italian campaign were to tie down as many German forces as possible while gaining a foothold in southern Italy that would put Allied Air Forces within striking distance of important Axis targets.[11] To get maximum advantage from the limited means at his disposal, Eisenhower proposed that part of Eighth Army land on the toe of Italy before the main invasion at Salerno by Lieutenant General Mark Clark's Fifth Army.

The night of September 3, 1943, two divisions of Eighth Army slipped across the Messina Straits and landed between Reggio and San Giovanni. The Italian coast defense units surrendered after token resistance, but the next day the British began to meet German opposition. Fighting was light, but the retreating Germans made extensive use of demolitions to hamper the British advance. Every bridge, culvert, and tunnel had to be rebuilt as the Eighth Army worked its way northward. Six days after the initial landings, the British First Airborne Division occupied the Italian naval base at Taranto. Bari, an important harbor on Italy's east coast, was quickly seized. In less than two weeks Eighth Army had secured a firm hold on southern Italy.

Clark's Fifth Army had more trouble.[12] The Italian armistice was announced as the assault forces were approaching Salerno Bay, but German troops met the Allied invaders. The factors which had

---

[10] The "long terms" were signed on September 28, 1943. On October 13 the Badoglio government declared war on Germany and became a co-belligerent.

[11] Ehrman, *Grand Strategy*, Vol. V, pp. 58–66.

[12] For the Salerno assault and subsequent fighting, see Morison, *Sicily—Salerno—Anzio;* Clark, *Calculated Risk;* Starr, *From Salerno to the Alps.*

determined Salerno as the invasion site—aircraft range and suitable beaches—were as obvious to the Germans as to the Allies, and for days the 16th Panzer Division had been in the area setting up guns, laying mines, and building strongpoints. As the Allies struggled ashore on September 9, they met fierce resistance. On the extreme left (north) of the assault area, a force of Commandos and Rangers landed unopposed and moved inland to seize the vital passes that offered access to the Naples area to the north. To the right of the Commandos the British X Corps fought its way ashore and established a tenuous beachhead, while eight miles further south the U.S. VI Corps did the same. By the end of D-day the initial assault forces were ashore, but losses had been high and objectives had not been met.

On September 10 the Germans concentrated against the British X Corps to protect the route to Naples. That day and the next the U.S. VI Corps made progress inland. Salerno was occupied on the 10th, and an airfield was taken on the 11th, but neither could be used by the Allies since German artillery was well sited in the ring of hills and mountains that surrounded the narrow coastal plain. Salerno set the pattern for the war in Italy, a war of bitter fighting for control of the hills. After two days of grueling battle, the Fifth Army had penetrated only ten miles at its deepest point, while on the northern flank the beachhead was only a mile deep. Between the two corps was a thinly manned and vulnerable gap, and in that area Kesselring, with elements of six German divisions, opened a vigorous attack designed to throw the Allies back into the sea. VI Corps began to retreat and infantry lines began to break. Alexander moved quickly to strengthen the defense with a massive air assault and an intense naval bombardment of the German positions. By nightfall of the 13th the German counterattack had been stopped, and the next day German efforts to renew it were broken up. Fifth Army was in Italy to stay.

By the end of the first week of October, the initial objectives of the Italian campaign had been met. Fifth Army had reached the Volturno River and the Eighth Army, which had advanced from the toe of the peninsula, had secured the Foggia airfields. Meanwhile the Germans had evacuated Sardinia (September 18) and Corsica (September 18–October 3). The Allied forces in Italy could best support the

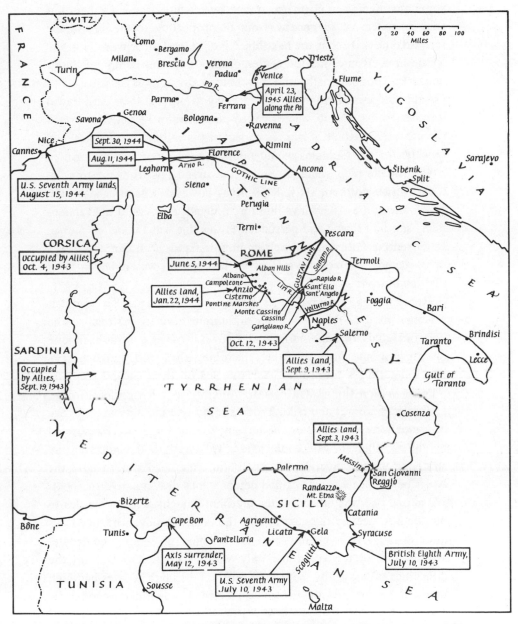

ITALIAN CAMPAIGN

coming campaign in northern France by reaching the Po valley, but such an extensive advance was out of proportion to the size of the force. Rome was set as the next objective.[13] Good airfields were in the Rome area. Rome was the center of the road and communications network, and politically and psychologically it was a prize. The German forces in Italy must be kept busy to prevent their withdrawal to other fronts, and it was logical to concentrate the activity toward the capture of Rome. Planners expected that Rome would be taken quickly, for the Germans would doubtless withdraw to the north of Italy to make their stand. Rommel had urged this from the time he took over in northern Italy. Kesselring, however, encouraged by the small size of the Allied invading force, decided he could hold indefinitely south of Rome and persuaded Hitler this was the better course. In November Hitler put Kesselring in command of all German forces in Italy and Rommel, having shown less spunk, was removed from the Italian front.

Rome lay one hundred miles north of the Volturno River, but it was one hundred miles of rugged mountains and swift streams. The boot of Italy is long and narrow, and down it runs a central backbone of craggy mountains, called the Apennines, that sends out hundreds of smaller ranges toward the Adriatic Sea on the east and the Tyrrhenian Sea on the west. Coastal plains are marshy, roads are few, and winters are wet and cold. Troop supply and mobility and the use of armor were restricted by the terrain; the air forces were restricted by the weather. It was country ideally suited to defend. German strategy for the remainder of the Italian campaign was to hold the Allies behind a series of fortified defense lines drawn across the boot. When one line was breached, the Germans fought delaying battles to buy time to occupy the next line to the rear. To advance, the Allies must dislodge their enemy from his fortified positions, and frontal assault was all too often the only way of approach. Despite the difficulties presented by the terrain, Fifth and Eighth Armies had high hopes of capturing Rome before year's end. The first defensive hurdle on Fifth Army's front was the Volturno River line, and it was crossed early in October. The Germans then withdrew to their main defensive lines, a series of fortifications in depth utilizing the Sangro, Rapido,

[13] Eisenhower, *Crusade in Europe*, pp. 199–200.

and Garigliano Rivers and the hills and natural barriers around them. The defenses up to the river barriers were termed the Winter Line, while those beyond, guarding the approaches to Rome through the valley of the Liri River, were called the Gustav Line. Majestic Monte Cassino, rising out of the valleys of the Rapido and the Liri and crowned with the massive Benedictine monastery, was the key to the Gustav Line. In this small section of central Italy the Allies and the Germans were to battle each other until late May 1944.

Anzio Conceived

The last months of 1943 witnessed bitter fighting around the Winter Line. Allied progress was slow and costly. Frontal assaults on fortified positions are almost certain to be difficult; to break the Winter and Gustav Lines at less cost in men and time, planners proposed an amphibious "end run" at Anzio. Code-named SHIN-GLE, the plan was to land one division at Anzio, sixty miles behind the main battle line. It would be too risky to land such a small force behind enemy lines if a rapid link-up with the main army was not assured, so when the Fifth Army advance was stopped by the Winter Line defenses, SHINGLE was abandoned. At the end of December the operation was put back into Allied plans at Churchill's urging, and its force was strengthened from one division to two.[14]

The reinstatement of the SHINGLE operation coincided with a change in the Mediterranean command. In January Eisenhower went to England to assume Supreme Command of OVERLORD, the cross-Channel invasion. Named to succeed him as Supreme Commander in the Mediterranean was General Sir Henry Maitland-Wilson, who had commanded the British forces in Greece and served admirably in the Mediterranean theater for the past few years. General Alexander remained as Commander-in-Chief for Italy; General Clark remained with Fifth Army; Montgomery was called to England and his place with Eighth Army was taken by Lieutenant General Sir Oliver Leese. With Wilson's appointment, the executive direction of

[14] Churchill, *Closing the Ring*, pp. 426–37.

the Mediterranean campaign passed to the British,[15] and on January 2, 1944, Alexander issued the orders for the Anzio landings. At the same time Clark's Fifth Army was ordered to "make as strong a thrust as possible towards Cassino and Frosinone shortly prior to the assault" and then to create a breach in the front to link up "rapidly" with the Anzio force.[16] Part of the Eighth Army was transferred to the Fifth Army front, while a weakened Eighth Army was to keep the enemy on the east pinned down.

General Clark's orders to Fifth Army called for a series of closely coordinated attacks. On January 12 the Free French Expeditionary Corps under General Juin (newly arrived at Fifth Army) was to launch a drive on the far right of the front, above Cassino, toward Sant' Elia. On January 15 the II Corps, in the center of the line, was to fight its way out of the mountains and clear the way to the Rapido River. Two days later the X Corps on the far left of the front was to cross the Garigliano River and push toward the Liri valley. On January 20 the II Corps would cross the Rapido about five miles below Cassino, near Sant' Angelo. If each phase of the offensive succeeded, Cassino would be under assault from both sides. Finally, on January 22, VI Corps would land at Anzio. Hopes were high that the diversion in their rear would cause the Germans to withdraw forces from the Gustav Line and Fifth Army could break through.

The German Tenth Army, under General Vietinghoff, had been ordered to defend the Gustav Line to the last, and his army dramatically illustrated obedience to military discipline. The Germans fought at Cassino with an intensity that turned the name into a synonym for tenacious defense.

The Battle of Cassino

The Battle of Cassino began on a note of optimism for Fifth Army, for the opening attacks met with some success. By January 15 the French had forced the Germans out of Sant' Elia and II Corps had cleared the way to the Rapido River. On schedule the X Corps

---

[15] Matloff, *Strategic Planning for Coalition Warfare 1943–44*, p. 414.
[16] Starr, *From Salerno to the Alps*, p. 83.

pushed across the Garigliano, but it met such heavy counterattacks that it was unable to expand its bridgehead. After three weeks X Corps was pressed into a defensive posture that it held until May.

While the X Corps was battling across the Garigliano, Major General Fred Walker's 36th Division was scheduled to force a crossing of the Rapido River. The Rapido is narrow, swift, and deep, with steep banks covered with brush. The near side of the river was protected by minefields, and the ground on the far bank, which sloped up into bluffs affording the Germans observation of the entire area, was a mass of pillboxes, trenches, bunkers, barbed wire, and machine-gun emplacements. The 36th Division was unable to seize a bridgehead. Despite two days of bitter struggle, the Rapido crossing ended in disastrous failure.[17]

Since neither the Garigliano nor the Rapido assault had achieved breakthrough, General Clark directed the U.S. 34th Division to cross the Rapido north of Cassino and with the French mount an enveloping attack on Monte Cassino from the north. This bridgehead was obtained, and the next objective was the mass of hills north and west of Monte Cassino, an area of roughly six square miles that blocked the way to the Liri valley. For two weeks the soldiers fought without respite in these hills. German engineers had blasted machine-gun emplacements and shelters in the rocky slopes and had built bunkers of steel, railroad ties, and concrete that were so secure the German soldiers inside could enjoy a game of cards during an intensive artillery barrage. Such defenses fanatically held are hard to overcome, and the Americans were unable to break through. By February 12 they had reached the limit of physical endurance, and the fresh New Zealand Corps moved in to take over.

The New Zealand Corps enjoyed a reputation for high morale and keen professionalism. Under General Freyberg, the Corps consisted of three of the finest divisions in the British forces, the 2nd New Zealand, the 78th British, and the 4th Indian. Freyberg and his divisional commanders asked that the huge stone monastery atop Monte Cassino be bombed, and on February 15 heavy bombers from the Strategic Air Forces reduced it to rubble. Controversy raged about the wisdom and morality of the act, and tragically enough, the

17 Starr, *From Salerno to the Alps*, p. 97. See Majdalany, *The Battle of Cassino*.

destruction of the monastery did not immediately ease the military situation.

Freyberg's plan for overcoming the Cassino defenses was for the 4th Indian Division to take Monastery Hill and the Abbey and then sweep down the mountain to Highway 6, which led to Rome. Simultaneously, in the valley the 2nd New Zealand Division would seize the railway station about a mile from the town of Cassino. The German defenses would then be pinched out and the reserves could burst through to the Liri valley. Freyberg's attempt also ended in bitter failure. In the mountains, attacking forces were cut to pieces by German fire, and in the valley the New Zealanders were unable to hold the railway station.

The exhausted soldiers enjoyed a brief respite until mid-March, when the battle was renewed from a different approach. The town of Cassino was reduced to rubble by heavy bombers—the first time they had been used for such a small target in support of infantry. Unfortunately the resulting rubble protected the surviving Germans and hampered the Allied advance. As the New Zealanders worked their way slowly through the demolished town, other units attempted to take Monastery Hill by way of the hills that rose against its base behind the town. After a week of exhausting combat it was obvious that this effort too had failed. Allied gains from January through March were disappointing and costly, and the Gustav Line remained essentially intact.

The Anzio Beachhead

During the bitter battle at Cassino, a concurrent battle raged at Anzio. Few operations of the entire war were as controversial. Originally conceived as a flanking maneuver within supporting distance of the main army, it was launched even though the main army was still stalemated roughly sixty miles away. Anzio was a gamble that offered the possibility of dazzling success; it was a gamble that failed. For four months the Allied forces were contained in their beachhead, unable to exploit the amphibious landing.[18]

[18] Morison, *Sicily—Salerno—Anzio,* p. 317.

SHINGLE was under the command of Major General John P. Lucas. His forces were the VI Corps, composed of the British 1st Division (Major General W. R. C. Penny) and the U.S. 3rd Division (Major General Lucian K. Truscott, Jr.), plus follow-up forces and reserves. The actual landings went perfectly and by the end of D-day all looked promising, except that the Fifth Army was pinned down at the Gustav Line and General Lucas had to decide what to do next. His orders were to establish a beachhead and advance on the Alban Hills, but he also was told that the advance should not be considered so binding that he must sacrifice his corps to achieve it.[19] Rome was only forty miles away and the German opposition was as yet not organized. A dashing drive to seize the Alban Hills and advance on to Rome might succeed, but would not his force be cut off from the beachhead? It was not realistic to expect that the Germans would allow two divisions to wander unopposed throughout central Italy. Feeling that his first responsibility was to secure his beachhead, General Lucas advanced slowly and carefully and concentrated on consolidating the rear areas to insure continuing supply for his forces. After VI Corps had consolidated its position, it prepared for an orderly attack toward Cisterna and Campoleone. The advance began January 30, eight days after the landings, and by that time Field Marshal Kesselring was ready. From northern Italy, Germany, France, and Yugoslavia German troops had rushed to Anzio. Only a few were pulled out of the Gustav Line. Despite concentrated air attacks on railways and roads, the Germans were able to move with speed and efficiency. The assembled troops came under General Eberhard von Mackensen as the Fourteenth Army.

General Lucas's planned attack was a two-pronged drive, with the 1st Division advancing on Albano and the 3rd Division on Cisterna. The latter thrust was spearheaded by the Rangers, who crept toward the town through a large, half-dry irrigation ditch. When they left the ditch at dawn they were surrounded and ambushed. Only 6 Rangers out of 767 got safely back to Allied lines.[20] A sobered 3rd Division continued its attack for three days, but was unable to reach Cisterna. The 1st Division drove a salient to Campoleone, but armored units

[19] Blumenson, Anzio: *The Gamble that Failed,* pp. 66–68.
[20] *Ibid.,* p. 100.

bogged down in the muddy fields, and the sturdy stone farmhouses provided the defending Germans with excellent and numerous small fortresses. By the afternoon of February 1 Generals Alexander and Clark decided VI Corps must go on the defensive, for a German counterattack seemed imminent. VI Corps was reinforced, and the men took up positions behind barbed wire and minefields to await the German onslaught.

The coastal plain between Anzio and the Alban Hills was part of the Pontine Marshes that had been reclaimed in one of Mussolini's more admirable endeavors. On the extreme right of the Anzio beachhead, a deep canal and flooded marshes gave VI Corps a reasonably secure right flank, while the far left of the front could be ably supported by naval gunfire. The critical areas were the roads leading from Anzio to Cisterna and Albano. The irrigation ditches and marshy land between them made control of the roads necessary for rapid movement. Kesselring and von Mackensen methodically concluded their preparations for a battle of psychological importance. Germany's military position was deteriorating. The Russians held all the initiative in the east; North Africa was lost and the Allies were in Italy; all signs pointed to an invasion of France in the coming months. Hitler, enraged by the Anzio landings, called the beachhead an "abscess" which must be cut out and ordered the troops to fight with "holy hatred." [21] As a preliminary operation, the Germans eliminated the 1st Division's salient at Campoleone, and as pressure against them intensified, VI Corps began to appreciate its peculiar difficulties of defense. The beachhead was too shallow (roughly 14 miles) to permit much maneuver or defense in depth; a breakthrough by the Germans would put them in the vulnerable rear areas. The shallowness of the beachhead also meant that the entire area came under German artillery fire, expertly controlled from observation posts in the Alban Hills.

The main battle to cut out the "abscess" began on February 16. For four days the VI Corps fought for its life. The Germans had more troops (approximately 125,000) and more heavy artillery; the Allies had air and naval superiority.[22] Kesselring expected victory in three

[21] Trevor-Roper, *Blitzkrieg to Defeat*, p. 158. Hitler's Order of the Day, January 28.
[22] Blumenson, *Anzio: The Gamble that Failed*, p. 117.

days, and at first it appeared he would achieve it. The Allies were pushed back to the final beachhead line—a line beyond which Lucas ordered no retreat. Here the weary infantry held. By February 20 the offensive power of the Germans was expended and the beachhead, though battered, was intact.

After the February crisis General Lucas left Anzio, tired, discouraged, and disheartened. General Truscott assumed command and VI Corps settled down to its ordeal of hanging on to the beachhead until enough force could be mustered to break through the Cassino defenses and rout the Germans. Though SHINGLE had failed, there was never a question of having to evacuate the beachhead.[23] Thanks in part to the excellent preparation Lucas had made, the Navy kept supplies pouring into Anzio harbor. The garrison was not only sustained, but reinforced to support the major breakthrough that came in May.

The Drive to Rome

During March and April General Alexander pondered the problem of reorganizing his forces to achieve the breakthrough so far denied. More force must be applied, and on a broader front. To achieve the necessary concentration, the forces on the Adriatic coast were reduced to a bare minimum and the Eighth Army was moved west of the Apennines to take over the narrow part of the front directly facing Cassino and the Liri valley. Fifth Army's sector was narrowed to a strip thirteen miles wide from the sea to the Liri valley, plus the beachhead at Anzio. Separating the two parts of Fifth Army was roughly sixty miles of tangled, rugged mountain with only one major road, Highway 7, leading toward Rome. Since previous attempts to gain control of valleys and roads had been thwarted, Fifth Army planned to advance over the hills themselves. While Fifth Army advanced on the left of the front, Eighth Army would make the main attack facing the Liri valley, break through the Cassino defenses, and open Highway 6 to Rome. They hoped to do this by crossing the Rapido in strength below Cassino, while on the far right the newly

[23] *Ibid.,* pp. 166–67. See also Morison, *Sicily—Salerno—Anzio.*

arrived Polish Corps took Monte Cassino from the mountains on the north. Preparations were methodical and determined; reinforcements arrived; supplies were stockpiled; roads were improved. The Battle of Cassino was building up to a decisive climax. D-day was May 11; H-hour was just before midnight.

Although the May 11 offensive caught the Germans by surprise, no immediate breakthrough was obtained despite the heavier concentration of force on the front. On the far left, the Americans made only token progress the first night; in the middle two British divisions crossed the Rapido but their bridgeheads remained insecure. On the far right the Polish Corps was repulsed with heavy losses after a gallant attempt to take Monte Cassino from the north. The French met with the most positive success. Starting from the bridgehead across the Garigliano River secured the preceding winter, they attacked across the mountains—mountains so rugged the Germans had not considered it necessary to fortify them heavily. Many of the components of General Juin's Free French Expeditionary Corps were native mountaineers, and their morale was high. This was the first real chance for the French to fight back since the humiliation of 1940. They made impressive gains, and by May 17 had pushed so far toward the rear they threatened the entire German line. By that time the other attacks were also on the move.

The British continued to fight doggedly and to force their way into the Liri valley; on May 17 and 18 the Poles renewed the assault on Monte Cassino. The Polish II Corps, under General Wladyslaw Anders, was similar to the French in its determination to fight for the honor of its homeland, a homeland occupied by two separate enemies. Anxious to strike back at the forces which had loosed catastrophe on their nation, the Poles had endured incredible hardships to reach the Middle East and form the Polish Corps.[24] Unlike the Americans, who felt little personal hatred for their enemy, the Poles had personal reason to hate, and they assaulted Monte Cassino with cold fury. This time Cassino fell. The morning of the 18th the Poles and British joined forces around Monte Cassino and the Poles occupied the ruined Abbey on its summit. Cassino, symbol of German

[24] For the story of the Polish Army see Anders, *An Army in Exile*.

resistance and Allied stalemate for almost half a year, had fallen. The next job was to get on to Rome.

By the 23rd of May the Germans were in retreat all along the front, and the next defense line behind the Gustav Line was carried by the momentum of the Allied advance. Also on the 23rd the forces at Anzio, built up to six divisions, broke out of their beachhead. Two days later they made contact with the II Corps, which had advanced along the coast against light opposition. General Clark ordered Fifth Army to advance on Rome with all speed. The Germans held briefly around the Alban Hills, but then withdrew to the north. Rome was declared an open city and the Fifth Army entered it on June 4, 1944.

Two days later OVERLORD became a reality as Allied forces stormed the shores of Normandy. Twenty-six German divisions that might otherwise have opposed them were facing the Allied armies in Italy.[25] Had these divisions been free to meet the cross-Channel invasion, would OVERLOAD have succeeded?

[25] Jackson, *The Battle for Italy,* p. 340, Appendix F; p. 247.

Russia Recovers Her Losses

DURING the months that the Western Allies fought from Tunisia to Sicily and up the Italian peninsula to Rome, the Russian armed forces maintained the initiative seized at Stalingrad and began a steady drive westward toward Berlin.

The Battle of Kursk

In March 1943 the Eastern Front had become stabilized along the Donetz River, and the battlefields were quiet until July. The Russian lines were east of Orel and Kharkov but bulged out to the west of Kursk, forming a salient approximately a hundred miles square. Such bulges offer tempting military possibilities, for simultaneous attacks on both sides of the bulge can pinch off the enemy forces. Such was the course the German High Command decided to follow, and the Russians expected it. In April Zhukov and his Chief of Staff, Vasilievsky, the team which had masterminded the Stalingrad tri-

192

RUSSIAN GAINS

Nov. 19, 1942 – July 4, 1943

July 5, 1943 – Nov. 30, 1943

Dec. 1, 1943 – June 22, 1944

June 22, 1944 – Dec. 15, 1944

Dec. 15, 1944 – May 7, 1945

0   100   200   300
Miles

RUSSIAN OFFENSIVES, 1942–1945

umph, moved to the Kursk front. Accurately anticipating the German assault, they alerted and reinforced the armies of Generals Vatutin and Rokossovsky, while to their rear General Koniev formed an armored reserve.

The German High Command delayed opening the Kursk offensive to amass great quantities of armor, especially their new Porsche and Panther tanks, unprecedented in armor and size. Not until July did von Kluge, who planned to strike from the north, and von Manstein, who would strike from the south, have at their disposal the final force —17 armored divisions, 10 infantry divisions, and about 1000 aircraft. The Russians had made good use of the delay to fortify the bulge and gather a comparable force. The Battle of Kursk, intense and severe, was the last German offensive on the Eastern Front and the greatest tank battle of history. At its height three thousand tanks were in action.[1]

The battle began on July 4, 1943. The Germans advanced against the bulge from north and south in dense armored wedges. Hoth, directing the southern pincer, had nine divisions concentrated on a thirty-mile front. The Russian outer defenses were penetrated, for the Porsche and Panther were relatively immune to the Russian anti-tank guns, but by the morning of July 5 the German forces found themselves embroiled in a savage slugging match with a well-prepared enemy equally strong in firepower. The heavy tanks, lacking small firepower, were vulnerable to the Russian infantryman, who emerged from his slit trench to squirt flamethrowers into the armored monsters' ventilator slats. The battle reached its climax on July 12, when the Russian armored reserve was unleashed. By then the German armored divisions were badly depleted and exhausted, and the Russian reserves were fresh and their tanks in good repair. By evening the Russians controlled the field, and the next day Hitler called off the battle, doubtless influenced by the crisis in the west, where the British and Americans had just invaded Sicily.

The Russian Offensive, July 1943–June 1944

The German High Command had hoped that the Battle of Kursk would weaken the Russian forces to such an extent that they could

[1] Clark, *Barbarossa*, p. 322. See also Manstein, *Lost Victories*.

not seriously hamper German operations for the remainder of the summer. The result was the opposite. Not even waiting for the outcome of the Kursk battle, the Russians began an attack toward Orel that marked the beginning of their first successful summer offensive. Much of its effort was exerted against General von Manstein's Army Group South, and of the campaign, von Manstein wrote that the initiative having passed to the Russians, "Southern Army Group found itself waging a defensive struggle which could not be anything more than a system of improvisations and stop-gaps." [2]

Stop-gap measures were necessary because the Russians, capitalizing on the long, thinly held line, began striking all along the front from Leningrad to the Crimea. The Russian soldiers would concentrate force for a breakthrough; penetration and exploitation would follow. If the Germans moved enough troops to contain that effort, the Russians attacked elsewhere, content with shallow thrusts that crumpled the German lines and pushed them back on a broad front.

Russian cities and villages, and the farmland and industrial areas of the Ukraine were reclaimed. The Germans yielded Orel and Belgorod the first week in August; at the end of the month von Manstein evacuated Kharkov rather than sacrifice an army in its defense. Protesting that if he could not have substantial reinforcements, he must withdraw to the Dnieper River to shorten his line and establish a defense, von Manstein found his hands tied by Hitler, to whom retreat was anathema. Both von Manstein's and von Kleist's Army Groups bulged eastward, and the Russians exploited their vulnerability. Finally, when the German front was in danger of collapse, Hitler authorized a limited retreat to the Dnieper. It was too late. Fortifications and defenses had not been prepared, and any hopes the Germans entertained for a reprieve on the Dnieper were shattered when the Russians forced the river at several points in dramatic, nighttime operations. From their bridgeheads on the west bank the Russians proceeded to reclaim Kiev (November 6) and exert pressure on Zhitomir and other railroad centers that would cut the German communications to von Manstein's and von Kleist's Armies. While fighting desperately to hold Zhitomir, von Manstein continued to plead for operational flexibility, but Hitler remained unmoved. He

[2] Manstein, *Lost Victories*, p. 450.

needed the Crimea because from it the Allies could bomb the Ploesti oilfields; he needed the Nikopol and Krivoy Rog area because of the manganese and iron.

By the third winter of the Russian war the Wehrmacht was obviously declining in strength. Replacements did not keep up with losses; equipment was overworked; fuel and ammunition were in short supply. Overall direction was uncertain. Hitler held complete control over his armies, even to the smallest operational detail, and his commanders, to obtain permission for operations, had to endure long and tedious conferences with him that often decided nothing. The steady retreat that began in August was hard on German morale, especially as winter drew near.

The Russian soldier, bolstered by advance and victory, gained confidence and skill. Field Marshal von Kleist later said that the Russians were "first-rate *fighters* from the start, and we owed our success simply to superior training. They became first-rate *soldiers* with experience." [3] The Russian Command became a capable organization. Russian armed strength was growing. Whereas Germany dispersed her effort by developing new and more powerful tanks, Russia was content to rely on a high production of only two models. Lend-Lease materials were bolstering Russian production. Trucks were putting infantry on wheels and simplifying their supply as the Russians advanced.

Throughout the winter and spring the Russians continued their successful pattern of the previous summer: fighting numerous local operations conducted where chances of success were good. All along the Eastern Front, from Leningrad to Odessa, the Germans met one defeat after another. (See map, page 193.)

Russia's Leningrad operation, though a minor portion of the broad offensive, was emotionally gratifying. The German Army Group North, weak because strength had been sent to more active sectors, based its defenses on water barriers and fortifications. The water barriers were assailed in January 1944, when the Russians attacked across the ice of Lake Ilmen and its neighboring swamps, while at the same time breaking out of a small beachhead at Oranienbaum, west of Leningrad. The double operation achieved success, and at the end

[3] Liddell-Hart, *The German Generals Talk,* p. 220. Italics are Liddell-Hart's.

of January the 28-month siege of Leningrad was ended. The Germans fell back, first to the Luga River, then to the area around the Narva River, Lake Peipus, and Lake Pskov.

More dramatic were Russian gains in the south, from the Pripet Marches to the Black Sea. Here von Manstein was fighting against Zhukov. It was a mild, wet winter, and the Russians, whose equipment could operate in the mud more effectively than the German's, kept up a constant pressure. Russian reserves grew while von Manstein's shrank, and von Manstein continued to be restricted by Hitler's orders not to retreat.

Von Manstein's forward salient, toward the Nikopol-Krivoy Rog area, came under heavy attack early in the year. Vatutin and Koniev executed an encirclement at Korsun and cut off some eight German divisions. By February 7 Nikopol was in Russian hands; Krivoy Rog followed. During March and April the Russians crossed, in quick succession, the barriers of the Bug, Dniester, and Pruth Rivers. Hitler dismissed von Manstein from command and replaced him with Field Marshal Walter Model. Model's forces were renamed Army Group North Ukraine, but the changes did not alter the desperate situation. The German forces in the south were divided by the Russian's strong wedge between the Carpathian Mountains on the south and the Pripet Marshes on the north, and there seemed no way of stopping the Russians from driving straight on to Lwow, Cracow, and Warsaw.

In April the Russians drove the German Seventeenth Army out of the Crimea, and by the end of May, when the Russian advance slowed to a temporary halt, the German-Soviet armies faced each other along a line running roughly from the Gulf of Finland to northern Rumania and Bessarabia. Although the Germans still held the Baltic countries as well as a large bulge penetrating Belorussia, most of the economically valuable Ukraine was again in Russian hands. The Germans had had a bad year.

Hitler's New Order

As Germany's occupied areas were gradually reclaimed, evidence of how Hitler had intended to establish his New Order in Europe came to light. The Nazi occupation was harsh in all of the conquered countries, but most severely oppressed were the nations of central and eastern Europe; most systematically exterminated were the Jews.[4] Nazi oppression of the Jews began even before the war commenced, and as the German conquest spread, so did the oppression. Obsessed by the idea that the Germans were the "Master Race," Hitler intended to exterminate both Jews and Slavs, since he saw them as being *"Untermenschen,"* or sub-humans. The Jews were first rounded up and herded into ghettos, wherein it was expected that many would die from malnutrition, overcrowding, and disease.

When the German armies began advancing into Russia in the summer of 1941, the policy of exploitation and extermination was extended to the Russians with a special virulence, for Hitler wanted to eliminate the population of European Russia to obtain *Lebensraum,* or living space, for the Germans. Not only were prisoners of war deliberately neglected so that thousands died of starvation or exposure, but the Slavs were recruited for slave labor in the Reich, where they were worked as long as they were able and then murdered. The Gestapo, or SS, was charged with "Special Tasks" to eliminate the Jews, and in Russia massacre followed massacre. Thousands of persons were shot and their bodies consigned to mass graves. The ultimate in genocide came with the "Final Solution"—the establishment of mass extermination camps, where victims died in gas chambers and were then cremated in huge crematories. The nature of the slaughter was such that an accurate count of victims cannot be made, but the round number 6,000,000 is generally accepted as the number of Jews murdered by the Reich. It is possible the number was much lower,[5] but the scope of the tragedy cannot be reduced.

The Big Three at Teheran

During the first two years of the war, Stalin had been cool toward the Western Allies, but by 1943 a friendship was growing. As the

---

[4] The basic sources of information are in the records of the war crimes trials. See Shirer, *The Rise and Fall of the Third Reich,* Chapter 27.

[5] Reitlinger, *The Final Solution,* pp. 489–501, Appendix I.

far-flung theaters of war began to converge and political matters assumed more importance, an agreement between the major allies seemed essential. Roosevelt and Churchill urged Stalin to meet with them, and a preliminary meeting of Foreign Ministers (V. M. Molotov, Cordell Hull, and Anthony Eden) took place in October 1943. Molotov made it clear that Russia's main concern was that a Second Front be opened in 1944. He was assured that it would be done. A Four-Nation Declaration (including China) was signed, pledging cooperation and joint action in concluding the war and settling post-war problems. The European Advisory Commission (EAC) was established as a committee of diplomatic representatives of the three countries. It was authorized to make studies and advise on political problems. General agreement on other matters was reached, and on November 27 the first meeting of the "Big Three" convened in Teheran, Iran (Persia).[6] Churchill and Roosevelt, after preliminary conferences at Cairo, were anxious to come to an understanding with Stalin on three main areas: (1) the issue of the Second Front, (2) the several complex political situations arising, and (3) the nature of the post-war international security organization. Assured that the Second Front would be opened in May 1944, Stalin agreed to open a simultaneous offensive on the Eastern Front. Stalin, in turn, assured Roosevelt that after the defeat of Germany, Russia would help to defeat Japan. Stalin also put in his claim for concessions in the Far East—a warm water port, the Kurile Islands, half of Sakhalin, and recognition of the status quo in Outer Mongolia—but he accepted China as one of the "Big Four" in the preliminary discussions that later evolved into the Security Council of the United Nations, and he seemed willing to accept U.S. efforts to bolster the Chinese Nationalists at the expense of the Chinese Communists.

One of the most complicated political issues discussed at Teheran was Poland. Russia and Germany had cooperated in the Polish partition of 1939, and at that time the Polish government took refuge in London. In 1941, after Germany had captured Russian-held Poland, diplomatic relations were restored between the London Poles

---

[6] Churchill, *Closing the Ring,* Book II, Chapters 2, 3, 4, and 5; Feis, *Churchill, Roosevelt, Stalin,* Chapters 25, 26, 27, and 28; Sherwood, *Roosevelt and Hopkins,* pp. 776–99.

and the Russians. The Poles wanted assurance that the Polish boundaries set by the German-Russian partition were not binding, but Russia refused to make any commitment. In April 1943 Russian-Polish relations became strained when Germany revealed a mass grave, in the Katyn Forest near Smolensk, containing the bodies of more than twelve thousand Polish officers the Germans claimed the Russians had murdered. The Russians insisted the massacre was done by the Germans, but used the episode as an excuse to break off relations with the London Poles. Shortly thereafter Russia established a rival Polish government in Russia, called the Union of Polish Patriots. Efforts by the British to settle Polish-Russian differences brought few results, and at Teheran Churchill agreed in principle to Stalin's demand that Russia's boundaries be moved west at the expense of Poland. Poland's boundaries would then be moved west at the expense of Germany. It remained for the London Poles to agree, but a solution mutually acceptable to Russians and Poles seemed unlikely.[7]

Even though the Teheran conference produced no agreement on how to handle one major problem—what to do with Germany after the country was defeated—Roosevelt left Teheran encouraged that his hope for a peaceful post-war world, based on continued friendship and cooperation among the three major allies, might be realized.

[7] See Churchill, *The Second World War*, all volumes. For the Polish viewpoint, see Mikolajczyk, *The Rape of Poland;* Anders, *Army in Exile;* Bor-Komorowski, *The Secret Army.*

Progress in the Pacific

THE 1942 AND EARLY 1943 Allied victories at Midway, Guadalcanal, and Papua were so effective in halting Japan's initial offensive that the Pacific Allies could begin offensive actions of their own. Although the Casablanca conference in January had reaffirmed the principle of "Germany first" and had produced no long-range plans for the defeat of Japan, planners agreed that the Allies must keep Japan from regaining the initiative, must secure bases for future operations, and must reduce Japanese strength through attrition.

CARTWHEEL Preliminaries

As the second year of the Pacific war began, Allied forces were concentrated in the South and Southwest Pacific. Guadalcanal and Buna were their forward gains. From there, Rabaul, a major Japanese air and naval base on the eastern tip of New Britain, made a logical target, but both MacArthur and Halsey estimated its seizure would take more forces than the Joint Chiefs of Staff were prepared to allot. In March 1943 the Joint Chiefs selected objectives in the Solomon Islands and in New Guinea that would take Allied base power closer to Rabaul.[1] MacArthur was to have overall strategic command of the campaign, and Halsey was to retain operational command of the South Pacific. The arrangement gave Halsey "two hats," for Admiral Nimitz at Pearl Harbor controlled Halsey's forces while MacArthur directed his strategy. What could have been an awkward and frustrating state of affairs turned out to be workable and functional, primarily because Halsey and MacArthur respected one another and got along well.[2]

Rabaul can be viewed as the apex of a triangle with one leg drawn down the Solomons to Guadalcanal, another leg stretching along New Guinea to the Huon peninsula, and the third reaching from the Vitiaz Strait along New Britain back to Rabaul. Halsey's South Pacific forces were to advance up the leg of the Solomons to southern Bougainville. MacArthur's Southwest Pacific forces were to seize the Trobriand Islands (Woodlark and Kiriwina), the Lae-Salamaua-Finschhafen-Madang area of New Guinea, and the western tip of New Britain. Named CARTWHEEL, the campaign involved a number of operations, some on a small scale, and all scattered over a broad area of unfamiliar territory. The Solomons, New Guinea, and New Britain were inhabited by primitive Melanesians and were largely untouched by modern civilization. The military bases were little islands of busy humanity, sprinkled throughout the dense jungle. Living conditions were crude. Cities and roads did not exist. The rations were monotonous, the weather was hot and muggy, disease was prevalent, and the enemy was near. Troop movement and supply was largely dependent on air and naval forces, and this shaped the nature of the campaign. CARTWHEEL was a series of amphibious or airborne advances, each conducted within range of Allied air cover. After each hop, the Allies literally hacked a clearing in the jungle, built an airbase (or took over a Japanese base), and brought in the planes to support the next step. As the process continued, along

[1] Morton, *Strategy and Command: The First Two Years,* Chapter 19. See also background material in Miller, *Cartwheel,* and Morison, *Breaking the Bismarcks Barrier.*

[2] Halsey and Bryan, *Admiral Halsey's Story,* pp. 154–55.

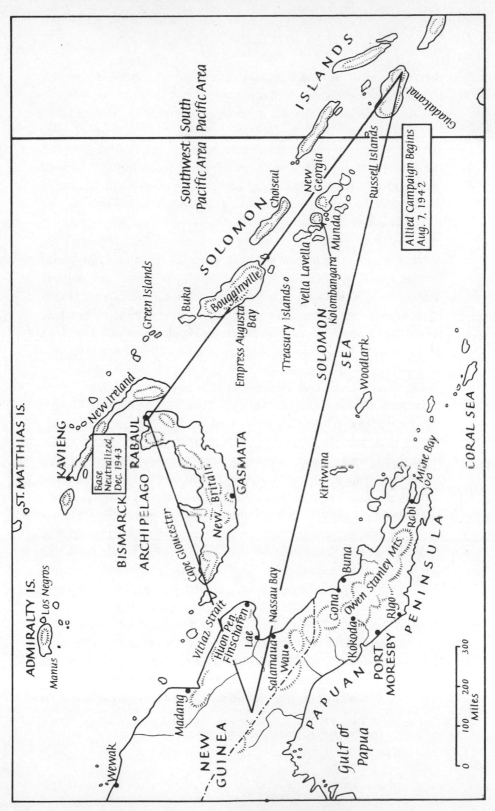

ST. MATTHIAS IS.

ADMIRALTY IS.
Manus
Los Negros

BISMARCK ARCHIPELAGO

KAVIENG
New Ireland
RABAUL
Base Neutralized, Dec. 1943

Green Islands

Buka
Bougainville
Empress Augusta Bay

SOLOMON

Choiseul

New Georgia

Vella Lavella
Kolombangara Munda
Treasury Islands

Russell Islands

ISLANDS

Guadalcanal

Allied Campaign Begins
Aug. 7, 1942

Southwest
Pacific Area

South
Pacific Area

SOLOMON
SEA

Woodlark

Cape Gloucester
New Britain
GASMATA

Vitiaz Strait
Huon Pen.
Finschafen
Lae
Salamaua
Wau

Nassau Bay

Buna
Gona
Kokoda
Owen Stanley Mts.
Rigo

Kiriwina

Milne Bay
Rabi

CORAL SEA

PAPUAN
PENINSULA

PORT
MORESBY

Gulf of Papua

PAPUAN

NEW GUINEA
Madang
Wewak

0   100   200   300
Miles

SOUTH AND SOUTHWEST PACIFIC

the two axes of advance, control of the air was attained and the bomber line moved closer to Rabaul.

CARTWHEEL itself did not get underway until the end of June, but in February 1943 South Pacific forces occupied the Russell Islands. While the Americans developed bases on Guadalcanal and the Russells, they sought to weaken Japanese bases in the Solomons preparatory to the next advance. The result was an almost constant war of attrition, especially in the air. The Allies disposed of Japanese planes at a favorable ratio,[3] and during April the Japanese made a major effort to regain the initiative in the air. Admiral Yamamoto, utilizing naval as well as army planes, conducted an intense aerial bombardment on both the Solomons and New Guinea. It did not achieve its aim, and on April 18 Japanese morale received a severe blow when Admiral Yamamoto, enroute to Bougainville by bomber, was blasted from the skies by P-38's from Henderson Field. His place at the head of the Combined Fleet was taken by Admiral Mineichi Koga, who shared Yamamoto's conviction that the war would be won or lost by a decisive clash between the U.S. and Japanese Fleets.

In New Guinea, after the fall of Buna in January 1943, the Japanese began reinforcing their garrisons at Lae and Salamaua. Inland from Lae, at Wau, a small Australian force represented the only Allied ground troops in contact with the enemy in New Guinea. When the Japanese began a vigorous assault on Wau the Australians were reinforced by plane and repelled the attack. From Wau they began to fight their way through jungle and over mountains, "One of the most difficult and unpleasant areas ever to confront troops,"[4] to threaten Lae and Salamaua. They got their supplies by air drop, and air support took the place of artillery in their advance. Japanese losses in New Guinea were heavy, and the commanders at Rabaul decided to send a major reinforcement convoy to Lae. Lieutenant General George C. Kenney, commanding the Fifth Air Force, divined Japanese intentions and was well prepared. On March 3, when the Japanese convoy came within range, Kenney committed almost his entire air strength against it. The clash, known as the Battle of the Bismarck Sea, was successful beyond all hopes. Out of a convoy of 16

[3] Craven and Cate, *The Army Air Forces in World War II*, Vol. IV, pp. 212–25.
[4] Dexter, *The New Guinea Offensives*, p. 21.

ships, 12, including all the transports, were destroyed.[5] Thereafter the Japanese supply lines to New Guinea were manned by submarines and barges, supplemented by air transport.

In May attention shifted from MacArthur's theater to the Aleutian Islands, where the American 7th Infantry Division landed on Attu. The Japanese had occupied Attu and Kiska in June 1942 as part of their Midway campaign. In subsequent months American forces harassed the Japanese as much as weather would permit. Despite the forbidding cold and fog, which hampered all operations, plans were drafted to dislodge the Japanese. By-passing more heavily defended Kiska, the Americans assaulted Attu on May 11. Two main landings, on the south and north shores, were to meet in the middle of the island and close on the Japanese. Although the Americans had a comfortable margin of superiority, the Japanese defended themselves stoically, and the campaign was not over until the end of the month. The Japanese evacuated Kiska under cover of the notorious Aleutian mists, and when landings were made there later in the summer, the island was found deserted.

CARTWHEEL Launched

On June 30, 1943, both South and Southwest Pacific areas erupted in a spurt of activity, with simultaneous landings on the Trobriand Islands, at Nassau bay in New Guinea, and on New Georgia. The landings on the Trobriands were unopposed, and went so smoothly they became the template for future operations of Rear Admiral Daniel E. Barbey's Amphibious Force of the Seventh Fleet. Airfield construction began at once, and by mid-July they were operating.

The Nassau Bay landings were part of MacArthur's campaign against Lae and Salamaua. A heavy surf got the landings off to a poor start, and the advance inland was slow, but by July 13 the advancing troops had linked up with the Australians fighting toward Salamaua from the interior. By concentrating against Salamaua, MacArthur hoped to cause the Japanese to reinforce it at the expense of taking

[5] Craven and Cate, *The Army Air Forces in World War II*, Vol. IV, pp. 146–49; Morison, *Breaking the Bismarcks Barrier*, pp. 62–63.

forces off of Lae. The ruse succeeded, and when the Australian 9th Division landed at Lae on September 4, it met a reduced Japanese garrison. On September 5, 1700 paratroopers were landed at Nadzab to cut off the Japanese escape route up the Markham River valley, and after hasty preparation of the airfield, troop transports brought in the Australian 7th Division.[6] It advanced down the valley toward Lae, about twenty miles away, and by September 16 both Lae and Salamaua were in Allied hands.

In a quick follow-up of the Lae-Salamaua success, Finschhafen was assaulted from the sea on September 22, and by October 2 it, too, was in Australian hands. While pounding the Japanese air bases, especially a major one at Wewak, Kenney began developing his own forward bases. Nadzab was to be a major one, and to insure its supply by sea as well as by air, engineers carved a road through the jungle to connect Nadzab with Lae.

Meanwhile Halsey advanced up the chain of the Solomons.[7] Landings in New Georgia on June 30 launched a bitter campaign that lasted until the end of August. Its aim was to obtain airfields to cover the advance into Bougainville, and as the Japanese had a sizable and well-defended air base at Munda Point, Halsey decided not to assault Munda directly, but to land at several points and fight an overland battle to the strip itself. Under the direction of Rear Admiral Richmond Kelly Turner, the amphibious landings went well, but the Japanese wanted to hold New Georgia as a key outpost protecting Bougainville, and they responded to the invasion with vigor. The Tokyo Express steamed down the Slot by night, only to be met by the destroyers and cruisers of Halsey's Third Fleet. The Japanese excelled at night fighting and had a superior torpedo. Losses on both sides were high. Ashore, the American soldiers found operations difficult because of the tangled jungle, craggy hills, swollen streams, and reeking mangrove swamps, as well as a tenacious Japanese defense. The advance was slow and illness was high. By August 5 Munda was in American hands, and its airfield subsequently became the best and most-used field in the Solomons.

[6] Craven and Cate, *The Army Air Forces in World War II*, Vol. IV, pp. 181–86.
[7] Rentz, *Marines in the Central Solomons;* Craven and Cate, *The Army Air Forces in World War II*, Vol. IV.

The Munda operation had been slow and costly to both sides. The Japanese could ill afford the losses they had sustained and they were frustrated in their intention to make the Americans fight that long and severely for every island bastion on the route to Japan. In mid-August Halsey began leap-frogging. Kolombangara, which was heavily defended, was by-passed, and South Pacific forces landed on lightly defended Vella Lavella instead. Kolombangara was then neutralized by air attacks and naval blockade, and the Japanese were forced to evacuate.

The New Georgia phase of CARTWHEEL was successfully concluded in August, and, coupled with the September success in New Guinea, it paved the way for future operations by providing the vital forward airfields. The cooperation between forces of the South and Southwest Pacific became closer and more effective. Brigadier General Nathan Twining's South Pacific Air Forces, (Air Command, Solomons) and Kenney's Fifth Air Force alternated their efforts in support of the two axes of advance. Halsey planned to move into Bougainville November 1; MacArthur planned to move to Cape Gloucester the end of December. During October and November Kenney concentrated his efforts on Rabaul while Twining prepared Bougainville. After Bougainville was secured, Twining's forces kept Rabaul pounded down while Kenney's turned to tactical preparation.

On November 1 South Pacific forces landed in force at Empress Augusta Bay, Bougainville. The object was to seize and hold a perimeter large enough to protect airfields built within it. The Japanese forces on Bougainville numbered some 37,500 soldiers and 20,000 sailors,[8] but most of them were concentrated in the southern portion of the island, and the opposition at Empress Augusta Bay was not serious. During the succeeding weeks the 3rd Marine Division and the 37th Infantry Division fought numerous small actions to expand and fortify their perimeter.

Again Japanese air and naval opposition was lively. Rabaul was only 215 miles to the northwest. The Japanese came off second best in the Battle of Empress Augusta Bay on November 2, but Admiral Koga responded to the Bougainville threat by sending a force of seven

[8] Miller, *Cartwheel*, p. 235. See also Rentz, *Bougainville and the Northern Solomons*.

heavy cruisers from Truk to Rabaul. The cruiser force posed a serious threat to the landings, and Halsey sent Vice Admiral Raymond A. Spruance and the newly formed Fifth Fleet to attack them on November 5. Koga's heavy forces sustained enough damage to cause him to pull them back to Truk. Of more consequence, Koga had reluctantly committed his carrier planes to Rabaul's defense, and by November 20, when the Americans landed in the Gilbert Islands, he had lost so many carrier planes that he was almost powerless to interfere.

Tarawa

The November 20 landings in the Gilbert Islands marked the beginning of a new Central Pacific offensive that made Tarawa, Kwajalein, Eniwetok, Saipan, Guam, Tinian, Peleliu, Iwo Jima, and Okinawa take their place in American military history. MacArthur opposed the plan, for he thought the best approach to Japan was along the New Guinea-Mindanao axis, where each phase of the assault could be covered by land-based planes. Those supporting the Central Pacific drive argued that the new fast aircraft carriers could effectively take the place of land-based air cover; the New Guinea advance had been torturously slow; the more favorable climate of the Central Pacific would get the men out of the steaming, malarial jungles; and the Central Pacific advance would utilize the growing Pacific Fleet and protect the right flank of the New Guinea-Mindanao drive. At the QUADRANT Conference of August 1943 the Combined Chiefs of Staff adopted a plan to approach Japan from two directions. CARTWHEEL would continue, but the Central Pacific drive, primarily a naval effort directed by Admiral Nimitz with the carriers providing air cover and the U.S. Marines as assault troops, was to have priority if conflict arose over allocation of resources.[9]

A large part of the Gilbert's assault—and the others to follow— was the planning, organization, and training that preceded it. An amphibious assault against a defended beach demands close timing

[9] Morton, *Strategy and Command: The First Two Years,* Chapters 25, 26.

and coordination of a number of specialized units. During the Pacific operations such vast distances from base to target were involved that logistics alone posed a formidable hurdle. Tarawa, for instance, is 2100 miles from Pearl Harbor, the Pacific Fleet's main supply base. A far-reaching and efficient system of mobile supply bases and mid-ocean fueling stations was inaugurated to cope with supplies, while other phases of the preparation went forward in bases scattered from Hawaii to the Ellice Islands. Admiral Spruance's Fifth Fleet, containing the bulk of the Pacific's naval strength and built around the new aircraft carriers, was the key. Central Pacific tactics were to assault a position with overwhelming force and to capture it quickly, preferably within four days, during which time the carrier planes provided air cover. Land-based planes could then fly in to the newly conquered bases, and the Fleet could retire before the Japanese could amass forces to counterattack in strength.

The Gilbert Islands, a sprinkling of coral atolls with poor soil and sparse vegetation but excellent airfield sites, were the first target. On November 20 Admiral Turner's Fifth Amphibious Force landed the 27th Infantry Division (Major General Ralph C. Smith) at Makin and the 2nd Marine Division (Major General Julian C. Smith) at Tarawa. Overall command of the ground forces rested with Marine Major General Holland M. Smith. Makin was lightly defended and secured by November 23. Casualties were light.

Tarawa proved a vivid contrast. The landings were made on Betio Island, 291 acres of well-fortified real estate. The Japanese garrison numbered approximately 3000 top-notch combat troops prepared to defend it to the death.[10] Violent opposition was anticipated. Prior to the landings carrier planes struck at Tarawa's defenses, and the morning of the invasion warships delivered a two-and-a-half hour bombardment that was expected to neutralize the garrison. However, the Japanese defenses, made of coconut logs, coral sand, and concrete, proved more durable than anticipated, and when the Marines began approaching the beach they found it far from neutralized.

From the beginning operations went badly. A scheduled air strike did not come in on time; the timetable for the landings went awry. A

[10] Crowl and Love, *Seizure of the Gilberts and Marshalls*, p. 73. Including labor and base troops, Japanese strength was more than 4800.

choppy sea plus strong winds and currents slowed the amphibious tractors (LVT's), and the first assault waves met murderous opposition from rifle pits, machine-gun nests, bunkers, pillboxes, and snipers hiding in the tops of coconut palms. A dodging tide prevented succeeding waves of landing craft from closing the beaches, and the men had to wade ashore in the face of enemy fire. If a man stumbled or was wounded it often meant death by drowning. Once on the beach the Marines were pinned against a seawall by enemy barricades and heavy fire. The day was a nightmare, but the Japanese also suffered, and a counterattack that might have thrown the Marines back into the lagoon that night did not materialize.

D+1 was no better. Communications and command organization, though improving, were still "snafu" (Situation Normal, All Fouled Up). Somehow the Marines pressed on, attacking with grenades, blocks of TNT, and flamethrowers. Tanks shelled the pillboxes and as communications improved, ship's guns and planes were able to provide more direct support. By afternoon the judgment was, "We are winning." [11] Throughout the 22nd, in intense heat, amid the stench of the dead, and often without food or water, the Marines continued their methodical reduction of the Japanese defenses. That night the Japanese launched a series of suicidal banzai attacks in which they lost heavily, and on the afternoon of November 23 Betio and its airfield were pronounced secured.

Although the price paid for Tarawa was high—more than a thousand dead and twice as many wounded— [12] most planners and historians who analyzed the assault concluded that it was necessary and justified. The Gilbert Island bases played an important role in future Central Pacific operations, and losses, while high for the 2nd Marine Division, were within acceptable limits when viewed in terms of the total force employed. More important, the theory of amphibious assault had been tested and proven, and the difficulties caused by tactical errors or lack of suitable equipment could be remedied. The Central Pacific planners looked ahead to their next objective—the Marshall Islands.

[11] Stockman, *The Battle for Tarawa*, p. 40.
[12] Stockman, *The Battle for Tarawa*, p. 72, Appendix B. Japanese dead numbered 4690.

Kwajalein, Eniwetok, and Truk

The Marshall Islands, coral atolls scattered over eight hundred square miles of ocean, lie north and west of the Gilberts. The Japanese had dotted them with air and naval bases, and Admiral Nimitz suggested leap-frogging to land deep within the Marshalls on Kwajalein. The bases which would be by-passed would be neutralized by air strikes. During the weeks before the Kwajalein landings, Allied land-based and carrier planes eliminated Japanese air power in the Marshalls, and three days before the landings Allied warships began giving Kwajalein's defenses an intense bombardment. When the assault began on February 1, it moved with gratifying precision. Kwajalein Island was to be taken by Major General Charles Corlett's 7th Infantry Division. Covered by an intense, short-range naval bombardment, the assault troops assembled in their craft. An hour before H-hour heavy bombers from Tarawa gave the beaches an additional pounding with 2000-pound bombs. Carrier planes bombed and strafed, and then the warships renewed their pounding. As the waves of landing craft neared the shore, naval fire rolled inland ahead of the advancing troops, who went ashore at the rate of 100 per minute [13] —a far cry from the situation at Tarawa. Across the lagoon, the 4th Marine Division (Major General Harry Schmidt), in action for the first time, landed on Roi, an island little larger than its three-runway airfield. The naval bombardment had already shattered its defenses, and before sundown it was secured. Namur, connected to Roi by a sand spit and causeway, posed more problems, but by February 2 the Roi-Namur operation was over.

By that time the fighting on Kwajalein had become intense. The 7th Division encountered little opposition on the beaches or in the initial advance inland. Although an estimated 50 percent of the Japanese defenders were killed in the bombardment, as the U.S. soldiers advanced they were held up by clusters of survivors hidden among the debris of the devastated island. The Japanese succeeded

[13] Morison, *Aleutians, Gilberts and Marshalls,* p. 260.

only in delaying the 7th Division's progress, and by late afternoon, February 4, the island was cleared. The remaining atolls, most of them "harder to pronounce than to capture," [14] were quickly occupied. An assessment of the Marshalls' campaign brought out marked differences from that of Tarawa. Although Kwajalein had been less heavily defended and fortified, its defensive strength was by no means light. Nearly 8000 Japanese died defending Kwajalein, while American casualties were less than 400 dead and 1500 wounded. [15]

The Central Pacific Command moved quickly to seize Eniwetok atoll, located at the far western edge of the Marshalls. Between February 17 and 22 Engebi, Eniwetok, and Parry Islands were secured and the Marshall Islands campaign was over. American forces were now in position to threaten the Japanese inner defense line drawn through the Caroline Islands.

Truk, the most important Japanese base in the Carolines, is only 670 nautical miles from Eniwetok. Truk differed from the other coral atolls, for within the lagoon were numerous volcanic islands that provided sufficient ground area for airstrips and shore facilities. There was enough protected anchorage for a sizable fleet, and since July 1942 it had been the headquarters and advance base for the Japanese Combined Fleet as well as a submarine and air base. Even more than Rabaul, Truk was the key to Japan, and as late as the Eniwetok operation, American planners had not decided what to do about it. Assault would doubtless be costly. In any event, Truk's planes must be kept from interfering with the invasion of Eniwetok, and so as a vital part of that operation Rear Admiral Marc Mitscher's Task Force 58 (the carrier force of the Fifth Fleet) was to see how much damage could be done at Truk. Mitscher's raid of February 17 and 18 is important in the history of carrier tactics because it was the largest raid yet conducted, and it was the first time that carrier forces attempted to knock out a major enemy base without assistance from land-based planes or a follow-through by amphibious forces.

Mitscher concentrated first on Japanese air power and then on shipping. Thirty strikes were conducted, and each of them was

---

[14] Proehl, *The Fourth Marine Division*, p. 33.
[15] Morison, *Aleutians, Gilberts and Marshalls*, p. 278.

stronger than the two Japanese strikes that hit Pearl Harbor on December 7.[16] Damage was so heavy that Truk was rendered untenable as a base for the Combined Fleet. Mitscher had demonstrated the potential of carrier forces and had convinced American planners that air power could keep Truk in an inoperable condition.

CARTWHEEL Concluded

By late 1943 it was apparent that Rabaul's offensive threat had been neutralized, and direct assault would be unnecessary. Nevertheless, the planned landings on the western tip of New Britain were still important for obtaining air and naval control of the Vitiaz and Dampier Straits, and Lieutenant General Walter Krueger with his Alamo Force (Sixth Army) conducted the landings at the end of December. Rabaul is on the eastern tip of New Britain, but the remainder of the crescent-shaped island was largely jungle. Japanese opposition to the landings was light. The airfield was secured on the third day and a defensive perimeter was gradually established around it, but the rain, damp rot, mold, mud, swamps, and jungle made the campaign a miserable one. Ironically, historians, judging with hindsight, have claimed that the war in the Southwest Pacific had accelerated to such an extent by that time that the operation was probably unnecessary.[17]

Capitalizing on the growing momentum of the Allied advance, MacArthur directed Krueger to land a division (the 32nd Infantry of Papuan fame) at Saidor, New Guinea, on January 2, 1944. The Japanese in New Guinea were already in retreat before the advancing Australians, and the Saidor operation helped to accelerate the process. Thousands of Japanese died of starvation, disease, or exhaustion during their forced march through jungle and mountains. The Australians secured Madang in April, and the Huon peninsula was in Allied hands.

[16] Morison, *Ibid.*, p. 321.
[17] Morton, *Strategy and Command: The First Two Years*, p. 582; Morison, *Breaking the Bismarcks Barrier*, p. 370.

CARTWHEEL was essentially completed. After Halsey's South Pacific forces occupied the Green Islands on February 15, 1944, the Americans were only a little more than a hundred miles from Rabaul. February 19 was later selected as the date for victory in the air war over Rabaul, as it was the last day that Rabaul sent up a sizable interception force against air attack.[18] The end of February, a month ahead of schedule, MacArthur moved into the Admiralties, and after March 4, when the last major Japanese counterattack was repulsed, these islands were essentially secure. They offered two airfields and suitable sites for more, and Seeadler Harbor was developed as a major base to service the Third, Fifth, and Seventh Fleets. On March 12, with the Marshalls and the Admiralties in Allied hands and Truk and Rabaul neutralized, the Joint Chiefs of Staff issued a revised directive to Nimitz and MacArthur. CARTWHEEL had been designed to put forces in position to assault Rabaul, but Allied sights were now on the Philippines. MacArthur was directed to isolate Rabaul and the Japanese base at Kavieng with a minimum force, move into Hollandia by April 15, take other New Guinea objectives as feasible, and plan to invade Mindanao on November 15. Ahead lay Luzon, with a tentative target date of February 15, 1945. Nimitz and the Central Pacific forces were to take the Marianas June 15, the Palaus September 15, and then plan for Formosa in February 1945.[19] The tempo was accelerating. It began to look as though MacArthur would return to the Philippines earlier than he had expected.

Late in March 1944 South Pacific forces occupied Emirau, northwest of Kavieng, and thereby completed their portion of CARTWHEEL. South Pacific forces, now out of objectives, were divided between MacArthur and Nimitz, and the South Pacific came under MacArthur's command. Later in the year the Australians took responsibility for the Solomons, New Britain, and eastern New Guinea. The remaining Japanese were no longer a strategic threat, but they were often in sizable numbers and mopping up was a nasty chore. Leaving it to the Australians, MacArthur's forces looked ahead to new objectives.

[18] Craven and Cate, *The Army Air Forces in World War II*, Vol. IV, p. 354.
[19] Crowl and Love, *Seizure of the Gilberts and Marshalls*, p. 373; Smith, *The Approach to the Philippines*, pp. 11–12.

Hollandia, Wakde, Biak

First in a series of operations that would see the Southwest Pacific forces on the Vogelkop in July was RECKLESS, a plan to by-pass Wewak and other Japanese strongpoints and strike outside the range of land-based air cover at Hollandia, in Dutch New Guinea. The Fifth Fleet came south to provide the air cover, and on April 22 General Eichelberger led the 24th and 41st Infantry Divisions against Tanahmerah and Humboldt bays. They were separated by some 25 miles, and between them, inland, was a plain suitable for airfields. A smaller landing was made at Aitape to seize airfields within supporting distance. Japanese resistance was scattered and uncoordinated. By April 26 the inland airfield area was reached, and though mopping up proceeded for some weeks it did not seriously interfere with the Allied engineering efforts to turn the Hollandia area into a major air, naval, and logistic base to support future operations. At Aitape the Japanese made a major effort to retake the area and thwart the Allied advance, but the reinforced units at Aitape fought a grim defensive battle that ultimately inflicted a major defeat on the Japanese.[20] Indicative of growing Allied strength and confidence, the next move to the west was undertaken even before the expected Japanese counterattack against Aitape developed.

Beyond Hollandia, the island of Biak, more than three hundred miles northwest in Geelvink Bay, was selected as the next major air-base site. An intermediate operation was planned for the Wakde Island-Sarmi area, which was roughly halfway between Biak and Hollandia, for there the Japanese were amassing strength sufficient to pose a threat to the Allied flank, and Wakde would be useful as a fighter base to support the Biak landings. Southwest and Central Pacific forces were coming within supporting distance of one another, and the advanced airfields were needed so Southwest Pacific air forces would be able to support Nimitz's move into the Marianas in mid-June. The Wakde and Biak landings were scheduled for May 17 and 27, respectively.

[20] Smith, *The Approach to the Philippines*, Chapters 5–8; see especially pp. 204–5.

Wakde was secured in two days. The airfields were put into use at once, and when the Biak fields were not secured as quickly as anticipated, Wakde's airfields were enlarged and used far beyond original plans. On the mainland across from Wakde a protracted struggle developed as the Allied forces began advancing toward Sarmi to clear out the Japanese resistance. The operation was not considered over until September, but the struggle at Wakde-Sarmi did not slow MacArthur's progress and on May 27 the remainder of the 41st Infantry Division landed on Biak. The island was surrounded by a coral reef which posed landing problems, but the force achieved tactical surprise and the Japanese offered little resistance as the men began advancing toward the coveted Japanese airfields. During the succeeding days, however, it became painfully obvious that the Biak defenses were well planned, well sited, manned with determination, and would be tough to break. The bulk of the Japanese combat troops (4000 out of a total of 11,400 men) [21] on Biak were a crack regiment commanded by Colonel Naoyuki Kuzume, whose orders were to hold the island as long as possible. He planned to do this by holding the cave-riddled cliffs overlooking the airfields, which would be useless to the Allies as long as Japanese artillery was zeroed in on them from the high ground. The frustrating battle at Biak went on until late August, even though its most important phases were over and Allied planes were using the field by the end of June.

The success of CARTWHEEL during 1943 had prompted the Japanese leaders to make a realistic appraisal of their prospects,[22] and in September 1943 they had adopted a "New Operational Policy" designed to trade space for time. Japan had not only lost heavily in planes, but American submarines, in the little publicized Battle of the Pacific, had inflicted such heavy losses on Japanese merchant shipping that Japan was faced with economic strangulation. Time was required to replace her losses in aircraft and merchant shipping. Under the New Operational Policy, the Japanese military leaders privately relinquished their outpost areas—the eastern New Guinea, northern Solomons, Gilbert and Marshall Islands perimeter—and proposed an "absolute national defense sphere" fortified with im-

[21] *Ibid.,* p. 300.
[22] Morton, *Strategy and Command: The First Two Years,* Chapter 27.

pregnable defenses, beyond which there would be no retreat. The new line would roughly correspond to Japan's minimum war aims, the Greater East Asia Co-Prosperity Sphere, stretching from the Kurils through the Bonins, Marianas, and Carolines to western New Guinea, thence around the Netherlands East Indies to Burma. This line must be heavily reinforced and held, while prolonged and determined delaying actions were fought in front of it. The delaying battles would buy time to build the ships and planes and strengthen the restricted perimeter.

When Alamo Force landed on Biak, the Commander of the Japanese Combined Fleet, Admiral Soemu Toyoda (Admiral Koga had been killed in a plane crash in March), ordered two giant battleships, *Yamato* and *Musashi,* plus other elements of the Combined Fleet, to Biak's support. The next day, however, when Admiral Mitscher's Task Force 58 struck Guam and Saipan, Admiral Toyoda changed his mind about defending Biak. Believing an assault on the Marianas to be imminent, he ordered all ships of the Combined Fleet to rendevous in the Philippine Sea.[23] Biak was reprieved, and one of the war's most dramatic naval engagements was at hand.

Saipan and the Philippine Sea

On June 15, 1944, the 2nd and 4th Marine Divisions began an assault on Saipan, one of the larger and southernmost of the islands in the Mariana group. It soon became apparent that fighting was going to be severe and prolonged. Although 20,000 assault troops got ashore on D-day, casualties were high and the first day's objectives were not attained.[24] When Admiral Spruance received reports on June 16 that the Japanese surface fleet was steaming toward Saipan, he promptly canceled the assault on neighboring Guam, scheduled for June 18, and held the Guam force in reserve. The Saipan reserve was ordered to land on Saipan at once so the transports could withdraw eastward to safer waters. Other portions of the supporting force joined Mitscher's Task Force 58 and deployed to meet the Japanese Fleet.

[23] Morison, *New Guinea and the Marianas,* pp. 131–32, 220–21.
[24] Morison, *New Guinea and the Marianas,* pp. 186–205. For amphibious phase see Isely and Crowl, *U.S. Marines and Amphibious War.*

Two years ago, at Midway, a numerically inferior American force had dealt the Japanese Navy a resounding defeat. The Americans began this second major encounter with a two to one superiority in naval aircraft and light carriers, while the ratio in fleet carriers and battleships was 5 Japanese to 7 American.[25] The Japanese Fleet, commanded by Vice Admiral Jisaburo Ozawa, was supported by land-based planes, whereas the Americans, because of Kuzume's stubborn defense at Biak, were dependent on carrier planes. Ozawa's naval aircraft had a longer range than did the American counterpart, and Ozawa was not burdened with the additional task of protecting an amphibious landing in progress. The decisive factor, however, was that the American carrier pilots went into battle with at least two years of sound training behind them, while the Japanese pilots were woefully ill-prepared. The Japanese training and replacement system had broken down. The fracas that broke on June 19 was so one-sided that the Americans called it the "Great Marianas Turkey Shoot."

Using the longer range of his planes to advantage, Ozawa held his carriers out of the Americans' reach and sent his planes, in four waves, against Mitscher's force. The American pilots soon sensed they were dealing with an enemy who had lost his tactical efficiency and offensive ardor. That day the Japanese lost more than 300 planes; the Americans lost 30.[26]

U.S. submarines played an important role in the Battle of the Philippine Sea, for Vice Admiral Charles A. Lockwood, who commanded the Pacific submarine forces and directed the quiet but deadly underseas war on Japanese merchant shipping, had ordered submarine patrols into the area where the Japanese Fleet might be found. Early on June 19 *Albacore* met success. Commander J. W. Blanchard took steady aim on the Japanese carrier *Taiho,* and when the mechanical sightings failed, he upped his periscope and fired six torpedoes by "seaman's eye." He submerged to escape, and not until some months later did the Americans learn that Blanchard's eye-balled torpedo had sent Japan's newest and largest carrier to a watery grave. Also on June 19 Lieutenant Commander Kossler in *Cavalla* destroyed the carrier *Shokaku.*

[25] Morison, *New Guinea and the Marianas,* p. 233.
[26] *Ibid.,* p. 277.

Although the submarines had done well, Task Force 58 had fought a defensive battle and had not touched the enemy fleet. In fact Spruance and Mitscher were uncertain just where the Japanese Fleet was, and not until late on the afternoon of June 20 did Mitscher receive definite word of Ozawa's location. He immediately committed a large strike. His pilots accounted for 65 more Japanese planes and 2 oilers, inflicted mortal damage on the carrier *Hiyo* and lesser damage on *Zuikaku,* at the low cost of 20 of their own planes.

The next day Spruance ordered a leisurely pursuit of the retiring Japanese force. Many downed aviators were found and taken aboard. One of them had witnessed the sinking of *Hiyo,* so the tally for the battle was sizable, and Task Force 58 could return to Saipan with its victory banners flying. The Japanese left the Philippine Sea with only 35 operational carrier planes.[27]

By the time the Battle of the Philippine Sea was over, the Marines and soldiers on Saipan had secured a beachhead but were far from securing the island. The naval success assured eventual victory, for with control of the sea and air the Americans could pour in reinforcements, but Saipan was a hard-fought battle of annihilation over difficult terrain and against a fanatical defense. American planners knew that Saipan would be different and difficult. It had been Japanese territory since the turn of the century, and the native population was loyal to Japan, unlike the politically detached Melanesians. Saipan was part of Japan's inner defense line and a strategic Japanese base. It was a larger land mass than the other Central Pacific objectives, and well suited to defense. Its terrain was similar to that of Biak —high ridges, deep ravines, precipitous cliffs, and numerous caves.

Although the assault phase went slower than desired, by June 20 General Holland Smith had his headquarters ashore; Aslito airfield, a major objective, had been captured; and units of the 4th Marine Division had reached the east coast. It was time for a wheeling movement and an advance northward to clear the island. As the troops started toward their first objectives, Major General Thomas E. Watson's 2nd Marine Division, on the left (west), faced a rough, distorted, volcanic mountain, Mount Tapotchau, where the Japanese "resisted our advance from every cliff, cave and cranny in which they

[27] *Ibid.,* p. 319.

219

could hide with a rifle, a machine gun or, in some cases, field pieces which they dragged in and out of their caves."[28] In the center, elements of Major General Ralph C. Smith's 27th Infantry Division faced a plateau flanked by the sheer cliffs of Mount Tapotchau on one side and a thickly wooded ridge on the other. On the far right of the front, Major General Harry Schmidt's 4th Marine Division faced less taxing terrain. When the attack began, both Marine divisions made more rapid progress than did the Army division in the center, and gradually the Marines were endangered by their exposed flanks as the line took the shape of a giant U, with the 27th Division at the bottom. The fighting was difficult and slow, but by June 25 Mount Tapotchau and Kagman peninsula were in American hands. The most vicious terrain was behind the Americans, and the Japanese were rapidly losing their capability to present an organized defense. The night of July 6 Lieutenant General Yoshio Saito, the Japanese commander, exhorted the remainder of his men to die in a last, desperate banzai charge. Their attack fell on units of the unfortunate 27th Division, which were poorly deployed to meet it. Wave after wave of screaming Japanese broke through, and before the attack was contained it had surged some distance behind the lines, creating much havoc. Casualties on both sides were high, but for the Japanese the attack resulted in a major slaughter. After the Americans reclaimed the battle area, 4300 Japanese dead were counted on the battlefield.[29] The banzai charge, the largest of the war, was Saipan's dying gasp. Two days later, as the Marines closed in on Marpi Point and hundreds of Japanese hurled themselves over the cliffs to die on the rocks below, Holland Smith proclaimed the island secured, although much mopping up remained to be done.

Saipan, a battle called by its Marine historian "the beginning to the end,"[30] was costly. More than 3400 Americans were killed or missing and 13,000 were wounded. Almost 24,000 Japanese gave their lives for Saipan,[31] but despite their sacrifice the Japanese were defeated on their own territory. In Tokyo responsible leaders, certain that victory

---

[28] Smith, *Coral and Brass*, p. 160.
[29] Hoffman, *Saipan: The Beginning of the End*, pp. 233–235.
[30] *Ibid.*
[31] Morison, *New Guinea and the Marianas*, p. 339; Hoffman, *Saipan: The Beginning of the End*, pp. 268–69, Appendix III.

was no longer attainable, began cautious moves toward a negotiated settlement of the war. The first step was to break the power of the militarists, and on July 18 General Tojo, under quiet but firm pressure, resigned as Premier. The Japanese people, who had never been given a truthful account of Japanese defeats, were told that Saipan was lost. General Kuniaki Koiso formed a new cabinet, but although he and others in it desired peace, they feared the power of the militarists and committed themselves to prosecuting the war.[32]

Guam and Tinian

The Guam and Tinian operations that followed Saipan were quicker and less costly. Guam was given the most meticulous pre-invasion bombardment the Pacific islands had yet experienced, and although the landings on July 21 were opposed, Japanese strength had been greatly reduced. Guam was not secured until August 10, but by the end of the first week Apra harbor, Orote peninsula, and the old Marine barracks were again in American hands. Thereafter, the Japanese put up only sporadic resistance.

Holland Smith called Tinian "the perfect amphibious operation."[33] Like Guam it received careful preparation from warships, planes, and artillery sited on Saipan, three miles away. The assault plans were carefully drawn, tactical surprise was achieved, and on July 24 the landings were faultlessly executed. By nightfall more than 15,000 men (primarily from the 4th Marine Division) were ashore,[34] and nine days later the American flag flew over the island. Tinian marked the first time forces had been employed so soon after another major operation or landed on so narrow a front. Fire bombs, combining napalm jelly and gasoline, were first used experimentally on Tinian and later employed extensively on the Japanese mainland. Tinian is remembered, however, as a major Pacific air base, for it was from this island, just over a year after it had fallen into American hands, that the B-29 carrying the atom bomb took off for Hiroshima.

[32] Butow, *Japan's Decision to Surrender*, pp. 27–41.
[33] Smith, *Coral and Brass*, p. 201.
[34] Morison, *New Guinea and the Marianas*, pp. 360–64.

Strategic Air Warfare

TO APPRECIATE the significance of the capture of the Marianas, it is necessary to take a close look at the employment of air power. Much of the Pacific campaign involved action by naval, air, and ground forces to seize forward bases for land-based planes. With each advance, the Allied bomber line moved within reach of new objectives, and when U.S. forces reached the Marianas, the mainland of Japan lay within striking range of U.S. very-long-range bombers. A new element, strategic bombing, entered the Pacific war.

Strategic Bombing of Japan, June 1944–March 1945

Although missions sometimes overlap, air power is employed in two ways—tactical and strategic. As a tactical weapon, planes operate in close coordination with surface forces and assist the surface advance by such means as reconnaissance, preventing enemy planes from attacking the surface forces, destroying enemy vehicles or strongpoints, or interdicting a battle area. Important as these functions are, many airmen conceive the primary purpose of air power to be its strategic employment. Not necessarily tied to the surface advance, planes strike far behind enemy lines at a nation's industrial base, munitions and armaments plants, fuel supplies, cities and civilian population. Although some air enthusiasts felt strategic air power alone could defeat the enemy, as used in World War II strategic bombing was only one way of bringing about the Axis collapse.

Strategic bombing began in Europe shortly after the war commenced. In the Pacific, because of the great distances involved, strategic bombing depended on capturing forward bases and the development of the very-long-range (VLR) or very-heavy bomber (VHB), the B-29. Work on the B-29 began in 1939,[1] when General Henry H. Arnold, Chief of the Air Corps, urged the development of a four engine bomber of a 2000-mile range. Hemisphere defense played a large part in early plans for its use, but by 1943 home defense no longer seemed critical. Nor was the Superfort needed in Europe, where the strategic campaign was already underway and the targets were within reach of the B-17's and B-24's. In the Pacific the B-29 could be put to many uses, however, and based in either China or the Marianas, it could begin bombing Japan. In September 1943 airmen urged the capture of the Marianas,[2] and late in the year the Joint Chiefs of Staff approved the move. It would be late 1944 before bases could be developed there, and partly to put the B-29 into early use, the Joint Chiefs decided to send the first B-29's to the CBI theater.

CBI (China, Burma, India) was the stepchild of the Allied Command. Distant and isolated from the sources of Allied strength, it had received only minor support designed primarily to keep China from giving up. Playing host to the first Superforts would boost Chinese morale as well as get the B-29's into action. The first wing of Superforts would fly from bases in India and China to attack Japan. The project was named MATTERHORN. It flew its first mission on June 15, 1944, when fifty B-29's from Calcutta bombed the Imperial Iron and Steel Works at Yawata, Kyushu. The strategic bombard-

[1] See Arnold, *Global Mission,* and Craven and Cate, *The Army Air Forces in World War II,* Vol. V, Chapter 1, for the development of the B-29 and the decision on its employment.
[2] Craven and Cate, *The Army Air Forces in World War II,* Vol. V, p. 19.

ment of Japan was underway.

MATTERHORN was a controversial operation. The B-29 was a new weapon, and MATTERHORN was its shakedown. It was also the test of a unique command system, for General Arnold, Commanding General of the Army Air Forces, decided to keep the B-29 under his command. A special organization, the Twentieth Air Force, was established to direct the B-29's strategic operations. Control of the Twentieth Air Force rested in Washington with the Joint Chiefs of Staff. Arnold, as their executive agent, directed the employment of the Superforts.[3]

Special airfields had to be built. In India, and to a greater extent in China, this was a tremendous task. Lacking heavy equipment or modern transport, the Chinese built the fields by hand. The area selected, near Chengtu, was a delta that had to be drained. Some three to five hundred thousand Chinese laborers carried sand from the streams in buckets balanced on yokes over their shoulders. They hauled rocks in wooden wheelbarrows or in carts pulled by men or women. They crushed stones by hammer and set them by hand. A correspondent called Chengtu "a saga of the nameless little people of China," who built the fields with "hand, muscle and goodwill."[4] The fields were completed, at a cost in money and endeavor impossible to determine,[5] and the bombers were flown to their new bases from Salina, Kansas, a distance of 11,500 miles. Five planes were lost and four seriously damaged, but the bulk of the 150 planes reached India safely.[6] Twentieth Air Force personnel who came to Calcutta by boat spent as much as ten weeks enroute.

The distance from the United States to India and China, plus the limited or non-existent communication facilities, posed huge logistic problems. Supply lines stretched from the United States to the base port of Karachi, India. From there, goods were moved by railway, water, plane, truck, bullock cart, or coolie to reach the combat forces. Materials needed in China had to be transported by air "over the

[3] *Ibid.*, pp. 33–41.

[4] New York *Times*, 17 June, 1944. Quoted in *Ibid.*, p. 68.

[5] The estimated cost of the Calcutta bases was $20,000,000. The total sum $210,000,000 paid to China included items in addition to the fields. See *Ibid.*, pp. 65, 70.

[6] The accident rate dropped after the first flight. Of the total 405 B-29's ferried to Calcutta before March 1945, only 8 were total losses. *Ibid.*, pp. 78–79.

Hump" or over the Himalayan peaks. The difficulty in moving up supplies limited the number of missions flown by MATTERHORN, for the transport facilities of the theater were already heavily taxed and plans for the B-29's to ferry their own fuel and supplies proved impractical.

Despite its problems, the XX Bomber Command, led (after August 1944) by Major General Curtis E. LeMay, attempted to meet expectations. Raids were conducted over Kyushu, on steel works in Manchuria, and one very long mission was staged through Ceylon against the Palembang oil complex in Sumatra. Both night and high-altitude daylight strikes were conducted. Training and reorganization to meet the special needs of the giant bomber took time and effort; fuel and supplies were short; adjustments had to be made on the planes themselves. In all, the strategic missions flown by MATTER-HORN were few and did Japan slight harm. The most substantial result of the operation was the combat testing of the B-29.[7] When a Japanese offensive in China threatened the security of the Chengtu bases late in 1944, the XX Bomber Command withdrew from China. It continued to fly tactical missions from Calcutta, supporting the Philippine invasion, until March 1945, when the planes flew to the Marianas to become part of XXI Bomber Command.

The Marianas were secured in July 1944, and base construction began at once. Eventually five B-29 fields were built, two each on Guam and Tinian, one on Saipan. The XXI Bomber Command, under Brigadier General Haywood S. Hansell, began its mission on November 24 when more than one hundred of the giant bombers headed for Tokyo. It was the first air raid on the Japanese capital since the Doolittle strike of April 1942, and the raid bolstered Allied morale. However, only 24 planes dropped their bombs on the primary target, the Musashino aircraft engine plant at Tokyo.[8]

During its initial period of operations, between November 1944 and March 1945, the results of XXI Bomber Command were disappointing. The B-29's conducted primarily high-altitude, daylight precision attacks on Japan's aircraft industry. Unfavorable weather in the Marianas delayed missions, and frequently cloud cover forced the planes to bomb by radar or seek other targets. Unusually strong

[7] See *Ibid.*, pp. 169–75 for evaluation.   [8] *Ibid.*, p. 558.

winds in the high altitudes over Japan posed problems for navigation and fuel supply as well as for bombing accuracy. The number of planes that aborted (turned back before reaching target) because of mechanical difficulties was high, as was the number ditched in the ocean on the long flight back to base. Washington was impatient with the limited results. In January 1945 Hansell was replaced by LeMay,[9] but repeated strikes on specified targets failed to bring better results. The Japanese aircraft engine plants had been given top priority as strategic targets, but even though they were concentrated around Tokyo, Nagoya, and Osaka, the high-altitude, daylight precision attacks failed to knock them out. The Washington headquarters of the Twentieth Air Force considered a change in tactics. Airmen believed that Japan's cities would be especially vulnerable to incendiary attacks, and some test raids, dropping incendiary bombs, were ordered. On February 25, 1945, an incendiary raid on Tokyo destroyed or damaged about one square mile of urban area. Beginning the night of March 9, 1945, LeMay switched XXI Bomber Command from daylight precision attacks to low-altitude, nighttime incendiary attacks against Japan's urban industrial areas.[10]

Strategic Bombing, Europe

By spring 1945, when the strategic bombardment of Japan began to bring decisive results, the strategic air forces in Europe, whose campaign had begun with the war itself, could see victory ahead. Lacking manpower or continental bases for the employment of large armies, Britain adopted early the principle of strategic bombardment and based her defense plans around a naval blockade to weaken Germany, while Bomber Command struck directly at the German economy. At first planners had reservations about bombing heavily populated areas, but after the Germans bombed Rotterdam in May 1940 the War Cabinet gave Bomber Command permission to strike the Ruhr, an industrial area.[11] The first British raids were small and did little damage, but on the night of May 30, 1942, Bomber

[9] *Ibid.*, p. 568.
[10] See *Ibid.*, pp. 608–14 for decision to change tactics.
[11] Webster and Frankland, *The Strategic Air Offensive,* Vol. I, p. 144.

Command committed almost its entire strength (1046 bombers from both first line and training forces) [12] to deliver a saturation raid on Cologne. Some six hundred acres of the city were destroyed,[13] and for the next 36 months the German cities were subjected to an intense aerial pounding. By the end of the war every major German city was partially a heap of rubble, while a few, such as Hamburg, were almost completely destroyed.

Even before the United States entered the war, the Joint Staff talks (March 1941) had settled that the USAF would join the RAF in strategic bombardment.[14] The U.S. Eighth Air Force was activated early in 1942 and began moving into East Anglia that spring, but it was more than a year before the Combined Bomber Offensive got underway. One delaying factor was that the USAF and the RAF differed in their approach to strategic bombing. By 1942 the RAF had essentially abandoned daylight, precision attacks on specific targets because of the operational difficulties involved.[15] The USAF favored high-altitude, daylight attacks on specific military or industrial targets. Confident that their heavily armed and armored bombers could penetrate deep into Germany, if necessary without fighter escort, the USAF was eager to put precision bombing to the test.

During 1942 the air forces tested their tactics and weapons. The RAF estimated that their first saturation raid on Cologne destroyed 12 percent of the city's industrial and residential areas,[16] but as evaluation techniques improved, they found their nighttime area raids were not obtaining expected results. Far from suffering crippling damage, Germany's industrial production was actually increasing. The British worked to develop more destructive bombs and to increase bombing accuracy. Pathfinder Squadrons were organized late in 1942. The Pathfinders flew ahead to locate the target and mark it with flares that guided the remainder of the mission. Radar and navigation devices were improved, but the Germans devised countermeasures, including an early warning radar system and an improved

[12] *Ibid.*, pp. 403–4.   [13] *Ibid.*, p. 407.
[14] Craven and Cate, *The Army Air Forces in World War II*, Vol. II, p. 210; Vol. I, p. 240.
[15] Webster and Frankland, *The Strategic Air Offensive*, Vol. I, pp. 447–48.
[16] Craven and Cate, *The Army Air Forces in World War II*, Vol. II, p. 298.

night fighter, and the aerial struggle grew steadily more intense.

The U.S. Eighth Air Force was slow to get started. Bad weather, shortages, and the allotment of strength to other theaters kept its missions in 1942 small and insignificant, but the Eighth Air Force found (as the Twentieth did later) that daylight precision bombing was often very inaccurate. By the Casablanca Conference of January 1943, the air forces could show no decisive results from their strategic bombing campaign, but the big bombers were still the only weapon that could touch the German homeland, and the cross-Channel invasion was still more than a year away. Consequently, at Casablanca the Combined Chiefs of Staff restated their commitment to a strategic bombing campaign and issued the Casablanca Directive that formally initiated the Combined Bomber Offensive. The air forces were advised that their primary object was the "progressive destruction and dislocation of the German military, industrial, and economic system, and the undermining of the morale of the German people to a point where their capacity for armed resistance is fatally weakened." [17]

The Combined Bomber Offensive, January 1943–June 1944

The strategic air war in Europe fell into three phases. Until the Casablanca Directive it was groping, growing, and becoming organized. After January 1943 it was a major part of the Allied war effort, and during 1943 and the first half of 1944 the Allied air forces wrested air superiority away from the Luftwaffe and paved the way for a successful cross-Channel invasion as well as a purely strategic air campaign, the third phase, that began after June 1944. Seventy-two percent of the bombs that fell on Germany fell after July 1, 1944,[18] but the final phase of the Combined Bomber Offensive (a campaign that paralleled similar strategic bombardment of Japan) against Germany's war-making capacity could not have been successfully conducted without the achievements of 1943 and early 1944 as a base. The middle phase had two goals: to reduce Germany's war-

---

[17] Webster and Frankland, *The Strategic Air Offensive*, Vol. II, p. 12.
[18] Craven and Cate, *The Army Air Forces in World War II*, Vol. III, p. 787.

making ability and to gain air superiority over Europe. Air superiority, a term subject to various interpretations, basically means that it is possible to carry out effective ground, naval, and air operations despite the opposition of the enemy air force. Essential for the success of both the cross-Channel invasion and the bombing offensive deep within Germany territory, air superiority could be attained by destroying the German aircraft industry and by fighting and defeating the German pilots. When the industries were attacked, the German pilots rose to protect them, and a steady campaign of attrition in the air proceeded.

The Eighth Air Force, under Major General Ira Eaker, favored a selective campaign against specific economic objectives, such as the ball-bearing industry, on the theory that it was better to cause much destruction in a few vital industries than small damage to many. The Commander-in-Chief of the RAF Bomber Command, Air Chief Marshal Sir Arthur Harris, did not agree that there were any key targets, and he saw Bomber Command's mission as dislocating the entire German economy by striking any objective operationally feasible.[19] Each followed its separate schedule of operations, though their goals were the same. Patience was essential in the air war, for there was no apparent progress in the bombing campaign. It was "flat, repetitive, without climax."[20] The men flew mission after mission, yet the war seemed to go on as before. Certain raids stood out only because of the intensity of the opposition, the high rate of loss, or the difficulty and daring of the strike.

Between March and July 1943 the RAF concentrated against industrial and munitions centers in the Ruhr. RAF Wing Commander Guy Gibson and his Dambusters Squadron made aviation history in May with a daring attack on the Mohne, Eder, and Sorpe dams. The mission was planned with care. Specially designed bombs were delivered in an unprecedented precision, low-level, nighttime attack that ruptured two of the dams. Although the losses were high and the effects on the German economy were not serious, the potential of precision night raids had been vividly demonstrated.[21]

[19] Webster and Frankland, *The Strategic Air Offensive*, Vol. II, p. 5.
[20] Craven and Cate, *The Army Air Forces in World War II*, Vol. II, p. ix.
[21] Webster and Frankland, *The Strategic Air Offensive*, Vol. II, pp. 168–78.

Aviation history was also made late in July with Operation GO-MORRAH, a series of night raids on Hamburg. Improved radar sets were in use, and another product of the Wizard War was used for the first time. "Window" consisted of filling the sky with tiny strips of tinfoil which threw a confusing pattern on the German radar-warning screens. On four nights between July 24 and August 2, the RAF bombed Hamburg. The USAF supplemented the attacks by day. Many incendiaries were used, and Hamburg became a vast cauldron of destruction. So many fires were burning at once that a column of hot air 1.5 miles in diameter rose 2.5 miles high. The column sucked in cooler air along the ground until winds reached tornado velocity, making a phenomenon called a fire storm. The storm roared through the city destroying all flammable material in its path. An estimated 6200 acres (out of a total of 8382) were devastated.[22] Thousands were killed, thousands were left bereft and homeless. Joseph Goebbels, German Minister of Propaganda, recorded in his diary that the raid had presented Germany with "problems that are almost impossible of solution." [23]

The German problems caused by the air war intensified. On August 1 USAF bombers raided the Rumanian oil refineries at Ploesti. Oil was a crucial weakness in the German war economy and was the prime target for the later phase of the bombing campaign, but the profitable targets were widely scattered and deep within the Axis stronghold. The Ploesti raid was carried out by Liberators from the U.S. Ninth Air Force in the Middle East and involved a round trip of some 2400 miles. The 177 B-24's streaked toward Ploesti unescorted, counting on surprise to reduce their casualties. A navigational error reduced surprise, and although they flew at tree-top height to escape radar detection, they encountered both fighters and flak. Damage was done, though it was difficult to say how much, and one third of the force did not return.[24]

In mid-August 1943 the Eighth Air Force celebrated the anniversary of its first mission (12 B-17's against Rouen, August 17, 1942)

[22] USSBS, *Overall Report,* p. 93; Webster and Frankland, *The Strategic Air Offensive,* Vol. II, p. 48.
[23] *Goebbels' Diaries,* p. 478.
[24] Brereton, *The Brereton Diaries,* p. 200–5. See Dugan and Stewart, *Ploesti,* for a detailed account of the raid and the fate of the prisoners.

by striking the Messerschmitt factory at Regensburg and the ball-bearing industry at Schweinfurt. Almost 400 B-17's were dispatched for the combined mission, which was not only the Eighth's largest to date but its furthest from base. The bomb run was successful, but 60 planes did not return.[25] Unescorted daylight raids continued to endure a high casualty rate, despite changes in combat formation or other tactics.

On October 14 the Eighth flew its second Schweinfurt mission, with 291 B-17's. They were escorted as far as the fighters could go, but once on their own they came under heavy attack. Wave after wave of German fighters swarmed over the bombers, firing rockets and large bore cannon, conducting air-to-air bombing, and concentrating on one group at a time, or on stragglers. The tactics were not new, "but never before had the enemy made such full and such expertly coordinated use of these tactics." Schweinfurt was bombed, but the Eighth lost 60 bombers with crews, climaxing a week in which four attacks had cost 148 planes.[26] Obviously, unescorted daylight raids were too costly. The British, faced earlier with the same conclusion, had switched to nighttime area bombing. The Americans instead sought the answer in a long-range fighter. It was an important decision, for German night fighters soon began to disrupt the night bombing campaign, and the success of the air war then depended on being able to defeat the German Air Force by day. The P-51, called the Mustang and believed by many airmen to be the outstanding plane developed during the war, was the long-range fighter that eventually escorted the B-17's to Berlin, but it was March 1944 before there were enough Mustangs to begin escorting large daylight raids into the heart of Germany.

In addition to the operational difficulties encountered, the strategic air forces were frustrated by the necessity to divert effort to targets other than those judged to be vital to the German war economy. The German submarine bases along the French coast received much of the big bombers' attention, for security in the Atlantic was prerequisite for the success of any other campaign. Tons of bombs were dropped on the submarine pens, but they had a negligible effect on the U-boat

[25] Craven and Cate, *The Army Air Forces in World War II,* Vol. II, p. 682.
[26] *Ibid.,* pp. 699–705.

war. The pens were so heavily reinforced with steel and concrete that even direct hits caused slight damage.

A second frustrating diversion, and again one of debatable value, came late in 1943. The Germans were developing a long-range missile, and the British spotted its testing site, Peenemunde on the Baltic Sea, early in 1943. In August the RAF bombed it, but with questionable results, and the Germans dispersed the industry. When launching sites began to appear along the French and Belgian coasts, the strategic air forces were assigned the task of disabling them. The campaign, begun in December 1943, was called CROSSBOW. The shape and construction of the rocket launching sites made them difficult targets, hard to damage by bombing. It was impossible to forecast the new weapon's destructive potential, but the possibility that it might disrupt the cross-Channel invasion indicated that drastic measures were needed. CROSSBOW was carried out with determination, but even after the war it was difficult to evaluate its success. Most estimates credit CROSSBOW with delaying the missile attack from three to six months.[27] The first flying bomb, the V-1, landed in England on June 12, just one week after the cross-Channel invasion began. The V-weapon sites continued to be a top priority target for the air forces until the sites were overrun in the course of the ground battle late in 1944.

By January 1944 the U.S. Air Force had grown to an impressive size, and reorganization put Lieutenant General Carl Spaatz at the head of the United States Strategic Air Forces in Europe. Spaatz coordinated the activities of the Fifteenth Air Force in Italy (Major General Nathan Twining) and the Eighth Air Force in England (Lieutenant General James H. Doolittle). The Fifteenth would hit targets in the Balkans and southern Germany, and the Eighth plus the RAF Bomber Command would strike western Europe and northern and central Germany. In February the Combined Chiefs of Staff issued a directive charging the Strategic Air Forces with the destruction of the German Air Force. On February 20, 1944, the Allied air forces began Operation ARGUMENT, a "Big Week" of concentrated bombing on the German aircraft industry. The RAF pounded by night and the USAF by day, paralyzing the German aircraft

[27] *Ibid.*, Vol. III, p. 106.

industry. The German fighters, taking mounting losses, began to oppose only the larger raids. As the destruction of German fighter strength was of utmost importance, Allied fighters, rather than flying in close support of the bombers, began to range over the skies in offensive search-and-destroy missions. The P-51 Mustang proved an able fighter in combat, and the Luftwaffe pilots tried to avoid dog-fights with it. Raids, especially on Berlin, were designed deliberately to draw the German fighters into the air.

Berlin, Nazi Germany's political center and an important transportation and industrial city, had been bombed by the RAF by night since November 1943. The Luftwaffe devoted much of its production and training effort to night fighters for the defense of Berlin and the other cities, and by spring 1944 the RAF raids were becoming so costly that the Berlin battle was turned over to the day bombers of the Eighth Air Force. In March Berliners first saw fighter-escorted bombers over their capital by day. German air superiority was a thing of the past. By April 1944 the Allies had air superiority over Germany and western Europe. The cross-Channel invasion was scheduled for early June, and during April and May the strategic air forces cooperated with the tactical air forces in a campaign against the German transportation system designed to isolate the area of the approaching battle. Due to the combined efforts of the RAF and USAF, General Eisenhower, on the eve of D-day, was able to tell his soldiers, "If you see a plane overhead, it'll be ours." [28]

[28] Brereton, *The Brereton Diaries,* p. 279.

PART III

The War Ends

The Second Front

B Y T H E middle of 1944 the Axis powers were on the defensive on all fronts. American forces were in the Marianas. Italy was out of the war; the Allies entered Rome on June 4. On Germany's Eastern Front Zhukov and Konicv were poised at the southeastern corner of Poland, ready to swoop on to Warsaw. From the air Allied bombers were reducing Germany's cities and industries to shambles. The U-boats had yielded control of the Atlantic to the Allied navies. On June 6, 1944, Allied forces stormed ashore in France, and the final campaign that would bring about Germany's defeat began.

Preparations for D-Day

That Allied forces would carry the war into Germany was part of British and American strategy from the first months of war. The demands of other fronts, shortages of men and equipment, differing views on strategy, the uncertain situation in the Atlantic, and the need to weaken Germany beforehand all contributed to delays in setting up the Second Front, but during 1943 the cross-Channel invasion was scheduled for the following spring.

OVERLORD, the largest amphibious assault in history, was largely shaped by British Lieutenant General Sir Frederick E. Morgan, who early in 1943 was appointed Chief of Staff to the Supreme Allied Commander (designate).[1] Morgan and his joint staff (COSSAC) incorporated all available information, data, and plans and produced an initial outline of OVERLORD that called for landings in Normandy on a three-division front. It was approved, with recommendations for strengthening it, by the Combined Chiefs of Staff at the Quebec Conference in August 1943.

Only OVERLORD's Supreme Commander could give the outline final form. Churchill and Roosevelt agreed that the preponderance of American strength for the final campaign called for an American commander, and General Marshall seemed the obvious choice. He was respected by Churchill, Roosevelt, and the Combined Chiefs as a soldier of unusual stature and strategic insight. Roosevelt, however, decided Marshall could not be spared from Washington, where he was directing the entire global struggle, and in December 1943 Roosevelt named Eisenhower to command OVERLORD.[2] In January 1944 Eisenhower went to London to establish SHAEF, Supreme Headquarters, Allied Expeditionary Forces. Air Chief Marshal Sir Arthur Tedder became Eisenhower's Deputy Supreme Commander, while General Bedell Smith continued as Eisenhower's Chief of Staff. Admiral Sir Bertram Ramsay commanded the Allied Naval Expeditionary forces; Air Chief Marshal Sir Trafford Leigh-Mallory commanded the Allied Expeditionary Air Force, composed of the U.S. Ninth Air Force (Brereton) and the British Second Tactical Air Force (Coningham). The strategic air forces (Doolittle's Eighth Air Force and Harris's RAF Bomber Command) were placed under Eisenhower's operational control for OVERLORD, and Tedder was

[1] For the evolution of OVERLORD, see Harrison, *Cross-Channel Attack;* Ellis, *Victory in the West,* Vol. I; Morgan, *Overture to Overlord.* To fit OVERLORD into the strategic picture, see Matloff and Snell, *Strategic Planning for Coalition Warfare 1941–42;* Matloff, *Strategic Planning for Coalition Warfare 1943–44;* Ehrman, *Grand Strategy,* Vol. V.

[2] Harrison, *Cross-Channel Attack,* pp. 112–14; Sherwood, *Roosevelt and Hopkins,* pp. 770–71, 803.

assigned the coordination of all air operations. General Montgomery came to London to take command of the assaulting land forces (the U.S. First Army under Bradley and the British Second Army under Dempsey). Once the invasion was a reality and the build-up began, Montgomery was to command a British Army Group and Bradley an American Army Group, while Eisenhower would assume direct command of land operations.

Eisenhower and Montgomery agreed that a three-division front was too narrow and weak, and the assault was expanded to a five-division, fifty-mile front, even though accumulating the additional landing craft and equipment meant delaying D-day from May until June, and postponing a landing in southern France originally planned as a simultaneous assault. Debate arose about preliminary air operations. The strategic air forces, having established air superiority over the continent, were anxious to proceed with a purely strategic campaign against the German oil industry. SHAEF wanted them employed in conjunction with the tactical air forces to conduct a massive attack on the continental communications system. OVERLORD differed from most other amphibious operations of the war in that the target area could not be kept isolated from enemy reinforcement by sea power, and the assaulting forces were only a small proportion of the total force to be committed. German strength on the continent was formidable, and with good land communications, the Germans could throw overwhelming force against an Allied landing. SHAEF considered it essential to disrupt the railway systems in France and Germany so that the Germans could not bring up reinforcements by land faster than the Allies could build them up by sea. SHAEF's viewpoint won. A systematic destruction of rail centers and marshalling yards was climaxed by a campaign against bridges, and after D-day the Allies were able to reinforce by sea faster than the Germans could reinforce by land.[3]

During the late winter and spring, the German defense measures intensified. The entire Western Front was under the command of von Rundstedt, who since 1942 had been preparing for the Allied invasion and building the Atlantic Wall—coastal defenses ordered by Hitler and designed to make Europe a fortress. Von Rundstedt had

[3] Craven and Cate, *The Army Air Forces in World War II*, Vol. III, p. 160.

two Army Groups, B in the north and G in the south. In January Hitler gave Rommel command of Army Group B, stationed in northern France, Belgium, and Holland, and charged him with meeting and repelling the invasion. Although nominally under von Rundstedt, Rommel had direct access to Hitler and enjoyed an unusual influence and popularity with both the Fuehrer and the German people. This confused command structure was further complicated because much of Rommel's armor was grouped under the separate command of General Geyr von Schweppenburg, the Luftwaffe and Navy were practically independent, and Himmler held restrictive control over the SS divisions.[4]

Rommel and von Rundstedt were not in complete agreement. Von Rundstedt had little faith in the Atlantic Wall and wanted to hold the mobile forces back from the coast to fight a battle of maneuver after the Allies were ashore. Rommel had already fought where the Allies held air superiority, and insisted that the Allied control of the air would render a battle of mobility impossible. Germany's only hope was to defeat the invasion force on the beaches at its most vulnerable moment. Fortifications must be prepared and the armored and mobile divisions must be held close to the beaches so they could be employed with rapidity during the first forty-eight hours of attack. Neither Field Marshal could move without Hitler's concurrence, and neither succeeded in persuading the Fuehrer completely to his point of view. The result was a compromise defense, based primarily on Rommel's concepts, but fatally weakened because the German High Command retained direct control over Schweppenburg's panzer divisions. Although nearly sixty German divisions awaited the Allied assault, very few, and only one armored division, would see action during the first forty-eight hours that Rommel deemed decisive.[5]

Work on the coastal fortifications was stepped up. Until early 1944, the Pas de Calais, the bulge of France-Belgium closest to England, had received the most attention. Fortifications along the Normandy coast were now emphasized. The Allied air offensive against transportation hampered construction, supplies were short,

---

[4] Analysis of German strength and command in Ellis, *Victory in the West*, Vol. I, Chapters 3 and 6; Harrison, *Cross-Channel Attack*, Chapter 7.

[5] Harrison, *Cross-Channel Attack*, pp. 242–58; Liddell-Hart, *The Rommel Papers*, pp. 453–57, 468–70.

and the defenses were far from complete by June 6. Nevertheless they posed a forbidding obstacle to a landing force. The beach obstacles typically consisted of a row of steel or timber ramps furthest to sea, followed by two rows of steel stakes. Inside the stakes were many-pointed steel obstructions that the Allies called "Hedgehogs." All the obstacles were covered at high tide. The landing craft, trying to cross the fortifications, would be ripped open by the obstacles or blown to bits by the shells and mines with which they were wired. Men who reached the beach faced barbed wire, minefields, and enfilading fields of fire from concrete gun emplacements. Allied planes photographed these obstacles, and Commandos, slipping ashore from submarines, stole samples of them to study. The landings were scheduled for the best tide conditions to allow Underwater Demolition Teams time to destroy them. Gun emplacements along the coast were carefully identified. Inland, tall stakes, wired and mined, began to sprout in the fields behind the beaches. They were dubbed "Rommel's Asparagus," for Rommel, expecting airborne landings, designed the stakes to destroy gliders.

Southern England became one huge military camp. The air forces had effectively isolated the battle area. The ships were loaded and ready to embark. The men were briefed. D-day would be June 5, and only one thing could stop it—the weather. June 5, 6, and 7 offered the optimum conditions of moonlight for the airborne troops, darkness for the convoys to cross the Channel, daylight for shore bombardment and air neutralization of beaches, and low tides for the landing craft and Underwater Demolition Teams. If the operation could not get underway then, it would have to wait at least two weeks, or possibly a full month, for ideal conditions to reoccur. On June 3 SHAEF's senior meterologist, Group Captain J. M. Stagg, predicted that June 5 would be overcast and stormy, with high winds and rough seas.[6] The invasion would be too hazardous if the air forces were grounded, and Eisenhower postponed the operation for twenty-four hours. Monday, June 5, the "camp was shaking and shuddering under a wind of almost hurricane proportions and the accompanying rain seemed to be traveling in horizontal streaks."[7] Unperturbed, Captain

[6] Wilmot, *The Struggle for Europe*, pp. 220–26.
[7] Eisenhower, *Crusade in Europe*, p. 250.

241

Stagg predicted a period of relatively good weather beginning the following morning. The long-term forecast was not good, but the consequences of a delay might be worse. The decision was Eisenhower's. OVERLORD was to go on June 6.

Invasion

Before midnight, June 5, planes headed for France to launch the largest airborne operation ever conducted.[8] The air assault was a vital part of the larger assault from the sea, and failure now could mean disaster later. The invasion beaches were named SWORD, JUNO, GOLD, OMAHA, and UTAH. The first three were assigned to the British, the latter two to the Americans. On the far left of the front, SWORD edged up to the Orne River and a parallel canal that connected Caen to the sea. The German 21st Panzer Division near Caen was a threat not only to the SWORD landings, but to the entire left flank of the assault. To protect the flank, part of the British 6th Airborne Division was to land in the pre-dawn hours of June 6, capture the bridges over the Orne and the canal, destroy five bridges over the River Dives, and secure the high ground between the Dives and Orne Rivers. The initial air-drop was to be reinforced on June 6 by Commandos landing from the sea and the remainder of the division coming in gliders. The operation went well. Gliders crash-landed against the bridge defenses and seized them before the Germans could fire their demolitions. Parachute brigades cleared the fields of Rommel's Asparagus and gliders landed reinforcements. A battery of guns sited to fire on the seaborne forces was silenced; the bridges over the Dives River were destroyed. By dawn the desired flank position was secured.

At the opposite end of the front, behind UTAH beach, the U.S. 82nd and 101st Airborne Divisions suffered more difficulty. UTAH beach lay at the base of the Cotentin peninsula and was separated from OMAHA beach by a marshy lowland through which the Douve and Vire Rivers empty into the sea. Behind UTAH was a wide lagoon, passable only by a few causeways. If the enemy controlled the causeways, the landing force would be bottled up in its beachhead. A

[8] See Wilmot, *The Struggle for Europe,* pp. 233–45; Marshall, *Night Drop.*

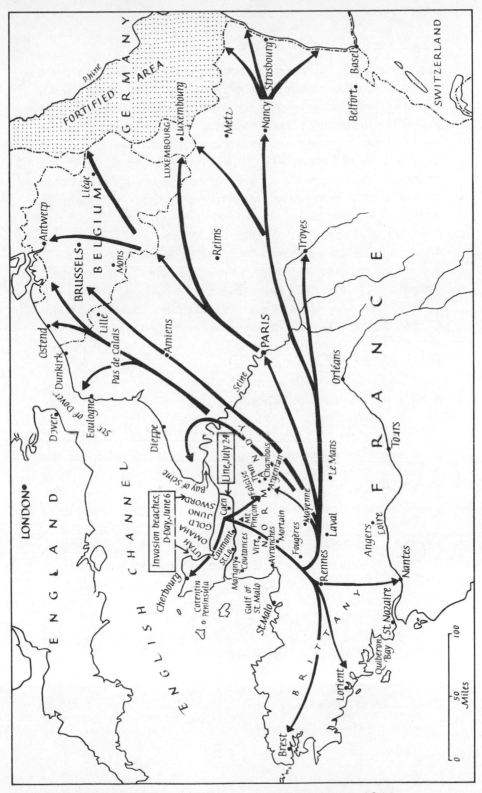

ALLIED CAMPAIGN IN WESTERN EUROPE, 1944

"miserable beach," [9] UTAH was included in the assault plan because it was essential to capture Cherbourg without delay. The Cotentin peninsula, with Cherbourg at its tip, was joined to the mainland by an area of marshy lowlands that the Germans could easily use to halt an Allied advance into the peninsula. To forestall that eventuality, Major General Lawton Collins' VII Corps would land on the peninsula itself, at UTAH, and move at once to take Cherbourg. To make the UTAH assault feasible, the two airborne divisions were to drop inland and seize the vital beach exits and road junctions. The mission was a success, although it did not unfold exactly as planned. The 101st, with the primary task of seizing the beach exits, was badly scattered in the drop. Anti-aircraft fire drove pilots off course; cloud obscured drop zones. The 101st spilled out over an area more than 25 by 15 miles wide. Units were badly broken up, and by dawn Major General Maxwell Taylor, who had jumped with his men, had collected less than one sixth of his total force. The vital beach exits were seized and held, but secondary objectives were not achieved. Because the drop had been widely scattered, German forces were for some hours at a loss to pinpoint the invasion area, and in the confusion the air-drop appeared greater than it actually was.

Major General Matthew Ridgway's 82nd Division also suffered from dispersion in the drop, and met vigorous enemy opposition. Its primary mission was to secure a bridgehead across the Merderet River and hold it against German threats to the beachhead. The leading regiment landed within three miles of their drop zone, rallied quickly, and by 4:00 a.m. had taken its objective, St. Mére Eglise, and blocked the Cherbourg-Carentan road. The other regiments were scattered about the countryside and found themselves in the midst of a German infantry division. Yet even though a compact bridgehead was not established, the main purpose, to keep the enemy from molesting the seaborne forces, was accomplished.

Admiral Ramsay's naval plan was a masterpiece of detail and coordination. More than 1200 warships and 4000 landing ships and craft were involved.[10] The Eastern Task Force, under Rear Admiral

[9] Eisenhower, *Crusade in Europe*, p. 240.
[10] Roskill, *The War at Sea*, Vol. III, Part II, pp. 18–19. See also account of OVERLORD in Morison, *The Invasion of France and Germany*.

Sir Philip Vian, was to land the British Second Army on SWORD, JUNO, and GOLD. The Western Task Force, under Rear Admiral A. G. Kirk, was to land the U.S. First Army on OMAHA and UTAH. Each ship, craft, and crew had a specific task, target, and schedule. As they sailed from their loading ports and assembled in "Piccadilly Circus," the area marking the start of the swept Channel, they knew both their own role and the larger plan.

Beginning before dawn, heavy, medium, and fighter bombers worked over the beach defenses. At daybreak the warships offshore opened the naval bombardment. Overhead flew fighter cover for the vessels plying the Channel, the ships offshore, and the beaches themselves. The assault waves formed and the landing craft began the run for the beaches. The seas were rough. Some craft were swamped. Others were driven off course, but by H-hour men were going ashore all along the fifty-mile front. Opposition varied from beach to beach. At UTAH, where great difficulty was expected, casualties were lightest and the landings smoothest. By a fortunate accident part of Major General Raymond Barton's 4th Division landed a mile off its assigned sector, found the area only lightly defended, and by 1:00 p.m. had made contact with the airmen of the 101st, holding their causeway exits. By evening more than 21,000 men and tons of stores were ashore. Casualties had been less than 200.[11] Although contact had not been made with the 82nd Airborne, the 4th Division was in a good position to begin offensive action the next day.

In the British sector the landings went almost as well. The British made good use of a number of specialized vehicles and weapons, especially amphibious tanks and flail tanks to clear minefields ashore. Even though the heavy seas caused some losses and disrupted landing schedules, and despite congestion on the beaches that slowed unloading, by evening the situation was well in hand. Behind GOLD and JUNO the 50th British Division and the 3rd Canadian Division joined to form a common beachhead twelve miles wide and six to seven miles deep, the most successful penetration of the day. The 3rd British Division landed at SWORD and experienced the only D-day raids by the Luftwaffe and the German Navy, as well as meeting and

[11] Morison, *The Invasion of France and Germany*, p. 134; Harrison, *Cross-Channel Attack*, p. 329.

repelling an attack by the 21st Panzer Division. Hitler, thinking the Normandy landings were a diversion to protect larger landings elsewhere, did not release the other panzer divisions.

At OMAHA heavy seas, cloud cover, naturally defensible beaches, and heavy German opposition turned the landings into a fierce and costly struggle. The naval bombardment, limited to a half hour because of the daylight and tide schedules, was insufficient to knock out the German strongpoints. The bombers scheduled to strike the beach defenses were hampered by cloud and mist. Fearful of bombing their own troops, they dropped their bombs too far inland to destroy the beach defenses. A German strongpoint on Pointe du Hoe caused the ships to anchor further to sea than was necessary at the other beaches. In the choppy seas many of the small craft were swamped. Many DUKW's carrying supporting artillery never reached shore, and even more critical was the loss of many of the amphibious tanks. Although tanks were forced ashore on the western end of OMAHA, on the eastern sector only 5 out of 32 reached the beach.[12] A lateral current pulled the landing craft off their targets. Units did not land together. Heavy machine-gun fire began hitting the landing craft before they debarked the troops. The men who reached shore were pinned down behind obstacles, under the sea wall, or at the base of a bank of loose stone. The difficulties experienced by the first assault waves affected those to follow, for obstacles and routes off the beach were not cleared. Succeeding waves of vehicles and craft piled up or milled around in confusion. Enemy fire continued to be heavy and accurate; the Germans reported that the landings were thwarted.

That a beachhead was seized can be attributed to the weight of the air and naval support and to the courage of individual leaders, afraid or fearless, who knew that the men must be led off the beach or face certain death. A colonel shouted, "Two kinds of people are staying on this beach, the dead and those who are going to die." [13] Small groups began to work their way inland, knocking out defenses, clearing routes through the minefields, and finding routes up the bluffs behind the beach. Landing craft rammed the beach obstacles and their guns

---

[12] Morison, *The Invasion of France and Germany*, p. 134; Harrison, *Cross-Channel Attack*, p. 309.

[13] Ryan, *The Longest Day*, p. 290.

supported the infantry. Destroyers closed the beach, and under cover of their supporting fire, engineers bulldozed routes through the sand dunes and cleared minefields. The Underwater Demolition Teams, taking heavy casualties, cleared the underwater obstacles and opened channels for succeeding waves of craft. By evening there was a beachhead, only a mile and a half deep at best, but a beachhead nonetheless. The better part of five regiments was ashore.

By the end of D-day 132,000 British, Canadian, and American troops had landed from the sea on Normandy.[14] Behind them Allied naval and air superiority assured a steady build-up of men and equipment, but ahead lay a frustrating struggle to strengthen the beachhead before the Allied armies could begin the final drive to Germany.

The Battle of the Beachhead

A critical and frustrating period of constant and heavy fighting began on June 7 and lasted until the end of July. While the Allies battled to land men and supplies and enlarge their beachhead, the Germans sought to contain them within Normandy. Once the Allies broke through the Normandy defenses, no prepared defense lines existed in front of the German border. To relinquish Normandy would mean relinquishing France.

The Germans' difficulty was compounded because they did not know the Allies' intentions. Elaborate deceptive measures had been taken, both before and after the Normandy invasion, to convince the Germans that Normandy was merely a diversion before a larger landing was launched on the Pas de Calais. To meet this expected assault, the German High Command retained their Fifteenth Army in the Pas de Calais, and to maintain contact between the Normandy forces and the Fifteenth Army, they applied the bulk of their remaining strength against the eastern end of the Allied beachhead. There the British Second Army faced Caen, and if they could force their way through the Caen bottleneck they would be in open country,

[14] Roskill, *The War at Sea,* Vol. III, Part II, p. 53.

suitable for massive tank and air operations, leading straight to Paris. The bulk of the German armor was concentrated on the Caen sector to prevent this, while the infantry divisions were given the task of containing the remainder of the beachhead.

Fortunately for the German endeavor, much of Normandy's terrain is well suited for defense. Its numerous small fields are surrounded by earth banks overgrown with brush and trees. Infantry and weapons, dug in and concealed in the hedgerows, could effectively hold up a much larger advancing force. Swamps, marshes, and bogs further canalized the Allied advance, which became a slow and costly battle for one hedgerow after another. The infantryman carried the burden of battle, for the hedgerows restricted observation and made accurate use of artillery almost impossible. Tanks were nearly useless, since when they started over a hedgerow their vulnerable underbellies were exposed to enemy fire and their own guns were pointed skyward.

While the British Second Army kept the bulk of the German strength employed near Caen, the American First Army moved to take Cherbourg (accomplished by June 26) and to expand the beachhead perimeter to the south. The American advance soon became bogged down in small-unit battles for the hedgerows. Gains were slight and casualties high. The build-up continued—by the end of June roughly a million men had been landed—but before they could be decisively employed they must seize a suitable line from which to open a major drive. By July, when it became apparent that the line they had hoped to reach would not be attained as soon as was hoped, General Bradley began working on plans for a breakout from positions further to the rear.

The night of June 12 the Germans opened a new blitz on London and the surrounding area with the V-1, the first of Hitler's "miracle weapons" with which he hoped to wrest victory from defeat. A flying bomb, the V-1 was pilotless, jet-propelled, approximately 25 feet long, had a wing span of 16 feet, and carried a 2000-pound explosive warhead. British defensive measures came into play and at once enjoyed appreciable success. Only one fourth of the roughly 10,000 V-1's launched toward London reached their target, and by September, when the main launching sites on the coast of France had been overrun, the worst of the V-1 attacks was over. Civilian casualties, while not as high as those resulting from the conventional bombing, numbered some 24,000 killed or seriously wounded during the V-1 campaign.[15]

Despite stalemate in Normandy and the new bombing attack on England, Germany's situation was precarious. On June 17 von Rundstedt and Rommel conferred with Hitler. Rommel urged withdrawing and reforming on a defensible line. Hitler would have none of it. Seeing only defeat ahead, Rommel urgently requested that the war be brought to an end. Hitler admonished him to confine his worries to his own front.[16] Again on June 29 von Rundstedt and Rommel appealed to Hitler to end the war before Germany was destroyed. Hitler, unmoved, relieved von Rundstedt of command and replaced him with von Kluge, who soon agreed with Rommel that little could be done.

A group of anti-Hitler conspirators, which had begun to form as early as 1938, contacted Rommel, since he was the obvious person to assume leadership in trying to make peace with the Western Allies if Hitler were got out of the way. Rommel, having concluded his loyalty lay with his country rather than with his Fuehrer, was receptive, but he was never made privy to the conspirator's plans. On July 20 a bomb, planted by Count Berthold von Stauffenberg, exploded in Hitler's headquarters. Though others were killed or seriously hurt, Hitler sustained only minor injury. The attempted overthrow of the Nazi government was a miserable failure. Incensed by the attempt, Hitler ordered a purge that showed neither justice nor mercy. Thousands were hailed before a People's Court and doomed to the firing squad, imprisonment, or hanging. Rommel became suspect. On July 17, as he was returning from a trip to the front, he was wounded when an Allied plane strafed his car. Rommel was in the hospital when von Stauffenberg's bomb exploded, but his name was associated with the conspirators. In October Hitler's Secret Police, the SS, gave Rommel the choice of taking poison or going to Berlin to stand trial. Rommel took the poison after being assured that if he did so, his family would not be molested. It was announced that he had died of his earlier wound.[17]

[15] Collier, *The Defense of the United Kingdom*, pp. 527–28.
[16] Freidin, *The Fatal Decisions*, p. 218. Shirer, *The Rise and Fall of the Third Reich*, pp. 1039–40.
[17] See Wheeler-Bennett, *Nemesis of Power*; Goerlitz, *The German General Staff*; Liddell-Hart, *The Rommel Papers*.

The Russian Drive, June 23–August 7

On June 23, 1944, two and a half weeks after D-day in Normandy, the Russians opened a massive offensive in Belorussia. On a front more than three hundred miles wide, a hundred divisions blasted their way forward with a staggering concentration of artillery (reportedly as high as four hundred cannon or heavy mortars per mile) and an overwhelming number of tanks.[18] The Germans were caught off-balance and were ill prepared, largely because of Hitler's misjudgment. By late spring 1944 the German front line in the east still stretched from the Gulf of Finland to the Black Sea in the shape of a giant reversed S. North of the Pripet Marshes the line protruded into Russia, while south of the Marshes it bulged the other direction, into Poland and northern Rumania. (See map, page 193.) Some in the German High Command urged withdrawal in the north to form a shorter, more defensible line which would run from Riga to Rumania. This actually became the line to which the Russians pushed them during June and July, but Hitler refused to tighten the line at this time although it would have given the Germans a strategic reserve, particularly if some of the occupation troops were recalled from Norway, Greece, or Crete. But even this late in the war Hitler refused to yield a yard of conquered soil. Lindemann's Army Group North and Busch's Army Group Center stayed in the Baltic and Belorussia, where certain vital communications hubs were designated "fortresses" that must be defended to the last man. Busch's Army Group Center was weakened to send reinforcements to Model's Army Group North Ukraine, against which the Russian advance between the Carpathian Mountains and the Pripet Marshes seemed most likely to continue.

The Russian offensive, not against Model, but against Busch, tore open a 250-mile gap in the German lines through which the armies poured. In encirclement maneuvers the Russian armies, coordinated by Marshals Zhukov and Vasilievski, cut off and destroyed 350,000 men—a numerical loss greater than that at Stalingrad.[19] On June 28

[18] See Werth, *Russia at War*, pp. 860–61; Clark, *Barbarossa*, p. 382. German and Russian figures differ on degree of Russian superiority.
[19] Werth, *Russia at War*, p. 864; Guderian, *Panzer Leader*, p. 336.

Hitler rushed Model to command a combined Army Group Center and Army Group North Ukraine, but restrained from shortening his lines, Model could do little but wait for the Russian advance to run its course.

For some days it appeared the Russians might not stop until Poland and Germany were overrun. The Russians were in Brest and Lublin by late July and in the suburbs of Warsaw by July 31. Nor was the drive confined to the center of the long front. On July 10 it erupted against the northern and southern flanks. Between July 12 and August 7 the Russians drove a wedge to Riga that isolated Army Group North in Estonia, while to the south Koniev took Lwow by July 27, not stopping until he reached the Vistula River south of Warsaw.

The first week in August the massive offensive slowed, then halted. Model had rallied his shattered forces, and the Russians had outrun their supplies. In places the Russian advance had been as much as 350 miles, and the cessation of battle would have raised no question had it not coincided with an underground uprising in Warsaw.

As the Poles watched the Russian advance, they wondered whether they were being liberated, or were merely exchanging one occupying authority for another. On July 25 the Russians announced the formation of the Polish National Liberation Committee (later called the Lublin Committee) to manage Polish affairs in Soviet-liberated Poland. The Lublin Committee was recognized by the Russian-sponsored Union of Polish Patriots. It denounced the London Poles; it was vague about its relation to Moscow. On July 29, as the Russian armies approached Warsaw's suburbs, the Russian radio broadcasted to the citizens of Warsaw a message urging them to rise against the Germans.[20] The London Polish government, with the help of its underground army in Warsaw, hoped to seize control of their capital before the Russians moved in and destroyed the chances for an independent Poland. On August 1 the Polish underground army, led by General Bor-Komorowski, attacked the German forces in Warsaw. By August 6 the Poles were in control of most of their capital, but two days later the SS moved in. Between August 8 and October 2,

[20] Bor-Komorowski, *The Secret Army*, p. 212.

when Bor-Komorowski surrendered, the entire city of Warsaw was razed. During those weeks, when the Warsaw patriots fought with makeshift weapons against one of the most brutal operations ever conducted by the SS, the Russian armies across the Vistula did nothing. The Western Allies were powerless to help the Poles. A few planes flew from bases in Italy to drop supplies, but their help was negligible. The Russians refused permission for British and American planes to land behind the Russian lines. Churchill repeatedly urged Stalin to extend some assistance to Warsaw, and on August 20 Roosevelt and Churchill sent a joint appeal, but no aid was forthcoming. On August 16, Moscow informed the U.S. Ambassador that "the Soviet Government do not wish to associate themselves either directly or indirectly with the adventure in Warsaw." [21]

The episode aroused bitter controversy. The Russians contended that heavy German counterattacks not only halted their advance but forced a retreat, and they were powerless to go to the Poles' assistance.[22] The Poles interpreted the Russian halt as intentional, a move to destroy the vestiges of an independent Poland and establish the Lublin Committee as the Polish government. Many Americans and British agreed. The political differences between Russia and the Western Allies, submerged during a brief period of military interdependence, became more marked. Warsaw was a turning point for the Allied coalition. The British in particular became more suspicious of Stalin's ambitions in eastern Europe and the Balkans; [23] Roosevelt continued to feel the only chance for a peaceful post-war Europe was to have a cooperative Russia as a leading force in the United Nations.

[21] Churchill, *Triumph and Tragedy*, p. 133. See also Feis, *Churchill, Roosevelt, Stalin*, pp. 378–90. For Polish position see Mikolajczyk, *The Rape of Poland*.
[22] See excerpts from the official Russian history quoted in Werth, *Russia at War*, Part VII, Chapter 8.
[23] Ehrman, *Grand Strategy*, Vol. V, pp. 367–76.

Drive to Germany

IN THE last half of 1944, the ring around Germany tightened. The Western Allies made a second landing in the south of France; the Russians drove through the Balkans; Alexander's forces in Italy pressed northward toward the Po valley; the Normandy forces broke out of their beachhead and drove for the Rhine.

Breakout

During July the Western Allies continued their frustrating battle among the hedgerows and orchards of Normandy. The British Second Army captured Caen on July 10, but a breakout did not follow. The American First Army took Saint-Lô on July 18, but the two-week battle cost 11,000 casualties.[1] All along the line the German defense was stubborn, Allied progress slow and costly. To make a breakout possible, General Omar Bradley proposed that the heavy bombers of

[1] Pogue, *The Supreme Command*, p. 193. See Johns, *The Clay Pigeons of St. Lô*.

the strategic air forces neutralize a portion of the German defenses just south of Saint-Lô. At Cassino and Caen heavy bombers had sought to clear the way for ground troops, but their success was limited. Profiting from these lessons, Bradley proposed to hold the infantry close enough to the target area that the ground assault could immediately follow the bombardment. Dropping small bombs would reduce the cratering that impeded advance. The air forces would saturate a carpet of roughly six square miles. As the bombers withdrew, three divisions of infantry, from General Collin's VII Corps, would advance through the carpet to seize the small towns of Marigny and Saint Gilles, holding open a corridor some three miles wide. While the tactical air forces kept the battle area isolated, one motorized infantry and two armored divisions would pour through the gap to drive west and encircle those Germans north of Coutances.

Bad weather delayed the attempt, and on July 24 the bombers started but had to turn back. A few planes did not get word the mission was canceled and dropped their bombs. Some fell among the waiting infantry, killing 25 and wounding 131. Bradley was shocked. After taking precautionary measures to prevent a recurrence of the short bombing, the commanders reset the attack for the next day. On July 25 more than 2400 Allied planes dropped more than four thousand tons of bombs on the carpet south of Saint-Lô. Dust and smoke obscured the landmarks and again American bombs fell on American troops. More than 100 were killed, nearly 500 wounded.[2] Despite shock, anger, and dismay over the bombing errors, the infantry advanced, and although the area was badly battered the men found opposition. The bulk of the air attack had fallen on the German Panzer Lehr Division, and though it had sustained as many as a thousand casualties and had lost most of its tanks and vehicles, survivors fought. Although the advance units did not reach their objectives, Collins ordered the armored thrusts to begin on schedule the morning of July 26. The German situation was much worse than it appeared. On the night of July 25, von Kluge reported that "the front has burst."[3] By night of the 27th the Americans held the key

[2] Blumenson, *Breakout and Pursuit*, pp. 222, 229, 234, 236; Craven and Cate, *The Army Air Forces in World War II*, Vol. III, pp. 228–38.
[3] Blumenson, *Breakout and Pursuit*, p. 240.

bridges and roads, and the Allied front broke into frenzied motion to exploit the opening wedge. While VII Corps exploited the break-through, the American VIII, XIX, and V Corps pushed against the disintegrating German lines. The British joined with an attack south of Caumont.

General Bradley and Major General Elwood Quesada of the IX Tactical Air Command, who was convinced that air power could play an important part in tactical support of ground operations, had worked out a system of ground-air cooperation whereby the planes acted as guides and scouts for the tanks, apprising them of enemy strongpoints and knocking out enemy positions ahead of the armored columns. Planes and tanks, in constant communication by radio, made an extremely effective team, and it was these armored columns with air cover that spearheaded the breakout. By August 1 the Americans had reached the base of the Cotentin peninsula at Avranches, and General George Patton and his newly activated Third Army burst through the Avranches gap, out of the Cotentin into Brittany. Patton's flamboyant armored drive in Sicily had demon-strated his talent for leading mobile, armored warfare, and Eisen-hower had accordingly given Patton the task he was most suited to perform.

Patton visualized the Brittany operation as a broad and rapid sweep to the objective—the Brittany ports. He employed two ar-mored divisions. Patton instructed Major General R. W. Grow (com-mander of the 6th Armored Division) simply to "take Brest," [4] and gave him five days in which to do it. The 6th Armored set off, its goal 200 miles away, its orders simple, its communications with rear headquarters dubious at best, and a road map of Brittany its guide. The French kept it informed of the location of German concentra-tions, which Grow skirted and left in the rear. To Grow's south Major General John S. Wood and his 4th Armored Division swept across Brittany to bring Saint-Nazaire and Lorient under siege. Although the 6th Armored reached Brest by August 6, the Germans intended to hold the Brittany ports, and the German defenses at Brest required a costly siege that did not end until September 19. The German garri-sons holed up at Lorient and Saint Nazaire were merely contained;

[4] *Ibid.*, p. 370.

they held out until the end of the war. The garrison at Saint-Malo was reduced after bitter fighting, but the Brittany ports, thought to be essential for supplying the armies, lost their importance as the battle to the east developed more rapidly than expected. During the week that Patton cleared Brittany, the battle around Avranches took a dramatic turn.

The Falaise Pocket

On August 1, when Third Army became operational, Bradley took command of the U.S. 12th Army Group, and Lieutenant General Courtney H. Hodges replaced Bradley at the head of First Army. Montgomery's 21st Army Group now controlled both the Second Army (Lieutenant General Miles Dempsey) and the First Canadian Army (Lieutenant General Sir Henry Crerar). The U.S. Ninth and the British Second Tactical Air Forces had almost completed their move to the continent, and the sizable Allied force was ready to move.

When Patton's VIII Corps began its advance into Brittany, the other corps of Patton's Third Army were ordered to protect its flank and enlarge the Avranches gap toward Fougeres and Mayenne. (See map, page 243.) Meanwhile, Hodges's First Army attacked toward Vire and Mortain, while the British and Canadians advanced on Mount Pinçon and Falaise. All forces except Third Army continued to meet stubborn, well-organized resistance, but Third Army's progress was rapid and the opposition negligible. Exploiting the situation, Dempsey, Crerar, and Hodges continued to exert pressure from the north and west while Patton swung the Third Army around the Germans' exposed left flank to swoop through Angers on the Loire with XX Corps, Laval and Le Mans with XV Corps. Patton wanted to thrust north to encircle the German armies, and on August 7 the Germans practically invited him to do so by launching a counterattack against the First Army at Mortain.

The German counterattack was Hitler's idea. In failing health, suspicious and mistrustful, convinced that he only had the will and the ability to direct the war, he insisted on making all decisions himself. He ordered von Kluge to attack from the Vire-Mortain area to Avranches, split the First and Third Armies, and restore the conditions for static warfare. With little hope of success, the German commanders ordered an attack at Mortain the night of August 7.

The U.S. 30th Division caught the main force of the German attack, but after yielding Mortain and small areas to its north and south, the Americans held. As more and more of the Germans were drawn into the Mortain battle, both Bradley and Montgomery intensified the attacks on the German flanks. Von Kluge sensed encirclement, but Hitler refused to divert forces from the Mortain battle to stop the flank penetrations. The First Canadian Army on the north and the Third Army on the south came daily closer to the road junctions at Argentan and Falaise. If they could meet, and if Third Army's long left flank could hold, the German Seventh and Fifth Panzer Armies would be trapped.

Von Kluge was helpless. By August 13 the gap between Americans and Canadians was only twenty miles wide. Patton reached Argentan and was eager to push on to Falaise to meet the Canadians, but Bradley ordered him to stop at Argentan. This decision caused controversy later on, for the Canadians did not take Falaise until August 16 and the Argentan-Falaise gap was never completely closed. Bradley ordered Patton to halt because his flanks were exposed, thinly held, and might not safely be stretched further; the Argentan-Falaise area was within 21st Army Group's sector of operations, and Montgomery, the ground forces commander, did not change it; and the confusion resulting from an American advance beyond Argentan might inadvertently bring Americans and Canadians into a head-on clash.[5]

For von Kluge, the slight gap between Argentan and Falaise was scant comfort, and on August 15 he went to the front to confer with his field commanders. The Germans were under constant air and artillery bombardment, communications were almost non-existent, coordinated action was impossible, and supply through the gap had almost ceased. Hitler, perhaps suspecting that von Kluge had been trying to parley with the Allies, ordered Model to the Western Front. Model took command August 18, and von Kluge, after writing his

[5] *Ibid.*, pp. 506–9; Bradley, *A Soldier's Story*, pp. 376–77.

Fuehrer urging him to end the war, swallowed potassium cyanide and died.

Model tried to salvage what he could from the shrinking Falaise pocket. Hitler finally sanctioned withdrawal, but further to the east the Allies were drawing a wider circle around the eastern end of the pocket at Trun and Chambois, and Patton's Third Army was streaking east to close off escape routes over the Seine. The night of August 19 the Germans began pouring through the gaps in the Trun-Chambois line. The next day rain kept the Allied air forces grounded, and the Allied units in the Trun-Chambois area became little islands of resistance trying to stop the escaping Germans. Before the line was closed an unknown number of Germans escaped (estimated between 20,000 and 40,000), but they left behind an estimated 50,000 comrades who became prisoners of war and approximately 10,000 dead on the battlefields of Falaise.[6]

Falaise was the beginning of an Allied flood that by the end of August covered France north of the Loire and west of the Seine. Part of Patton's Third Army drove south and east to seize bridgeheads over the Seine, north and south of Paris, while other elements wheeled north along the west bank of the Seine to ensnare the Germans escaping from the Falaise pocket. On August 20 Model combined the remnants of the Seventh and Fifth Panzer Armies under General Sepp Dietrich's command and ordered him to hold west of the Seine. Caught between Dempsey and Crerar on the west, Hodges and Patton to the south and pressing him toward the coast, Dietrich had to pull back over the Seine. Many of his men escaped on rafts and barges, but they saved almost none of their equipment.

On August 25 Paris was liberated. It had not been planned. In fact, it had been planned not to happen. Partly because of the complicated political situation,[7] partly because of the possible destruction to the city if the Germans chose to defend it, partly because the operation would consume precious supplies better used in the advance to the east, SHAEF planners had intended to by-pass the capital and wait for its garrison to surrender. But they reckoned without the French

---

[6] Blumenson, *Breakout and Pursuit*, pp. 555–58.

[7] Shortly before OVERLORD, de Gaulle proclaimed his National Committee of Liberation to be the provisional government of the French Republic. It the Allies entered Paris, de Gaulle's government would follow. See *ibid.*, for liberation of Paris.

partisans. The Free Forces of the Interior rose against their German occupiers and began fighting to free their capital. They could not do it alone, and General Jacques Philippe Leclerc's 2nd Armored Division was sent to their assistance. American units helped, and on the morning of August 25 Allied soldiers met on the Champs Elysées amid the fervent rejoicing of the population. The Germans surrendered, and de Gaulle returned to Paris.

Pursuit

During August the Allied High Command decided to press on across the Seine to Germany. Original plans had called for a halt at the Seine to consolidate and build up a sound supply base, but the Germans were disorganized, in retreat, and had no prepared defenses west of the German border. Logistical requirements might necessitate a halt, but if the Allied armies could push through the Siegfried Line (West Wall) and establish footholds across the Rhine River before the Germans had time to recover, the campaign would be greatly accelerated.

The end of August and the first two weeks of September saw four Allied armies racing east to liberate France, most of Belgium and Luxembourg, and part of Holland. Everywhere the advancing Allies were met with an exuberant welcome. The freed citizens assisted their liberators by seizing bridges, rounding up straggling parties of Germans, and affording whatever help was in their power. Crerar's First Canadian Army cleaned up the coast; they opened its ports to the Allies and captured the V-weapons's sites along the Pas de Calais. The German Fifteenth Army was forced to retreat. Dempsey's Second Army liberated Brussels September 3 and the next day secured Antwerp with its harbor facilities intact. Hodges's First Army plunged across southern Belgium, pocketing a sizable number of German prisoners at Mons and sweeping on through Liége to seize a foothold over the German border. Patton's Third Army drove through Reims and across the Meuse to threaten Metz, Nancy, and the Moselle River Line. Third Army was stretched out across the entire east-west width of France, and although the German forces on its south were not threatening, Third Army exposed a long flank. Patton gave the job of protecting it to the XIX Tactical Air Command, under Brigadier General O. P. Weyland. XIX Tactical was so aggressive that it received the surrender of some 20,000 Germans who did not even come in contact with Third Army ground forces at all.[8]

Getting supplies to the continent was becoming a serious problem. Cherbourg was not ready for use until mid-July, so most Allied supplies continued to come in over the Normandy beaches. Food, medicine, clothing, spare parts and replacements for vehicles and weapons, ammunition, fuel, sometimes even drinking water had to be transported from supply depots to the men in the field. After the liberation of Paris, a tremendous supply effort was required to feed the civilians. Highways were made one-way, and traffic moved practically bumper to bumper twenty-four hours a day, but as the Allies advanced, the distance between depot and army increased, and more fuel was consumed enroute. Fuel was the most critical item. During the week of August 20 the U.S. First and Third Armies, both on the move, had a daily consumption of more than 800,000 gallons.[9] Although PLUTO was operating by mid-August, pipelines could not be laid fast enough to keep up with the advancing armies.

More controversial than the supply situation was the strategy involved in the movement of the armies. Eisenhower's directive from the Combined Chiefs of Staff left him broad discretion in determining how the defeat of Germany was to be accomplished. After the breakout SHAEF set the Ruhr, the heart of Germany's iron and steel industry that lay along the Rhine north of Cologne, as the next goal. SHAEF recommended approaching it by a dual thrust through Liége on the north and Metz on the south. Although the Allied forces would be split, the Germans would also be forced to divide their strength. The southern thrust would threaten the Saar basin, another industrial area, but the northern thrust would be the main effort. The orientation of the armies made it logical for Montgomery's 21st Army Group to take the northern route and Patton's Third Army the southern. Hodges's First Army (and later Simpson's Ninth), in between, was to throw the bulk of its weight north of the Ardennes Forest area, but also advance south of the forest in support

[8] Sunderman, *World War II in the Air: Europe,* p. 254.
[9] Blumenson, *Breakout and Pursuit,* p. 691.

of Patton. The Allied armies would thus close the Rhine on a broad front, from the Netherlands to Switzerland.

Montgomery disagreed with the broad-front strategy and urged that the entire Allied strength go to the northern route.[10] The broad-front strategy ruled, but neither Patton nor Montgomery was completely satisfied. Each felt that with sufficient logistical support, he could achieve a significant victory and bring the war to a speedy end.

By mid-September the Allied armies were on the German frontier, eight months ahead of their anticipated advance, but they were running out of supplies and the German resistance had stiffened. Von Rundstedt was reinstated as Commander-in-Chief, West, on September 6, though Model retained command of Army Group B. Even though the Germans had lost at least 1,200,000 men since June,[11] (mostly on the Russian front, but some 500,000 in the west), von Rundstedt's return to command improved German morale, and as the German divisions retreated, their remnants rallied and turned to fight. The Allies had one more chance to outflank the Siegfried Line before a halt. It failed, but in imaginative daring it was one of the outstanding operations of the war.

MARKET-GARDEN

On September 8 the first V-2's, the second of Hitler's miracle weapons, began to fall on London from launching sites in western Holland. The V-2 was a gyroscopically stabilized rocket, finned, 46 feet long, carrying 1650 pounds of explosives, and moving at the speed of sound.[12] Its approach was unseen and unheard. The British had no defense against it. The V-2 attacks would not end until the launching sites were overrun in March 1945.

In September Montgomery proposed that the newly organized First Allied Airborne Army, under Lieutenant General Lewis H. Brereton, be dropped along a corridor into the Netherlands to seize key bridges over the Meuse and Rhine and hold them for the advance of the British Second Army. If successful, the operation would put the

[10] See Ehrman, *Grand Strategy*, Vols. V and VI; Pogue, *The Supreme Command*.
[11] Blumenson, *Breakout and Pursuit*, pp. 669–70.
[12] Collier, *The Battle of the V-weapons*, pp. 180–81; Collier, *The Defense of the United Kingdom*, pp. 406–21, 527.

British over the Rhine and in position to drive on the Ruhr, as well as cut off the German Fifteenth Army in western Holland. The operation was scheduled for September 17. It was composed of two parts.[13] Operation MARKET called for the U.S. 101st Airborne Division to seize numerous bridges and hold open the highway around Eindhoven; the U.S. 82nd Airborne Division was to seize Grave and Nijmegen. The British 1st Airborne Division, landing deepest within enemy territory, was to seize and hold the bridges over the lower

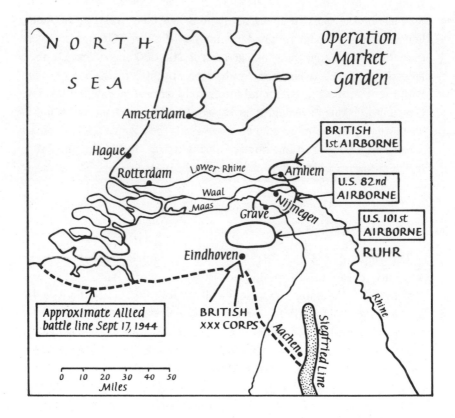

---

[13] MacDonald, *The Siegfried Line Campaign*, Chapters 6–8; Gavin, *Airborne Warfare*, pp. 90–121; Wilmot, *The Struggle for Europe*, Chapters 25–27.

Rhine at Arnhem. The complementary operation, code-named GAR-DEN, called for the XXX Corps of the British Second Army to drive through the corridor seized by the airmen and press on to the Zuider Zee. Because of the numerous waterways and soft lowland areas, the soldiers must advance along a single road for a distance of some sixty miles.

The initial phase of MARKET-GARDEN, the largest airborne operation yet conducted, went beautifully. Elements of the three divisions were dropped on target and with negligible losses. Some objectives were seized immediately, and XXX Corps began driving toward Eindhoven. Thereafter each day brought increasing difficulty. Vigorous German opposition and congestion on the highway forced XXX Corps to move more slowly than planned. Bad weather delayed the build-up and resupply of the airborne forces. Although one battalion fought its way to the northern end of the Arnhem bridge, other units failed to join it, reinforcements did not arrive in time, and German opposition was heavier than expected. The 1st Airborne could not take the Arnhem bridges, and XXX Corps could not seize a bridgehead over the Rhine. The night of September 25 the ultimate objectives of MARKET-GARDEN were abandoned and the remnants of the 1st Airborne were withdrawn from the north bank of the Rhine.

Winter Frustration

After MARKET-GARDEN, the Allied forces had to consolidate their gains and build up their supply base before making another major attempt to drive into Germany. Montgomery had to clear the Schelde estuary and Walcheran and South Beveland Islands so that Antwerp could be opened to Allied supply ships. On Montgomery's right, Bradley was directed to push the First and Ninth Armies toward Aachen and Cologne, while on the far right, supplies permitting, Allied forces would move forward to threaten the Saar and upper Rhine.

Without exception the winter battles were hard fought and brought slow gain.[14] The First Canadian Army, fighting on Walcheran and Beveland Islands, faced formidable terrain and a strong defense that succeeded in denying the Allies the use of Antwerp until the end of November. The Eindhoven-Nijmegen salient was enlarged and the Netherlands were cleared west and south of the Maas (Meuse) River. The U.S. First Army, despite heavy support from the air forces, made slow gain in the Aachen sector, where the Siegfried Line defenses were strong. Though Aachen itself was in American hands by October 21, the advance continued to be laborious. Unusually bad weather hampered air and armored support, and the burden of battle fell on the wet and cold infantry. In mid-November the offensive was renewed, for the steady attrition would weaken the German capacity to withstand a major breakthrough, and by exploiting local weaknesses, bridgeheads valuable for future operations might be seized. While the First and Ninth Armies fought through the Huertgen Forest and moved up to the Roer River defenses, on the far right of the front Allied forces fought to the upper Rhine and began battering on the Siegfried Line denying them access to the Saar basin. Allied commanders meanwhile worked on plans for a decisive offensive into Germany to begin early in 1945. No one anticipated that the battered German armies could prevent its opening on schedule.

ANVIL-DRAGOON

Ten weeks after D-day in Normandy, on August 15, 1944, United States and French troops landed on the south coast of France between Cannes and Toulon in one of the most beautifully executed amphibious assaults of the war.[15] Its success was spectacular, its cost was slight. Vice Admiral Kent Hewitt's Western Task Force transported Lietuenant General Alexander Patch's Seventh Army, composed of Lieutenant General Lucian Truscott's VI Corps (the assault troops) and General Jean de Lattre de Tassigny's French II Corps. Hewitt's task force laid on an intensive bombardment, supplemented by air strikes from both the XII Tactical Air Command and the strategic bombers of the Fifteenth Air Force. Airborne troops and

[14] See MacDonald, *The Siegfried Line Campaign;* Cole, *The Lorainne Campaign.*
[15] Morison, *The Invasion of France and Germany*, p. 221. See also Pogue, *The Supreme Command.*

Commandos captured key inland areas, and the soldiers swarmed ashore against light opposition. While the French liberated Toulon and Marseilles, the Americans spread up the Rhone valley.

In southern France the German General Johannes Blaskowitz had Army Group G, eleven divisions. He was ordered to leave units to defend the ports and retire with the main forces toward the Vosges mountains. The French overcame German resistance in Toulon and Marseilles on August 28, and by the first week of September, Allied supplies were entering France through the two ports. On September 11 advance patrols of Truscott's VI Corps linked up with patrols of Patton's Third Army, and on September 15, one month from the landings, ANVIL-DRAGOON was over. Patch's Seventh and Tassigny's First French Armies became Lieutenant General Jacob L. Dever's 6th Army Group, which came under Eisenhower's command and took over on the far right of the Allied front.

The success of ANVIL-DRAGOON has been eclipsed by controversy about its political and military goals.[16] Landings in the south of France, code-named ANVIL, were planned during 1943. ANVIL would tie down the Germans, protect the southern flank of the OVERLORD forces, and open the ports of southern France as additional sources of supply. ANVIL was originally planned to coincide with OVERLORD, but when SHAEF enlarged the latter operation, ANVIL was postponed. But opinion was divided about ANVIL. The British felt the effort could more profitably be made elsewhere, and at Teheran, in November 1943, Churchill proposed making the southern drive through the Aegean Sea and the Balkans. Stalin urged the execution of ANVIL as planned, and Churchill reluctantly concurred. When operations at Anzio proved more costly than expected, Churchill and General Wilson, Supreme Commander in the Mediterranean, proposed that ANVIL be scrapped, since landing craft in particular were needed for the Italian campaign.

Monte Cassino fell in May; Rome fell on June 4; the Italian situation ceased to be critical. American planners, who had been unenthusiastic about the Italian campaign, continued to favor ANVIL

[16] Greenfield, *Command Decisions*, Chapter 13; Churchill, *Triumph and Tragedy*, pp. 57–71. Wilmot, *The Struggle for Europe*, Chapter 23, is critical of U.S. decisions. Eisenhower, *Crusade in Europe*, pp. 281–84, present Eisenhower's views. Clark, *Calculated Risk*, pp. 348–51, argues against ANVIL.

rather than a vigorous pursuit in Italy. Churchill was opposed, and when the Combined Chiefs of Staff met in June he and General Wilson argued to use Mediterranean strength to push the Germans out of Italy, proceed through the Ljubljana gap, link up with the Yugoslav partisans, and drive on to the Hungarian plain. The war might be ended at Budapest or Vienna, and the Italian thrust would support OVERLORD as much as would ANVIL. The Americans were unmoved, and the June conference ended in indecision. Finally, when Roosevelt declared that he could not agree to employ U.S. forces in the Balkans, Churchill gave tentative agreement to ANVIL. At this point the code-name was changed to DRAGOON, reportedly because Churchill had been "dragooned" into it.

Although purely political reasons for the thrust through Italy and the Balkans were not advanced, it is the political issue that makes the ANVIL controversy remain alive. Shortly after the Germans occupied the Balkans, partisan bands were organized to disrupt the German rear areas and tie down occupation troops that Germany might otherwise have employed for offensive action. Much of the partisan movement was closely controlled by the Communist Party with the aim of insuring a Communist-dominated government in territory the Russians might liberate from the Germans.[17] Had the Western Allies moved into the Balkans before the Russians did, the post-war control of those countries might have been different. The Balkans were liberated by the Russians during the last half of 1944; Nazi authority was replaced by Soviet authority. Later, the Iron Curtain dropped in front of Rumania, Bulgaria, Hungary, and Yugoslavia.

Russian Drive through the Balkans

On August 20 the Eastern Front broke into activity, this time at the southern end of the long Soviet-German line. The armies of Malinovsky and Tolbukhin struck at Rumania, where Germany's Army Group South Ukraine could muster only two German and two Rumanian armies. The rest had been sent north to strengthen the Warsaw front. The initial Russian blows, carefully planned and pre-

[17] See Dixon and Heilbrunn, *Communist Guerilla Warfare.*

pared, fell against the Rumanian Armies and met almost no resistance. The Rumanians had long since had their fill of the war and were seeking the best way out. The German Sixth Army was surrounded within 48 hours, the bulk of its 15 divisions lost. As the Russians swept on toward Bucharest, Rumania's King Michael, who had been in touch with the Allies for some months,[18] interned Antonescu, tool of the Nazi alliance, and appointed General Sanatescu to head the government. King Michael and Sanatescu accepted a Russian armistice which called for breaking with Germany, for Rumanian armed forces to turn on Germany, and for restoration of the 1940 Soviet-Rumanian border. Russia agreed to the return to Rumania of that part of the country Hitler had given Hungary in 1940. The Germans bombed and shelled Bucharest, but the Russian forces relieved the capital on August 31.

The Russian avalanche moved from Rumania into Bulgaria early in September. Though Bulgaria had never declared war on the Soviet Union, her proclamations of neutrality were not trusted. When Soviet troops moved into Bulgaria, the government requested an armistice (granted September 9), and declared war on Germany.

The Russians then advanced into Yugoslavia, where the partisan movement, led by a young Communist named Tito, was especially active. The Russian armies joined forces with Tito's partisans and after entering Belgrade on October 20, wheeled north toward Hungary. Hitler was furious at his erstwhile allies, and made frantic efforts to pull his forces out of Crete, Greece, and Yugoslavia to hold a firm line in Hungary. Although the first Soviet troops reached Budapest's defenses early in November, not until December 27 was the city surrounded. Two days later a Soviet-sponsored provisional Hungarian government declared war on Germany. The fighting around Budapest was so heavy that the city was not in Russian hands until February 13, 1945.

Germany's satellite armies, the oil of Ploesti, the grain of the Rumanian plains, metallic ores and other raw materials of the Balkans—all were gone. Even Finland was no longer Germany's reluctant ally. During June the Russians had pushed their Finnish border back to its post-Winter War boundaries, and the Finns had requested

18 Feis, *Churchill, Roosevelt, Stalin*, pp. 218, 336.

an armistice. It was signed in September.

The rapid liberation of the Balkans persuaded Churchill to fly to Moscow in October to confer with Stalin. At Dumbarton Oaks the post-war peace organization, the United Nations, was beginning to take shape, but its prospects would be slim indeed if such matters as the future government of Poland and the political alignment of the Balkans tore the United Nations apart before the war was over. Although Churchill and Stalin made little progress in settling Polish affairs, a short-term agreement was reached for the Balkans. Russia was to have final say about Rumania. Greece was placed under British influence during the coming months of liberation and transition. In Hungary, Bulgaria, and Yugoslavia, Russia and the Western Allies would share responsibility and authority.[19]

Subsequent British action in Greece was firm. Rival bands of Greek partisans, experienced in guerrilla warfare, were prepared to contest for power, and when the Germans pulled out the British sent troops into Athens to keep order until the Greek government and army could return to its homeland. The Communist-led partisans resisted, and street fighting erupted in Athens during December. On Christmas Day Churchill flew to the Greek capital to arrange a compromise government that would bring the rival Greek factions together and tide Greece through a difficult transition.

The Italian Campaign, June–December, 1944

After the fall of Rome in June 1944, seven divisions were withdrawn from Clark's Fifth Army to conduct ANVIL. Reorganizing the front so that the Eighth Army was responsible for a larger portion, Alexander directed his depleted forces northward. German policy was to delay their advance, while working diligently to complete the next major defensive position, the Gothic Line. Utilizing the natural features of the high northern Apennines, the Germans turned the area into a bastion of military strength, using concrete and steel, mines,

---

[19] Churchill, *Triumph and Tragedy*, pp. 206–21, 226–43; Feis, *Churchill, Roosevelt, Stalin*, pp. 441–53. For British decisions regarding Greece, see Churchill, *Triumph and Tragedy*, pp. 283–325; Ehrman, *Grand Strategy*, Vol. VI, pp. 57–64.

guns, and booby traps. To defend his position, Kesselring had 22 divisions, divided between the Fourteenth and Tenth Armies.[20] Although under strength, they occupied a formidable position, and despite the efforts of the Allied air forces to interdict the area, the German supply routes through the Brenner Pass continued to function.

The Battle of the Gothic Line began late in August and progress was good. The main effort was made on the Adriatic coast by the Eighth Army. When their assault got underway Kesselring pulled some of his strength away from the center of the line to halt it. The Fifth Army began to follow up and exploit the enemy's withdrawals. Although the offensive was marked by fighting all along the wide front, the main points of effort were by Eighth Army on the coast and units of Fifth Army at Il Giogo Pass. By the end of September the Gothic Line had crumbled, the victim of a beautifully executed offensive characterized by good concentration of strength, surprise, timing, and coordination.

Breaking the Gothic Line put the Allies on the threshold of victory, since just beyond lay the Po valley. There was terrain where armor could play a decisive role, and where roads were adequate to maintain the supply of an army. While the main defensive line guarding the valley had been broken, 15 to 20 miles of mountains still separated the Allies from the valley. The troops were tired and the divisions under strength, but reinforcements were not available because the main Allied effort was striving to close the Rhine River. Supply lines were long and the mountain roads poor. Just as had happened south of the Gustav Line the year before, the fall rains began and winter showed signs of coming early. Despite the handicaps, the two Allied armies made a final and desperate attempt to clear the mountains before winter set in. Advances were made, but by the end of October the men had to take up defensive positions for another long, cold winter at the front, although the Po valley was in sight of some of the forward units. Not until April 1945 would the 15th Army Group break into the Po valley to rout the Germans out of Italy.

[20] Jackson, *Italy*, p. 341, Appendix F. Kesselring had 4 other divisions in the Adriatic area. 15th Army Group could muster 20 divisions.

Command changes in December sent Wilson to Washington, and Alexander, promoted to Field Marshal, became Supreme Commander, Mediterranean Theater. General Clark replaced Alexander as head of the 15th Army Group, the most heterogeneous of the Allied Army Groups. Under its command fought contingents of 26 nationalities.[21]

The Battle of the Bulge

Hitler decided that the German Army would end the year 1944, a year of unbroken reversals, with a dramatic offensive in the west, and on December 16 three German armies (20 divisions with 5 more in reserve) began assaulting the American lines on a 70-mile front in the Ardennes between Monschau and Echternach.[22] On the north, SS General Sepp Dietrich's Sixth Panzer Army hoped to break through

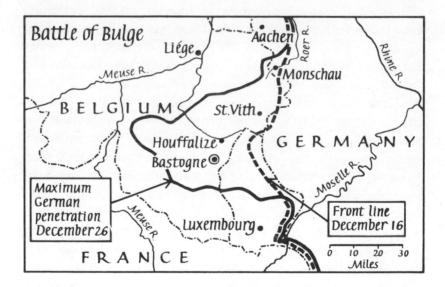

---

[21] See Alexander's *Memoirs,* p. 155.
[22] See Cole, *The Ardennes: Battle of the Bulge;* Marshall, *Bastogne, The First Eight Days.*

the Allied lines, cross the Meuse River between Liège and Huy, and drive on to Antwerp. To its south, General Hasso von Manteuffel's Fifth Panzer Army struck through the middle of the Ardennes toward Saint-Vith and Bastogne, intending to sweep on across the Meuse and drive to Antwerp on Dietrich's left flank. On the far south, General Erich Brandenberger's Seventh Army was to protect the southern flank of the German salient. Success would mean splitting the Allied forces, denying them the use of Antwerp for supply, and regaining German initiative in the west.

The German assault broke over General Hodges's First Army, which held a long portion of the front. To concentrate strength for offensive action in the Aachen-Roer River sector and in the Saar, the Ardennes area, less suited for military action, was held with a minimum of troops. The risk was acceptable because the Allies had overwhelming strength to both north and south, and the mobility to move quickly should a German threat materialize. A major threat to this area was considered unlikely,[23] and the strength of the December offensive was not immediately grasped. The battle began in confusion, since it was shrouded by dense cloud cover that kept Allied air power grounded for the first week. Allied communications were broken and decisions were made by divisions and smaller units more often than by higher headquarters.

Dietrich's Army, the spearhead of the assault, made slow gains against General Gerow's V Corps in the Elsenborn-Malmedy-Stavelot area. On the far south, Brandenberger also met a vicious reception, and to both northern and southern sides of the developing bulge Bradley sent armored divisions to strengthen the defense. The shoulders began to hold, but in the middle, von Manteuffel's Fifth Panzer Army made distressing progress against Major General Troy Middleton's thinly spread VIII Corps. As Middleton's divisions were surrounded or shattered, the battle in the middle Ardennes became a battle of small skirmishes. The "Bulge" gradually took shape. Strong resistance on the shoulders of the salient limited its width and denied Dietrich his planned route of advance to the northwest. Von Manteuffel's progress in the center was halted because in the initial

---

[23] Pogue, *The Supreme Command*, pp. 361–72; Baldwin, *Battles Lost and Won*, Chapter 10.

confusion American eyes had become riveted on Bastogne as a place that must be held.

The rugged terrain of the Ardennes made the roads essential, for without them the Germans could not sustain the momentum of their advance. On the southern side of the Bulge, seven major roads met at Bastogne. On December 19 the 101st Airborne Division, commanded by Brigadier General Anthony C. McAuliffe (General Taylor was on leave), arrived in Bastogne and proceeded to set up a defensive perimeter around it. Von Manteuffel's advance toward Bastogne was delayed by a series of small battles and roadblocks, and rather than take time to reduce them all, von Manteuffel by-passed Bastogne and directed his Fifth Army onward. By December 21 the Bastogne garrison was an island in a sea of Germans streaming west on both sides. Too late, von Manteuffel realized he must have the Bastogne road net to support his advance. He directed his Fifth Panzer Army to seize it, but by then the 101st, bolstered by an assortment of small units that had gathered from the east, was prepared to defend it, and General Patton's Third Army was moving north to Bastogne's relief.

By December 19 the shape of the German penetration was clear, and Eisenhower and his commanders conferred to plan countermeasures. The forces on the north of the salient [24] were hard pressed to contain the main German effort, but on the south Patton could disengage his Third Army in the Saar and counterattack toward Bastogne. By the morning of the 22nd one corps of Third Army began fighting north, but it was not just a matter of driving an armored column through to the besieged city. Rather, a corridor must be seized, which would be wide enough to reclaim and hold Bastogne within the Allied lines. Progress was slow and the 101st was running out of ammunition.

On the 23rd the weather cleared. Cargo planes dropped ammunition and supplies to Bastogne, fighters and fighter bombers began

[24] To simplify command, Eisenhower put Montgomery in command of all forces north of the German salient, Bradley in command to the south. Although a temporary arrangement and a practical one, it was extremely unpopular and raised a storm of protest and hard feelings. At a later press conference Montgomery tactlessly implied that the American Command had failed and the British had to step in to rescue it. The British press revived a demand for giving Montgomery command of all ground forces, and the American commanders were acutely resentful. See Eisenhower, *Crusade in Europe*, pp. 355–57; Wilmot, *The Struggle for Europe*, pp. 591, 610–11; Bradley, *A Soldier's Story*, pp. 476–78, 483–88.

working over the German columns crowding the roads, and the heavy bombers began striking further back at supply routes and rear areas. December 26 brought the crest of the German advance. The 4th Armored Division from Third Army drove through to Bastogne, while to the northwest the 2nd Armored Division, part of General Collins's VII Corps, cut off and destroyed the point of the German armored spearhead. The Bulge had attained a maximum depth of sixty airline miles; it never reached the Meuse. Casualties on both sides were high—an estimated 77,000 for the Allies and more than 100,000 for the Germans.[25] Losses in materiel were also high, but whereas the Allies could quickly make them good, Germany could not. The Western Allies' offensive into Germany was delayed, for it took most of January 1945 to eliminate the Bulge and resume the effort to close to the Rhine River. By that time the Russian offensive in the east was steamrolling toward Berlin, and the reserves with which the Germans might have stopped it had been chewed to bits in the Ardennes.

[25] Estimates on German casualties run as high as 120,000, Shirer, *The Rise and Fall of the Third Reich*, p. 1095. See Cole, *The Ardennes: Battle of the Bulge*, p. 674; Pogue, *The Supreme Command*, p. 396.

Return to the Philippines

I F T H E last half of 1944 was a decisive and dramatic period in the European war, it was no less so in the Pacific. By the time the Battle of the Bulge was over and Allied forces were preparing for their final drive into Germany, the Philippines were partially reclaimed and the war against Japan had moved into its final phase.

Leyte Preliminaries

When Guam was captured on August 10, the Marianas campaign was over. The strategic decision—which land mass should be used to launch the final assault on Japan—had yet to be made. Possibilities were Formosa, China, or Luzon.[1] Neither the Joint Chiefs of Staff nor the various commanders were in agreement as to the best course. China posed logistical difficulties, and Formosa lacked adequate an-

[1] See Greenfield, *Command Decisions,* Chapter 18; Matloff, *Strategic Planning for Coalition Warfare, 1943–1944,* Chapter 21.

chorages and port facilities. That left the Philippines, which MacArthur had urged from the beginning, and on September 13 Admiral Halsey backed him up.

Halsey and the Third Fleet [2] appeared in the Pacific in mid-summer. In support of the Morotai and Peleliu landings, scheduled for September 15, Halsey had been striking Japanese air bases in the vicinity, and with the cooperation of the air forces, had thoroughly bombed the Japanese air bases. Raids on Mindanao and Leyte drew so little resistance that Halsey concluded those islands might be lightly held. Why not cancel all scheduled operations, including Mindanao, and give MacArthur the combined resources of both the Central and Southwest Pacific to hurl into Leyte at once? Although Leyte was out of range of land-based planes, Halsey could cover it with his carriers until airfields were established ashore. MacArthur agreed, and within hours the decision had been approved by the Joint Chiefs of Staff. MacArthur would return to the Philippines as he had promised, and the biggest leap-frogging maneuver of the Pacific war would take place October 20. Leyte would be followed by Luzon in December, Iwo Jima and Okinawa in January and March 1945.

By September MacArthur's forces had completed the New Guinea campaign. From Biak and other islands in Geelvink bay, they had jumped to Noemfoor (July 2) and on to the Mar-Sansapor area of the Vogelkop (July 30). Both operations met negligible opposition, and now Allied air bases surrounded and neutralized the remaining Japanese in New Guinea.[3] MacArthur turned north, and he and Halsey planned a series of operations as preliminaries to Mindanao. Although some of them could now be canceled, three were not. Morotai was needed as an advance air-base site for staging planes into the Philippines. Peleliu had one of several Japanese airfields in the southern Palaus that posed a threat to the flank of the forces that would move into the Philippines, and Ulithi, in the Carolines, was needed as an advance fleet anchorage.

[2] The U.S. had only one Fleet in the Central Pacific. When Halsey was in command, it was called the Third Fleet; when Spruance was in command, the Fifth. Rotating commands and staffs made for greater efficiency. The Seventh Fleet, sometimes called "MacArthur's Navy," was designed to transport and protect MacArthur's forces. It had no carriers.

[3] See Smith, *Approach to the Philippines*.

Morotai was lightly contested and Ulithi not at all.[4] At Peleliu, however, the battle began on September 15 and, because of a succession of misfortunes and difficulties, dragged on until the end of November. It was costly (almost 2000 American dead),[5] took months rather than days (as the commanding general predicted),[6] and might have been avoided (Halsey opposed the operation from the first, and with the benefit of hindsight others agreed).[7] The 1st Marine Division (Major General William H. Rupertus), which had borne the brunt of Guadalcanal and Cape Gloucester, was assigned to Peleliu. The main objective, the airfield, was secured within a week, and the assault phase was pronounced over on October 12, but ahead lay six weeks of some of the toughest fighting of the Pacific war.

Peleliu was made of coral and limestone formed into precipitous cliffs and contorted ridges. The island was full of underground rock faults that formed a labyrinth of caves.[8] The Japanese had enlarged and improved the caves, fissures, and faults, and they formed the basis of their defensive system. So far Japanese efforts to defeat amphibious landings on the beaches had met complete failure, and the desperate banzai attacks had merely hastened the end of resistance. On Peleliu they used different tactics. Colonel Kunio Nakagawa was in command. His aim was to delay the invaders as long as possible. No man or weapon was ever needlessly exposed. The caves, with multiple entrances and connecting passageways, were planned to be almost unassailable. The Americans could blast one cave entrance while the occupants merely scooted to safety through another exit on the other side of the ridge. The Americans were vulnerable, for the coral surface of Peleliu had so little topsoil the men could not dig foxholes for protection. As part of the southern Palaus campaign, the 81st Infantry Division secured the nearby island of Angaur between September 17 and 20, and then assisted the Marines on Peleliu. The island was gradually cleared, but the new Japanese tactics were a

---

[4] *Ibid.,* Chapter 20; Morison, *Leyte,* Chapters 2 and 3; Craven and Cate, *The Army Air Forces in World War II,* Vol. V, pp. 311–16.

[5] Hough, *The Assault on Peleliu,* p. 183; Smith, *Approach to the Philippines,* p. 573. Figures are for Peleliu plus Angaur, which was less costly.

[6] Hough, *The Assault on Peleliu,* p. 35.

[7] Halsey and Bryan, *Admiral Halsey's Story,* pp. 194–95.

[8] See Hough, *The Assault on Peleliu;* Smith, *Approach to the Philippines;* Morison. *Leyte.*

preview of Iwo Jima and Okinawa.

The operation on Peleliu marked the end of a phase of the Pacific war called "the approach to the Philippines." Halsey, MacArthur, and Nimitz had pushed American front lines from Pearl Harbor to Leyte Gulf, where, between October 23 and 25, the Third Fleet fought the second major naval battle of 1944, while American soldiers stormed the beaches of Leyte.

The Battle of Leyte Gulf

When General Krueger's Sixth Army began landing on Leyte on October 20, the Japanese responded by committing their Combined Fleet. If their plan, involving a series of naval actions over a wide expanse of ocean, failed, Japan stood to lose her entire fleet. Commander-in-Chief Toyoda felt the gamble had to be taken, for if the Philippines were lost, the fleet would be cut off from its fuel supplies and be useless.[9] His plan was for Admiral Kurita (Center Force) to debouch from San Bernadino Strait into Leyte Gulf and fall on the American transports. Admirals Shima and Nishimura (Southern Force) were to advance on Leyte Gulf through Surigao Strait on the south. A new weapon, the suicide plane, would neutralize the American escort carriers, while Admiral Ozawa's main carrier force, almost stripped of planes and consequently on a suicide mission, would lure Halsey's Third Fleet up north and out of the way.

American submarines located Kurita's Center Force and sank three heavy cruisers in the Palawan passage early on October 23.[10] When Kurita's force reached the Sibuyan Sea on October 24, it was met by Mitscher's pilots, who sank the battleship *Musashi,* damaged another cruiser, and inflicted minor damage on other ships. Kurita began to withdraw.

Meanwhile the Japanese Southern Force was spotted enroute to Surigao Strait. Vice Admiral T. C. Kincaid, Commander of the Seventh Fleet, ordered Rear Admiral Jesse B. Oldendorf and the Seventh Fleet's fire support ships to meet it. On October 25 Olden-

[9] USSBS, *Interrogations of Japanese Officials,* Vol. II, p. 317.
[10] See Morison, *Leyte.*

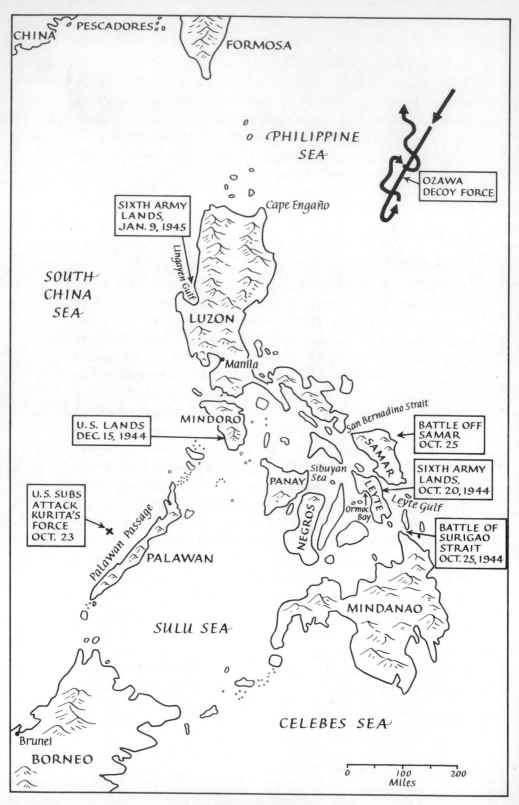

CHINA
PESCADORES
FORMOSA

PHILIPPINE
SEA

Cape Engaño

OZAWA
DECOY
FORCE

SIXTH ARMY
LANDS,
JAN. 9, 1945

Lingayen Gulf

SOUTH
CHINA
SEA

LUZON

Manila

U.S. LANDS
DEC. 15, 1944

MINDORO

San Bernadino Strait

BATTLE OFF
SAMAR
OCT. 25

SAMAR

U.S. SUBS
ATTACK
KURITA'S
FORCE
OCT. 23

Palawan Passage

PANAY

Sibuyan
Sea

LEYTE

SIXTH ARMY
LANDS,
OCT. 20, 1944

Leyte Gulf

Ormoc
Bay

NEGROS

BATTLE OF
SURIGAO
STRAIT
OCT. 25, 1944

PALAWAN

SULU SEA

MINDANAO

Brunei

BORNEO

CELEBES SEA

0   100   200
Miles

THE PHILIPPINES

dorf formed his cruisers, battleships, and supporting destroyers into battle line across the fifteen-mile expanse where Surigao Strait empties into Leyte Gulf and sent two divisions of destroyers into the Strait to deliver torpedo attacks. Although the destroyers crippled the Japanese ships, Admiral Nishimura steamed on toward Leyte Gulf, and his "T" was crossed by Oldendorf's battle line.[11] Nishimura escaped with only a cruiser and a destroyer. The second group of the Southern Force, under Admiral Shima, nosed into the battle area, but after assessing the situation, Shima decided to withdraw. The Battle of Surigao Strait, in which naval air power played no part, marked the end of an era of naval warfare as well as the end of the southern pincer on Leyte Gulf.

Admiral Halsey's orders read that if an opportunity arose, he was to annihilate the main Japanese Fleet, so after the Battle of the Sibuyan Sea, he hastened north to find Ozawa. Thinking the Center Force was no longer a threat, Halsey left not even a picket boat to guard San Bernadino Strait. However, at dawn on October 25, a group of Seventh Fleet's escort carriers came under attack by Kurita's Center Force. Escort carriers are not designed to fight; their protection is provided by other units of the fleet. Because of a misunderstanding, Admiral Kincaid thought the carriers were guarded by Admiral Lee and his battleships from Halsey's Third Fleet. The mistake resulted partly because two fleets were operating off Leyte— Kincaid's Seventh and Halsey's Third. Kincaid was responsible to MacArthur, Halsey to Nimitz. Kurita's force of 4 battleships, 6 heavy cruisers, and numerous destroyers took on Rear Admiral Clifton Sprague's group of 6 escort carriers and their destroyer escorts. Although it was a one-sided match, the American planes and destroyers sank 3 of Kurita's heavy cruisers and so badly disrupted his force that Kurita withdrew. American losses were serious (1 carrier, 2 destroyers, and 1 destroyer escort), but Kurita had failed to annihilate the Seventh Fleet, and to the north Halsey had Ozawa's force under attack.

Third Fleet pilots began striking Ozawa's force when it was about

---

[11] "Crossing the T" is standard battle line tactics. The enemy, steaming in single column, forms the stem of the "T." It is crossed by a line of ships steaming at right angles to the stem. All the broadsides of the crossing ships can be concentrated on the leading enemy ship, whereas only her forward guns can be brought to bear.

two hundred miles off Cape Engano on October 25. By mid-afternoon Third Fleet had flown 527 sorties and had sunk a destroyer and four carriers—one of the ships destroyed was *Zuikaku,* the last survivor of the Pearl Harbor raid. Halsey had hoped to send Admiral Lee's battle line against Ozawa's force after the planes had crippled it, but when Sprague's carriers came under attack, Kincaid appealed to Halsey for aid, and Halsey dispatched Admiral Lee and his battleships to Leyte Gulf. They arrived too late to catch the retiring Kurita, and off Cape Engano the remaining cruisers and destroyers proved insufficient to complete the annihilation of Ozawa's force. Although Ozawa escaped with the remnants of his fleet, the Battle of Cape Engano, as well as the other battles that comprised the Battle of Leyte Gulf, was a Japanese defeat. Japanese hopes now lay with the air and ground forces, and on October 21 General Tomoyuki Yamashita, charged with the defense of the Philippines, decided to make a major stand on Leyte.[12]

Struggle for Leyte

For the invasion of Leyte, the Allies amassed the greatest concentration of force yet seen in the Pacific. Admiral Kincaid's Seventh Fleet numbered more than 700 ships; Halsey's Third Fleet of 18 fleet carriers and supporting battleships, cruisers, and destroyers, made the total armada the greatest ever assembled.[13] Lieutenant General Walter Krueger's Sixth Army landed four divisions in the Dulag-Tacloban area on October 20. They moved quickly against the Japanese resistance (only 1 division of Japanese was on Leyte on D-day), and by November 2 the Leyte valley, the first objective, was in American hands. Complications developed, and despite the naval victory of Leyte Gulf and satisfactory progress on land, the Leyte operations soon bogged down into a grim struggle that lasted well into the following May. MacArthur and Krueger planned to use the Leyte valley as an air and logistical base to support the remainder of the

[12] Cannon, *Leyte: The Return to the Philippines,* pp. 93–94, 103.
[13] Morison, *Leyte,* p. 113. The record was broken for Luzon and Okinawa.

campaign,[14] but the water table was so high and the subsoil so unstable that heavy military traffic turned roads into bogs that threatened to halt all operations. The airfields, easily captured, were abandoned when it became apparent they could never fulfill the need. New ones had to be built, but there was a shortage of suitable sites, engineering personnel, metaling materials, and, of course, roads to move men, equipment, and supplies. Until the airstrips were operational, the land-based planes of General Kenney's Far Eastern air forces could not move in with sufficient strength and speed to provide effective air cover and direct support for ground operations.[15] Consequently the Japanese were able to reinforce Leyte, and the supporting naval forces, detained in Philippine waters longer than intended, fell victim to the Kamikaze Corps.

By barge, transport, and destroyer, Japanese soldiers began converging on Leyte from the other islands in the Philippines. Between October 23 and December 11 nine convoys landed roughly 45,000 Japanese in the vicinity of Ormoc Bay, on the western side of Leyte. (See map, page 278.) Although Allied planes managed to sink approximately 80 percent of the transport vessels, most of the troops got ashore,[16] and they were sufficient to make the battle for Leyte a prolonged and vicious struggle.

All through November and December Allied planes from New Guinea, Biak, Morotai, and Angaur pounded Japanese fields in the southern and central Philippines. Although the Japanese lost fairly heavily,[17] the lack of sufficient facilities on Leyte to accommodate the desired amount of land-based air support was keenly felt. MacArthur asked Halsey to retain Task Force 38 (the carriers of Third Fleet) in the area, especially to keep Japanese bases on Luzon pounded down. Halsey complied, but it was a costly and exhausting mission for the Third Fleet, because at Leyte the Japanese began to employ their final, most desperate weapon, the suicide planes.

The Kamikaze Corps was an air corps of pilots who conducted suicide missions by crashing their planes, filled with bombs, into an

[14] Cannon, *Leyte: The Return to the Philippines*, Chapter 3.
[15] Craven and Cate, *The Army Air Forces in World War II*, Vol. V, pp. 373–75, 384–85.
[16] Cannon, *Leyte: The Return to the Philippines*, pp. 99–102.
[17] Craven and Cate, *The Army Air Forces in World War II*, Vol. V, p. 375.

enemy ship. Difficult to defend against, the Kamikaze was a guided missile with human controls. Kamikaze means "divine wind," and the name was taken from an event in Japanese history in which a typhoon blew away an invasion force and saved Japan. Presumably, if enough young men were willing to sacrifice their lives to create a new "divine wind," the war could be won. Pilots were plentiful, for to the Japanese it was an honor to die in battle and a disgrace to meet defeat. Aircraft carriers were the prime targets for the Kamikaze planes, and two were sunk during the Leyte battles. Many other ships sustained damage, and by the end of November Halsey, judging that he was achieving nothing by remaining at Leyte, took his Task Force 38 to Ulithi for repairs.

By the time the battered Navy withdrew, the ground operations on Leyte were nearing their climax. All through November the fighting had been constant and difficult. After seizing the eastern valley, Krueger's forces began a two-pronged drive on Ormoc, the port on the west of the island through which most of the Japanese reinforcements were arriving. Major General Franklin C. Sibert's X Corps was to take Limon and advance down the Ormoc valley to meet Major General John R. Hodge's XXIV Corps, moving north along the western coast. Progress was slow. Throughout much of November a shortage of direct air support continued to hamper American operations, while Japanese troops continued to flow into Ormoc. Some of Japan's best divisions were committed to Leyte, and under the command of Lieutenant General Sosaku Suzuki, they fought with discipline and skill. Nevertheless, as the days went by the chances of a Japanese victory diminished. As early as November 10 General Yamashita recommended to his High Command that the Leyte campaign be abandoned and that their remaining strength be concentrated on Luzon.[18] When his suggestion was denied, Yamashita reapplied himself to helping Suzuki. His main worry was the potential threat of American air power in the Leyte valley, within range to sever the lifelines between Japan and the Netherlands East Indies. The resources of the Indies, especially oil, were essential, and in early December the Japanese launched an offensive that they hoped would destroy the Leyte fields and the Americans' growing air power. The

[18] Morison, *Leyte*, pp. 353–54.

offensive failed,[19] and the same day the Americans conducted an amphibious landing on the west coast near Ormoc. The 77th Infantry Division, by landing near Ormoc and rapidly moving to secure the town (December 10), defeated the Japanese in western Leyte. Ten days later the two corps of Sixth Army joined forces in the Ormoc valley, and on Christmas day General MacArthur pronounced Leyte secured. The next day General Eichelberger's Eighth Army began relieving Sixth Army, and continued to battle the recalcitrant Japanese on Leyte until well into May 1945.

The Philippine campaign did not wait for Eichelberger to finish mopping up on Leyte. On December 15 American forces landed on Mindoro to set up an advance base for the assault on Luzon, and on January 9, 1945, Krueger's Sixth Army began going ashore in Lingayen Gulf. The outcome was not in doubt. Yamashita wrote that "After the loss of Leyte . . . I realized that decisive battle was impossible." [20]

Luzon

Yamashita might not have the means to wage decisive battle, but he could still exact a high toll of casualties by husbanding his troops. During the amphibious and support phase of the landings, Kamikaze planes plagued the U.S. ships, and commanders were baffled as to how to defend themselves. A determined pilot could maneuver as rapidly and as easily as a ship. Radar often failed to pick up the Kamikazes, since they would fly low over the land for their approach. Individual planes sneaked in close to the fleet by hiding in groups of American planes. Although Combat Air Patrol and anti-aircraft fire splashed three out of every four Kamikazes, one out of every four found a target and one out of every 33 sank a ship.[21] The only solution was the complete elimination of Japanese air power, and that was accomplished on Luzon by January 13, by the combined efforts of Third and Seventh Fleets and Kenney's land-based planes. There-

[19] Cannon, *Leyte: The Return to the Philippines*, pp. 294–305.
[20] *Ibid.*, p. 370.
[21] Morison, *The Liberation of the Philippines*, p. 53.

after the Navy was free to support and supply the Army without being forced to fight at the same time.

Four divisions of Sixth Army landed in Lingayen Gulf January 9,[22] almost three years after the Japanese had invaded the area. Part of Yamashita's forces were deployed to meet the invaders, and since the Americans must secure the Lingayen Gulf area for the continuing supply of its Luzon force, Major General Innis P. Swift and his I Corps were assigned to defeat them. The Japanese gradually retired into the mountain redoubts to the north, and while I Corps was engaged in reducing their strongholds, Major General Oscar W. Griswold and the XIV Corps moved down the central plain toward Clark Field. A second portion of Yamashita's strength contested the Clark Field area before withdrawing into the mountains to the east, and the fighting was severe and slow. MacArthur moved his headquarters into Tarlac and urged Krueger to make haste, but it was the first of February before XIV Corps was ready to move on Manila.

To seal off the Bataan peninsula, one division landed on the south side of the entrance to Manila Bay, while XI Corps landed on the west coast just above Subic Bay. Stranded Japanese naval forces took control in Manila and met the converging Americans with grim determination. It took a month—until the end of February—for the Americans to liberate Manila. Thereafter the Sixth Army continued to press Yamashita's forces back into the hills, and Eichelberger's Eighth Army, transported by the Seventh Fleet, spread over the southern and central Philippines. Philippine guerrillas helped where they could, and the liberating process was still going on when the Japanese surrendered in August. Although MacArthur did not declare Luzon secure until July 4, by the middle of March the outlook was good. Yamashita's forces, coralled into their mountain strongholds, could effectively tie down numerous American forces, but they could not prevent the Americans from turning Luzon into a major staging base for the invasion of Japan. Clark Field and its excellent airstrips were once again taken over by the U.S. Army Air Forces. Work was begun to clear Manila bay and to rebuild the harbor facilities. Corregidor was reclaimed by a brilliantly executed airborne and amphibi-

[22] See Smith, *Triumph in the Philippines*, and Morison, *The Liberation of the Philippines*.

ous assault.[23] Some of the bloodiest battles of the Pacific war lay ahead, but U.S. planners felt that victory was assured. Even on the mainland of Asia, where the Allies had made their lowest priority effort, the Japanese were meeting defeat.

[23] See Gavin, *Airborne Warfare;* Belote and Belote, *Corregidor: The Saga of a Fortress.*

China, Burma, India

Since 1941 China, isolated from her allies and exhausted by internal struggles as well as by the war against Japan, had played a small role in the war. At first, the Allies considered the mainland of China one possible approach to Japan, but the difficulties were great. When the Central Pacific offensives began to move rapidly, the importance of Chinese bases decreased and operations on the Asian mainland were relegated to a supporting role. Nevertheless, since both the people and what happened in the CBI (China, Burma, India) theater were of a nature to hold the public interest, this area attracted much attention.

Defensive

China had been fighting the Japanese for a decade before Japan's aggression of 1941 brought the United States and other powers into the war in the Far East. Even though she had not been able to prevent Japan from seizing Manchukuo in 1931 and occupying the

286

bulk of eastern China between 1937–41, China had kept Japan from winning a conclusive victory. A sizable portion of Japan's military strength was deployed in China, and Chiang Kai-shek, as Generalissimo of the Chinese armies, continued to direct opposition from his capital at Chungking, deep in China's interior. Chiang's position was far from secure. The collapse of the ancient Manchu Dynasty in 1911 had been followed by a period of civil strife, and Chiang and his Kuomintang (Chinese Nationalists) did not assume leadership of a united China until 1927. Four years later, when the Japanese marched into Manchuria, the Kuomintang was still engaged in a desperate struggle to establish a unified Chinese Republic.

Most notable among the forces in opposition to the Republic were the Chinese Communists.[1] The Chinese Communist Party came into being in the early twenties. Relations between the Kuomintang and the Communists fluctuated from cooperation to open warfare, but in 1937 the two groups joined forces to present a united defense against Japanese aggression. It was an uneasy truce. The military forces under Communist control were concentrated in the north of China, and as time went by Chiang, more and more suspicious that the Communists intended to overthrow the Republic, concentrated Kuomintang forces to contain them. The Communists not only held political control in the north of China, but in the eastern areas the Communists were especially successful at waging guerrilla warfare against the Japanese. In effect China was divided into three parts: (1) Chiang's Republic, (2) the areas held by the Communists, and (3) those areas occupied by the Japanese. At Chungking, internal rivalries for both political power and the control of military forces weakened the Republic and weakened its effectiveness in the war against Japan.

President Roosevelt felt that Chiang's Kuomintang offered the best hope of revitalizing China and bringing her into the world family of nations as a viable post-war power that could afford stability in Asia. After the Japanese conquests of 1941–42, when it was impossible to assess when or how the military situation might be restored, the United States decided they must make every possible effort to support

[1] Houn, *A Short History of Chinese Communism*, Chapters 1–4; Chinese Ministry of Information, *China Handbook 1937–1943*, pp. 147–54, Chapter 9; Romanus and Sunderland, *Stilwell's Mission to China*, p. 5.

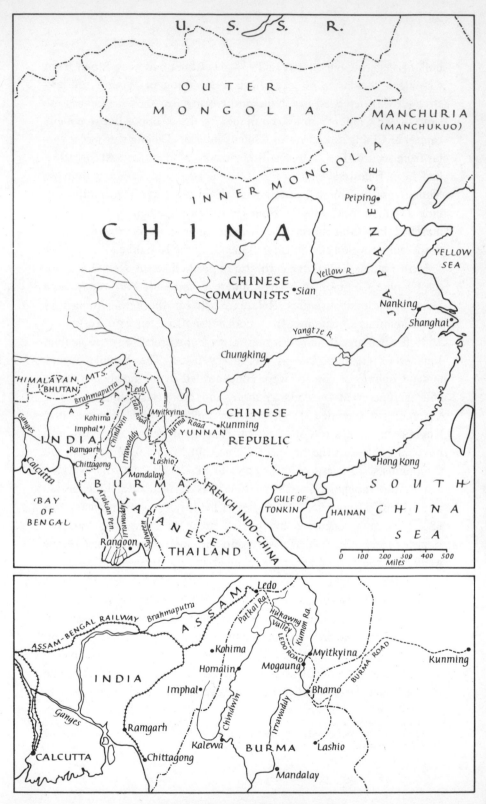

CHINA-BURMA-INDIA THEATER

China and keep her in the war.[2] When the conquest of Burma cut China's land routes to her allies, materials and supplies for the Chinese were sent by air over the Himalayan mountains. A difficult and hazardous route, the Hump airlift, as it was called, became a major strategic commitment designed to keep China from collapsing.

The disposition of supplies flown into China was another matter. Two American generals—Joseph W. Stilwell and Claire Chennault—were stationed in China. Chennault had come to China in 1937 at the invitation of Madame Chiang Kai-shek to help develop a Chinese air force. In 1941 he had organized the American Volunteer Group, a flying foreign legion called the "Flying Tigers." Using aggressive tactics, the Flying Tigers did what they could to counter Japanese air mastery over China, and these flyers became heroes to the Chinese. In June 1942, after the Japanese conquest of Burma, Chennault and his flyers were incorporated into the U.S. Army Air Force.

Stilwell had been in China since March 1942. At the ARCADIA conference in December 1941, the Combined Chiefs decided to ask Chiang Kai-shek to be Supreme Commander of a United Nations China theater. Chiang accepted and asked for a U.S. officer to serve as his Chief of Staff. Stilwell was sent. He had had experience in China, knew the language, and was a brilliant soldier, but he was not known for either his tact or his diplomacy. His mission, to improve the combat efficiency of the Chinese Army and "support China," proved full of frustrations. "Peanut," as Stilwell called the Generalissimo, tended to promise one thing but to fulfill another. In 1942 Stilwell was given command of two Chinese armies to help hold the Japanese in Burma. The Chinese were no match for the Japanese, the officers were involved in intrigue, and Stilwell's orders often were not obeyed. The Chinese armies became part of the general rout that marked the end of the Burma campaign. Nevertheless Stilwell felt the Chinese Army could be built up into an effective fighting force that could make a meaningful contribution in the war against Japan. Much reorganization and training were needed, for units were understrength, poorly led and trained, often unpaid and unfed, and lacking the bare essentials to make them a fighting force. Stilwell hoped to take thirty divisions, give them proper training, equipment, and lead-

[2] See Feis, *The China Tangle;* Romanus and Sunderland, *Stilwell's Mission to China, Stilwell's Command Problems, Time Runs Out in CBI; The Stilwell Papers.*

ership, and seize the initiative from the Japanese.

Conflict developed between Stilwell and Chennault. Chennault saw China as an air theater, and he wanted the Combined Chiefs of Staff to give him 105 fighters, 30 medium bombers, and 12 heavy bombers. With such an air force he claimed he could "accomplish the downfall of Japan," and "destroy the effectiveness of the Japanese Air Force." [3] Chennault was confident, and many of the Chinese supported him. Stilwell, backed by General Marshall, insisted the air offensive was impracticable until the Chinese ground forces were built up sufficiently to protect the airfields. Otherwise the Japanese would disrupt Chennault's plans by capturing his bases. In the spring of 1943 Roosevelt and Marshall called Stilwell and Chennault to Washington for a conference, and Chennault's plan was given approval.

Stilwell, an infantryman, saw CBI in a different way. He championed a campaign to retake Burma, at least the northern part, and reopen the land route to China. This would solve the problem of limited supplies and enable both ground and air operations to proceed. A Burmese campaign would necessitate the cooperation of Chinese, British, and Indian forces. Chiang Kai-shek refused to commit the Chinese Army unless the British promised sufficient naval support to conduct a simultaneous amphibious assault. India, in the throes of a famine as well as in political turmoil, had little to spare for a Burmese campaign. The British, who did not share the U.S. concern for China,[4] opted to wait for landing craft and attack from the sea rather than become involved in a land campaign in the Burmese jungle. The landing craft were not available, and Stilwell, bucking British reluctance, Chinese apathy, and the U.S. commitment to the Central Pacific, became more and more the acid figure known as "Vinegar Joe."

Offensive

In August 1943 Admiral Lord Louis Mountbatten went to India to head up the newly established Southeast Asia Command.[5] Stilwell

[3] Chennault, *Way of a Fighter*, pp. 212–16; Romanus and Sunderland, *Stilwell's Mission to China*, pp. 250–54.
[4] Churchill, *The Hinge of Fate*, pp. 133, 785–86, and *Closing the Ring*, pp. 560–61.
[5] Ehrman, *Grand Strategy*, Vol. V, pp. 135–53; Romanus and Sunderland, *Stilwell's Mission to China*, pp. 355–60.

became his Deputy, as well as continuing to serve as Chief of Staff to Chiang Kai-shek. Stilwell also maintained his position as commander of U.S. ground forces in CBI, and continued to manage Lend-Lease to China. The Combined Chiefs of Staff promised the new command support and supplies, including landing craft, and SEAC planned a campaign to open communications with China. The landing craft were delayed, and Burma was reconquered by a difficult land campaign that got underway late in 1943 and lasted until May 1945.

Burma, a land of mountains, rivers, jungle, and few roads, is well sited to resist a land campaign. Of necessity the campaign involved many simultaneous and scattered operations rather than a concentrated struggle on one front. In northern Burma, American engineers were constructing a road which would run from the railhead at Ledo, in Assam, India, across the Patkai mountain range, down the Hukawng and Mogaung valleys, and connect eventually with the old Burma Road beyond Myitkyina. It would provoide the desired land route to China. (See map, page 278.) The Ledo Road traversed towering mountains, lowlands often flooded by the heavy rains, and streams that turned into torrents during the monsoons.[6] The road was not only a challenge to the engineers, but, if it was to go through, the Japanese holding northern Burma must be routed out. Only one Japanese division was in northern Burma, but it was the crack 18th, veterans of Malaya. Stilwell had two Chinese divisions, trained since 1942 by American officers at Ramgarh, India. Other Chinese armies were in Yunnan province, China, and Stilwell urged that Chiang order them to attack in conjunction with the Ramgarh forces, but Chiang refused to commit them. Frustrated by the lack of decisiveness and the constant shortages, Stilwell left his headquarters and went to the front to take personal command of his forces.[7]

Two special forces fought with Stilwell in north Burma. British Major General Orde C. Wingate pioneered the Long-Range Penetration Group, designed to operate behind enemy lines while receiving supplies by air. Wingate's Chindits (named after a mythical winged beast who guards the Burmese temples) were flown by glider into the

[6] See Anders, *The Ledo Road.*

[7] Romanus and Sunderland, *Stilwell's Mission to China,* pp. 384–85; *Stilwell's Command Problems,* Chapter 2. For a critical view of Stilwell, see Ehrman, *Grand Strategy,* Vol. V, pp. 141–43; see also General Marshall's assessment of Stilwell in Romanus and Sunderland, *Stilwell's Command Problems,* p. 29.

heart of Burma, where they took up positions astride the railway that constituted the Japanese 18th Division's main supply line. The second force, Merrill's Marauders (named for their commander, Major General Frank D. Merrill) operated with Stilwell's Chinese. The Chinese would meet the Japanese in a frontal attack, and the Marauders would move through the jungle to hit the Japanese flanks and hasten their withdrawal.[8]

While Stilwell led operations in northern Burma, British forces operated on Burma's western frontier.[9] In November 1943 the British began a campaign to recover the Arakan peninsula of southern Burma. At first it went well, but in February the Japanese counterattacked in strength. The British positions were cut off and surrounded, but rather than retreat, they held fast. They received supplies by air and held out until the Japanese eventually withdrew. North of Arakan, Lieutenant General Sir William Slim's Fourteenth Army abandoned plans for an offensive into Burma in order to counter a Japanese invasion of India. The Japanese drive got underway in March 1944. Its objective was to disrupt the entire Allied campaign. If the Japanese could break across the British forces holding Imphal and Kohima and cut the railroad behind the Imphal plain, they would sever Stilwell's and Slim's supply lines and be in a position to sweep into India. There, exploiting local unrest, they might be able to wrest India out of Allied hands. Slim anticipated the Japanese offensive and planned to meet it in the plain of Imphal, where fighting conditions would favor the Allies. The Japanese disrupted his plans and soon had Kohima and Imphal under siege. Assuring Stilwell that he need not worry about his threatened supply line, Slim kept the besieged forces supplied by air until the siege could be lifted. By May the Fourteenth Army was pushing the Japanese out of India.

Meanwhile Stilwell's Chinese divisions continued to advance, and the Marauders were forcing their way over the Kumon Hills toward Myitkyina, a key area for completion of the Ledo Road. Stilwell's forces were strained almost beyond endurance, and both Stilwell and Roosevelt urged Chiang to commit his Yunnan divisions to the battle

[8] Ogburn, *The Marauders.*
[9] For British action in Burma see Owen, *The Campaign in Burma* and Slim, *Defeat into Victory.*

so that a decision might be reached before the monsoon broke in May. Chiang was reluctant. He feared a Japanese attack on China, and he also believed that the Chinese Communists were hoping he would exhaust his army against the Japanese so that the Communists could overthrow his Republic. For some time the Americans had contended that Chiang could best strengthen his Republic by a combination of internal reforms, reorganization of his army, and cooperation with the Allies to break the blockade. Since CBI had been low on the list of material priorities, Roosevelt had attempted to boost Chinese morale by political guarantees that China would be granted a place among the great powers at the end of the war. China was expected to do something to earn the position offered.[10] Chiang reluctantly ordered the Yunnan forces to advance, but his directive came too late to bring success in the spring of 1944. A few weeks later, on May 17, the sick and exhausted force of Marauders took the Myitkyina airstrip. The Japanese quickly besieged them, and not until early August was Myitkyina secure. The campaign in northern Burma continued through the remainder of 1944, and at the end of January 1945 the Ledo Road was opened to traffic. Vinegar Joe Stilwell, whose driving force had been the major factor in its completion, was not there to see the convoys begin. In October 1944 he was recalled from CBI at Chiang Kai-shek's insistence.

In April 1944 the Japanese had begun an offensive in eastern China, and one by one the eastern airfields used by Chennault's Fourteenth Air Force were lost. The possibility had been foreseen by Stilwell and Marshall, and was the main reason they had urged building up the ground forces before developing the air force. The situation became critical. The transport aircraft sent to India to carry supplies to Chennault were needed in Europe, where the Allies had taken Rome and had landed on the Normandy beaches.[11] Roosevelt and Marshall agreed that drastic measures were necessary. In July Roosevelt urged Chiang to give Stilwell (promoted to full general) command over all forces in China, including those of the Chinese Communists, which Chiang had repeatedly refused to use against the

---

[10] Feis, *The China Tangle*, Chapter 11.
[11] Romanus and Sunderland, *Stilwell's Command Problems*, pp. 379, 454.

Japanese.[12] Chiang resorted to the tactic of delay. The military and political situation in eastern China deteriorated, and Chiang threatened to withdraw his Yunnan force from the battle in Burma, a step that would jeopardize the entire effort to reopen a land route to China. In September Roosevelt wrote Chiang a firm letter insisting that he continue the effort on the Burma front and give Stilwell "unrestricted command" of all Chinese forces. Chiang was bitter and angry, and his wrath fell on Stilwell.[13] Chiang pledged to cooperate with any qualified American officer Roosevelt might send, but Stilwell had to go. In October CBI theater was divided into Burma-India and China, and Major General Albert C. Wedemeyer became Commander of U.S. forces in China. Chiang had won his point, but at the expense of impairing relations with the Americans.[14]

Shortly after Stilwell left Burma, the Allied campaign began to show the results of the months of plans, preparations, and effort. On December 2 Slim's Fourteenth Army took Kalewa on the Chindwin River, and two weeks later Lieutenant General Dan I. Sultan, who now commanded the northern armies, united with Slim's forces to make a joined front pressing into Burma from west and north. To the east, the Chinese force advanced over the Salween River and in January 1945 it, too, linked up with Sultan's forces. In March Chiang recalled his Chinese divisions to China, but Slim's forces continued alone. Mandalay fell in late March and on May 2, 1945, Rangoon fell to an amphibious assault. The arduous Burmese campaign was over.

[12] *Ibid.*, pp. 383–84.
[13] Text of Roosevelt's message in *Ibid.*, pp. 445–46; Chiang's reaction pp. 446–53. See also Feis, *The China Tangle*, Chapter 19.
[14] *Ibid.*, pp. 468–71.

War Ends in Europe

In 1945 from east, south, and west Allied armies moved across the borders of the Reich to defeat the Wehrmacht on its home ground, while from the air Allied bombers rained destruction on the German homeland.

Advance from the East

On January 12, 1945, Marshal Koniev's First Ukranian Front burst from its bridgehead over the Vistula south of Warsaw and began a steamrolling offensive. Within four weeks the Russians had crossed the Oder River near Breslau and had cut off the industrial area of the upper Silesia, chief source of the Reich's coal since Allied air attacks had demolished the Ruhr. On January 14 Zhukov's Front opened a massive offensive heading toward Warsaw, while further north massed Russian artillery began bombarding East Prussia. Russia's largest offensive to date, some 180 divisions against the Germans' 75, broke through and swept past the German resistance to open a 350-mile breach in the German lines. Armored spearheads followed by infantry pushed the lines forward as much as forty miles per day.[1] Warsaw fell on January 17, and Zhukov by-passed the German stronghold at Poznan, not halting until he reached German soil on the lower Oder River, barely forty miles from Berlin, at the end of January. On Zhukov's north, Rokossovsky's Front drove toward the Baltic coast and reached it by January 26, cutting off the German forces east of Danzig in their East Prussian redoubt. Temporarily halted along the Oder-Niesse Rivers in the west, the Russians pressed north toward the Baltic Sea on a wide front. The fighting for Danzig and Koniegsberg was severe (Danzig held out until March 30, Koniegsberg until April 9), and the Germans were able to evacuate some of their East Prussian forces by sea.

The Russians also advanced on the Balkan end of their long front. The Germans fought doggedly for Budapest, but it finally fell to the Russians on February 13, and the three Fronts of Yeremenko, Malinovsky, and Tolbukhin moved up the valley of the Danube to threaten Vienna and to pierce the Reich from the south. To defend Budapest and counter the southern advances Hitler, much to Guderian's disgust, committed the bulk of his reserves, including his best mobile and armored divisions.

In July 1944 General Heinz Guderian had been appointed Chief of Staff of the Army and was responsible for the entire Eastern Front. He warned Hitler that the Front was a "house of cards" poised to collapse, but Hitler refused either to reinforce or to withdraw his troops. When Guderian tried to organize a counterattack on the north, Hitler tied his hands by giving command of the Army Group to Himmler, Chief of the Gestapo, who had little military training. The attack failed, and by January 27 the Russian offensive was a "complete disaster." [2] Guderian, fighting Hitler and the High Command as openly as the Russians, talked to Foreign Minister von Ribbentrop about arranging a peace with the West. Hitler was furious. Guderian then urged a counterattack to sever Zhukov's spearhead and insisted

[1] Allen and Muratoff, *The Russian Campaigns of 1944–1945*, pp. 259–317; Clark, *Barbarossa*, Chapter 21; Werth, *Russia at War*, pp. 951–63.
[2] Guderian, *Panzer Leader*, pp. 387, 405.

it be directed by a competent officer. Hitler finally approved, but the forces were far from adequate and the counterattack met rapid defeat. As February drew to an end, the spring thaws brought the Germans a welcome, though temporary, respite in the east.

Attack from the Air

After the Normandy invasion the strategic air forces returned to their campaign against Germany's war-making capacity. Since air superiority had been attained, the bombers could now strike Germany's synthetic oil industry. Planners had long felt the oil campaign would be decisive, but the results exceeded expectations. The oil, rubber, chemical, and explosives industries were closely connected, and the destruction of one hurt the others. Within six months the output of aviation gasoline and nitrogen (important also in making explosives) had fallen off by 90 percent, while production of other grades of oil had fallen off 50 percent. After May 1944 German oil consumption consistently exceeded production.[3] From Italy, the Fifteenth Air Force destroyed the oil complex at Ploesti, depriving Germany of her last source of natural petroleum. As one by one the synthetic refineries were knocked out, German oil reserves began to disappear.

An Allied assault on the transportation system began in September 1944. Bridges, railroads, marshalling yards, and rolling stock were destroyed, compounding the difficulty of getting what little fuel Germany could produce to the fronts. Not only the ground forces, but also the Luftwaffe was affected. Even though early in 1945 the Luftwaffe unleashed another miracle weapon—the jet plane—most of the new German jets were destroyed on the ground. Not enough fuel existed to keep them in action, or to provide their crews with adequate training.[4] By the beginning of 1945 the German economy was on the verge of collapse. As the Russians began their January offen-

[3] Webster and Frankland, *The Strategic Air Offensive Against Germany*, Vol. IV, p. 324; USSBS, *Overall Report*, p. 37; Craven and Cate, *The Army Air Forces in World War II*, Vol. III, Chapter 20.

[4] See Galland, *The First and the Last*, for a German view of the decline of the Luftwaffe.

sive, the strategic air forces struck at Germany's cities and transportation centers facing the Eastern Front. On February 13 the last massive area attack of the European war was made on Dresden, where the fire storm and resulting devastation on the refugee-swollen city were unusually severe. Leipzig, Chemnitz, and Berlin also came under intense assault, for Air Chief Marshal Harris thought a final, culminating blow to German morale might precipitate a surrender.[5]

By mid-April 1945 the strategic air forces declared their campaign at an end and turned their efforts to direct support of the advancing armies. General Spaatz and the U.S. Eighth Air Force began moving into the Pacific. Germany's oil production was at an estimated 6 percent of normal, production of coal and steel had been drastically reduced, and what remained could not be moved because the transportation system was wrecked.[6]

Advance from the West

During January 1945 the Western Allies eliminated the German bulge into the Ardennes by coordinated drives from the northern and southern flanks that met at Houfflaize on January 16 and proceeded to push the Germans back to the Siegfried Line. The Allies then began a three-stage Rhineland offensive to complete the approach to the Rhine River. First, Montgomery would clear the west bank of the Rhine from Nijmegen to Dusseldorf, and Bradley would capture the Roer dams with First Army. In the next phase, Montgomery would prepare for a major assault over the lower Rhine, while Bradley would clear the west bank of the Rhine from Dusseldorf to Coblenz. Finally, Third Army and Seventh Army would clear the Saar-Palatinate area, west of the upper Rhine.

Plagued by cold and snow, rain and mud, the Rhineland campaign [7] opened in early February as the First Army drove on the

---

[5] Webster and Frankland, *The Strategic Air Offensive Against Germany*, Vol. III. Casualties for the Dresden raid are estimated at 135,000, which would make it the costliest air raid in terms of human lives, but the Dresden fire storm engulfed a smaller area than the Tokyo fire of March 9. See p. 315, note 20.

[6] USSBS, *Overall Report*, p. 37; Webster and Frankland, *The Strategic Air Offensive Against Germany*, Vol. III, p. 110.

[7] See Eisenhower, *Crusade in Europe;* Montgomery, *From Normandy to the Baltic.*

Roer dams. When they reached the last dam on February 9, the Germans jammed the locks and flooded the Roer valley, preventing Simpson's Ninth Army from crossing the Roer River on February 10 as planned. Simpson had to wait, but on schedule the First Canadian Army broke out of the Nijmegen bridgehead and struck southeast between the Roer and the Rhine. The Germans had fortified the area thoroughly, and the ablest of the German divisions, led by General Student, opposed their advance. The terrain ranged from dense forest to lowlands so marshy and flooded that amphibious craft were often necessary. The two-week struggle ended successfully after Simpson crossed the flooded Roer on February 23, achieving a surprise attack. He advanced to the Rhine at Dusseldorf and contacted the Canadians to the north by March 3.

The Rhineland offensive, picking up momentum, rolled to the south. Part of Hodges's First Army now thrust toward Cologne (reached on March 6) while other units turned southeast to sweep down the west bank of the Rhine and make contact with Third Army. Patton, who during February had been hammering away on the Siegfried Line, left his newly won bridgehead near Prum, and together First and Third Armies claimed the Rhineland north of the Moselle. West of the Rhine the German defense was becoming confused and disorganized, and on March 7 First Army captured, intact, a bridge over the Rhine at Remagen.[8] A bridgehead on the east bank was seized at once. Hitler was furious that von Rundstedt had let the Remagen bridge be taken and dismissed him. Field Marshal Kesselring was called from Italy to take von Rundstedt's place. His mission was to "Hang on!," but he later wrote, "The best general cannot make bricks without straw."[9]

Meanwhile the Rhineland campaign swept southward. On the far right of the front, General Devers had been busy during January and February holding a German offensive to limited gains and then clearing his area west of the Siegfried Line. Now, in March, General Patch's Seventh Army, coordinated with Patton's Third, made a major bid to capture the Saar-Palatinate area and force the last of the Germans east of the Rhine. As Seventh Army fought its way through

[8] See Toland, *The Last 100 Days,* Chapter 11.
[9] Kesselring, *A Soldier's Record,* pp. 286, 297.

the Siegfried Line, Third Army drove southeast to the Germans' rear. Germany's Army Group G, refused permission to withdraw east of the Rhine, was surrounded and most of it destroyed as Patton and Patch proceeded to clear the Rhineland south of the Moselle. Capitalizing on his momentum and the Germans' confusion, Patton's 5th Division crossed the Rhine at Oppenheim the night of March 22. Patton expanded his bridgehead and proceeded to seize another near Boppard two days later. The Rhineland campaign cost Germany 250,000 men in prisoners alone, and Germany now had only the equivalent of 26 divisions with which to hold back the Allies, who were more than three times as strong.[10]

For two weeks, before Montgomery crossed the lower Rhine, the air forces had isolated the area from German reinforcement, and an intense artillery barrage paved the way for the assault, using four divisions, on March 23. Opposition was lighter than expected, and on the 24th two airborne divisions were dropped east of the Rhine to support the rapidly expanding bridgehead. Churchill, on hand to witness the Rhine assault, expressed the feelings of all when he cried, "The German is whipped. We've got him. He is all through." [11] The Rhine had been crossed against the best opposition the Germans could muster, and the road across Germany was open.

Between March 23 and April 1 the Allied armies surrounded the Ruhr. Exploiting the bridgeheads at Remagen and Oppenheim and seizing others as needed, 12th Army Group poured over the Rhine, captured Frankfurt on the Main, and swept northeast to connect with Ninth Army near Lippstadt. Leaving 18 divisions to subdue Field Marshal Model and his troops trapped in the Ruhr, Montgomery went northeast to seal off Holland and Denmark and secure the Baltic ports, and Bradley headed for the Elbe River near Dresden and Leipzig. Devers advanced more slowly, bearing southeast to protect Bradley's flank. The Ruhr pocket, reduced by April 18, gave the Allies more than 317,000 prisoners.[12] Model, rather than join their ranks, committed suicide. American forces were by then on the Elbe River and the Russians had opened a major drive on Berlin.

In the fall of 1944 SHAEF had decided that once the Rhine was

[10] Pogue, *The Supreme Command*, p. 427.
[11] Eisenhower, *Crusade in Europe*, p. 390.
[12] Pogue, *The Supreme Command*, pp. 436–40.

crossed, the main drive would be through the north German plain to Berlin. By the time the Rhine was crossed the situation was changed. The Russians were some thirty miles from Berlin and no doubt could take the city when they chose. The Western Allies, still some 200 miles west of the German capital, could make the most effective contribution to Germany's military defeat by driving through central Germany rather than on to Berlin. This drive would wipe out Germany's remaining industrial potential, cut the German armed forces into northern and southern pockets, and eliminate any possibility that the Germans would withdraw into the mountainous south to hold out in a fortified redoubt. Accordingly, on March 28, Eisenhower announced that the main drive would be by Bradley, in central Germany, rather than by Montgomery to the north.[13]

The British objected. Churchill pled for the Western Allies to seize Berlin if possible. Not only was it of "high strategic importance," but if the Russians took Berlin, as well as Austria and Vienna, they might feel they had been the "overwhelming contributor to our common victory"—an attitude that might pose future political difficulties.[14] The matter involved not only the post-war political climate, but the question of confidence in the Supreme Commander, the complex difficulties of an Allied Command, an equitable share in prestige and public acclaim, and a basic difference in the U.S. and British approach to the conduct of military affairs. The U.S. leaders favored a rapid military conclusion to the war, directed with maximum freedom by the Supreme Commander as the one best qualified to judge how a military decision could be most efficiently attained. The British favored a closer integration of military and political strategy. Both British and Americans were concerned about Russia's political maneuverings, for as military victory came closer, political agreements seemed further away than ever before.

In early February Churchill, Roosevelt, and Stalin met at Yalta for the last of their Big Three conferences. Most of the agenda was political, and although the rift between East and West was apparent, agreements were reached on certain post-war problems. During the succeeding weeks Russia's actions were often in direct violation of

[13] *Ibid.*, Chapters 23 and 24; Greenfield, *Command Decisions*, Chapter 19; Ehrman, *Grand Strategy*, Vol. VI, pp. 131–46, 151–61; Churchill, *Triumph and Tragedy*, pp. 455–68.

[14] Churchill, *Triumph and Tragedy*, p. 465.

those agreements.[15] Hopes for the post-war world were based on cooperation and trust through the United Nations. Would it be better to display trust, or move boldly and hope to force the Russians to abide by their commitments? On April 7 Eisenhower expressed his views in a message to General Marshall: [16]

> I regard it as militarily unsound at this stage of the proceedings to make Berlin a major objective, particularly in view of the fact that it is only 35 miles from the Russian lines. I am the first to admit that a war is waged in pursuance of political aims, and if the Combined Chiefs of Staff should decide that the Allied effort to take Berlin outweighs purely military considerations in this theater, I would cheerfully readjust my plans and my thinking so as to carry out such an operation.

The Combined Chiefs of Staff did not direct Eisenhower toward Berlin, and the final operations were planned to achieve a sound military decision. The Elbe was chosen as the forward line of advance for Allied forces because it was easily recognizable and would help prevent the catastrophe of Russian and American armies clashing in a head-on attack. Even so, the Elbe lay within the post-war zone of occupation already assigned to the Russians. Political decisions, reached during 1944 and confirmed at Yalta, had divided Germany into occupation zones controlled by the major Allies, and the western boundary of the Russian zone ran one to two hundred miles west of Berlin.

On April 12 Franklin Roosevelt died. His last message to Churchill urged that they "minimise the general Soviet problem as much as possible," while continuing to be firm.[17] Since he had met with the leaders at Yalta, Roosevelt's health had been failing, but his death came as a shock. Harry S Truman, taking up the task of guiding the nation, pledged his continued support of Roosevelt's war and peace policies.[18]

---

[15] Feis, *Churchill, Roosevelt, Stalin*, pp. 561–80.
[16] Pogue, *The Supreme Command*, p. 446; Greenfield, *Command Decisions*, p. 381.
[17] Churchill, *Triumph and Tragedy*, p. 454.
[18] Truman, *Year of Decisions*, pp. 11–13, 42; Feis, *Churchill, Roosevelt, Stalin*, 596–600.

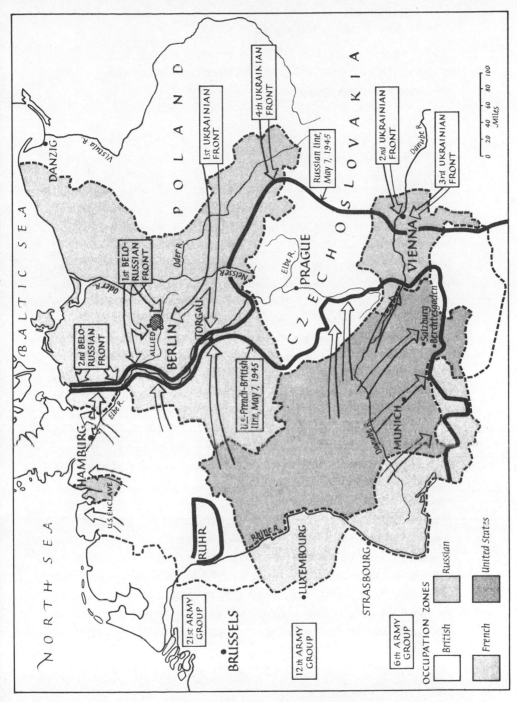

BALTIC SEA

DANZIG

Vistula R.

P O L A N D

1st UKRAINIAN FRONT

4th UKRAINIAN FRONT

Russian line, May 7, 1945

2nd UKRAINIAN FRONT

3rd UKRAINIAN FRONT

Danube R.

Miles
0 20 40 60 80 100

Oder R.

Neisser R.

Elbe R.

PRAGUE

C Z E C H O S L O V A K I A

VIENNA

Oder R.

1st BELO-RUSSIAN FRONT

2nd BELO-RUSSIAN FRONT

BERLIN

TORGAU

ALLIED

Salzburg

Berchtesgaden

U.S.-French-British line, May 7, 1945

MUNICH

Danube R.

BALTIC SEA

Elbe R.

HAMBURG

U.S. ENCLAVE

NORTH SEA

RUHR

Rhine R.

LUXEMBOURG

STRASBOURG

21st ARMY GROUP

BRUSSELS

12th ARMY GROUP

6th ARMY GROUP

OCCUPATION ZONES

Russian

United States

British

French

FINAL DEFEAT OF GERMANY

Advance from the South

On April 1, as the Allies closed the circle around the Ruhr, Generals Alexander and Clark, with the 15th Army Group, began offensive operations designed to defeat the Germans in the Po valley.[19] Eighth Army (General Sir Richard McCreery), on the right, opened the drive, and Fifth Army (Lieutenant General Lucien S. Truscott), on its left, joined a few days later. These armies were outnumbered, but Vietinghoff, who had succeeded Kesselring in March, had no air support and was hampered by Hitler's orders not to yield ground. By April 20, however, he had to yield, because the Allied armies broke out of the mountains that had contained them since the winter before and began a sweep of the Po valley, taking many German prisoners before Vietinghoff pulled his shattered units north of the Po River. Pursued by Allied armor and pounded by Allied aircraft, the Germans could not hold at the Po, and the Allies crossed the river and moved into Austria to meet the advancing Russians.

On April 13 the Russians took Vienna. On April 16 Zhukov and Koniev, competing to reach Berlin first, opened their final, massive campaign. General Gotthard Heinrici, who had replaced Himmler as commander of the defending forces, could do little to halt them. Hitler continued to issue orders that bore no relation to the disintegration of the German armies or the scope of the Russian assault. By April 24 Berlin was surrounded and General Chuikov's Guards Army was forcing its way toward the Chancellery. On April 25 American and Russian advance patrols met at the Elbe River, and Germany was cut in two. Third Army was driving toward Czechoslovakia, while to the north the British Second Army had cleared the west bank of the lower Elbe and the First Canadian Army had sealed Holland off from the Reich. Germany was defeated.

[19] Jackson, *The Battle for Italy*, Chapter 17; Ehrman, *Grand Strategy*, Vol. VI, pp. 118–21; Clark, *Calculated Risk*, Chapter 18.

Collapse from Within

Even at the end of April, as the Western Allies reached the Elbe and the Russians drew closer daily to Berlin, Hitler refused to capitulate to end the suffering and death of the German people. He had taken refuge in a concrete bunker deep underground beneath the Chancellery, and on April 22 he vowed to remain there, defend Berlin to the end, and take his life at the last moment. From April 22 to May 2, when Grand Admiral Doenitz announced Hitler's death and his own succession, Germany was essentially without leadership. Hitler had abdicated responsibility, but he did not relinquish power. Goering, interpreting Hitler's decision to stay in Berlin as a directive to him, who was next in line, to assume leadership of the Reich, found himself stripped of all his offices and barely spared the death penalty. When Himmler approached the West about an armistice, Hitler, who considered the move treason, was enraged. By the end of April Hitler's followers had deserted him, and the Russian artillery was closing in on the Chancellery. As Zhukov's and Koniev's soldiers swarmed through the ruins of Berlin, Hitler married his mistress, Eva Braun, and wrote his will and testament. The latter expelled Goering and Himmler from the Party and appointed Doenitz Reich President and Supreme Commander of the Armed Forces. The heritage of power—what was left of it—would go to the German Navy, which even up to the last weeks of the war had continued its unrelenting campaign against Allied shipping. The next day, April 30, Hitler killed himself.[20]

The Reich survived its Fuehrer by one week, for when authority to act for the German government fell upon Doenitz, the military surrenders were already taking place. The first was made to Alexander's forces in Italy. Negotiations had been underway for some weeks. When the surrender was signed on April 29, nearly a million Germans laid down their arms, signaling the end of the Italian campaign

[20] See Trevor-Roper, *The Last Days of Hitler,* and Lev Bezymenski, *The Death of Adolf Hitler.*

—the longest (20 months) for any U.S. Army during the war.[21] On May 4 the German forces in the northern part of Germany, including Denmark and the Netherlands, surrendered to Montgomery's 21st Army Group. On May 5 the remains of Army Group G, in the south of Germany, capitulated to Devers's 6th Army Group, and on the same day an authorized German representative arrived at Eisenhower's headquarters at Reims to open final negotiations. The surrender was signed at 2:41 a.m. on May 7, 1945; in Europe the war was over.

[21] The Italian surrender negotiations were tedious and complex. See Ehrman, *Grand Strategy*, Vol. VI, pp. 122–31; Feis, *Churchill, Roosevelt, Stalin*, pp. 583–96; Churchill, *Triumph and Tragedy*, pp. 440–54. For the German capitulation see Pogue, *The Supreme Command*, pp. 475–94.

Climax in the Pacific

D U R I N G 1 9 4 5 Allied forces closed in on Japan by seizing Iwo Jima and Okinawa. At sea and in the air, the blockade and bombardment of Japan by U.S. forces weakened the Japanese power to resist.

Iwo Jima

An "island of sulphur, no water, no sparrow, and no swallow," [1] Iwo Jima is composed of black volcanic ash, rough ridges and gorges, and steaming fissures in rocks which are still being forced up from the sea. On its eight square miles, in 1945, nearly 28,000 Japanese and Americans died. [2] For the Japanese, the defense of Iwo Jima was the defense of their homeland. Their defensive perimeter, drawn up in

---

[1] Esposito, *The West Point Atlas of American Wars*, Vol. II, Map 162.

[2] Japanese deaths were nearly 21,000; roughly 1,000 of their total garrison surrendered. American casualties were more than 25,000, of which 6,800 were killed. Isely and Crowl, *The U.S. Marines and Amphibious War*, p. 483; Bartley, *Iwo Jima: Amphibious Epic*, pp. 210, 193, 218–21.

1941–42, was now pushed back to a front line running through southern Korea, Shanghai, Formosa, Okinawa, and Iwo Jima. The Japanese on Iwo, commanded by General Tadamichi Kuribayashi, were ordered to fight to the death and to make the battle as costly as possible. They honeycombed the island with defenses, which were so skillfully burrowed into the rock and ash that spotting them was nearly impossible. Every weapon was dug in and camouflaged. Pillboxes and bunkers were below ground. Living quarters and supply dumps were so far underground bombs and shells did not affect them, and the island was a maze of subterranean passages.[3]

The Americans wanted Iwo as an advance air base for the support of the B-29's operating out of the Marianas.[4] Not only would the Iwo base make it possible to provide fighter escort to Japan for the Superforts, but an emergency landing field on the island would save many crippled planes and pilots from a possible fatal splash in the sea. Eventually, Iwo more than fulfilled its purpose. The first crippled B-29, unable to make Tinian, landed on Iwo's unfinished fields on March 4, and before the vast bombing raids came to an end, 2400 more B-29's had done the same. Although not all of those planes and crews would necessarily have been lost had Iwo not been in American hands, 25,000 airmen made emergency landings there.

The Marines who took the island were from the Fifth Amphibious Corps—the Fourth, Fifth, and Third Marine divisions—commanded by Major General Harry Schmidt. General Holland Smith, now Commander of the Fleet Marine Force, was also on hand. Preliminary bombing and bombardment were carried out, and the assault waves began going ashore the morning of February 19, 1945.[5] They fought up terraced beaches of dark, volcanic ash, coarse in texture, light in weight, that shifted underfoot and slowed them to a tiring, lumbering walk. **Taking heavy losses**, the advance waves crawled and climbed inland, while behind them the succeeding waves of landing craft met beach congestion as well as enemy fire. Nevertheless, by nightfall 30,000 Marines had landed and secured a foothold stretching from

[3] See Isely and Crowl, *The U.S. Marines and Amphibious War*, pp. 483–88; Bartley, *Iwo Jima: Amphibious Epic*, pp. 11–18.

[4] Craven and Cate, *The Army Air Forces in World War II*, Vol. V, pp. 586–98.

[5] See Morison, *Victory in the Pacific*, Chapters 2 and 3 for assault phase. For action ashore see Isely and Crowl, *The U.S. Marines and Amphibious War*; Bartley, *Iwo Jima: Amphibious Epic*.

one side of the island to the other, across its narrowest part.

Iwo Jima is pear-shaped. From their beachhead, the Marines must wheel left and take Mount Suribachi, a cone-shaped, 550-foot volcano on the stem. At the same time, they had to wheel right to advance over the meaty portion of the pear. The island was 4.5 miles long. Optimists predicted four days for the operation. The attacks to both left and right got underway on February 20. On the right the Marines ran headlong into Kuribayashi's main defenses. Commanders soon realized they faced a defense in depth manned by disciplined soldiers, prepared to sacrifice their lives only at a high cost to their enemies. Fighting was vicious and gains were measured in yards. This type of fighting dragged on for 34 days.

Mount Suribachi, bristling with emplaced weapons and riddled with caves and passageways, was gradually overcome by tanks, flame-throwers, rockets, demolitions, and the fire of supporting warships. By the 23rd, the mountain was surrounded. A patrol of forty men, ordered to seize the crest, worked their way up the face of the mountain. One of them, who had brought a flag, affixed it to a length of pipe and thrust it into the soft ground of the crater. Suddenly two Japanese darted from a cave, brandishing grenades. A skirmish followed, but the Marines and the flag were atop Suribachi to stay.[6]

By the first of March roughly half the island was in American hands and the Seabees (Naval Construction Battalions) were feverishly converting the shambles of broken rock into usable airfields. By mid-March the island was pronounced secured, but heavy fighting continued for another ten days. As the mopping up on Iwo Jima began, news came that the Americans had invaded Okinawa.

Okinawa

April 1 was D-day for Okinawa, the largest Pacific operation to date.[7] Two corps of Lieutenant General Simon B. Buckner's Tenth Army began landing on Okinawa against light opposition. Objectives

[6] See Newcomb, *Iwo Jima*, Chapter 4.
[7] See Appleman, *Okinawa: The Last Battle;* Morison, *Victory in the Pacific;* Nichols and Shaw, *Okinawa: Victory in the Pacific.*

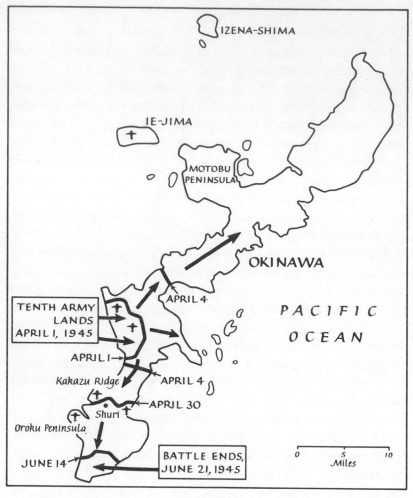

IZENA-SHIMA

IE-JIMA

MOTOBU PENINSULA

OKINAWA

APRIL 4

PACIFIC OCEAN

TENTH ARMY LANDS APRIL 1, 1945

APRIL 1→

Kakazu Ridge

APRIL 4

←APRIL 30

Shuri

Oroku Peninsula

JUNE 14→

BATTLE ENDS, JUNE 21, 1945

0   5   10
Miles

OKINAWA

scheduled for D+3 were secured before noon. The Japanese airfields were seized at once. Buckner directed one corps to clear the northern portion of the island, and within three weeks its mission was accomplished.

The landings had been made on the southern third of the long, irregular-shaped island, and when one corps turned north, General Hodges's XXIV Corps turned south. They at once found themselves battering formidable defenses, and efforts to seize the dominating Kakazu Ridge brought heavy casualties. On April 13 the Japanese hit the 96th Division with a counterattack—not a wild, disorganized banzai charge, but a well-planned and coordinated assault. The 96th held firm. The Japanese attack lost its momentum, and a lull fell over the battlefield for a week.

Under the direction of Lieutenant General Mitsuru Ushijima and his Chief of Staff, Lieutenant General Isamu Cho, the Japanese Thirty-Second Army had fortified the southern portion of the island with a view toward maximum delaying tactics. The terrain, naturally suited to defense, had been exploited to form three major defense lines stretching across the island from east to west. Behind the Kakazu Ridge was an even more formidable defense area pivoting around Shuri Castle, the ancient site of Okinawan kings, and behind the Shuri defenses was a third barrier exploiting the hilly terrain at the extreme southern end of the island. The Japanese hoped that while the Americans battered against their defenses in southern Okinawa, the Kamikaze Corps could drive away the American Navy, thus severing the American forces from their source of supply. Okinawa was only 350 miles from Kyushu, and the Japanese had enough planes on Kyushu and Formosa to ruin American plans. Before the invasion, American planes had blasted Japanese airfields and factories so that during the early days of the invasion the Japanese Air Force was helpless. By April 6, however, it had recovered sufficiently to strike the U.S. naval vessels off Okinawa with seven hundred planes. This was the first of ten massive Kamikaze attacks, the "Floating Chrysanthemums," on which the Japanese based their hopes for the Okinawan campaign.[8] Before Okinawa was secured, 36 American ships were sunk and nearly 400 damaged; more than 700 fleet aircraft were lost; 4800 sailors were wounded; 4900 were either killed or missing.[9] Yet although Okinawa was one of the costliest naval battles on record, the Kamikaze planes did not come close either to destroying the American Fleet or to driving it out of Okinawan waters.

On April 7 pilots from Task Force 58 sank *Yamato,* the largest, most dangerous, and most beautiful battleship afloat, thus ending the threat from the Japanese surface fleet. Although a few Japanese

[8] See Morison, *Victory in the Pacific,* Chapter 7 for April 6 attack; Chart on page 233 for strength of various assaults.
[9] *Ibid.,* p. 282.

submarines still prowled the seas, and one sank the heavy cruiser *Indianapolis* on July 29, the naval battle off Okinawa was a slugging match and endurance contest between ships and land-based aircraft. Especially hard hit were the destroyers which had been posted to a picket line around Okinawan waters to give advance warning of the approach of Japanese planes. The battered American ships held their posts and fought back, and by the end of May, when Halsey replaced Spruance and Fifth Fleet again became Third Fleet, there were signs that the ordeal was nearing its end.

The battle for Okinawa involved some of the nastiest fighting of the war. On April 19 three U.S. Army divisions struck in a simultaneous, full-scale attack that scarcely dented the Japanese lines, and not until the end of the month were the first Japanese defensive positions, including Kakazu Ridge, overcome. Casualties were heavy. Whole hills were tunneled out to make gigantic fortifications. Closely coordinated teams of infantrymen and supporting tanks carried the burden of battle, although they were ably assisted by artillery, close air support, and naval bombardment.

On May 4 General Cho launched a massive counterattack coordinated with a Kamikaze raid. Although at one point the Japanese penetrated almost a mile through the American front lines, their gains were insignificant, and after sustaining some 5000 casualties, Ushijima called off the offensive and thereafter restricted his men to defensive, attrition tactics. On May 11, three days after the end of the war in Europe, Tenth Army launched its first major assault on the Shuri defenses. Four divisions were now in the front lines, but it took ten days for the Japanese lines to begin to crumble. The battle was fought in torrential rain that made the supply situation critical, but Shuri Castle fell on the 29th. The Japanese made an orderly withdrawal to their final defensive positions, and held out for another three weeks.

During June the Sixth Marine Division eliminated one pocket of Japanese resistance on Oroku peninsula, while the other three divisions cleared the southern extremity of the island. For the final effort, a regiment of the Second Marine Division was brought in, and while visiting its forward observation post on June 18, General Buckner was killed. Four days later Major General Roy S. Gieger, who assumed temporary command of Tenth Army, pronounced Okinawa secured. Tenth Army losses, added to the Naval losses, put American casualties at more than 49,000 (12,500 killed). Japanese deaths were more than 100,000.[10]

Okinawa was the last land battle of the war. Anticipating that an invasion of Japan would be necessary, since the Japanese showed no signs of surrender, staff officers worked on plans for an invasion of Kyushu, scheduled for November 1, and Honshu, planned for sometime in March 1946.

Blockade and Strategic Bombardment

The Battle of the Pacific had begun on December 7, 1941, with an order from the Chief of Naval Operations, Admiral Stark, to "Execute unrestricted air and submarine warfare against Japan." [11] At that time the U.S. Navy had only 51 submarines in the Pacific—29 at Manila, 22 at Pearl Harbor. Japanese sea lanes were numerous and good use could be made of the protection of coastal waters. Thus, the submarine battle in the Pacific differed from its Atlantic counterpart, for the U.S. Pacific submarines, commanded during much of the war by Vice Admiral Charles A. Lockwood, Jr., operated individually or in small patrols. Although warships were their prime target, they preyed on merchant shipping as well. Japan, like Britain, was dependent on her seaborne lifelines for most raw materials and a good portion of her food. After the war, General Tojo judged that the successful submarine war the U.S. conducted against Japanese merchant shipping was one of the three main causes of Japan's defeat.[12]

Japan started the war with insufficient merchant tonnage to support civilian and military needs and exploit her military gains, and she did not inaugurate a vigorous shipbuilding program to replace her losses. The Japanese Navy's anti-submarine tactics and weapons were not good and did not improve. Convoys were not initiated at once and

[10] Appleman, *Okinawa: The Last Battle*, p. 473; Nichols and Shaw, *Okinawa: Victory in the Pacific*, p. 260; Morison, *Victory in the Pacific*, p. 282.
[11] Roscoe, *United States Submarine Operations in World War II*, p. 5.
[12] Morison, *Leyte*, p. 412. The other two were the leapfrogging strategy and the actions of the fast carrier forces.

were not used with maximum effectiveness, partly because of the shortage of escort vessels.[13] As early as April 1942 the balance of shipping available to Japan began to drop.[14] It continued to drop, even though the U.S. submarines were few and were severely handicapped by defective torpedoes. Not until autumn 1943 did U.S. submarines possess adequate torpedoes,[15] but even so, during 1943 alone they accounted for 22 Japanese warships and 296 merchant vessels. The latter represented for Japan a net loss of 718,000 tons, for shipping captured, salvaged, and constructed did not keep pace with that sunk.[16]

The campaign against Japanese shipping intensified in 1944, since the submarine fleet increased in numbers and the portion of the Pacific under Japanese control decreased. In 1944 Japan lost approximately two and a half million tons of merchant shipping to the submarines and a significant additional tonnage to Allied aircraft.[17] Much of that tonnage was in oil tankers, and Japan's oil imports dropped from 1,000,000 barrels in January to 600,000 in June. They continued to drop, for Japan had no tanker reserves to make up the loss.[18] By the end of the year Japan's merchant tonnage had dropped below the minimum deemed necessary to supply civilian needs alone.[19] By the beginning of 1945 Japanese commerce had been essentially driven off the seas, and more and more the submarines were employed to rescue downed aviators.

Before March 1945 the U.S. strategic bombardment of Japan, first from India and China and then from the Marianas, had produced few results in return for a huge investment in men, planes, and bases. In March General LeMay, head of the XXI Bomber Command in the Marianas, decided to abandon the unsuccessful high altitude, daylight

[13] Roscoe, *United States Submarine Operations in World War II*, pp. 209–10; USSBS, *Campaigns of the Pacific War*, p. 378; Morison, *The Two Ocean War*, pp. 496–97.
[14] See Chart, p. 384 of USSBS, *Campaigns of the Pacific War;* Roscoe, *United States Submarine Operations in World War II*, p. 155.
[15] Roscoe, *United States Submarine Operations in World War II*, Chapter 20; Morison, *Coral Sea, Midway and Submarine Actions*, pp. 191, 214, 221–22, 230–32; Morison, *New Guinea and the Marianas*, pp. 15–16.
[16] Roscoe, *United States Submarine Operations in World War II*, p. 298; Morison, *New Guinea and the Marianas*, p. 16; Morison, *The Two Ocean War*, p. 497.
[17] Roscoe, *United States Submarine Operations in World War II*, p. 432; USSBS, *Campaigns of the Pacific War*, Charts, pp. 384, 385.
[18] Roscoe, *United States Submarine Operations in World War II*, pp. 331, 334, 338.
[19] *Ibid.*, pp. 410, 434; USSBS, *Campaigns of the Pacific War*, p. 380.

precision raids and ordered, for the night of March 9, a low altitude, incendiary bomb raid on a densely populated area of Tokyo that housed home industries and feeder plants. More than three hundred B-29's conducted a three-hour raid against a city that had few night defenses and insufficient fire-fighting equipment. Approximately one fourth of the buildings in Tokyo were destroyed in the most destructive air attack of the war. More than a million people were left homeless; more than 83,000 killed; more than 40,000 wounded; more than 15 square miles of the city devastated.[20]

LeMay, feeling that air power so employed might bring about Japanese surrender before an invasion of Kyushu was necessary, decided to press the incendiary attacks against Japan with maximum effort.[21] Japan's industrial cities—Nagoya, Osaka, Kobe, Yokohama—were severely bombed. By mid-June, when the Okinawa campaign was over, the six most important industrial areas of Japan were almost completely destroyed. Fire raids were coupled with precision raids on specific industries and stocks of stores, and Japan's plight grew more and more desperate. The Japanese, still capable of inflicting high losses on their enemy, husbanded their remaining military strength to defend their homeland. But the war was lost, and the United States as well as Japan was seeking ways to bring about a settlement.

Surrender

One of the most tightly guarded secrets of the war was the development by Allied scientists of an atomic bomb.[22] By April 1945, when Truman became President, the bomb was nearly ready. The Secretary of War, Henry Stimson, suggested the formation of a committee of civilians to study the issues and advise how best the atomic power should be used. Their unanimous opinion, submitted on June 1, was that the bomb should be used against Japan as soon as possible, it

---

[20] Craven and Cate, *The Army Air Forces in World War II*, Vol. V, pp. 614–17. The more famous attack on Hiroshima with an atom bomb by comparison caused between 70–80,000 deaths and approximately the same number of wounded, while destroying 4.7 square miles of the city. *Ibid.*, p. 722.

[21] *Ibid.*, pp. 623–26.

[22] See Smyth, *Atomic Energy for Military Purposes*.

should be dropped on a military installation in a built-up area, and it should be used without specific warning.[23] Truman and his advisers felt that perhaps a sudden shock, emphasizing the futility of continued resistance, might precipitate a Japanese surrender. They concluded that if the bomb were successfully built, it should be used.

On July 16 Truman, Churchill, and Stalin assembled in Potsdam for the final summit conference of the war. Mainly, the agenda concerned post-war problems in Europe.[24] It was not a cordial conference. The military necessities that had held the coalition together were no longer binding, and conflicting goals set the participants at odds. Toward the end of the proceedings, Churchill was dealt a bitter defeat when the British, in a parliamentary election, voted him out and elected Clement Attlee to lead them through the post-war period. Attlee went to Potsdam for the concluding days of the conference, which adjourned on August 2.

On July 16 the atom bomb was successfully tested in the desert near Alamogordo, New Mexico. Atomic power was a reality, and the ultimate decision as to whether it would be used was Truman's. He did not hesitate. The Japanese would be asked to surrender. If they refused, the bomb would be dropped.[25] On July 26 the Potsdam Declaration was issued as a joint statement from Truman, Churchill, and Chiang Kai-shek. The Declaration warned Japan of the uselessness of continued resistance, and it stressed several points: (1) Japan's armed forces must surrender unconditionally, (2) Japan would be limited to her home islands, (3) militarism must be stamped out, and (4) Japan must submit to occupation. The Potsdam Declaration assured Japan that (1) the military forces would be allowed to return to their homes, (2) the Japanese nation would be neither enslaved nor destroyed, (3) industry and trade would not be banned, and (4) the occupation forces would withdraw when a "peacefully inclined" government was established. The atom bomb was not mentioned in unmistakable terms. The Declaration ended with the warning that Japan's alternative to surrender was "prompt

---

[23] Feis, *Japan Subdued*, p. 38. See Greenfield, *Command Decisions*, Chapter 20; Grew, *Turbulent Era*, Vol. II, esp. Chapter 36; Stimson and Bundy, *On Active Service in Peace and War*, p. 612 ff.

[24] See Feis, *Between War and Peace*.

[25] Truman, *Year of Decisions*, pp. 419, 421.

and utter destruction." [26]

In Japan, as in the summer and fall of 1941, two elements were vying for control of Japanese policy. One group, primarily the Army, was prepared to fight on the Japanese mainland rather than submit to unconditional surrender. A second group, realizing that the war was lost, favored peace, provided that their unique national polity, centered around the person of the Emperor, might be maintained.[27] Prominent among the latter group were the Lord Keeper of the Privy Seal, Marquis Kido, and senior statesman Prince Konoye. After 1942, when Japan began to suffer a succession of military defeats, the "peace party" grew, but so long as the Army controlled the government and favored prosecuting the war to complete destruction, they could do little but seek to break the Army's rigid control and pave the way for the Emperor to take a leading role in terminating the war.

In April 1945 Admiral Kantaro Suzuki, an elderly warrior with little political experience, was made Premier. The U.S. interpreted his appointment as a move toward peace, and Suzuki later claimed that he understood the Emperor wanted him to make peace as quickly as possible, but Suzuki followed a circuitous and hesitant route. When Germany surrendered in May, Truman's victory statement called on the Japanese to surrender and assured them of reasonable treatment, but the Japanese government announced that Germany's surrender would cause no change in Japan's policy, since her war aims were based on "self-existence and self-defense." [28] The only concession on Japan's part was a decision to approach Russia (who had earlier terminated her Neutrality Pact with Japan) with the dual purpose of persuading Russia against entering the war and seeking her services to mediate an end to the conflict on more favorable terms than unconditional surrender. To the Army as well as to the peace group, the retention of the Emperor was the minimum condition for peace.

Preliminary efforts to talk with the Russians came to naught, and in early June an Imperial Conference adopted as policy a commitment to continue fighting. On June 22, as the Okinawa campaign came to an end, Hirohito summoned his Supreme Council and urged

[26] The complete text is given in Butow, *Japan's Decision to Surrender*, p. 243, Appendix C.
[27] See Butow, *Japan's Decision to Surrender;* Kase, *Journey to the Missouri.*
[28] Butow, *Japan's Decision to Surrender,* p. 79.

them to seek a negotiated peace. Time was lost in tentative approaches, but in July the Japanese Ambassador in Moscow asked if the Russian leaders would receive a Japanese delegation, headed by Konoye. Konoye's mission would be to seek Russian help in ending the conflict short of unconditional surrender, which was the "only obstacle to peace." [29] Molotov did not give the Japanese Ambassador a definite answer, and shortly Molotov and Stalin left for Potsdam. During the Potsdam conference the Russians told the Americans of the Japanese diplomatic advances. No change was made in the plans to issue the Potsdam Declaration, and if Japan rejected it, to drop the bomb.[30] The Potsdam Declaration precipitated a desperate debate within the Japanese government. As the Declaration seemed to leave some room for interpretation, the peace advocates were able to influence the cabinet not to reject the Declaration, but rather to seek clarification of it, try to obtain an answer from the Russians about mediation, and to take an attitude of "wait and see." The word used in a statement to the press, when translated, was "ignore." The U.S. interpreted it as contemptuous rejection.[31]

In the Marianas, General Spaatz, Commanding General of the U.S. Army Strategic Air Forces, already had received his orders—to deliver the first atom bomb "as soon as weather would permit visual bombing after about 3 August." [32] When the Japanese chose to "ignore" the Potsdam Declaration, the order stood. The atom bomb was carried by *Enola Gay,* a B-29, operating out of the Marianas. Two other planes went along for observation. Their target was Hiroshima, Japan's eighth largest city, a military port and the headquarters of sizable army forces, and the home of war industries. The bomb was dropped at 8:15 a.m. (Hiroshima time) on August 6, 1945. Its explosive force was greater than twenty thousand tons of TNT. Truman warned the Japanese that if they did not now accept U.S. terms, "they may expect a rain of ruin from the air, the like of which has never been seen on this earth." [33] No surrender offer came.

---

[29] *Ibid.,* p. 130.

[30] *Ibid.,* pp. 130–32; Stimson, *On Active Service in Peace and War,* pp. 626–29; Byrnes, *Speaking Frankly,* pp. 205–7, 262.

[31] Butow, *Japan's Decision to Surrender,* pp. 142–49; Kase, *Journey to the Missouri,* pp. 209–10.

[32] Craven and Cate, *The Army Air Forces in World War II,* Vol. V, p. 714.

[33] Truman, *Year of Decisions,* p. 422.

General Spaatz was ordered to continue operations as planned unless otherwise instructed.

On August 8 Molotov summoned the Japanese Ambassador. Expecting to receive sanction for Konoye's mission, he was shaken when informed that on the following morning the Soviet Union would be at war with Japan. That night Soviet forces began pouring across the borders into Manchuria.

About 11:00 a.m. (Tokyo time) August 9, the second atom bomb fell on Nagasaki. Early in the morning of August 10 the Japanese sued for peace, on the condition that "the Prerogatives of His Majesty as a Sovereign Ruler" be not threatened.[34] The U.S., supported by Britain, Russia, and China, replied on August 11 that, "From the moment of surrender the authority of the Emperor and the Japanese Government to rule the state shall be subject to the Supreme Commander of the Allied powers." [35]

Even now the Japanese government was divided. The surrender offer of August 10 had been decided upon after a prolonged and bitter debate in which the Army spokesmen maintained that Japan could secure better terms after the enemy invasion. The deadlock in the cabinet was broken by the Emperor, who, in an unprecedented move, urged his ministers to accept the Potsdam Declaration on the sole condition that his authority be retained. When the reply came, the dispute was resumed. The Americans, impatient, on the morning of August 14 (Tokyo time) dropped leaflets over Tokyo to inform the people of the Japanese offer and the Allied reply. The Japanese could no longer delay their decision. The Emperor called an Imperial Conference and directed his government to accept the Allied terms. The message was sent through the Swiss government. It reached Washington the afternoon of August 14.

The formalities of surrender were held on the deck of the battleship *Missouri,* anchored in Tokyo Bay, on September 2, 1945. General MacArthur, as the Allied Supreme Commander charged with the occupation and rehabilitation of Japan, presided. His remarks were

[34] Complete text of reply in Butow, *Japan's Decision to Surrender,* p. 244, Appendix D. Acting Secretary of State Grew had urged the U.S. to make clear that the Emperor could be maintained. See Grew, *Turbulent Era,* Vol. II, Chapter 36.

[35] Complete text in Butow, *Japan's Decision to Surrender,* p. 245, Appendix E.

directed to a better future rather than the bitter past: [36] "The issues
. . . have been determined on the battlefields of the world and hence
are not for our discussion or debate. Nor is it for us here to meet . . .
in a spirit of distrust, malice or hatred. . . . It is my earnest hope and
indeed the hope of all mankind that from this solemn occasion a
better world shall emerge out of the blood and carnage of the past—a
world founded upon faith and understanding—a world dedicated to
the dignity of man and the fulfillment of his most cherished wish—for
freedom, tolerance and justice."

Reflections

On September 8, 1944, the first V-2 rocket landed in Britain and
on August 6, 1945, the first atomic bomb burst over Japan. As the
Second World War ended, its most significant new weapons ushered
in a new age. It is the way of wars that each spawns weapons to make
the next more destructive than its predecessor. The Second World
War was fought with the culminating developments of the First—armor and air power. The Third could be fought with atomic missiles.
Man has perfected his weaponry until its indiscriminate use can
destroy his world. This is the first inescapable legacy of the Second
World War.

The war left other legacies. The worldwide political structure
underwent drastic change. Great Britain expended more in strength
and treasure than she could afford, and consequently she lost both her
worldwide influence and her objective—to maintain the balance of
power in Europe. Russia emerged from the conflict a great power, her
regime tried and tested, her military potential proven. As she took advantage of military presence to convert central Europe into a vast satellite, Europe's center of gravity shifted to the east, and even yet the
continent has not made a comfortable adjustment to the change. The
United States abandoned her traditional policies of isolation and
non-entanglement to assume world leadership as a great power counterbalancing Russia's strength. In Asia, Japan, an aggressive power
for half a century, rejected war as an instrument of policy and set a

[36] Complete text in Whan, Editor, *A Soldier Speaks,* pp. 148–49.

course toward industrialization and population control to solve her immediate problems. China, who for centuries had asked nothing save to be left alone, succumbed to the promises and threats of Communism and set a militant course toward world revolution.

Colonialism, already dying, could not survive the stresses of the Second World War. All through Asia and Africa colonial peoples asserted their rights to independence, and the vacuum left by retiring colonialism has often been filled by competing forces that turn the new nations into battlegrounds. The post-war decades have been characterized by political instability, revolution, civil war, and power struggles as the world seeks a new structure to replace the old.

The war left a legacy of cynicism and bewilderment. War jolts the creative and social processes from their evolutionary pattern of change into an intense period of passionate, desperate haste. This process is disruptive; and the questions released by the Second World War are not easily answered. War itself, the traditional approach to settling disputes and solving problems, has come under re-examination. When war reaches a certain point in destructiveness, are there any winners? The air war, which killed thousands of non-combatants, raised troubling issues of morality. The mass murder of millions of Jews and Slavs by the Third Reich shook mankind's faith in the supposedly moral civilization he had created. The war crimes trials that followed the war opened up Pandora's Box: are man's responsibilities to the laws of his state or to a higher authority? The search for answers goes on.

The war also left a legacy of hope. When the need for cooperation became compelling, men learned to cooperate. The Allied coalition is a splendid example of how personal and national interests can be subordinated to those of a higher cause, provided the motivation is sufficient. Given a second chance to form a world organization to keep the peace, the participants made the United Nations stronger than the League of Nations had been. Given the choice of destroying a defeated enemy or helping him recover, the Americans extended aid. The scientific and industrial developments spurred by the war have made possible, in part of the world, a rise in the standard of living to heights once considered unattainable. Rockets do not have to carry explosive warheads; they can take man to the moon and be-

321

yond. Atomic energy does not have to be used in bombs; it can provide an almost inexhaustible source of power for pursuits of a peaceful nature. The problems of the post-war atomic-space age are vast and complex, but the potential exists for achievement as well as tragedy.

Appendix I

World War II Deaths

As many as fifty-five million people died as a result of World War II. Estimates for economic costs run so high they become meaningless. The exact cost in neither resources nor lives can be ascertained with precision.

Any effort to assign economic value to destroyed property quickly bogs down in complexities. Robert Goralski, in *The World War II Almanac* (Putnam's, 1981), lists expenditures of $878,972,000,000 (in U.S. dollars) directly related to the war, with the United States heading the list with $288 billion. Arthur Guy Enock, in *This War Business* (The Bodley Head, 1951), arrives at £223,342,859,543. Enock's book includes detailed compilations.

Considerable variation exists, even among reliable sources, for casualty figures. Military deaths, more accurately tallied than civilian deaths, differ according to whether they represent battle deaths alone, or whether they include those in the service who died from disease or accident, died later from wounds, died as prisoners of war, the missing and presumed dead, or civilians who fought as guerrillas. The number of civilians killed in air raids is hard to determine, but when civilian casualties include noncombatants who were worked to death as forced labor, victims of atrocities, or those who died from famine or disease caused by the war's disruption, the figures skyrocket. John Dower, analyzing casualties in *War Without Mercy* (Pantheon, 1986), points out that total estimates often do not include Asian nations other than China and Japan, yet millions in those other Asian nations died.

In the following list, casualties for the Asian nations come from *War Without Mercy*. The military deaths for most non-Asian nations come from *The Encyclopedia Americana* (1984 edition); *The World War II Almanac* provided the source for civilian casualties and for some additional nations.

Nation	Military dead	Civilian dead
Australia	29,395	
Austria	380,000	145,000 (inc. 60,000 Jews)
Belgium	7,760	75,000 (inc. 25,000 Jews)
Brazil	943	
Britain	244,723	60,595
British colonies	21,805	
Bulgaria	10,000	
Canada	37,476	
China (from 1937)	1,324,516	10,000,000 (estimate only)
	(estimated as high as 2,850,000)	
Czechoslovakia	6,683	310,000 (inc. 250,000 Jews)
Denmark	3,006	
Estonia		140,000
Finland	82,000	
France	210,671	173,260 (inc. 65,000 Jews)
Germany	3,500,000	3,063,000 (inc. 170,000 Jews and 56,000 foreign civilians in Germany)
Greece	16,357	155,300 (inc. 60,000 Jews)
	(The *Americana*, which does not list civilian deaths, includes guerrilla fighters among 73,700 military dead)	
Hungary	140,000	280,000 (inc. 200,000 Jews)
India	40,000	140,000
Indochina		1,000,000
Indonesia		4,000,000
Italy	279,820	93,000 (inc. 8,000 Jews)
	(numbers vary widely; includes 17,400 fighting against the Axis)	
Japan (from 1937)	1,740,955	353,000 (conservative figure)
Korea		70,000
Latvia		120,000
Lithuania		170,000
Netherlands	13,700	236,300 (inc. 104,000 Jews)
New Zealand	10,023	
Norway	4,780	5,417
	(inc. merchant seamen)	(inc. guerrillas)
Philippines	30,000	90,000
Poland	320,000	6,028,000 (inc. 3,200,000 Jews)
Rumania	300,000	465,000 (inc. 425,000 Jews)
South Africa	6,840	
United States	407,318	
	(292,131 battle, 115,187 other)	
U.S.S.R.	13,600,000	7,720,000 (inc. 1,720,000 Jews)
Yugoslavia	410,000	1,355,000 (inc. 55,000 Jews)

Appendix II

Chronology of Major Events, September 1939–August 1945

EUROPE, AFRICA, ITALY	RUSSIAN FRONT	FAR EAST	ATLANTIC AND U.S.
1939			**1939**
Sept. 1 Germany invades Poland			
Sept. 17 Russia invades Poland			
	Nov. 30 Russia invades Finland		Dec. 17 *Graf Spee* scuttled
1940			**1940**
	Mar. 12 Finland capitulates		
		Jan.–June Japan begins pressuring Netherlands East Indies	
Apr. 9 Denmark conquered, Norway invaded			
May 10 Germany invades Holland, Belgium, Lux.			
May 14 Holland capitulates			
May 26–June 4 Dunkirk evacuation			
May 28 Belgium capitulates			
June 9 Norway capitulates		June Japan begins pressuring Indo-China	
June 10 Italy enters war			
June 25 France capitulates			
	Aug. 1–8 Estonia, Latvia, Lithuania admitted to USSR		
Aug. 15 Battle of Britain begins			
Sept. 7 London Blitz begins			
Sept. 13 Italians begin advance into Egypt		Sept. 27 Japan signs Tripartite Pact	
Oct. 8 Italy invades Greece			Nov. FDR elected third term

EUROPE	AFRICA, ITALY	RUSSIAN FRONT	FAR EAST	ATLANTIC AND U.S.
1941				1941
	Feb. 5 British victory of Beda Fomm			Mar. 11 Lend-Lease; Hull-Nomura talks begin
	Mar. 31 Rommel launches offensive			
	Apr. 6 Germany invades Greece, Yugoslavia		Apr. 13 Russo-Japanese Treaty	
	Apr. 10 Siege of Tobruk begins			
	Apr. 17 Yugoslavia capitulates			
	Apr. 24 Greece capitulates			
	May 27 Crete capitulates			May 27 *Bismarck* sunk
		June 22 BARBAROSSA opens		
		Sept. Siege of Leningrad begins		Sept. *Greer* incident
			Oct. Tojo becomes Premier	
	Nov. British offensive begins			
		Dec. 6 Russian counteroffensive before Moscow		
			Dec. 7 Japanese attack Pearl Harbor	
			Dec. 8 Japanese attack Hong Kong, Wake, Malaya, Philippines	
	Dec. 10 Siege of Tobruk lifted		Dec. 23 Wake falls	
			Dec. 25 Hong Kong falls	
			Dec. 31 Retreat into Bataan	
				Dec. 24–Jan. 14 ARCA-DIA conference

Europe	Africa, Italy	Russian Front	Far East	Atlantic and U.S.
		July 4–12 Battle of Kursk		June 30 CARTWHEEL launched
	July 10–Aug. 17 Sicily	July 12 Beginning of Russian drive west		
	Sept. 3 Allies invade Italy			Nov. 20–23 Tarawa, Makin
		Nov. 27–30 Teheran conference		Dec. 26 Cape Gloucester landings

1944

Europe	Africa, Italy	Russian Front	Far East	Atlantic and U.S.
Jan. Eisenhower assumes supreme command	Jan. 22 Anzio landings	Jan. 27 Siege of Leningrad lifted		
			Jan. 31–Feb. 4 Kwajalein	
			Feb. 17–22 Eniwetok; Truk raid	
			Feb. 29 Admiralties	
			Apr. 22 Hollandia	
	May 11 Allies open drive on Rome		May 17–19 Wakde	
	June 4 Allies take Rome		May 27–June 22 Biak	
June 6 OVERLORD			June 15–July 9 Saipan	
		June 23–Aug. 7 Russians drive into Poland	June 19–20 Battle of Philippine Sea	
July 25 Breakout at Saint Lô			July 21–Aug. 10 Guam	
Aug. 20 Falaise pocket		Aug. 1–Oct. 2 Warsaw uprising	July 24–Aug. 1 Tinian	
Aug. 15 ANVIL-DRAGOON				

1944

EUROPE AFRICA, ITALY	RUSSIAN FRONT	FAR EAST	ATLANTIC AND U.S.
Aug. 25 Paris liberated		Sept. 15 Morotai, Peleliu	
Sept. 17 MARKET-GARDEN		Oct. 20–Dec. 25 Leyte	
Sept. 25 Gothic Line broken		Oct. 23–25 Battle of Leyte Gulf	
	Aug. 20 Russians begin drive through Balkans		Nov. FDR elected fourth term
Nov. Antwerp opened		Nov. 24 B-29 raids from Marianas begin hitting Japan	
Dec. 16 Battle of Bulge begins			
1945			1945
	Jan. 12 Russians open drive into Germany	Jan. 9 Luzon invaded	
	Feb. 4–11 Yalta conference	Jan. Ledo Road opened	
Feb.–Mar. Rhineland campaign		Feb. 19 Iwo Jima	
		Mar. 9 Fire raid, Tokyo	
Mar. 23 Rhine crossed		Apr. 1 Okinawa	
Apr. 1 Ruhr surrounded			
	Apr. 16 Russians open drive on Berlin		Apr. 12 FDR dies
Apr. 25 U.S. and Russians meet at Elbe			
May 7 German High Command surrenders		July 26 Potsdam Declaration	
July 17–Aug. 2 Potsdam conference		Aug. 6 Atom bomb, Hiroshima	
		Aug. 8 USSR declares war on Japan	
		Aug. 9 Atom bomb, Nagasaki	
		Aug. 14 Japan surrenders	

Bibliography

This bibliography represents books that have answered questions or met needs for me; it makes no claim to be comprehensive. Volumes marked with an asterisk are suggested for readers approaching the war with minimal background.

Official Histories, Reference

The individual titles of official histories cited in the text are listed by theater.

Commager, Henry S., ed. *Documents of American History*. New York: Appleton-Century-Crofts, 1963.

Esposito, Vincent J. *The West Point Atlas of American Wars, Vol. II*. New York: Praeger, 1959.

Foreign Relations of the United States. Documents published by the U.S. State Department; volumes by year and/or country.

Hearings Before the Joint Committee on the Investigation of the Pearl Harbor Attack, 39 vols. Washington: Government Printing Office, 1945-46.

History of the Second World War, United Kingdom Military Series. London: Her Majesty's Stationery Office.

Rosenman, Samuel I., ed. *The Public Papers and Addresses of Franklin Roosevelt*. New York: Random House, 1938-50.

The United States Army in World War II. Washington: Department of the Army.

United States Strategic Bombing Survey (USSBS). Washington: Government Printing Office. The 321 reports are listed and summarized in Gordon Daniels, ed. *A Guide to the Reports of the United States Strategic Bombing Survey*. London: Royal Historical Society, 1981.

Ziegler, Janet. *World War II: Books in English, 1945-65*. Stanford: Hoover Institution Press, 1971.

Causes, Background, Outbreak of War

Beasley, W.G. *The Modern History of Japan*. New York: Praeger, 1963.

Borton, Hugh. *Japan*. Ithaca, New York: Cornell University Press, 1951.

Brook-Shepherd, Gordon. *The Anschluss*. Philadelphia: Lippincott, 1963.

*Bullock, Alan. *Hitler: A Study in Tyranny*. New York: Harper, 1962.

Butow, Robert J. C. *Tojo and the Coming of the War*. Princeton: Princeton University Press, 1961.

Churchill, Winston S. *Step by Step*. New York: Putnam's, 1939.

———. *The Gathering Storm*. Boston: Houghton Mifflin, 1948.

Feiling, Keith. *The Life of Neville Chamberlain*. London: Macmillan, 1970.

*Feis, Herbert. *The Road to Pearl Harbor.* Princeton: Princeton University Press, 1950.

Finer, Herman. *Mussolini's Italy.* New York: Henry Holt, 1935.

Grew, Joseph C. *Ten Years in Japan.* New York: Simon & Schuster, 1944.

_____. *Turbulent Era.* Boston: Houghton Mifflin, 1952.

Heiden, Konrad. *Der Fuehrer.* Boston: Houghton Mifflin, 1944.

Henderson, Neville. *Failure of a Mission.* New York: Putnam's, 1940.

Kirkpatrick, Ivone. *Mussolini: A Study in Power.* New York: Hawthorn, 1964.

Langer, William L. and S. Everett Gleason. *The Challenge to Isolation.* New York: Harper, 1952.

_____. *The Undeclared War, 1940-41.* New York: Harper, 1953.

*Lash, Joseph P. *Roosevelt and Churchill, 1939-41: The Partnership that Saved the West.* New York: Norton, 1976.

Millis, Walter. *This Is Pearl!* New York: Morrow, 1947. See also Prange.

Morison, Samuel E. *The Rising Sun in the Pacific.* Boston: Little, Brown, 1955.

Morley, James William, ed. *The China Quagmire: Japan's Expansion on the Asian Continent, 1933-41.* New York: Columbia University Press, 1983.

Prange, Gordon W. *Pearl Harbor: The Verdict of History.* New York: McGraw-Hill, 1986.

Shirer, William L. *The Rise and Fall of the Third Reich: A History of Nazi Germany.* New York: Simon & Schuster, 1960.

Snell, John L., ed. *The Outbreak of the Second World War: Design or Blunder?* Boston: Heath, 1962. Readings giving conflicting views.

*Taylor, A.J.P. *The Origins of the Second World War.* New York: Atheneum, 1962.

Weinberg, Gerhard L. *Hitler's Germany: Starting World War II, 1937-39.* Chicago: University of Chicago Press, 1980.

Wheeler-Bennett, John W. *Munich: Prologue to Tragedy.* New York: Duell, Sloan and Pearce, 1948.

_____. *The Nemesis of Power: The German Army in Politics, 1918-1945.* New York: St. Martin's, 1964.

Works Spanning More Than One Theater

*Ambrose, Stephen E. *Eisenhower: Soldier, General of the Army, President Elect.* New York: Simon & Schuster, 1983.

Anders, Wladyslaw. *An Army in Exile.* London: Macmillan, 1949.

Baldwin, Hanson. *Battles Lost and Won.* New York: Harper & Row, 1966.

Blum, John Morton. *V Was for Victory: Politics and American Culture During World War II.* New York: Harcourt, Brace, Jovanovich, 1976.

*Blumenson, Martin. *Patton: The Man Behind the Legend.* New York: Morrow, 1985.

Bradley, Omar N. *A Soldier's Story.* New York: Holt, 1951.

Bryant, Arthur. *The Turn of the Tide.* Garden City, New York: Doubleday, 1957.

_____. *Triumph in the West.* London: Collins, 1959.

Byrnes, James F. *Speaking Frankly.* New York: Harper, 1947.

Churchill, Winston S. *Their Finest Hour.* Boston: Houghton Mifflin, 1949.

_____. *The Grand Alliance.* Boston: Houghton Mifflin, 1950.

_____. *The Hinge of Fate.* Boston: Houghton Mifflin, 1950.

_____. *Closing the Ring.* Boston: Houghton Mifflin, 1951.

_____. *Triumph and Tragedy.* Boston: Houghton Mifflin, 1953.

Dallek, Robert. *Franklin D. Roosevelt and American Foreign Policy, 1932-1945.* New York: Oxford University Press, 1979.

Cunningham, Andrew B. *A Sailor's Odyssey*. New York: Hutchinson, 1951.

De Gaulle, Charles. *The Complete War Memoirs*. New York: Simon & Schuster, 1964.

Eggleston, Wilfrid. *Scientists at War*. New York: Oxford University Press, 1950.

Ehrman, John. *Grand Strategy*. Vols. V and VI, *History of the Second World War, United Kingdom*. London: Her Majesty's Stationery Office, 1956.

Eisenhower, Dwight D. *Crusade in Europe*. New York: Doubleday, 1948.

Feis, Herbert. *Churchill, Roosevelt, Stalin: The War They Waged and the Peace They Sought*. Princeton: Princeton University Press, 1957.

*Flower, Desmond and James Reeves, eds. *The Taste of Courage*. New York: Harper, 1960. Vignettes and excerpts.

Freidin, Seymour and William Richardson, eds. *The Fatal Decisions*. New York: W. Sloan Associates, 1956.

Fuller, J.F.C. *The Second World War, A Strategical and Tactical History*. New York: Duell, Sloan and Pearce, 1949.

Fussell, Paul. *Wartime*. New York: Oxford University Press, 1989.

Gray, J. Glenn. *The Warrior: Reflections on Men in Battle*. New York: Harcourt, Brace, 1959.

*Greenfield, Kent Roberts, ed. *Command Decisions*. Washington: Department of the Army, 1960.

Guderian, Heinz. *Panzer Leader*. New York: Dutton, 1952.

Hull, Cordell. *The Memoirs of Cordell Hull*. New York: Macmillan, 1948.

Irving, David. *Hitler's War*. New York: Viking, 1977.

King, Ernest J. and Walter Muir Whitehill. *Fleet Admiral King: A Naval Record*. New York: Norton, 1952.

Liddell-Hart, B.H., ed. *The Rommel Papers*. New York: Harcourt, Brace, 1953.

Manstein, Erich von. *Lost Victories*. Chicago: Regency, 1958.

Matloff, Maurice. *Strategic Planning for Coalition Warfare 1943-44*. Washington: Department of the Army, 1959.

Matloff, Maurice and Edwin M. Snell. *Strategic Planning for Coalition Warfare 1941-42*. Washington: Department of the Army, 1953.

Morton, Louis. *Strategy and Command, the First Two Years*. Washington: Department of the Army, 1962.

Nalty, Bernard C. *Strength for the Fight: A History of Black Americans in the Military*. New York: Free Press, 1986.

Patton, George S. *War as I Knew It*. Boston: Houghton Mifflin, 1947.

Pogue, Forrest C. *The Supreme Command*. Washington: Department of the Army, 1954.

*_____. *George C. Marshall*. Vol. 2: *Ordeal and Hope, 1939-1943* (1966). Vol. 3: *Organizer of Victory, 1943-1945* (1973). New York: Viking, 1966-73.

*Sherwood, Robert. *Roosevelt and Hopkins*. New York: Harper, 1950.

*Snell, John L. *Illusion and Necessity: The Diplomacy of Global War, 1939-1945*. Boston: Houghton Mifflin, 1963.

Speer, Albert. *Inside the Third Reich*. New York: Macmillan, 1970.

Stimson, Henry L. and McGeorge Bundy. *On Active Service in Peace and War*. New York: Harper, 1947.

Trevor-Roper, H.R. *Blitzkrieg to Defeat: Hitler's War Directives*. New York: Holt, Rinehart, Winston, 1964.

Truman, Harry S. *Year of Decisions*. Garden City, New York: Doubleday, 1955.

Werth, Alexander. *De Gaulle: A Political Biography*. New York: Simon & Schuster, 1965.

*Wright, Gordon. *The Ordeal of Total War.* New York: Harper & Row, 1968.

*Young, Desmond. *The Desert Fox.* London: Harper & Row, 1950.

Western Europe

Bezymenski, Lev. *The Death of Adolf Hitler.* New York: Harcourt, Brace and World, 1968.

Blumenson, Martin. *Breakout and Pursuit.* Washington: Department of the Army, 1961.

Cole, Hugh M. *The Lorraine Campaign.* Washington: Department of the Army, 1950.

_____. *The Ardennes: Battle of the Bulge.* Washington: Department of the Army, 1965.

Collier, Basil. *The Defense of the United Kingdom.* London: Her Majesty's Stationery Office, 1957.

*Divine, A.D. *Dunkirk.* New York: Dutton, 1948.

Draper, Theodore. *The Six Weeks' War.* New York: Viking, 1944.

Eisenhower, Dwight D. *Crusade in Europe.* Garden City, New York: Doubleday, 1948.

Ellis, L.F. *The War in France and Flanders.* London: Her Majesty's Stationery Office, 1953.

_____. *Victory in the West. Vol. 1: The Battle of Normandy.* London: Her Majesty's Stationery Office, 1962.

Fleming, Peter. *Operation Sea Lion.* New York: Simon & Schuster, 1957.

*Frank, Anne. *The Diary of a Young Girl.* Garden City, New York: Doubleday, 1952.

Goebbels, Joseph. *The Goebbels Diaries,* edited by Louis P. Lochner. Garden City, New York: Doubleday, 1948.

Goerlitz, Walter. *History of the German General Staff.* New York: Praeger, 1953.

Harrison, Gordon A. *Cross-Channel Attack.* Washington: Department of the Army, 1951.

*Horne, Alistair. *To Lose a Battle: France 1940.* Boston: Little, Brown, 1969.

Johns, Glover S., Jr. *The Clay Pigeons of St. Lo.* Harrisburg, Penn.: Military Service Publishing Co., 1958.

Kennedy, Robert M. *The German Campaign in Poland, 1939.* Washington: Department of the Army Pamphlet No. 20-255, April 1956.

Langer, William L. *Our Vichy Gamble.* New York: Knopf, 1947.

Liddell-Hart, B.H., ed. *The German Generals Talk.* New York: Morrow, 1948.

MacDonald, Charles B. *The Siegfried Line Campaign.* Washington: Department of the Army, 1963.

*_____. *The Mighty Endeavor: American Armed Forces in the European Theater in World War II.* New York: Oxford University Press, 1969.

Marshall, S.L.A. *Bastogne: The First Eight Days.* Washington: Infantry Journal Press, 1946.

Montgomery, Bernard L. *From Normandy to the Baltic.* New York: Houghton Mifflin, 1948.

Morgan, Frederick. *Overture to Overlord.* Garden City, New York: Doubleday, 1950.

Morison, Samuel Eliot. *The Invasion of France and Germany.* Boston: Little, Brown, 1957.

Ryan, Cornelius. *The Longest Day: June 6, 1944.* New York: Simon & Schuster, 1959. Personal accounts.

Spears, Edward. *Assignment to Catastrophe.* London: Heinemann, 1954.

Taylor, Telford. *The March of Conquest*. New York: Simon & Schuster, 1958.
_____. *The Breaking Wave*. New York: Simon & Schuster, 1967.
Toland, John. *Battle: The Story of the Bulge*. New York: Random House, 1959.
_____. *The Last 100 Days*. New York: Random House, 1966.
Trevor-Roper, H.R. *The Last Days of Hitler*. New York: Macmillan, 1947.
*Wilmot, Chester. *The Struggle for Europe*. New York: Harper and Brothers, 1952.

North Africa, the Mediterranean, Italy

*Barnett, Correlli. *The Desert Generals*. New York: Viking, 1961.
Blumenson, Martin. *Anzio: The Gamble that Failed*. Philadelphia: Lippincott, 1963.
_____. *Kasserine Pass*. Boston: Houghton Mifflin, 1966.
Buckley, Christopher. *Greece and Crete, 1941*. London: Her Majesty's Stationery Office, 1952.
Ciano, Count Galeazzo. *The Ciano Diaries, 1939-1943*, edited by Hugh Gibson. New York: Doubleday, 1946.
Clark, Alan. *The Fall of Crete*. New York: Morrow, 1962.
Clark, Mark W. *Calculated Risk*. New York: Harper, 1950.
*Deakin, Frederick W. *The Brutal Friendship: Mussolini, Hitler, and the Fall of Italian Fascism*. New York: Harper & Row, 1962.
_____. *The Embattled Mountains*. New York: Oxford University Press, 1971. Resistance in Yugoslavia.
Garland, Albert N. and Howard McGaw Smyth. *Sicily and the Surrender of Italy*. Washington: Department of the Army, 1965.
Heckstall-Smith, Anthony. *Tobruk, The Story of a Siege*. New York: Norton, 1959.
Heckstall-Smith, Anthony and H.T. Baillie-Grohman. *Greek Tragedy, 1941*. New York: Norton, 1961.
Howe, George F. *Northwest Africa: Seizing the Initiative In the West*. Washington: Department of the Army, 1957.
Jackson, W.G.F. *The Battle for Italy*. New York: Harper & Row, 1967.
*Majdalany, Fred. *The Battle of Cassino*. Boston: Houghton Mifflin, 1957.
_____. *The Battle of El Alamein*. Philadelphia: Lippincott, 1965.
Montgomery, Bernard L. *El Alamein to the River Sangro*. New York: Hutchinson, 1948.
Moorehead, Alan. *The March to Tunis: The African War 1940-43*. New York: Harper & Row, 1967.
Morison, Samuel E. *Operations in North African Waters*. Boston: Little, Brown, 1947.
_____. *Sicily, Salerno, Anzio*. Boston: Little, Brown, 1954.
Playfair, I.S.O. *The Mediterranean and the Middle East*, 4 vols. London: Her Majesty's Stationery Office, 1954-66.
Starr, Chester G. *From Salerno to the Alps*. Washington: Infantry Journal Press, 1948.
Wiskemann, Elizabeth. *The Rome-Berlin Axis*. New York: Oxford University Press, 1949.

War in the Atlantic

Fergusson, Bernard. *The Watery Maze*. London: Collins, 1961.
Frischauer, Willi and Robert Jackson. *The Altmark Affair*. New York: Macmillan, 1955.
Grenfell, Russell. *The Bismarck Episode*. New York: Macmillan, 1949.
Morison, Samuel E. *The Battle of the Atlantic*. Boston: Little, Brown, 1947.
_____. *The Atlantic Battle Won*. Boston: Little, Brown, 1956.

*_____. *The Two-Ocean War*. Boston: Little, Brown, 1963.

Padfield, Peter. *Dönitz, The Last Fuehrer*. New York: Harper & Row, 1984.

Roskill, S.W. *The War at Sea 1939-1945*, 3 vols. London: Her Majesty's Stationery Office, 1954-61.

The Eastern Front

Allen, W.E.D. and Paul Muratoff. *The Russian Campaigns of 1941-1943*. New York: Penguin, 1944.

Anders, Wladyslaw. *Hitler's Defeat in Russia*. Chicago: Regnery, 1953.

Bor-Komorowski, T. *The Secret Army*. Nashville, Tenn.: Battery Press, 1984 (reprint of 1951 edition).

Chaney, Otto Preston, Jr. *Zhukov*. Norman, Ok.: University of Oklahoma Press, 1971.

Chuikov, Vasili I. *The Beginning of the Road*. London: Macgibbon & Kee, 1963.

*Clark, Alan. *Barbarossa*. New York: Morrow, 1965.

Dixon, C.A. and Heilbrunn, Otto. *Communist Guerrilla Warfare*. New York: Praeger, 1954.

Ehrenburg, Ilia. *The War: 1941-1945*. London: Macgibbon & Kee, 1964.

Erickson, John. *The Soviet High Command*. New York: St. Martin's, 1962.

_____. *The Road to Stalingrad*. New York: Harper and Row, 1975.

_____. *The Road to Berlin*. Boulder, Col.: Westview Press, 1983.

Goerlitz, Walter. *Paulus and Stalingrad*. London: , 1963.

Goure, Leon. *The Siege of Leningrad*. Stanford: Stanford University Press, 1962.

*Harriman, W. Averell and Elie Abel. *Special Envoy to Churchill and Stalin, 1941-46*. New York: Random House, 1975.

Jackson, W.G.F. *Seven Roads to Moscow*. New York: Philosophical Library, 1958.

Kennan, George F. *Russia and the West*. Boston: Little, Brown, 1961.

Kerr, Walter. *The Russian Army*. New York: Knopf, 1944.

Liddell-Hart, B.H. *The Red Army*. New York: Harcourt, Brace, 1956.

Mikolajczyk, Stanislaw. *The Rape of Poland*. New York: Whittlesey House, 1948.

Reitlinger, Gerald. *The Final Solution*. New York: A.S. Barnes, 1953.

Schroter, Heinz. *Stalingrad*. New York: Dutton, 1958.

*Skrjabina, Elena. *Siege and Survival: The Odyssey of a Leningrader*. Carbondale, Ill.: Southern Illinois University Press, 1971.

Tanner, Vaino A. *The Winter War*. Stanford: Stanford University Press, 1957.

Werth, Alexander. *Leningrad*. New York: Knopf, 1944.

_____. *The Year of Stalingrad*. New York: Knopf, 1947.

_____. *Russia at War*. New York: Dutton, 1964.

Zacharoff, Lucien. *The Voice of Fighting Russia*. New York: Alliance, 1942.

War in the Air

Arnold, H.H. *Global Mission*. New York: Harper, 1949.

Brereton, Lewis H. *The Brereton Diaries*. New York: Morrow, 1946.

Caidin, Martin. *Black Thursday*. New York: Dutton, 1960.

Collier, Basil. *The Battle of Britain*. New York: Macmillan, 1962.

_____. *The Battle of the V-Weapons 1944-1945*. New York: Morrow, 1965.

Craven, Wesley F. and James L. Cate, eds. *The Army Air Forces in World War II*, 7 vols. Chicago: University of Chicago Press, 1948-58.

Dugan, James and Carroll Stewart. *Ploesti*. New York: Random House, 1962.

*Galland, Adolf. *The First and the Last*. London: Methuen, 1955.

Gavin, James M. *Airborne Warfare*. Washington: Infantry Journal Press, 1947.

Giovannitti, Len and Fred Freed. *The Decision to Drop the Bomb*. New York: Coward McCann, 1965.

Glines, Carroll V. *Doolittle's Tokyo Raiders*. Princeton: Van Nostrand, 1964.

*Hastings, Max. *Bomber Command*. New York: DialPress/James Wade, 1979.

Marshall, S.L.A. *Night Drop*. Boston: Little, Brown, 1962.

Schaffer, Ronald. *Wings of Judgment*. New York: Oxford University Press, 1985.

Smyth, Henry De Wolf. *Atomic Energy for Military Purposes*. Princeton: Princeton University Press, 1946.

Sunderman, James F., ed. *World War II In the Air*. Vol 1: *The Pacific* (1962). Vol. 2: *Europe* (1963). New York: F. Watts, 1962, 1963.

*Townsend, Peter. *Duel of Eagles*. New York: Simon & Schuster, 1970.

Webster, Sir Charles and Noble Frankland. *The Strategic Air Offensive against Germany 1939-1945*, 4 vols. London: Her Majesty's Stationery Office, 1961.

Intelligence, Undercover

Beesley, Patrick. *Very Special Intelligence*. London: Hamish Hamilton, 1977. Ultra in the Battle of the Atlantic.

Bennett, Ralph. *Ultra in the West*. London: Hutchinson, 1979.

Hinsley, F.H. *British Intelligence in the Second World War*, 3 vols. London: Her Majesty's Stationery Office, 1979-88.

*Lewin, Ronald. *Ultra Goes to War*. New York: McGraw-Hill, 1978.

_____. *The American Magic*. New York: Farrar Straus Giroux, 1982.

Montagu, Ewen. *The Man Who Never Was*. Philadelphia: Lippincott, 1954.

Smith, Bradley F. *The Shadow Warriors: O.S.S. and the Origins of the C.I.A.* New York: Basic Books, 1983.

Stevenson, William. *A Man Called Intrepid*. New York: Harcourt, Brace, Jovanovich, 1976.

Welchman, Gordon. *The Hut Six Story: Breaking the Enigma Codes*. New York: McGraw-Hill, 1982.

Winterbotham, F. W. *The Ultra Secret*. New York: Harper & Row, 1974.

*Wohlstetter, Roberta. *Pearl Harbor: Warning and Decision*. Stanford: Stanford University Press, 1962.

The Pacific Theater

Appleman, Roy E. and James M. Burns. *Okinawa: The Last Battle*. Washington: Department of the Army, 1948.

Bartley, Whitman S. *Iwo Jima: Amphibious Epic*. Washington: U.S. Marine Corps, 1954.

Belote, James H. and William M. Belote. *Corregidor: The Saga of a Fortress*. New York: Harper & Row, 1967.

_____. *Titans of the Seas: The Development and Operations of Japanese and American Carrier Task Forces during World War II*. New York: Harper & Row, 1975.

Blair, Clay, Jr. *The Silent Victory: The U.S. Submarine War against Japan*. Philadelphia: Lippincott, 1975.

Brown, Cecil B. *Suez to Singapore*. New York: Random House, 1942.

*Butow, Robert J.C. *Japan's Decision to Surrender*. Stanford: Stanford University Press, 1954.

Cannon, M. Hamlin. *Leyte: The Return to the Philippines*. Washington: Department of the Army, 1953.

Chinese Ministry of Information, comp. *China Handbook 1937-45*. New York: Macmillan, 1947.

Crowl, Philip A. and Edmund G. Love. *Seizure of the Gilberts and Marshalls*. Washington: Department of the Army, 1955.

Dexter, David. *The New Guinea Offensives*. Canberra, Australia: Australian War Memorial, 1961.

*Dower, John W. *War Without Mercy*. New York: Pantheon, 1986.

Eichelberger, Robert L. *Our Jungle Road to Tokyo*. New York: Viking, 1950.

Falk, Stanley L. *The Bataan Death March*. New York: Norton, 1962.

Feis, Herbert. *Between War and Peace*. Princeton: Princeton University Press, 1960.

_____. *Japan Subdued*. Princeton: Princeton University Press, 1961.

*Fuchida, Mitsuo. *Midway: The Battle that Doomed Japan*. Annapolis: Naval Institute, 1955.

Griffith, Samuel B. *The Battle for Guadalcanal*. Philadelphia: Lippincott, 1963.

Halsey, William F. and J. Bryan. *Admiral Halsey's Story*. New York: Whittlesey House, 1947.

Heinl, Robert D. *The Defense of Wake*. Washington: U.S. Marine Corps, 1947.

*Hersey, John R. *Hiroshima*. New York: Knopf, 1946.

History of Marine Corps Operations In World War II, 5 vols. Washington: U.S. Marine Corps, 1963-70.

Hoffman, Carl W. *Saipan: The Beginning of the End*. Washington: Department of the Army, 1950.

Hough, Frank O. *The Assault on Peleliu*. Washington: Department of the Army, 1950.

Iriye, Akira. *Power and Culture: the Japanese-American War*. Cambridge: Harvard University Press, 1981.

*Isely, Jeter A. and Philip A. Crowl. *The U.S. Marines and Amphibious War*. Princeton: Princeton University Press, 1951.

James, D. Clayton. *The Years of MacArthur, 1941-1945*. Boston: Houghton Mifflin, 1975.

Kase, Toshikazu. *Journey to the Missouri*. New Haven: Yale University Press, 1950.

Kirby, Woodburn S. *The Loss of Singapore*. London: Her Majesty's Stationery Office, 1957.

Miller, John, Jr., *Guadalcanal: The First Offensive*. Washington: Department of the Army, 1949.

_____. *Cartwheel: The Reduction of Rabaul*. Washington: Department of the Army, 1959.

Milner, Samuel. *Victory in Papua*. Washington: Department of the Army, 1957.

Morison, Samuel E. *Aleutians, Gilberts and Marshalls*. Boston: Little, Brown, 1951.

_____. *New Guinea and the Marianas*. Boston: Little, Brown, 1953.

_____. *The Struggle for Guadalcanal*. Boston: Little, Brown, 1953.

_____. *Breaking the Bismarcks Barrier*. Boston: Little, Brown, 1955.

_____. *Coral Sea, Midway and Submarine Actions*. Boston: Little, Brown, 1955.

_____. *Leyte, June 1944-January 1945*. Boston: Little, Brown, 1958.

_____. *The Liberation of the Philippines*. Boston: Little, Brown, 1959.

_____. *Victory in the Pacific*. Boston: Little, Brown, 1960.

Morton, Louis. *The Fall of the Philippines*. Washington: Department of the Army, 1953.

*Newcomb, Richard F. *Iwo Jima*. New York: Holt, Rinehart, Winston, 1965.

Nichols, Charles S., Jr. and Henry I. Shaw. *Okinawa: Victory in the Pacific*. Washington: Department of the Army, 1955.

Proehl, Carl W. *The Fourth Marine Division in World War II*. Washington: U.S. Marine Corps, 1946.

Rentz, John N. *Bougainville and the Northern Solomons*. Washington: U.S. Marine Corps, 1948.

_____. *Marines in the Central Solomons*. Washington: U.S. Marine Corps, 1952.

Roscoe, Theodore. *United States Submarine Operations in World War II*. Annapolis: U.S. Naval Institute, 1949.

Sherrod, Robert. *Tarawa: The Story of a Battle*. New York: Duell, Sloan and Pearce, 1944.

Smith, Holland M. *Coral and Brass*. New York: Scribner's, 1949.

Smith, Robert Ross. *The Approach to the Philippines*. Washington: Department of the Army, 1953.

_____. *Triumph in the Philippines*. Washington: Department of the Army, 1963.

*Spector, Ronald. *Eagle against the Sun: The American War with Japan*. New York: Free Press, 1988.

Stockman, James R. *The Battle for Tarawa*. Washington: U.S. Marine Corps, 1947

Thorne, Christopher. *Allies of a Kind: The United States, Britain and the War against Japan*. New York: Oxford University Press, 1978.

*Toland, John. *But Not in Shame*. New York: Random House, 1961.

Tregaskis, Richard W. *Guadalcanal Diary*. New York: Random House, 1943.

Wainwright, Jonathan M. *General Wainwright's Story*. Garden City, New York: Doubleday, 1946.

Whan, Vorin E., ed. *A Soldier Speaks: Public Papers and Speeches of General of the Army Douglas MacArthur*. New York: Praeger, 1965.

Zimmerman, John L. *The Guadalcanal Campaign*. Washington: U.S. Marine Corps, 1949.

China, Burma, India

Anders, Leslie. *The Ledo Road*. Norman, Ok.: University of Oklahoma Press, 1965.

Byrd, Martha. *Chennault: Giving Wings to the Tiger*. Tuscaloosa, Ala.: University of Alabama Press, 1987.

Chennault, Claire Lee. *Way of a Fighter*. New York: Putnam's, 1949.

Davies, John Paton. *Dragon by the Tail*. New York: Norton, 1972.

*Feis, Herbert. *The China Tangle*. Princeton: Princeton University Press, 1953.

Houn, Franklin W. *A Short History of Chinese Communism*. Englewood Cliffs, N.J.: Prentice-Hall, 1967.

Ogburn, Charlton, Jr. *The Marauders*. New York: Harper, 1959.

Owen, Frank. *The Campaign in Burma*. London: Her Majesty's Stationery Office, 1946.

Romanus, Charles F. and Riley Sunderland. *Stilwell's Mission to China*. Washington: Department of the Army, 1953.

_____. *Stilwell's Command Problems*. Washington: Department of the Army, 1954.

_____. *Time Runs Out in CBI*. Washington: Department of the Army, 1959.

Slim, W.J. *Defeat into Victory*. New York: David McKay, 1961.

*Tuchman, Barbara. *Stilwell and the American Experience in China*. New York: Macmillan, 1970.

White, Theodore, ed. *The Stilwell Papers*. New York: William Sloane, 1948.

Index

The author

Historian Martha Byrd, a Phi Beta Kappa graduate of The University of North Carolina at Chapel Hill, holds a master's from The University of Tennessee, Knoxville. Her most recent book is *Chennault: Giving Wings to the Tiger* (University of Alabama Press, 1987). She and her husband live in Davidson, North Carolina.